Win32 System Programming
Second Edition

Win32 System Programming

Second Edition

A Windows® 2000
Application Developer's Guide

Johnson M. Hart

ADDISON-WESLEY

Boston • San Francisco • New York • Toronto • Montreal
London • Munich • Paris • Madrid
Capetown • Sydney • Tokyo • Singapore • Mexico City

The publisher offers discounts on this book when ordered in quantity for special sales. For more information, please contact:

Pearson Education Corporate Sales Division
One Lake Street
Upper Saddle River, NJ 07458
(800) 382-3419
corpsales@pearsontechgroup.com

Visit AW on the Web: www.awl.com/cseng/

Library of Congress Cataloging-in-Publication Data

Hart, Johnson M., 1944–
   Win32 system programming: a Windows 2000 application developer's guide / Johnson M. Hart—2nd ed.
      p. cm.
   Includes bibliographical references and index.
   ISBN 0-201-70310-6
   1. Application software—Development. 2. Microsoft Win32. 3. Microsoft Windows (Computer file) I. Title.

   QA76.76.A65 H37 2000
   005.26'8—dc21   00-056595

ISBN 0-201-70310-6
Text printed on recycled paper
1 2 3 4 5 6 7 8 9 10—CRW—0403020100
First printing, September 2000

Contents

Chapter 10   Advanced Thread Synchronization   275

Chapter 11   Interprocess Communication   301

Figures

xiii

Tables

Programs

Preface

This book shows how to use the Win32 Application Programming Interface (API) and the emerging Win64 API, concentrating on the core system services, including the file system, process and thread management, interprocess communication, network programming, and synchronization. User interfaces, internals, and I/O drivers, although important and interesting topics, are beyond the scope of this book. The examples concentrate on scenarios that are likely to arise in practice, and in many cases the examples can be used as bases for real applications.

The Win32 API is supported by Microsoft's family of 32-bit operating systems: Windows 2000, Windows NT, Windows 98, Windows 95, and Windows CE. Win64, to be supported as a 64-bit interface on Windows 2000, is very similar, and migration issues are discussed as required. There is no doubt that Win32, along with Win64,[1] is an important factor for application developers, in many cases replacing UNIX as the preferred API for application programs targeted at desktop and server systems. Many observers predict that Win32 will become the dominant programming interface, although it appears that UNIX and Win32 will continue to coexist and that each will find its own niche.

Regardless of the outcome of the operating system wars, many experienced programmers will want to learn the Win32 API quickly, and this book is designed to help them do so.

The first objectives are to explain what Win32 is, show how to use it in realistic situations, and do so as quickly as possible without burdening the reader with unnecessary detail. This book is, therefore, not comprehensive, but it explains the central features of the most important functions and shows how to use them in realistic programming situations. Equipped with this knowledge, the reader will be able to use the comprehensive Microsoft reference documentation to explore details, advanced options, and the more obscure functions as requirements or interests dictate. I have found the Win32 API easy to learn using this approach, and I have greatly enjoyed developing Win32 programs, despite occasional frustration. This enthusiasm will show through at times, as it should. This does not mean that I feel that Win32 is necessarily better than other operating system APIs, but it certainly has many attractive features.

Many Win32 books assume that the user is familiar only with 16-bit Windows 3.1 programming. These books spend a great deal of time explaining how pro-

---

[1] Win64 will be mentioned only if the distinction is important; nearly all statements apply to Win64 as well, and Win64 is likely be the API for large applications on servers and some workstations.

cesses, virtual memory, interprocess communication, and preemptive scheduling work without showing how to use them in realistic situations. A programmer experienced in UNIX, VAX VMS, IBM MVS, or another high-end operating system— that is, nearly anything other than the long-obsolete Windows 3.1 Win16 API— will be familiar with these concepts and will be impatient to find out how they are implemented in Win32. Most Win32 books also spend a great deal of space on user interface programming. This book avoids the user interface, beyond discussing simple character-based console I/O, in the interest of concentrating on the important core features.

This book takes the point of view that Win32 is just an operating system (OS) API, providing a well understood set of features. Many programmers, regardless of experience level, need to learn Win32 and the Windows operating systems quickly, and an understanding of Win32 is invaluable in discussing subjects such as Microsoft's Component Object Model (COM). The Windows systems, when compared with other systems, have good, bad, and average features and quality. The purpose of this book is to show how to use those features efficiently and in realistic situations to develop useful, high-quality, and high-performance applications.

Audience

- Anyone who has experience programming in UNIX or another operating system, even Windows 3.1, and who wants to learn about Win32 quickly.

- Programmers and software engineers who must port existing applications, often in UNIX, to Win32 for operation under Windows 2000 or any of the other Windows platforms. This book contains many comparisons among Win32, UNIX, and standard C library functions and programming models. All common UNIX functionality, including process management, synchronization, file systems, and interprocess communication, is covered in Win32 terms.

- Programmers who are developing servers or other systems or components in which management of resources such as processes and threads is of primary importance and in which the user interface is of secondary importance.

- Programmers using COM or DCOM will find much of the information here helpful in understanding COM's DLL usage, thread models, interfaces, and synchronization.

- Readers starting new projects who are not constrained by the need to port existing code. Many aspects of program design and implementation are covered, and Win32 functions are used to create useful applications and to solve common programming problems.

- Computer science students at the upperclass undergraduate or beginning graduate level in courses covering systems programming or application development. This book will also be useful to those who are learning multithreaded programming or need to build networked applications. This book would be a useful complementary text to a book such as W. Richard Stevens' *Advanced Programming in the UNIX Environment* (see the Bibliography) so that students could compare Win32 and UNIX. Students in operating systems courses will find this book to be a useful supplement as it illustrates how a commercially important operating system provides essential OS functionality.

The only other assumption, implicit in all the others, is a knowledge of C programming.

Organization

Chapters are organized topically so that the features required in even a single-threaded application are covered first, followed by process and thread management features, and finally network programming in a multithreaded environment. This organization allows the reader to advance logically from file systems to security, memory management, and file mapping, and then to processes, threads, and synchronization, followed by interprocess and network communication. This organization also allows the examples to evolve in a natural way, much as a developer might create a simple prototype and then add additional capability. The advanced features, such as asynchronous I/O, appear last.

Within each chapter, after introducing the functionality area, such as process management or memory-mapped files, we discuss important Win32 functions and their relationships in detail. Illustrative examples follow. Within the text, only essential parts of programs are listed; complete programs and the required include files, utility functions, and the like are in an appendix or on the disc provided with the book. Throughout, we identify those features supported only by Windows 2000 and NT, because Windows 98, 95, and CE do not implement many advanced features. Each chapter suggests related additional reading and gives some exercises. Many exercises address interesting and important issues that did not fit within the normal text, and others allow the reader to explore advanced or specialized topics.

Chapter 1 is a high-level introduction to the Windows OS family and Win32. A simple example program shows the basic elements of Win32 programming style and lays the foundation for more advanced Win32 features. Win64 and migration issues are introduced in Chapter 1, described extensively in Chapter 16, and included throughout the book as required.

Chapters 2 and 3 deal with file systems, console I/O, file locking, and directory management. Unicode, the extended character set used by Windows 2000/NT, is also introduced in Chapter 2. Examples include sequential and direct file processing and a directory traversal program. Chapter 3 ends with a discussion of registry management programming, which is similar in many ways to file and directory management.

Chapter 4 introduces Win32's Structured Exception Handling (SEH) capability, which will be used extensively throughout the book. Many books defer SEH to later chapters, but by introducing it early we will be able to use SEH throughout and thus simplify some programming tasks and improve quality.

Chapter 5 explains Windows NT object security, showing, in an example, how to emulate UNIX-style file permissions. Security upgrades can then be applied to the examples as appropriate. Although security is used in the later chapters, feel free to skip this chapter if you are not interested in this topic.

Chapter 6 treats Win32 memory management and shows how to use memory-mapped files both to simplify programming and for performance. This chapter also covers dynamic link libraries (DLLs).

Chapter 7 introduces Win32 processes, process management, and simple process synchronization. Chapter 8 then describes thread management in similar terms. Examples in each chapter show the many benefits, including program simplicity and performance, of threads and processes.

Chapters 9 and 10 provide an extended, in-depth treatment of Win32 thread synchronization, one of Win32's strong features. Synchronization is a complex topic, and these two chapters use extended examples and well understood models to help you obtain the programming and performance benefits of threads while avoiding many of the pitfalls.

Chapters 11 and 12 are concerned with interprocess and interthread communication and networking. Chapter 11 concentrates on the features that are properly part of Win32—namely, pipes, named pipes, and mailslots. Chapter 12 treats Windows Sockets, which allow interoperability with non-Windows systems using industry-standard protocols, primarily TCP/IP. Windows Sockets, while not strictly part of Win32, provide for network and Internet communication and interoperability, and the subject matter is consistent with the rest of the book. A multithreaded client/server system illustrates how to use interprocess communication along with threads.

Chapter 13 describes how Windows 2000 and Windows NT provide "NT services" that allow you to manage background servers, such as the ones created in Chapters 11 and 12. Some small programming changes will turn the servers into NT services.

Chapter 14 shows how to use overlapped I/O with events and completion routines. For file systems, this feature applies only to Windows 2000 and NT, and you can achieve much the same thing with threads. The closely related I/O completion ports are, however, necessary for scalable multithreaded servers, so this feature is illustrated with the servers created in Chapters 11, 12, and 13. Waitable timers are described, because they require concepts first introduced in Chapter 14.

Chapter 15 concludes with a survey of two specialized topics: Remote Procedure Calls (RPCs) and Microsoft's COM object model, which integrates many of the concepts in the book. Remote procedures and COM objects frequently use the features described throughout this book. Simple examples are included, and this chapter illustrates that readers now have the necessary information to learn other Win32 topics beyond the core system services.

Chapter 16 describes the Win64 programming issues and how to plan for application migration and portability.

There are three appendices. Appendix A describes the programs on the disc and how to use them. Appendix B contains several tables that compare Win32 functions with their counterparts in UNIX and the Standard C library. Appendix C compares the performance of alternative implementations of some of the examples in the text so that you can gauge the trade-offs between Win32 features, both basic and advanced, and the C library.

Notes on the Second Edition

The Second Edition includes extensive new material along with significant updating and reorganization. Objectives of the Second Edition include:

- Cover Windows 2000 and Win64 migration.

- Provide increased coverage of threads and synchronization. Chapter 10 is new, as are the examples in Chapter 9.

- Add coverage of sockets and remote procedure calls (Chapters 12 and 15) and NT services (Chapter 13), thereby dealing with issues that are important when developing services and servers, particularly for Windows 2000.

- Describe the performance implications of threads and synchronization in more depth (Chapters 9 and 10).

- Incorporate reader and student feedback to fix defects, improve explanations, improve the organization, and address numerous small details.

UNIX and C Library Notes and Tables

Within the text at appropriate points, we contrast Win32 style and functionality with the comparable UNIX (and LINUX) and ANSI Standard C library features.

Tables listing the comparable functions are presented in Appendix B. This information is included because many readers are familiar with UNIX and are interested in the comparisons between the two systems. Readers without a UNIX background should feel free to skip these paragraphs. Such discussions are indented, in a smaller font.

Examples

The examples are designed to do the following:

- Illustrate common, representative, and useful applications of the Win32 functions.

- Correspond to real programming situations encountered in program development, consulting, and teaching. Some of my clients and course participants have used the code examples as the bases for their own systems. During my consulting activities, I frequently encounter code that is similar to that used in the examples, and on several occasions I have seen code taken directly from the First Edition. (Feel free to do so yourself, and an acknowledgment in your documentation would be greatly appreciated.) Frequently, this code occurs as part of COM or C++ objects. The examples are "real-world" examples and solve "real-world" problems.

- Emphasize how the functions actually behave and interact, which is not always as you might first expect after reading the documentation. Throughout this book, the text and the examples concentrate on interactions between functions rather than the functions themselves.

- Grow and expand, adding new capability to a previous solution in an easy and natural manner and exploring alternative implementation techniques.

- In the earlier chapters, many examples implement UNIX commands, such as `ls`, `touch`, `chmod`, and `sort`, showing the Win32 functions in a familiar context while creating a useful set of utilities.[2] Different implementations of the same command will also give us an easy way to compare performance benefits available with advanced Win32 features. Appendix C contains the results of these performance tests.

---

[2] Several commercial and freeware products provide complete sets of UNIX utilities; there is no intent to supplement them. These examples, although useful, are primarily intended to illustrate the use of Win32 features. A reader who is not familiar with UNIX should not, however, have any difficulty understanding the programs or their functionality.

Examples in the early chapters are usually short, but the later chapters present longer examples when appropriate.

Exercises at the end of each chapter suggest alternative designs, subjects for investigation, and additional functionality that is important but beyond the scope of this book. Some exercises are easy, and a few are very challenging. Frequently, clearly labeled defective solutions are provided, because fixing the bugs is an excellent way to sharpen skills.

All examples have been debugged and tested under Windows 2000, Windows NT, and, where appropriate, Windows 98 and 95. For Windows NT testing we used Version 4.0, and although the bulk of the development was performed on single-processor, Intel-based systems, many programs were also tested on multiprocessor systems. The client/server applications have been tested using multiple clients simultaneously interacting with a server. Nonetheless, there is no guarantee or assurance of program correctness, completeness, or fitness for any purpose. Undoubtedly, even the simplest examples contain defects or will fail under some conditions; such is the fate of nearly all software. I will, however, gratefully appreciate any messages regarding program defects—and, better still, fixes.

Book errata, along with additional examples, reader contributions, additional explanations, and much more, will be maintained at my home page: `http://world.std.com/~jmhart`. The code will be updated as required when defects are found and fixed and as reader input is received. If you encounter any difficulties with the programs or any material in the book, check this location first, because there may already be a fix or explanation. If that does not answer your question, feel free to send e-mail to `jmhart@world.std.com`.

Acknowledgments

Numerous people have provided assistance, advice, and encouragement during the preparation of the second edition. In particular, I've received many excellent and invaluable suggestions from readers and reviewers; their contributions have added significantly to the book's accuracy and completeness.

Major contributors of material, ideas, insights, solutions, and explanations that have found their way into the Second Edition include Steve Evans, Mike Francis, Craig Hill, Mike Innes, Vadim Kavelerov, Thomas Ollson, David Poulton, Donna Reese, Andrew Tucker, and Christian Vogler. Numerous readers and students in the Win32 courses delivered using the First Edition have also contributed suggestions, fixed program bugs, and made intangible contributions too numerous to mention. The good parts of this book are often due to the influence of others; remaining faults are due to the author. Michael Slaughter and Gary Clarke have been excellent editors, providing just the right mix of encouragement and urging. The Addison-Wesley production staff have given excellent support. Elissa Armour, the compositor, contributed a high level of irreplaceable skill and patience in preparing the manuscript for production.

The Second Edition would not have been possible without the First Edition, and for that I remain grateful to (in alphabetical order) Ralph Davis, Ed Dekker, Bjørn Elstad, Alan Feuer, Peggy Harris, Carl Anton Holmboe, Shin-Wei Hwang, Shirley Kaltenbach, Joe Newcomer, Ali Rafieymehr, Edward Schiebel, and Larry Schmuhl.

The true inspiration and confidence required to write this book ultimately came from my parents, who taught me the importance, power, and enjoyment of the written word. I'll always be grateful for all that they have given.

Johnson (John) M. Hart
`jmhart@world.std.com`

1 | Getting Started with Win32 and Win64

This chapter introduces the Microsoft Windows family of operating systems—Windows 2000, Windows NT, Windows 98, Windows 95, and Windows CE—and the Win32 Application Programming Interface (API) used by all family members. The new 64-bit Win64 API is also described, and migration and portability between the two are discussed as required. From now on, we will speak mainly of Win32, but everything applies to Win64 as well unless noted otherwise.

The Win32 API, like any other operating system API, has its own set of conventions and programming techniques, which are driven by the Windows philosophy. A simple file copy example illustrates the Win32 programming style, and this same style is used for file management, process and memory management, and advanced features such as thread synchronization. The example is also shown coded using the Standard C library in order to contrast Win32 with more familiar programming styles.

The first step is to review the basic features that any modern operating system must provide and, from there, learn how to use these features in Win32.

Operating System Essentials

Win32 makes core operating system features available on systems ranging from laptop PCs to enterprise servers. Operating system features can be described by considering the most important resources that must be managed:

- **Memory**. The operating system (OS) manages a large, flat, virtual memory address space and transparently moves information between physical memory and disc storage.

- **File Systems**. The OS manages a named file space and provides both direct and sequential access as well as directory and file management. Most systems have a hierarchical name space.

- **Resource Naming and Location**. File naming allows for long, descriptive names, and the naming scheme is extended to objects such as devices, synchronization, and interprocess communication objects. The OS also locates and manages access to named objects.

- **Multitasking**. The OS must manage processes, threads, and other units of independent, asynchronous execution. Tasks can be preempted and scheduled according to dynamically determined priorities.

- **Communication and Synchronization**. The OS manages task-to-task communication and synchronization within single systems as well as communication between networked systems and with the Internet.

- **Security and Protection**. The OS provides flexible mechanisms to protect resources from unauthorized and accidental access and corruption.

The Win32 API supports all these features and makes them available to satisfy the normal OS requirements on a range of platforms. The Win32 API is supported on all the platforms, although there are limitations in some cases. The current platforms, collectively called "Windows," are:

- **Windows 2000**, which is expected to replace Windows NT and is targeted at servers and the high end of the desktop market.

- **Windows NT** 4.0 (3.51 is the most common predecessor version). NT Version 4.0 Service Pack 3 (SP 3) is assumed from now on when mentioning NT, because some features are missing in Version 3.51 and earlier service packs.[1] Version 5.0 is actually Windows 2000.

- **Windows 98** and **Windows 95** (or simply **Windows 9x**, because the distinction is rarely important), which are primarily desktop operating systems lacking, among other things, the NT and 2000 security features.

- **Windows CE**, which is targeted at smaller systems, such as palmtops and embedded processors, and provides a subset of Win32 features.

If that were all there was to it, however, Windows would not be unique. After all, numerous proprietary operating systems have these features, and UNIX has

---

[1] Microsoft releases service packs from time to time to fix bugs, add new features, and improve performance. SP4 is common, and SP5 is sometimes referred to as "NT embedded."

long been available on a wide range of systems. There are other advantages, both business and technical, to using Win32.

- Windows dominates the market, especially on the desktop. Therefore, Windows applications have a large target market, numbering in the tens of millions and dwarfing other desktop systems, including UNIX and the Macintosh.

- The market dominance of the Windows operating systems means that applications and software development tools are widely and inexpensively available for Windows. Furthermore, innovations often appear first on Windows systems.

- Windows applications can use a graphical user interface (GUI) that is familiar to millions of users.

- Windows is available for systems using Intel X86, Pentium, and compatible processors. NT is also available on Digital Alpha processor systems (2000 is portable but not available on non-Intel architectures), and Windows CE runs on a variety of processors. Symmetric multiprocessor (SMP) systems are also supported by 2000 and NT. Windows NT and 2000 are not confined to the desktop; they can also support departmental and enterprise servers and high-performance workstations.[2]

- Windows NT and 2000, but not Windows 9x and CE, are certified at the National Security Agency (NSA) C2 security level, something that is not standard in UNIX and many other systems.

- Most operating systems, other than UNIX, are proprietary to a few system architectures.

- The Windows operating systems have many features not available in standard UNIX, although they may be available in some UNIX implementations. Threads and C2-level security are two examples.

In summary, Windows provides modern operating system functionality and can run large applications formerly confined to UNIX, multiuser, or mainframe systems on cheap personal computers, exploiting a familiar user interface. Furthermore, Windows platforms scale from the desktop to the enterprise. Decisions to develop Win32 applications are driven by both technical features and business requirements.

---

[2] The range of Win32 host systems can be appreciated by considering that programs in this book have been tested on systems including an obsolete 486 system with 16MB of RAM to a four-processor, 2GB RAM, 500MHz Pentium III enterprise server.

Windows 3.1 as an Operating System

Windows 3.1 is not a consideration in this book, but it's worth noting that all Windows platforms retain features of, and backward compatibility with, Windows 3.1 and even DOS. By definition, Windows 3.1 and DOS, the once-common operating systems deployed by the tens of millions from the mid-1980s to the mid-1990s, are not fully functional operating systems. Their limitations stem from the fact that they were initially designed to meet the limited requirements of early PC applications and to operate efficiently on 16-bit CPUs. Limitations include the lack of true multitasking, the complexity of memory management based on a 16-bit architecture, limited file naming, and a lack of security.

Windows 3.1 and DOS, despite their great past success, long ago outlived their ability to support either the demands of larger applications or the capabilities of more powerful computer systems.

Win32 and Windows 2000, NT, 9x, and CE

Having several distinct 32-bit Windows operating systems can be confusing. From the programmer's perspective, they are similar. In particular, they all support the *identical* Win32 API. Programs developed for one system can, with considerable ease, run on another, providing source and, in most cases, binary portability.

For simplification, we'll use the terms "2000/NT" and "9x" when there is no need for differentiation. Including CE, there are then just three, rather than five, major Win32 family members.

Despite the similarities, there are a few differences and limitations.

- Windows 9x and CE do not have any security features.

- Windows 9x runs only on Intel systems.

- Only 2000/NT supports symmetric multiprocessing (SMP).

- Windows 9x does not support Unicode wide characters, whereas 2000/NT and CE use Unicode everywhere, including in file names.

- Numerous differences in Win32 API implementation and architecture can affect performance, and performance guidelines on one Windows platform may not apply to another.

- In general, Windows 9x and CE will not support as many resources, such as open files and concurrent processes.

- Windows 9x and CE have limited support for asynchronous I/O.

- A number of Windows 9x Win32 functions have restricted implementations, making them generally unusable.[3] The same is true for CE.

Windows 9x, then, can be viewed as the low-end desktop client platform. Windows 2000 and NT, on the other hand, can be viewed as the high-end client and server platforms, ready to take on the most demanding applications.[4] Finally, CE is targeted at the very low-end and embedded systems.

Other significant differences among the various operating systems are generally transparent to the programmer, because they relate to the implementation architecture.

Windows 2000 and NT are capable of supporting other "subsystem" environments, and the operating system kernel is truly protected from applications. Win32 is only one of several environments; POSIX subsystems are also available but are rarely used. The POSIX subsystem lacks essential features, such as networking (sockets) functions. Within the Win32 subsystem, Microsoft has provided a 16-bit Windows 3.1 and an MS-DOS environment. Windows 2000/NT can also support different underlying processor and system architectures and has a Hardware Abstraction Layer (HAL) to enable porting to different architectures, although this is not a direct concern for the application developer.

Win32, Standards, and Open Systems

This book is about developing applications using the Win32 API. For a programmer coming from UNIX and "open systems," it is natural to ask, "Is Win32 open?" "Is Win32 an industry standard?" "Is Win32 just another proprietary API?" The answers depend very much on the definitions of *open*, *industry standard*, and *proprietary*, as well as on the benefits that are expected from open systems.

The Win32 API is totally different from the standard UNIX API. Win32 does not conform to the X/Open standard or any other open industry standards formulated by standards bodies or industry consortia.

Win32 is controlled by one vendor. Although Microsoft solicits industry input and feedback, it remains the sole arbiter and implementor. This means that the user receives many of the benefits that open standards are intended to provide as well as other advantages:

---

[3] When we say that a system call function is "not implemented in Windows 9x," the function is actually available (your program will execute), but it returns results indicating that the call failed.

[4] Two major exceptions to this statement are worth noting. First, Win32 supports a 32-bit memory architecture, whereas 64-bit architectures are required for some applications. The 32-bit limitation will soon be removed, however, with Win64 and Intel IA-64 processors.

- Uniform implementations reach the market quickly.

- There are no proprietary "improvements" or "extensions" to baffle the programmer, although the differences among the various Win32 platforms must be considered.

- One vendor has defined and implemented competent OS products with all the required capabilities. Applications developers add value at a higher level.

- The underlying hardware platform is open. There are numerous Intel platform vendors to select from, and CE is available on several architectures.

Arguments will rage for years as to whether this situation is beneficial or harmful to users and the computer industry as a whole. This book will not settle the argument; it is merely intended to help the applications developer come up to speed quickly with Win32.

Windows systems do, however, support many essential standards. For example, Windows supports the ANSI Standard C library and a wide array of open interoperability standards. Thus, Windows Sockets provide a standard networked programming interface for access to TCP/IP and other networking protocols, allowing Internet access and interoperability with non-Windows systems. The same is true with Remote Procedure Calls (RPCs).[5] Diverse systems can communicate with high-level database management system (DBMS) protocols using Structured Query Language (SQL). Finally, Internet support with Web and other servers is a part of the total Windows offering. The key standards, such as TCP/IP, are supported by Windows, and many added-value options, including X Windows clients and servers, are available at reasonable cost in an active market of Windows solution suppliers.

In summary, Windows supports the essential interoperability standards, and, while the core API is proprietary, it is available cost-effectively on a wide variety of systems.

Compatibility Libraries

Compatibility libraries are possible and available, but are rarely used. There are two possibilities:

- A Win32 compatibility library can be hosted on UNIX, a Macintosh, or some other system, allowing source code portability from Win32.

---

[5] Windows Sockets and RPC are not properly part of Win32, but they are described in this book because they relate directly to the general subject matter and approach.

- A POSIX compatibility library can be hosted on top of the Win32 subsystem. Several commercial products do just this. Microsoft's Visual C++ development environment includes a limited compatibility library.

In summary, it is possible, but rare, to select one API and host portable applications on Win32, POSIX, or even Macintosh systems.

Win32 Principles

There are some basic Win32 principles to keep in mind. Furthermore, the Win32 API is different in many ways, both large and small, from other APIs such as the POSIX API familiar to UNIX programmers. Although Win32 is not inherently difficult, it requires some changes in coding style and technique.

Here are some of the major characteristics of Win32:

- Nearly every system resource is a *kernel object* identified and referenced by a *handle*. These handles play all the roles played by, for example, UNIX file descriptors and process IDs.[6]

- Kernel objects must be manipulated by Win32 APIs. There are no "back doors." This arrangement is consistent with the data abstraction principles of object-oriented programming, although Win32 is not object-oriented.

- Objects include files, processes, threads, pipes for interprocess communication, memory mapping, events, and many more. Objects have security attributes.

- Win32 is a rich and flexible interface. First, it contains many functions that perform the same or similar operations; in particular, convenience functions combine common sequences of function calls into one function. Second, a given function will often have numerous parameters and flags, many of which can normally be ignored. This book concentrates on the most important functions and options rather than being encyclopedic.

- Win32 offers numerous synchronization and communication mechanisms tailored for different requirements.

- Instead of a process, as in UNIX, the Win32 thread is the basic unit of execution. A process can contain one or more threads.

- Win32 function names are long and descriptive. The function names

---

[6] These handles are similar to, but not the same as, the HWND and HDC handles used in Windows GUI programming.

```
WaitForSingleObject

WaitForSingleObjectEx

WaitForMultipleObjects

WaitNamedPipe
```

illustrate function name conventions as well as Win32's variety. In addition to these features, there are a few conventions for type names.

- Predefined data types, required by the API, are in uppercase and are also descriptive. The following typical types occur frequently:

    BOOL (defined as a 32-bit object for storing a single logical value)

    HANDLE

    DWORD (the ubiquitous 32-bit unsigned integer)

    LPTSTR (a string pointer of either 8- or 16-bit characters)

    LPSECURITY_ATTRIBUTES

Many other data types will be introduced as required.

- The predefined types avoid the * operator and make distinctions such as differentiating LPTSTR (defined as TCHAR *) from LPCTSTR (defined as const TCHAR *). *Note*: TCHAR may be a normal char or a two-byte wchar_t.

- Variable names, at least in function prototypes, also have conventions. For example, lpszFileName might be a "long pointer to a zero-terminated string" representing a file name. This is the so-called Hungarian notation, which this book does not generally use for program variables. Similarly, fdwAccess is a double word (32 bits) containing file access flags; "fdw" denotes "flags in a double word."

Note: It is informative to look at the system include files where the functions, constants, flags, error codes, and so on are defined. There are many interesting files, such as the following, that are part of the Microsoft Visual C++ environment and are normally installed in the Program Files\Microsoft Visual Studio\ VC98\Include directory:

WINDOWS.H (this file brings in all the others)

WINNT.H

WINBASE.H

Finally, even though Win32 was designed from scratch, it is backward-compatible with the Windows 3.1 Win16 API. This has several effects that will annoy the 32-bit programmer. For example:

- There are anachronisms in types, such as `LPTSTR` and `LPDWORD`, which refer to the "long pointer" that is simply a 32-bit pointer. There is no need for any other pointer type. At other times, the "long" is omitted, and `LPVOID` and `PVOID` are equivalent.[7]

- The need for backward compatibility means that there are numerous 16-bit functions that are never used in this book, even though they might seem important. `OpenFile` is such a function; always use `CreateFile` to open an existing file.

Getting Ready for Win64

Win64, which can be supported by Windows 2000 on Intel's Itanium (formerly code named "Merced") processor, will be an increasingly important factor in the building of large applications. The essential difference between Win32 and Win64 is the size of pointer variables (64 bits in Win64) and the size of virtual address space.

Throughout this book, Win64 migration is discussed as appropriate, and the programs are built so that a simple compiler switch will enable you to build the programs as Win64 applications.

Most of the differences, from a programming point of view, concern the size of pointers and careful avoidance of the assumption that a pointer and an integer (`LONG`, `DWORD`, etc.) are of the same length. Thus, the types `DWORD32` and `DWORD64` are defined so that you explicitly control variable size. Two other types, `POINTER_32` and `POINTER_64`, control pointer size.

With a little care, you will find that it is fairly simple to ensure that your programs will run under either Win32 or Win64, and, in general, we will use "Win32," or sometimes "Windows," to refer to the API. Chapter 16 provides more information on Win64, including information on source and binary compatibility issues.

UNIX programmers will find some interesting differences. HANDLEs are "opaque." They are not integers allocated in sequential order. Thus, the fact that 0, 1, and 2

---

[7] The `include` files contain types, such as `PVOID`, without the prefix, but the examples conform to the usage in many other books and the Microsoft documentation.

are special file descriptor values, which is important to some UNIX programs, has no analogy in Win32.

Many of the distinctions between, say, process IDs and file descriptors go away. Win32 simply uses a HANDLE for both. Many important functions treat file, process, event, pipe, and other handles identically.

The UNIX programmer familiar with short, lowercase functions and parameter names will need to adjust to the more verbose Win32 style. The Win32 style is closer to that of VAX VMS, and VMS programmers will find many familiar features. One reason for the similarity to VMS is that the original VMS architect, David Cutler, assumed a similar role with NT and Win32.

Critical distinctions are made with such familiar concepts as processes. Win32 processes do not, for example, have parent-child or comparable process group relationships.

Finally, Windows text files represent the end-of-line sequence with CR–LF rather than with LF as in UNIX.

The Standard C Library: When to Use It for File Processing

Despite Win32's unique features, it is still possible to achieve most file processing (the subject of Chapters 2 and 3) using the familiar C programming language and its ANSI Standard C library. The C library (the adjectives ANSI and Standard are often omitted) also contains numerous indispensable functions that do not correspond to Win32 system calls, such as <string.h>, <stdlib.h>, <signal.h>, formatted I/O functions, and character I/O. Other functions, however, correspond closely to system calls, such as the fopen and fread functions in <stdio.h>.

When is the C library adequate, and when is it necessary to use native Win32 file management system calls? There is no easy answer, but portability to non-Windows platforms is a consideration in favor of the C library if an application needs only file processing and not, for example, process management or other Win32 capabilities. However, many programmers have formulated guidelines as to when the C library is or is not adequate, and these same guidelines should apply to Win32. In addition, given the increased power, performance potential, and flexibility provided by Win32, it is often convenient or even necessary to go beyond the C library, as we will see starting as early as Chapter 3. Win32 file processing features not available with the C library include file locking, memory mapping (required for memory sharing), asynchronous I/O, random access to very long files (more than 4GB in length), and interprocess communication.

The C library file management functions are often adequate for simple programs. With the C library, it is possible to write portable applications without learning Win32, but options will be limited. For example, Chapter 6 exploits memory-mapped files for performance and programming convenience, and this functionality is not included in the C library.

The following sections show short example programs implementing a simple sequential file copy program in three different ways:

1. Using the standard C library

2. Using Win32

3. Using a single Win32 convenience function, `CopyFile`

In addition to showing contrasting programming models, these examples will show the capabilities and the limitations of the C library and Win32. Alternative implementations will enhance the program to improve performance and increase flexibility.

What You Need to Use This Book

Before presenting the first examples, here is what you will need, both to build and to run the examples, and for the rest of the book.

First, of course, it is helpful to bring your knowledge of applications development in UNIX or some other OS, and knowledge of C programming is assumed. Before you tackle the exercises and examples, however, you will need hardware and software. These are the basics:

- A system running Windows 9x or Windows 2000/NT. One of each is even better. Only 2000/NT will run the asynchronous I/O, security, and named pipe server examples.

- A C compiler and development system, such as Microsoft Visual C++ Version 4.0 or greater. Version 6.0 was used for the examples and is recommended. Other vendors also supply development systems, but none has been tested with the examples. The Windows 2000 software development kit (SDK) is required if you wish to explore Win64 issues.

- Enough RAM and disc space for program development. Check the requirements for the development system. I have found that as little as 32MB RAM and 250MB free disc space are sufficient, if minimal, so system resources should not be a limiting issue.

- A CD-ROM drive, on either the system or the network, to install the development system.

- The on-line documentation, such as that provided with Microsoft Visual C++. It is recommended that this documentation be installed on the disc, because you will access it frequently.

- CE developers will most likely develop and emulate under 2000/NT or 9x before testing on an actual CE platform.

Example: A Simple Sequential File Copy

Sequential file processing is the simplest, most common, and most essential capability of any file system, and nearly any large program processes at least some files sequentially.

File copying, often with updating, and the merging of sorted files are common forms of sequential processing. Compilers and text processing tools are examples of other applications that access files sequentially.

Although sequential file processing is conceptually simple, efficient processing that achieves optimal speed can be much more difficult to achieve. It can require overlapped I/O, memory mapping, threads, or other techniques.

Simple file copying is not very interesting by itself, but comparing programs gives us a quick way to contrast different systems and to introduce Win32. The following examples implement a limited version of the UNIX cp command, copying one file to another where the file names are specified on the command line. Error checking is minimal, and existing files are simply overwritten. Subsequent Win32 implementations of this and other programs will address these and other shortcomings. *Note*: A UNIX implementation is included on the disc provided with this book.

File Copying with the Standard C Library

As illustrated in Program 1–1, the Standard C library supports stream FILE I/O objects that are similar to, although not as general as, the Win32 HANDLE objects shown in Program 1–2.

Program 1–1   cpC: File Copying with the C Library

```
/* Chapter 1. Basic cp file copy program.
   C library Implementation. */
/* cp file1 file2: Copy file1 to file2. */

#include <stdio.h>
#include <errno.h>
#define BUF_SIZE 256

int main (int argc, char *argv [])
{
    FILE *in_file, *out_file;
    char rec [BUF_SIZE];
```

```
    size_t bytes_in, bytes_out;
    if (argc != 3) {
        printf ("Usage: cpC file1 file2\n");
        return 1;
    }
    in_file = fopen (argv [1], "rb");
    if (in_file == NULL) {
        perror (argv [1]);
        return 2;
    }
    out_file = fopen (argv [2], "wb");
    if (out_file == NULL) {
        perror (argv [2]);
        return 3;
    }

    /* Process the input file a record at a time. */
    while ((bytes_in = fread (rec, 1, BUF_SIZE, in_file)) > 0) {
        bytes_out = fwrite (rec, 1, bytes_in, out_file);
        if (bytes_out != bytes_in) {
            perror ("Fatal write error.");
            return 4;
        }
    }
    fclose (in_file);
    fclose (out_file);
    return 0;
}
```

This simple example clearly illustrates some common programming assumptions and conventions that do not always apply with Win32.

1. Open file objects are identified by pointers to FILE structures (UNIX uses integer file descriptors). NULL indicates an invalid value. The pointers are, in effect, a form of "handle" to the open file object.

2. The call to fopen specifies whether the file is to be treated as a text file or a binary file. Text files contain system-specific character sequences to indicate situations such as an end of line. On many systems, including Windows, I/O operations on a text file convert between the end-of-line character sequence and the null character that C interprets as the end of a string. In the example, both files are opened in binary mode.

3. Errors are diagnosed with perror, which, in turn, accesses the global variable errno to obtain information about the function call failure. Alternatively, the

ferror function will return an error code that is associated with the FILE rather than the system.

4. The fread and fwrite functions directly return the number of bytes processed, rather than return the value in an argument, and this arrangement is essential to the program logic. A successful read is indicated by a non-negative value, and 0 indicates an end of file.

5. The fclose function applies only to FILE objects (a similar statement applies to UNIX file descriptors).

6. The I/O is synchronous so that the program must wait for the I/O operation to complete before proceeding.

7. The C library printf I/O function is useful for error messages and occurs even in the initial Win32 example.

The C library implementation has the advantage of portability to UNIX, Win32, and other systems that support ANSI C. Furthermore, as shown in Appendix C, C library performance for sequential I/O is competitive with alternative implementations. Nonetheless, programs are still constrained to synchronous I/O operations.

C library file processing programs, like their UNIX equivalents, are able to perform random access file operations (using fseek or, in the case of text files, fsetpos and fgetpos), but that is the limit of sophistication of Standard C library file I/O. *Note*: Visual C++ does provide nonstandard extensions that support, for example, file locking. Finally, the C library cannot control file security.

In summary, if simple synchronous file or console I/O is all that is needed, then use the C library to write portable programs that will run under Win32.

File Copying with Win32

Program 1–2 shows the same program using the Win32 API, and the same basic techniques, style, and conventions will be used throughout this book.

Program 1–2 cpW: File Copying with Win32, First Implementation

```
/* Chapter 1. Basic cp file copy program. Win32 Implementation. */
/* cpW file1 file2: Copy file1 to file2. */

#include <windows.h>
#include <stdio.h>
#define BUF_SIZE 256
int main (int argc, LPTSTR argv [])
{
```

```
    HANDLE hIn, hOut;
    DWORD nIn, nOut;
    CHAR Buffer [BUF_SIZE];

    if (argc != 3) {
        printf ("Usage: cpW file1 file2\n");
        return 1;
    }
    hIn = CreateFile (argv [1], GENERIC_READ, 0, NULL,
            OPEN_EXISTING, 0, NULL);
    if (hIn == INVALID_HANDLE_VALUE) {
        printf ("Cannot open input file. Error: %x\n",
                GetLastError ());
        return 2;
    }
    hOut = CreateFile (argv [2], GENERIC_WRITE, 0, NULL,
            CREATE_ALWAYS, FILE_ATTRIBUTE_NORMAL, NULL);
    if (hOut == INVALID_HANDLE_VALUE) {
        printf ("Cannot open output file. Error: %x\n",
                GetLastError ());
        return 3;
    }
    while (ReadFile (hIn, Buffer, BUF_SIZE, &nIn, NULL) && nIn > 0) {
        WriteFile (hOut, Buffer, nIn, &nOut, NULL);
        if (nIn != nOut) {
            printf ("Fatal write error: %x\n", GetLastError ());
            return 4;
        }
    }
    CloseHandle (hIn);
    CloseHandle (hOut);
    return 0;
}
```

This simple example illustrates some Win32 programming features that Chapter 2 will start to explain in detail.

1. <windows.h> is always included and contains all Win32 function definitions and data types.[8]

2. All Win32 objects are identified by variables of type HANDLE, and a single generic CloseHandle function applies to most objects.

---

[8] Appendix A shows how to exclude unwanted definitions to expedite compilations and save disc space.

3. It is recommended that all open handles be closed when they are no longer required so as to free resources. Nonetheless, the handles will be closed automatically when a process exits.

4. Win32 defines numerous symbolic constants and flags. Their names are usually quite long and often describe their purposes. INVALID_HANDLE_VALUE and GENERIC_READ are typical.

5. Functions such as ReadFile and WriteFile return Boolean values rather than byte counts, which are arguments. This alters the loop logic slightly.[9] The end of file is detected by a zero byte count and is not a failure.

6. System error codes, as DWORDs, can be obtained at any point through GetLastError. Chapter 2 will show how to obtain Win32-generated textual error messages.

7. Windows NT has a more powerful security system, described in Chapter 5. The output file in this example is not secured.

8. Functions such as CreateFile have a rich set of options, and the example uses default values.

File Copying with a Win32 Convenience Function

Win32 has a number of convenience functions that combine several functions to perform a common task. These convenience functions can also improve performance in some cases (see Appendix C). CopyFile, for example, greatly simplifies the program (Program 1–3). Among other things, there is no need to be concerned with the appropriate buffer size, which was arbitrarily set to 256 in the two preceding programs.

Program 1-3   cpCF: File Copying with a Win32 Convenience Function

```
/* Chapter 1. Basic cp file copy program. Win32 implementation
   using CopyFile for convenience and improved performance. */
/* cpCF file1 file2: Copy file1 to file2. */

#include <windows.h>
#include <stdio.h>

int main (int argc, LPTSTR argv [])
{
```

---

[9] Notice that the loop logic depends on ANSI C's left-to-right evaluation of logical "and" (&&) and logical "or" (||) operations.

```
    if (argc != 3) {
        printf ("Usage: cpCF file1 file2\n");
        return 1;
    }
    if (!CopyFile (argv [1], argv [2], FALSE)) {
        printf ("CopyFile Error: %x\n", GetLastError ());
        return 2;
    }
    return 0;
}
```

Summary

The three simple file copy programs, Programs 1–1, 1–2, and 1–3, illustrate many of the differences between C library and Win32 programs. Appendix C shows some of the performance differences among the various implementations. The Win32 examples clearly illustrate Win32 programming style and conventions but only hint at the functionality available to Win32 programmers.

Looking Ahead

Chapters 2 and 3 take a much more extensive look at I/O and the file system. Topics include console I/O, ASCII and Unicode character processing, file and directory management, file attributes, and advanced options, as well as registry programming. These two chapters develop the basic techniques and lay the groundwork for the rest of the book.

Additional Reading

Publication information about the following books is listed in the bibliography.

Win32

Mastering Windows NT Programming, by Brian Myers and Eric Hamer, *Win32 System Services*, by Marshall Brain, and *Programming Applications for Microsoft Windows* (formerly *Advanced Windows* in earlier editions), by Jeffrey Richter all cover Win32 programming subjects from varying perspectives. *Win32 Network Programming*, by Ralph Davis, gives shorter discussions of many of the same topics and is not limited to networking.

The hypertext on-line help available with Microsoft Visual C++ documents every function.

The Microsoft home page, http://www.microsoft.com, contains a number of technical papers covering different Win32 subjects. Start with the MSDN (Microsoft Developer's Network) section and search for any topic of interest. You'll find a variety of white papers, product descriptions, sample code, and other useful information.

The *Microsoft Windows NT Resource Kit* is a comprehensive information source for supporting NT. The resource kit contains source code for some helpful utility programs.

Win64

Few books discuss Win64, but you can also find a wealth of material on the Microsoft home page. See Chapter 16 for more information.

Windows NT Architecture

Inside Windows NT, by Helen Custer (second edition by David A. Solomon), referred to as "Custer/Solomon," is for the reader who wants to know more about NT design objectives or who wants to understand the NT architecture. The book discusses NT objects, processes, threads, virtual memory, the kernel, and I/O subsystems, and the discussion is largely applicable to Windows 2000. It does not, however, discuss the actual API functions or Windows 9x and CE. You may want to refer to Custer/Solomon as you read this book.

UNIX

Advanced Programming in the UNIX Environment, by the late W. Richard Stevens ("Stevens" from now on), discusses UNIX in much the same terms in which this book discusses Win32. Stevens is the standard reference on standard UNIX features, but the book does not discuss threads. UNIX standardization has progressed, but Stevens is a convenient working definition of what UNIX provides. This book also contrasts C library file I/O with UNIX I/O, and this discussion is relevant to Win32.

Windows GUI Programming

Windows user interfaces are not covered here. See Rector and Newcomer, *Win32 Programming*.

Operating Systems Theory

There are many good texts on general operating system theory. *Operating System Concepts*, by A. Silberschatz and P. Galvin, is one of the more popular.

The ANSI Standard C Library

The Standard C Library, by P. J. Plauger, is a comprehensive guide. For a quick overview, *The C Programming Language*, by B. W. Kernighan and D. M. Ritchie, lists and explains the complete library. These books can be used to help decide whether the C library is adequate for your file processing requirements.

Windows CE

SAMS Teach Yourself Windows CE Programming in 24 Hours by Makofsky, Nottingham, and Tucker is recommended for those who wish to apply the material in this book to Windows CE.

Exercises

1–1. Compile, build, and execute the three file copy programs. Other possibilities include using UNIX compatibility libraries, including the Microsoft Visual C++ library (a program using this library is included on the disc). *Note*: The source code is included on the disc. Appendix A gives some brief notes on getting started with Visual C++.

1–2. Become familiar with a development environment, such as Visual C++. In particular, learn how to build console applications. Also experiment with the debugger on the programs in this chapter.

1–3. Windows uses the carriage return–line feed (CR–LF) sequence to denote an end of line. Determine the effect on Program 1–1 if the input file is opened in binary mode and the output file in text mode, and conversely. What is the effect under UNIX or some other system?

1–4. Time the file copy programs on any large file. Obtain data for as many of the combinations as possible. Later, compare these times with enhanced Win32 versions of the programs. Needless to say, performance depends on many factors, but, by keeping other system parameters the same, it is possible to get helpful comparisons between the implementations. *Suggestion*: tabulate the results in a spreadsheet to facilitate analysis. Chapter 7 contains a program for timing programs, and Appendix C gives some experimental results.

2 Using the Win32 File System and Character I/O

The file system and simple terminal I/O are often the first operating system features that the developer encounters. Early PC operating systems such as MS-DOS did little except manage files and terminal (or *console*) I/O, and these resources are also central features of nearly every operating system.

Files are essential for the long-term storage of data and programs and are the simplest form of program-to-program communication. Furthermore, many aspects of the file system model apply to interprocess and network communication.

The file copy programs in Chapter 1 introduced the four essential sequential file processing functions:

```
CreateFile      WriteFile

ReadFile        CloseHandle
```

This chapter will explain these and other related functions and will also describe character processing and console I/O functions in detail. First, it is necessary to say a few words about the various file systems available and their principal characteristics. In the process, we'll show how to use Unicode wide characters for internationalization. The chapter concludes with an introduction to Win32 file and directory management.

The Win32 File Systems

There are three file systems to deal with, but only the first two will be important throughout this book.

1. The *File Allocation Table* (FAT) file system descends from the original MS-DOS and Windows 3.1 file systems. FAT has been extensively updated to support long file names (DOS and Windows 3.1 have an 11-character limit). This updated system is called the Virtual FAT (VFAT), but the distinction is omitted from now on. The FAT file system is the only one available on diskettes and Windows 9x discs (other than CD-ROMs). FAT32 is a variation that manages disc space more efficiently.

2. The *NT* file system (NTFS) is unique to 2000/NT. In addition to supporting long file names, it provides security, recoverability, compression, extended attributes, and support for very large files and volumes.

3. The *CD-ROM* file system (CDFS), as the name implies, is for accessing information provided on CD-ROMs. Windows NT and Windows 95 both support the CDFS.

All the file systems are accessed in the same way but with limitations. For example, only the NTFS supports security. This book will point out features unique to NTFS as appropriate.

Windows 2000/NT also allows the development of custom file systems, and NT 3.51 supports the so-called *High Performance* file system used with OS/2.

The format of a file system, as a disc volume or partition, is determined when a disc is partitioned. A disc can be partitioned with any combination of the first two file systems.

File Naming

Win32 supports hierarchical file naming, but there are a few subtle distinctions for the UNIX user and basic rules for everyone.

- The full pathname of a disc file starts with a drive name, such as A: or C:. The A: and B: drives are normally diskette drives, and C:, D:, and so on are hard discs and CD-ROMs. Network drives are usually designated by letters that fall later in the alphabet, such as H: and K:.

- Alternatively, a full pathname, or Universal Naming Code" (UNC), can start with a double backslash, indicating the global root, followed by a server name and a *share* name to indicate a path on a network file server. The first part of the pathname, then, is \\servername\sharename.

- The pathname *separator* is the backslash (\), although the forward slash (/) can be used in API parameters, which is more convenient in C.

- Directory and file names cannot contain any of the ASCII characters with values in the range 1–31 or any of these characters:

  < > : " |

  Names can contain blanks. However, when using file names with blanks on a command line, be sure to put each file name in quotes so that the name is not interpreted as naming two distinct files.

- Directory and file names are *case-insensitive*, but they are also *case-retaining*, so that if the creation name is `MyFile`, the file name will show up as it was created, but the file can also be accessed with the name `myFILE`.

- File and directory names can be as many as 255 characters long, and pathnames are limited to `MAX_PATH` characters (currently 260).

- A period (`.`) separates a file's name from its extension, and extensions quite often indicate the file's type. Thus, `atou.EXE` would be an executable file, and `atou.C` would be a C language source file.

- `.` and `..`, as directory names, indicate the current directory and its parent.

With this introduction, it is now time to learn more about the Win32 functions introduced in Chapter 1.

Opening, Reading, Writing, and Closing Files

The first Win32 function described in detail is `CreateFile`. It is used for opening existing files and creating new ones. This and other functions will be described first by showing the function prototype and then by describing the parameters and operation.

Creating and Opening Files

This is the first Win32 function, so it is described in some detail; later descriptions will frequently be much more streamlined. Nonetheless, `CreateFile` has numerous options not described here; this additional detail can always be found in the on-line help.

The simplest use of `CreateFile` is illustrated in Chapter 1's introductory Win32 program (Program 1–2), in which there are two calls, both of which rely on default values for `fdwShareMode`, `lpsa`, and `hTemplateFile`. `fdwAccess` is either `GENERIC_READ` or `GENERIC_WRITE`.

```
HANDLE CreateFile (
    LPCTSTR lpszName,
    DWORD fdwAccess,
    DWORD fdwShareMode,
    LPSECURITY_ATTRIBUTES lpsa,
    DWORD fdwCreate,
    DWORD fdwAttrsAndFlags,
    HANDLE hTemplateFile)

Return: A HANDLE to an open file object, or
        INVALID_HANDLE_VALUE in case of failure.
```

Parameters

The parameter names illustrate some Win32 conventions. The prefix fdw is used when a DWORD (32 bits, unsigned) contains flags, and lpsz ("long pointer to a zero-terminated string") is for pathnames and other strings, although the Microsoft documentation is not entirely consistent. At times, you need to use common sense or read the documentation carefully to determine the correct data types.

lpszName is a pointer to the null-terminated string that names the file, pipe, or other named object to open or create. The pathname is normally limited to MAX_PATH (260) characters, but Windows 2000/NT can circumvent this restriction if the pathname is prefixed with \\?\ to allow for very long pathnames (as long as 32K). The prefix is not part of the name. The LPCTSTR data type will be explained in an upcoming section; just regard it as a string data type for now.

fdwAccess specifies the read and write access, using GENERIC_READ and GENERIC_WRITE. Flag values such as READ and WRITE do not exist. The GENERIC_ prefix may seem redundant, but it is required. Numerous other constant names may seem longer than necessary.

These values can be combined with a bit-wise "or" (|), so to open a file for read and write access, use the following:

GENERIC_READ | GENERIC_WRITE

fdwShareMode is a bit-wise "or" combination of the following:

- 0—The file cannot be shared. Furthermore, not even this process can open a second handle on this file. (Uppercase HANDLE is used only when it is important to emphasize the data type.)

- FILE_SHARE_READ—Other processes, including the one making this call, can open this file for concurrent read access.

- FILE_SHARE_WRITE—This allows concurrent writing to the file.

By using locks or other mechanisms, the programmer must take care to prevent concurrent updates to the same file location. There will be much more about this in Chapter 3.

lpsa points to a SECURITY_ATTRIBUTES structure. Use NULL values for now; security is treated in Chapter 5.

fdwCreate specifies whether to create a new file, whether to overwrite an existing file, and so on. The individual values can be combined with the C bit-wise "or" operator.

- CREATE_NEW—Fail if the specified file already exists; otherwise, create a new file.

- CREATE_ALWAYS—An existing file will be overwritten.

- OPEN_EXISTING—Fail if the file does not exist.

- OPEN_ALWAYS—Open the file, creating it if it does not exist.

- TRUNCATE_EXISTING—The file length will be set to zero. fdwCreate must specify at least GENERIC_WRITE access.

fdwAttrsAndFlags specifies file attributes and flags. There are 16 flags and attributes. Attributes are characteristics of the file, as opposed to the open HANDLE, and are ignored when an existing file is opened. Here are some of the more important ones:

- FILE_ATTRIBUTE_NORMAL—This attribute can be used only when no other attributes are set (flags can be set, however).

- FILE_ATTRIBUTE_READONLY—Applications can neither write to nor delete the file.

- FILE_FLAG_DELETE_ON_CLOSE—This is useful for temporary files. The file is deleted when the last open HANDLE is closed.

- FILE_FLAG_OVERLAPPED—This attribute flag is important for asynchronous I/O, which is described in Chapter 14. It must be NULL for Windows 9x except for serial I/O devices.

Several additional flags also specify how a file is processed and help the Win32 implementation optimize performance and file integrity.

- `FILE_FLAG_WRITE_THROUGH`—Intermediate caches are written through directly to the file on disc.

- `FILE_FLAG_NO_BUFFERING`—There is no intermediate buffering or caching in user space, and data transfers occur directly to and from the program's buffers. Accordingly, the buffers are required to be on sector boundaries, and complete sectors must be transferred. Use the `GetDiskFreeSpace` function to determine the sector size when using this flag.

- `FILE_FLAG_RANDOM_ACCESS`—The file is intended for random access, and Windows will attempt to optimize file caching.

- `FILE_FLAG_SEQUENTIAL_SCAN`—The file is for sequential access, and Windows will optimize caching accordingly. These last two access modes are not enforced.

`hTemplateFile` is the handle of an open `GENERIC_READ` file that specifies extended attributes to apply to a newly created file, ignoring `fdwAttrsAndFlags`. Normally, this parameter is `NULL`. `hTemplateFile` is ignored when an existing file is opened. This parameter can be used to set the attributes of a new file to be the same as those of an existing file.

The two `CreateFile` instances in Program 1–2 use default values extensively and are as simple as possible but still appropriate for the task. It could be beneficial to use `FILE_FLAG_SEQUENTIAL_SCAN` in both cases. (Exercise 2–3 explores this option, and Appendix C shows the performance results.)

Notice that if the file share attributes and security permit it, there can be numerous open handles on a given file. The open handles can be owned by the same process or by different processes.

Closing Files

One all-purpose function closes and invalidates handles and releases system resources for nearly all objects. Exceptions will be noted. Closing a handle also decrements the object's handle reference count so that nonpersistent objects such as temporary files and events can be deleted. The system will close all open handles on exit, but it is still good practice for programs to close their handles before terminating.

Closing an invalid handle or closing the same handle twice will cause an exception (Chapter 4 discusses exceptions and exception handling). It is not necessary or appropriate to close standard device handles, which are discussed in the section entitled Standard Devices and Console I/O.

```
BOOL CloseHandle (HANDLE hObject)
```

Return: TRUE if the function succeeds; FALSE otherwise.

The comparable UNIX functions are different in a number of ways. The UNIX open function returns an integer file descriptor rather than a handle, and it specifies access, sharing, create options, and the attributes and flags in the single-integer oflag parameter. The options overlap, with Win32 providing a richer set.

There is no UNIX equivalent to fdwShareMode. UNIX files are always shareable.

Both systems use security information when creating a new file. In UNIX, the mode argument specifies the familiar user, group, and other file permissions.

close is comparable to CloseHandle, but it is not general purpose.

The C library <stdio.h> functions use FILE objects, which are comparable to handles (for disc files, terminals, tapes, and other devices) connected to streams. The fopen mode parameter specifies whether the file data is to be treated as binary or text. There is a set of options for read-only, update, append at the end, and so on. freopen allows FILE reuse without closing it first. Security permissions cannot be set.

fclose closes a FILE. Most stdio FILE-related functions have the f prefix.

Reading Files

```
BOOL ReadFile (
    HANDLE hFile,
    LPVOID lpBuffer,
    DWORD nNumberOfBytesToRead,
    LPDWORD lpNumberOfBytesRead,
    LPOVERLAPPED lpOverlapped)
```

Return: TRUE if the read succeeds (even if no bytes were read
    due to an attempt to read past the end of file).

Assume, until Chapter 14, that the file handle does *not* have the `FILE_FLAG_OVERLAPPED` option set in `fdwAttrsAndFlags`. For disc files, this assumption will always hold with Windows 9x and CE. `ReadFile`, then, starts at the current file position (for the handle) and advances the position by the number of bytes transferred.

The function fails, returning `FALSE`, if the handle is, or other parameters are, invalid. The function does not fail if the file handle is positioned at the end of file.

Parameters

Because of the long variable names and the natural arrangement of the parameters, they are largely self-explanatory. Nonetheless, here are some brief explanations.

`hFile` is a file handle with `GENERIC_READ` access. `lpBuffer` points to the memory buffer to receive the input data. `nNumberOfBytesToRead` is the number of bytes to read from the file.

`lpNumberOfBytesRead` points to the actual number of bytes read by the `ReadFile` call. This value can be zero if the handle is positioned at the end of file, and message-mode named pipes (Chapter 11) can have a zero-length message.

`lpOverlapped` points to an `OVERLAPPED` structure (Chapter 3 and Chapter 14). Use `NULL` for now.

Writing Files

```
BOOL WriteFile (
    HANDLE hFile,
    CONST VOID *lpBuffer,
    DWORD nNumberOfBytesToWrite,
    LPDWORD lpNumberOfBytesWritten,
    LPOVERLAPPED lpOverlapped)

Return: TRUE if the function succeeds; FALSE otherwise.
```

The parameters are familiar by now. Notice that a successful write does not ensure that the data actually is written through to the disc unless `FILE_FLAG_WRITE_THROUGH` is specified with `CreateFile`. If the handle is positioned at the file end, Win32 will extend the length of an existing file.

ReadFileGather and WriteFileGather allow you to read and write using a collection of buffers of different sizes.

UNIX read and write are the comparable functions, and the programmer supplies a file descriptor, buffer, and byte count. The functions return the number of bytes actually transferred. 0 on read indicates the end of file; –1 indicates an error. Win32, by contrast, requires a separate transfer count and returns Boolean values to indicate success or failure.

The functions in both systems are general purpose and can read from files, terminals, tapes, pipes, and so on.

The C standard I/O library fread and fwrite binary I/O functions use object size and object count rather than a single byte count as in UNIX and Win32. A short transfer could be caused by either an end of file or an error; test explicitly with ferror or feof. The library provides a full set of text-oriented functions, such as fgetc and fputc, that do not exist outside the C library in either OS.

Interlude: Unicode and Generic Characters

Before proceeding, it is necessary to explain how Windows processes characters and differentiates between 8- and 16-bit characters and generic characters.

Win32 supports standard 8-bit characters (type char or CHAR) and, in Windows 2000/NT, "wide" 16-bit characters (WCHAR, which is defined to be the C wchar_t type). The Microsoft documentation refers to the 8-bit character set as "ASCII," but it is actually the "Latin-1" character set; "ASCII" will be used for convenience. These types are capable of representing symbols and letters in all major languages, including English, French, Spanish, German, Japanese, and Chinese, using the Unicode representation.

Here are the steps to follow in order to write a generic Win32 application that can be built to use either Unicode or 8-bit characters:

1. Define all characters and strings using the generic types TCHAR, LPSTR, and LPCTSTR.

2. Include the definitions #define UNICODE and #define _UNICODE in all source modules to get Unicode wide characters (ANSI C wchar_t); otherwise, with UNICODE and _UNICODE undefined, TCHAR will be equivalent to CHAR (ANSI C char). The definition must precede the #include <windows.h> statement. The first preprocessor variable controls the Win32 function definitions, and the second one controls the C library.

3. Character buffer lengths—as used, for example, in ReadFile—must be calculated using sizeof (TCHAR).

4. Use the collection of generic C library string and character I/O functions in `<tchar.h>`. Representative functions that are available are `_fgettc`, `_itot` (for `itoa`), `_stprintf` (for `sprintf`), `_tstcpy` (for `strcpy`), `_ttoi`, `_totupper`, `_totlower`, and `_tprintf`.[1] See the on-line help for a complete and extensive list. All these definitions depend on `_UNICODE`. This collection is not complete. `memchr` is an example of a function without a wide character implementation. New versions are provided as required.

5. Constant strings should be in one of three forms. Use these conventions for single characters as well. The first two forms are ANSI C; the third—the `_T` macro (equivalently, `TEXT` and `_TEXT`)—is supplied with the Microsoft C compiler.

   ```
   "This string uses 8-bit characters"

   L"This string uses 16-bit characters"

   _T ("This string uses generic characters")
   ```

6. Include `<tchar.h>` after `<windows.h>` to get required definitions for text macros and generic C library functions.

Windows 2000/NT uses Unicode throughout, and NTFS file names and pathnames are represented in Unicode. If `UNICODE` is undefined, 8-bit strings will be converted to wide characters as required by calls to system functions. If the program is to run under Windows 95 or 98, which are not Unicode systems, *do not* define `UNICODE` and `_UNICODE`. Under NT, the definition is optional unless the executable is to run under both systems.

All future programs will use `TCHAR` instead of the normal `char` for characters and character strings unless there is a clear reason to deal with individual 8-bit characters. Similarly, the type `LPTSTR` indicates a pointer to a generic string, and `LPCTSTR` indicates, in addition, a constant string. At times, this choice will add some clutter to the programs, but it is the only choice that allows the flexibility necessary to develop the applications in either Unicode form or as 8-bit character programs that can be easily converted to Unicode at a later date. Furthermore, this choice is consistent with common, if not universal, industry practice.

It is worthwhile to examine the system include files to see how `TCHAR` and the system function interfaces are defined and how they depend on whether or not `UNICODE` and `_UNICODE` are defined. A typical entry is of the following form:

---

[1] The underscore character will indicate that a function or keyword is provided by Microsoft C. Other development systems provide similar capability but may use different names or keywords.

```
#ifdef UNICODE
#define TCHAR WCHAR
#else
#define TCHAR CHAR
#endif
```

Alternative Generic String Processing Functions

String comparisons can use `lstrcmp` and `lstrcmpi` rather than the generic `_tcscmp` and `_tcscmpi` to account for the specific language and region, or *locale*, at run time and also to perform *word* rather than *string* comparisons.[2] String comparisons simply compare the numerical values of the characters, whereas word comparisons consider locale-specific word order. The two methods can give opposite results for string pairs such as *coop/co-op* and *were/we're*.

There is also a group of Win32 functions for dealing with Unicode characters and strings. These functions handle local characteristics transparently. Typical functions are `CharUpper`, which can operate on strings as well as individual characters, and `IsCharAlphaNumeric`. Other string functions include `CompareString` (which is locale-specific) and `MultiByteToWideChar`. Multibyte characters in Windows 3.1 and 9x extend the 8-bit character set to allow double bytes to represent character sets for languages of the Far East. The generic library functions (`_tprintf` and the like) and the Win32 functions (`CharUpper` and the like) will be used in later examples to demonstrate their use. Examples in later chapters will rely mostly on the generic C library.

The Generic Main Function

The C main function, with its argument list (`argv [ ]`), should be replaced by the macro `_tmain`. The macro expands to either `main` or `wmain` depending on the `_UNICODE` definition. `_tmain` is defined in `<tchar.h>`, which must be included after `<windows.h>`. A typical main program heading, then, would look like this:

```
#include <windows.h>
#include <tchar.h>
int _tmain (int argc, LPTSTR argv [])
{
    ...
}
```

---

[2] Historically, the "l" prefix was used to indicate a long pointer to the character string parameters.

The Microsoft C _tmain function also supports a third parameter for environment strings. This nonstandard extension is also common in UNIX.

Function Definitions

A function such as CreateFile is defined through a preprocessor macro as CreateFileA when UNICODE is not defined and as CreateFileW when UNICODE is defined. The definitions also describe the string parameters as 8-bit or wide character strings. Consequently, compilers will report a source code error, such as an illegal parameter to CreateFile, as an error in the use of CreateFileA or CreateFileW.

Unicode Strategies

A programmer who is starting a Windows project, either to develop new code or to port existing code, can select from four strategies, based on project requirements.

1. **8-Bit Only**. Ignore Unicode and continue to use the char (or CHAR) data type and the Standard C library for functions such as printf, atoi, and strcmp.

2. **8-Bit but Unicode Enabled**. Follow the earlier guidelines for a generic application, but do not define the two Unicode preprocessor variables.

3. **Unicode Only**. Follow the generic guidelines, but define the two preprocessor variables. Alternatively, use wide characters and the wide character functions exclusively. The resulting programs will not run properly under Windows 9x.

4. **Unicode and 8-Bit**. The program includes both Unicode and ASCII code and decides at run time which code to execute, based on a run-time switch or other factors.

As mentioned previously, writing generic code, while requiring extra effort, allows the programmer to maintain flexibility and build separate Windows 9x and NT versions. The examples in this book are generic, using strategies 2 and 3, and have generally been tested both ways. Although all these strategies are in common use, strategies 2 and 3 are becoming increasingly popular.

The locale can be set at run time. Program 2–2 shows how the language for error messages is specified.

The POSIX XPG4 internationalization standard, provided by many UNIX vendors, is considerably different from Unicode. Among other things, characters can be represented by four bytes, two bytes, or one byte, depending on the context, locale, and so on.

Microsoft C implements the Standard C library functions, and there are generic versions. Thus, there is a _tsetlocale function in <wchar.h>. Windows NT uses UNICODE characters, and Windows 9x uses the same multibyte characters (a mix of 8- and 16-bit characters) used by Windows 3.1.

Standard Devices and Console I/O

Like UNIX, Win32 has three standard devices for input, output, and error reporting. UNIX uses well-known values for the file descriptors (0, 1, and 2), but Win32 requires handles and provides a function to obtain them for the standard devices.

```
HANDLE GetStdHandle (DWORD nStdHandle)

Return: A valid handle if the function succeeds;
    INVALID_HANDLE_VALUE otherwise.
```

GetStdHandle *Parameters*

nStdHandle must have one of these values:

- STD_INPUT_HANDLE
- STD_OUTPUT_HANDLE
- STD_ERROR_HANDLE

The standard device assignments are normally the console and the keyboard. Standard I/O can be redirected.

GetStdHandle does not create a new or duplicate handle on a standard device. Successive calls with the same device argument return the same handle value. Closing a standard device handle makes the device unavailable for future use. For this reason, the examples often obtain a standard device handle but do not close it.

```
BOOL SetStdHandle (
    DWORD nStdHandle,
    HANDLE hHandle)
```

Return: TRUE or FALSE indicating success or failure.

SetStdHandle *Parameters*

nStdHandle has the same possible values as in GetStdHandle. hHandle specifies an open file that is to be the standard device.

The normal method, then, for redirecting standard I/O within a process is to use SetStdHandle followed by GetStdHandle. The resulting handle is used in subsequent I/O operations.

There are two reserved pathnames for console input (the keyboard) and console output: "CONIN$" and "CONOUT$". Initially, standard input, output, and error are assigned to the console. It is possible to use the console regardless of any redirection to these standard devices; just open handles to "CONIN$" or "CONOUT$" using CreateFile.

UNIX standard I/O redirection can be done in one of three ways (see Stevens, pp. 61–64).

The first method is indirect and relies on the fact that the dup function returns the lowest numbered available file descriptor. Suppose you wish to reassign standard input (file descriptor 0) to an open file description, fd_redirect. It is possible to write this code:

```
close (STDIN_FILENO);
dup (fd_redirect);
```

The second method uses dup2, and the third uses the F_DUPFD on the cryptic and overloaded fcntl function.

Console I/O can be performed with ReadFile and WriteFile, but it is simpler to use the specific console I/O functions: ReadConsole and WriteConsole. The principal advantages are that these functions process generic characters (TCHAR) rather than bytes, and they also process characters according to the console mode, which is set with the SetConsoleMode function.

```
BOOL SetConsoleMode (
    HANDLE hConsole,
    DWORD fdevMode)
```

Return: TRUE if and only if the function succeeds.

SetConsoleMode *Parameters*

hConsole identifies a console input or screen buffer, which must have GENERIC_WRITE access even if it is an input-only device.

fdevMode specifies how characters are processed. Each flag name indicates whether the flag applies to console input or output. On creation, all flags except ENABLE_WINDOW_INPUT are set.

- ENABLE_LINE_INPUT—A read function (ReadConsole) returns when a carriage return character is encountered.

- ENABLE_ECHO_INPUT—Characters are echoed to the screen as they are read.

- ENABLE_PROCESSED_INPUT—This flag causes the system to process backspace, carriage return, and line feed characters.

- ENABLE_PROCESSED_OUTPUT—This flag causes the system to process backspace, tab, bell, carriage return, and line feed characters.

- ENABLE_WRAP_AT_EOL_OUTPUT—Line wrap is enabled for both normal and echoed output.

If SetConsoleMode fails, the mode is unchanged and the function returns FALSE. GetLastError will, as is always the case, return the error code number.

The ReadConsole and WriteConsole functions are similar to ReadFile and WriteFile.

```
BOOL ReadConsole (HANDLE hConsoleInput,
    LPVOID lpvBuffer,
    DWORD cchToRead,
    LPDWORD lpcchRead,
    LPVOID lpvReserved)
```

Return: TRUE if and only if the read succeeds.

The parameters are nearly the same as with `ReadFile`. The two length parameters are in terms of generic characters rather than bytes, and `lpvReserved` must be `NULL`. Never use any of the reserved fields that occur in some functions. `WriteConsole` is now self-explanatory. The next example shows how to use `ReadConsole` and `WriteConsole` with generic strings and how to take advantage of the console mode.

A process can have only one console at a time. Applications such as the ones developed so far are normally initialized with a console. In many cases, such as a server or GUI application, however, you may need a console to display status or debugging information. There are two simple parameterless functions for this purpose.

```
BOOL FreeConsole (VOID)

BOOL AllocConsole (VOID)
```

`FreeConsole` detaches a process from its console. Calling `AllocConsole` then creates a new one associated with the process's standard input, output, and error handles. `AllocConsole` will fail if the process already has a console; to avoid this problem, precede the call with `FreeConsole`.

Note: Windows GUI applications do not have a default console and must allocate one before using functions such as `WriteConsole` or `printf` to display on a console. It's also possible that server processes may not have a console. Chapter 7 shows how a process can be created without a console.

There are numerous other console I/O functions for specifying cursor position, screen attributes (such as color), and so on. This book's approach is to use only those functions needed to get the examples to work and not to wander further than necessary into user interfaces. Additional functions will be easy for you to learn from the reference material after you see the examples.

For historical reasons, Windows is not terminal- and console-oriented in the way that UNIX is, and not all the UNIX terminal functionality is replicated by Win32. Stevens dedicates a chapter to UNIX terminal I/O (Chapter 11) and one to pseudo terminals (Chapter 19).

Serious Win32 user interfaces are, of course, graphical, with mouse as well as keyboard input. The GUI is outside the scope of this book, but everything we discuss works within a GUI application.

Example: Printing and Prompting

Function `ConsolePrompt`, which is used in Program 2–1, is a useful utility that prompts the user with a specified message and then returns the user's response. There is an option to suppress the response echo. The function uses the console I/O functions and generic characters. `PrintStrings` and `PrintMsg` are the other entries in this module; they can use any handle but are normally used with standard output or error handles. The first function allows a variable-length argument list, whereas the second one allows just one string and is for convenience only. `Print-Strings` uses the `va_start`, `va_arg`, and `va_end` functions in the Standard C library to process the variable-length argument list.

Example programs will use these functions and the generic C library functions as convenient. *Note*: The code on the disc included with this book is thoroughly commented and documented. Within the book, most of the comments are omitted for brevity and to concentrate on Win32 usage.

This example also introduces an include file developed for the programs in the book. The file, "`Envirmnt.h`" (listed in Appendix A), contains the UNICODE and _UNICODE definitions and related preprocessor variables to specify the environment.

Program 2–1 `PrintMsg`: Console Prompt and Print Utility Functions

```
/* PrintMsg.c: ConsolePrompt, PrintStrings, PrintMsg */

#include "Envirmnt.h" /* #define or #undef UNICODE here. */
#include <windows.h>
#include <stdarg.h>

BOOL PrintStrings (HANDLE hOut, ...)

/* Write the messages to the output handle. */
{
    DWORD MsgLen, Count;
    LPCTSTR pMsg;
    va_list pMsgList; /* Current message string. */
    va_start (pMsgList, hOut); /* Start processing messages. */
    while ((pMsg = va_arg (pMsgList, LPCTSTR)) != NULL) {
        MsgLen = _tcslen (pMsg);
            /* WriteConsole succeeds only for console handles. */
        if (!WriteConsole (hOut, pMsg, MsgLen, &Count, NULL)
                /* Call WriteFile only if WriteConsole fails. */
            && !WriteFile (hOut, pMsg, MsgLen * sizeof (TCHAR),
                &Count, NULL))
            return FALSE;
    }
    va_end (pMsgList);
```

```
    return TRUE;
}

BOOL PrintMsg (HANDLE hOut, LPCTSTR pMsg)

/* Single message version of PrintStrings. */
{
    return PrintStrings (hOut, pMsg, NULL);
}
BOOL ConsolePrompt (LPCTSTR pPromptMsg, LPTSTR pResponse,
        DWORD MaxTchar, BOOL Echo)

/* Prompt the user at the console and get a response. */
{
    HANDLE hStdIn, hStdOut;
    DWORD TcharIn, EchoFlag;
    BOOL Success;
    hStdIn = CreateFile (_T ("CONIN$"),
            GENERIC_READ | GENERIC_WRITE, 0,
            NULL, OPEN_ALWAYS, FILE_ATTRIBUTE_NORMAL, NULL);
    hStdOut = CreateFile (_T ("CONOUT$"), GENERIC_WRITE, 0,
            NULL, OPEN_ALWAYS, FILE_ATTRIBUTE_NORMAL, NULL);
    EchoFlag = Echo ? ENABLE_ECHO_INPUT : 0;
    Success =
            SetConsoleMode (hStdIn, ENABLE_LINE_INPUT |
                EchoFlag | ENABLE_PROCESSED_INPUT)
            && SetConsoleMode (hStdOut,
                ENABLE_WRAP_AT_EOL_OUTPUT | ENABLE_PROCESSED_OUTPUT)
            && PrintStrings (hStdOut, pPromptMsg, NULL)
            && ReadConsole (hStdIn, pResponse,
                MaxTchar, &TcharIn, NULL);
    if (Success) pResponse [TcharIn - 2] = '\0';
    CloseHandle (hStdIn);
    CloseHandle (hStdOut);
    return Success;
}
```

Notice that `ConsolePrompt` returns a Boolean success indicator, exploiting ANSI C's guaranteed left-to-right evaluation of logical "and" (&) where evaluation stops on encountering the first FALSE. This coding style may appear compact, but it has the advantage of presenting the system calls in a clear, sequential order without the clutter of numerous conditional statements. Furthermore, `GetLastError` will return the error from the function that failed. Win32's Boolean return values (for many functions) encourage the technique.

The function does not report an error; the calling program can do this if necessary.

The code exploits the documented fact that WriteConsole fails if the handle is redirected to something other than a console handle. Therefore, it is not necessary to interrogate the handle properties. The function will take advantage of the console mode when the handle is attached to a console.

Also, ReadConsole returns a carriage return and line feed, so the last step is to insert a null character in the proper location over the carriage return.

Example: Error Processing

Program 1–2 showed some rudimentary error processing, obtaining the DWORD error number with the GetLastError function. A function call, rather than a global error number, such as the UNIX errno, ensures that system errors can be unique to the threads (Chapter 8) that share data storage.

The function FormatMessage turns the message number into a meaningful message, in English or one of many other languages, returning the message length.

Program 2–2 shows a useful general-purpose error-processing function, ReportError, which is similar to the C library perror and to err_sys, err_ret, and other functions in Stevens (pp. 682ff). ReportError prints a message specified in the first argument and will terminate with an exit code or return, depending on the value of the second argument. The third argument determines whether the system error message should be displayed.

Notice the arguments to FormatMessage. The value returned by GetLastError is used as one parameter, and a flag indicates that the message is to be generated by the system. The generated message is stored in a buffer allocated by the function, and the address is returned in a parameter. There are several other parameters with default values. The language for the message can be set at either compile time or run time. FormatMessage will not be used again in this book, so there is no further explanation in the text.

ReportError can simplify error processing and will be used in nearly all subsequent examples. Chapter 4 modifies this function to generate exceptions.

Program 2–2 introduces the include file EvryThng.h. As the name implies, this file includes <windows.h>, Envirmnt.h, and the other include files explicitly shown in Program 2–1. It also defines commonly used functions, such as PrintMsg, PrintStrings, and ReportError itself. All subsequent examples will use this single include file, which is listed in Appendix A.

Notice the call to the function HeapFree near the end of the program. This function will be explained in Chapter 6.

Program 2–2   ReportError for Reporting System Call Errors

```
#include "EvryThng.h"
VOID ReportError (LPCTSTR UserMessage, DWORD ExitCode,
      BOOL PrintErrorMsg)

/* General-purpose function for reporting system errors. */
{
    DWORD eMsgLen, LastErr = GetLastError ();
    LPTSTR lpvSysMsg;
    HANDLE hStdErr = GetStdHandle (STD_ERROR_HANDLE);
    PrintMsg (hStdErr, UserMessage);
    if (PrintErrorMsg) {
        eMsgLen = FormatMessage
                (FORMAT_MESSAGE_ALLOCATE_BUFFER |
                FORMAT_MESSAGE_FROM_SYSTEM, NULL, LastErr,
                MAKELANGID (LANG_NEUTRAL, SUBLANG_DEFAULT),
                (LPTSTR) &lpvSysMsg, 0, NULL);
        PrintStrings (hStdErr, _T ("\n"), lpvSysMsg,
                _T ("\n"), NULL);
        /* Free the memory block containing the error message. */
        HeapFree (GetProcessHeap (), 0, lpvSysMsg); /* See Ch 6. */
    }
    if (ExitCode > 0)
        ExitProcess (ExitCode);
    else
        return;
}
```

Example: Copying Multiple Files to Standard Output

Program 2–3 illustrates standard I/O and extensive error checking as well as user interaction. This program is a limited implementation of the UNIX cat command, which copies one or more specified files—or standard input if no files are specified—to standard output.

Program 2–3 includes complete error handling. The error checking is omitted or minimized in most other programs, but the disc contains the complete programs with extensive error checking and documentation. Also, notice the Options function (listed in Appendix A), which is called at the start of the program. This function, included on the disc and used throughout the book, evaluates command line option flags and returns the argv index of the first file name. Use Options in much the same way as getopt is used in many UNIX programs.

Program 2–3   cat: File Concatenation to Standard Output

```
/* Chapter 2. cat. */
/* cat [options] [files] Only the -s option, which suppresses error
   reporting if one of the files does not exist. */

#include "EvryThng.h"
#define BUF_SIZE 0x200

static VOID CatFile (HANDLE, HANDLE);
int _tmain (int argc, LPTSTR argv [])
{
    HANDLE hInFile, hStdIn = GetStdHandle (STD_INPUT_HANDLE);
    HANDLE hStdOut = GetStdHandle (STD_OUTPUT_HANDLE);
    BOOL DashS;
    int iArg, iFirstFile;

    /* DashS will be set only if "-s" is on the command line. */
    /* iFirstFile is the argv [] index of the first input file. */
    iFirstFile = Options (argc, argv, _T ("s"), &DashS, NULL);
    if (iFirstFile == argc) { /* No input files in arg list. */
                            /* Use standard input. */
        CatFile (hStdIn, hStdOut);
        return 0;
    }
/* Process each input file. */
    for (iArg = iFirstFile; iArg < argc; iArg++) {
        hInFile = CreateFile (argv [iArg], GENERIC_READ,
                0, NULL, OPEN_EXISTING, FILE_ATTRIBUTE_NORMAL, NULL);
        if (hInFile == INVALID_HANDLE_VALUE && !DashS)
            ReportError (_T ("Cat file open Error"), 1, TRUE);
        CatFile (hInFile, hStdOut);
        CloseHandle (hInFile);
    }
    return 0;
}

/* Function that does the work:
/* read input data and copy it to standard output. */
static VOID CatFile (HANDLE hInFile, HANDLE hOutFile)
{
    DWORD nIn, nOut;
    BYTE Buffer [BUF_SIZE];
    while (ReadFile (hInFile, Buffer, BUF_SIZE, &nIn, NULL)
            && (nIn != 0)
            && WriteFile (hOutFile, Buffer, nIn, &nOut, NULL));
    return;
}
```

Example: ASCII to Unicode Conversion

Program 2–4 builds on Program 1–3, which used the `CopyFile` convenience function. File copying is familiar by now, so this example also converts a file to Unicode, assuming it is ASCII; there is no test. The program also includes some error reporting and an option to suppress replacement of an existing file, and it replaces the final call to `CopyFile` with a new function that performs the ASCII to Unicode file conversion.

This program is concerned mostly with ensuring that the conversion can take place successfully. The operation is captured in a single function call at the end. This boilerplate, similar to that in the previous program, will be used again in the future but will not be repeated in the text.

Notice the call to `_taccess`, which tests the file's existence. This is a generic version of the `access` function, which is in the UNIX library but is not a part of the Standard C library. It is defined in <io.h>. More precisely, `_taccess` tests to see whether the file is accessible according to the mode in the second parameter. A value of 0 tests for existence, 2 for write permission, 4 for read permission, and 6 for read-write permission. The alternative to test for the file's existence would be to open a handle with `CreateFile` and then close the handle after a validity test.

Program 2–4   `atou`: File Conversion with Error Reporting

```
/* Chapter 2. atou - ASCII to Unicode file copy. */

#include "EvryThng.h"

BOOL Asc2Un (LPCTSTR, LPCTSTR, BOOL);
int _tmain (int argc, LPTSTR argv [])
{
    DWORD LocFileIn, LocFileOut;
    BOOL DashI = FALSE;
    TCHAR YNResp [3] = _T ("y");

/* Get the command line options and the index of the input file. */
    LocFileIn = Options (argc, argv, _T ("i"), &DashI, NULL);
    LocFileOut = LocFileIn + 1;

    if (DashI) { /* Does output file exist? */
        /* Generic version of access function to test existence. */
        if (_taccess (argv [LocFileOut], 0) == 0) {
            _tprintf (_T ("Overwrite existing file? [y/n]"));
            _tscanf (_T ("%s"), &YNResp);
            if (lstrcmp (CharLower (YNResp), YES) != 0)
                ReportError (_T ("Will not overwrite"), 4, FALSE);
        }
```

```
    }
    /* This function is modeled on CopyFile. */
    Asc2Un (argv [LocFileIn], argv [LocFileOut], FALSE);
    return 0;
}
```

Program 2–5 is the conversion function `Asc2Un` called by Program 2–4.

Program 2–5 `Asc2Un` Function

```
#include "EvryThng.h"
#define BUF_SIZE 256

BOOL Asc2Un (LPCTSTR fIn, LPCTSTR fOut, BOOL bFailIfExists)

/* ASCII to Unicode file copy function.
   Behavior is modeled after CopyFile. */
{
    HANDLE hIn, hOut;
    DWORD fdwOut, nIn, nOut, iCopy;
    CHAR aBuffer [BUF_SIZE];
    WCHAR uBuffer [BUF_SIZE];
    BOOL WriteOK = TRUE;

    hIn = CreateFile (fIn, GENERIC_READ, 0, NULL,
            OPEN_EXISTING, FILE_ATTRIBUTE_NORMAL, NULL);

    /* Determine CreateFile action if output file already exists. */
    fdwOut = bFailIfExists ? CREATE_NEW : CREATE_ALWAYS;
    hOut = CreateFile (fOut, GENERIC_WRITE, 0, NULL,
            fdwOut, FILE_ATTRIBUTE_NORMAL, NULL);
    while (ReadFile (hIn, aBuffer, BUF_SIZE, &nIn, NULL)
            && nIn > 0 && WriteOK) {
        for (iCopy = 0; iCopy < nIn; iCopy++)
            /* Convert each character. */
            uBuffer [iCopy] = (WCHAR) aBuffer [iCopy];
        WriteOK = WriteFile (hOut, uBuffer, 2 * nIn, &nOut, NULL);
    }
    CloseHandle (hIn);
    CloseHandle (hOut);
    return WriteOK;
}
```

Performance

Appendix C shows that the performance of the file conversion program can be improved by using such techniques as providing a larger buffer and by specifying FILE_FLAG_SEQUENTIAL_SCAN with CreateFile. Appendix C also contrasts performance on FAT and NTFS file systems.

File and Directory Management

This section introduces the basic functions for file and directory management.

File Management

Win32 provides a number of functions, which are generally straightforward, to manage files. The following functions delete, copy, and rename files. There is also a function to create temporary file names.

Delete files by specifying the file names. Recall that all absolute pathnames start with a drive letter or a server name. It is not possible to delete an open file in Windows 2000/NT, but it is possible in Windows 9x and UNIX; attempting to do so in NT will result in an error. This limitation is hardly a loss; it is actually a beneficial feature.

```
BOOL DeleteFile (LPCTSTR lpszFileName)
```

Copy an entire file using a single function.

```
BOOL CopyFile (
    LPCTSTR lpszExistingFile,
    LPCTSTR lpszNewFile,
    BOOL fFailIfExists)
```

CopyFile copies the named existing file and assigns the specified new name to the copy. If a file with the new name already exists, it will be replaced only if fFailIfExists is FALSE.

A pair of functions is available to rename, or "move," a file. These functions also work for directories (`DeleteFile` and `CopyFile` are restricted to files).

Win32 does not support any file linking whereby two file names can indicate the same actual file. Close examination of Microsoft documentation will show a "number of links" member field in the `BY_HANDLE_FILE_INFO` structure. This field is used by the POSIX subsystem—which must implement links—and is not relevant to Win32.

Shortcuts are supported by the Windows shells, which interpret the file contents to locate the actual file, but not by Win32. Shortcuts provide linklike features, but only to shell users.

```
BOOL MoveFile (
    LPCTSTR lpszExisting,
    LPCTSTR lpszNew)

BOOL MoveFileEx (
    LPCTSTR lpszExisting,
    LPCTSTR lpszNew,
    DWORD fdwFlags)
```

`MoveFile` fails if the new file already exists; use `MoveFileEx` for existing files. Also, Windows 9x does not usefully implement `MoveFileEx`; it will just return a `FALSE`, indicating an error.

Parameters

`lpszExisting` specifies the name of the existing file *or* directory.

`lpszNew` specifies the new file or directory name, which cannot exist in the case of `MoveFile`. A new file can be on a different file system or drive, but new directories must be on the same drive. If `NULL`, the existing file is deleted.

`fdwFlags` specifies options as follows:

- `MOVEFILE_REPLACE_EXISTING`—Use this option to replace an existing file.

- `MOVEFILE_WRITETHROUGH`—Use this option to ensure that the function does not return until the copied file is flushed through to the disc.

- `MOVEFILE_COPY_ALLOWED`—When the new file is on a different volume, the move is achieved with a `CopyFile` followed by a `DeleteFile`.

- MOVEFILE_DELAY_UNTIL_REBOOT—This flag, which cannot be used in conjunction with MOVEFILE_COPY_ALLOWED, is restricted to administrators and ensures that the file move does not take effect until the system restarts.

There are a couple of important limitations when you're moving (renaming) files.

- Since Windows 9x does not implement MoveFileEx, you must perform a CopyFile followed by a DeleteFile. This means that two copies will exist temporarily, which could be a problem with a nearly full disc or a large file. The effect on file time attributes is different from that of a true move.

- Wildcards are not allowed in file or directory names. Specify the actual name.

UNIX pathnames do not include a drive or server name; the slash indicates the system root. The Microsoft C library file functions also support drive names as required by the underlying Win32 file naming.

UNIX does not have a function to copy files directly. Instead, you must write a small program or fork a process to execute the cp command.

unlink is the UNIX equivalent of DeleteFile except that unlink can also delete directories.

rename and remove are in the C library, and rename will fail when attempting to move a file to an existing file name or a directory to a directory that is not empty. A new directory can exist if it is empty.

As mentioned previously, Win32 does not support the concept of links.

Directory Management

Creating or deleting a directory involves a pair of simple functions.

```
BOOL CreateDirectory (
    LPCTSTR lpszPath,
    LPSECURITY_ATTRIBUTES lpsa)

BOOL RemoveDirectory (LPCTSTR lpszPath)
```

lpszPath points to a null-terminated string with the name of the directory that is to be created or deleted. The security attributes should be NULL for the time being. Only an empty directory can be removed.

A process has a current, or working, directory, just as in UNIX. Furthermore, each individual drive keeps a working directory. The programmer can both get and set the current directory. The first function sets the directory.

```
BOOL SetCurrentDirectory (LPCTSTR lpszCurDir)
```

lpszCurDir is the path to the new current directory. It can be a relative path or a fully qualified path starting with either a drive letter and colon, such as D:, or a UNC name (such as \\ACCTG_SERVER\PUBLIC).

If the directory path is simply a drive name (such as A: or C:), the working directory becomes the working directory on the specified drive. For example, if the working directories are set in the sequence

```
C:\MSDEV
INCLUDE
A:\MEMOS\TODO
C:
```

then the resulting working directory will be

```
C:\MSDEV\INCLUDE
```

The next function returns the fully qualified pathname into a buffer provided by the programmer.

```
DWORD GetCurrentDirectory (DWORD cchCurDir,
    LPTSTR lpszCurDir)
```

Return: The string length of the returned pathname, or the required buffer size if the buffer is not large enough; zero if the function fails.

Parameters

cchCurDir is the character (not byte) length of the buffer for the directory name. The length must allow for the terminating null character. lpszCurDir points to the buffer to receive the pathname string.

Notice that if the buffer is too small for the pathname, the return value tells how large the buffer should be. Therefore, the test for function failure should test both for zero and for the result being larger than the cchCurDir argument.

This method of returning strings and their lengths is common in Win32 and must be handled carefully. Program 2–6 illustrates a typical code fragment that performs the logic. Similar logic occurs in other examples. The method is not always consistent, however. Some functions return a Boolean, and the length parameter is used twice; it is set with the length of the buffer before the call, and the function changes the value. LookupAccountName in Chapter 5 is one of many examples.

An alternative approach, illustrated with the GetFileSecurity function in Program 5–4, is to make two function calls with a buffer memory allocation in between. The first call gets the string length, which is used in the memory allocation. The second call gets the actual string. The simplest approach in this case is to allocate a string holding MAX_PATH characters.

Example: Printing the Current Directory

Program 2–6 implements a version of the UNIX command pwd. The MAX_PATH value is used to size the buffer, but an error test is still included to illustrate GetCurrentDirectory.

Program 2–6 pwd: Printing the Current Directory

```
/* Chapter 2. pwd - Print working directory. */

#include "EvryThng.h"
#define DIRNAME_LEN MAX_PATH + 2

int _tmain (int argc, LPTSTR argv [])
{
    TCHAR pwdBuffer [DIRNAME_LEN];
    DWORD LenCurDir;

    LenCurDir = GetCurrentDirectory (DIRNAME_LEN, pwdBuffer);

    if (LenCurDir == 0) ReportError
        (_T ("Failure getting pathname."), 1, TRUE);
    if (LenCurDir > DIRNAME_LEN)
        ReportError (_T ("Pathname is too long."), 2, FALSE);
    PrintMsg (GetStdHandle (STD_OUTPUT_HANDLE), pwdBuffer);
    return 0;
}
```

Summary

Win32 supports a complete set of file processing and character processing functions. In addition, you can write portable, generic applications that will operate under all Windows platforms.

The Win32 functions resemble their UNIX and C library counterparts in many ways, but the differences are also apparent. Appendix B contains a table showing the Win32, UNIX, and C library functions, noting how they correspond and pointing out some of the significant differences.

Looking Ahead

The next step, in Chapter 3, is to discuss direct file access and to learn how to deal with file and directory attributes such as file length and time stamps. Chapter 3 also shows how to process directories and ends with a discussion of the registry management API, which is similar to the directory management API.

Additional Reading

Unicode

Developing International Applications for Windows 95 and Windows NT, by Nadine Kano, shows how to use Unicode in practice, with guidelines, international standards, and culture-specific issues.

The Microsoft home page has several helpful articles on Unicode. *Unicode Support in Win32* is the basic paper; a search will turn up others.

UNIX

Stevens covers UNIX files and directories in Chapters 3 and 4 and terminal I/O in Chapter 11.

UNIX in a Nutshell, by Daniel Gilly, is a useful quick reference on the UNIX commands.

For information on the POSIX international character set and its use, as well as general internationalization issues, see *Programming for the World*, by Sandra O'Donnell.

NTFS

Inside the Windows NT File System, by Helen Custer, is a short monograph describing the goals and implementation of the NTFS. This information is helpful in both this chapter and the next.

Exercises

2–1. Write a short program to test the generic versions of `printf` and `scanf`.

2–2. Modify the `CatFile` function in Program 2–3 so that it uses `WriteConsole` rather than `WriteFile` when the standard output handle is associated with a console.

2–3. `CreateFile` allows you to specify file access characteristics so as to enhance performance. `FILE_FLAG_SEQUENTIAL_SCAN` is an example. Use this flag in Program 2–5 and determine whether there is a performance improvement for large files. Appendix C shows results on several systems. Also try `FILE_FLAG_NO_BUFFERING`.

2–4. Determine whether there are detectable performance differences between the FAT and NTFS file systems when using `atou` to convert large files.

2–5. Run Program 2–4 with and without `UNICODE` defined. What is the effect, if any, under Windows 2000/NT and Windows 9x?

2–6. Compare the information provided by `perror` (in the C library) and `ReportError` for common errors such as opening a nonexisting file.

2–7. Test the `ConsolePrompt` (Program 2–1) function's suppression of keyboard echo by using it to ask the user to enter and confirm a password.

2–8. Determine what happens when performing console output with a mixture of generic C library and Win32 `WriteFile` or `WriteConsole` calls. What is the explanation?

2–9. Write a program that sorts an array of Unicode strings. Determine the difference between the word and string sorts by using `lstrcmp` and `_tcscmp`. Does `lstrlen` produce different results from those of `_tcslen`? The remarks under the `CompareString` function entry in the Microsoft on-line help are useful.

2–10. Extend the `Options` function implementation so that it will report an error if the command line option string contains any characters not in the list of permitted options in the function's `OptionString` parameter.

3 | Advanced File and Directory Processing, and the Registry

File systems provide more than sequential processing; they must also provide direct access, file locking, directory processing, and file attribute management. Starting with direct file access, which is required by database, file management, and many other systems, this chapter shows how to manage file pointers to access files at any location. In particular, it is necessary to show how to use Win32's 64-bit file pointers, because the NTFS is capable of supporting very large files.

The next step is to show how to scan directory contents and how to manage and interpret file attributes, such as time stamps, access, and size. Finally, file locking protects files from concurrent modification by more than one process.

The final topic in this chapter is the Windows registry, a centralized database that contains configuration information for applications and for the system itself. Registry access functions and program structure are similar to the file and directory management function, as shown by the last program example.

The 64-Bit File System

Win32 and Win64, with the NTFS, support 64-bit file addresses so that files can, in principle, be as long as 2^{64} bytes.

The 2^{32}-byte length limit of 32-bit file systems constrains file lengths to 4GB (4×10^9 bytes). This limit is a serious constraint with some applications, including large database and multimedia systems, so any complete modern operating system must support much larger files.

Needless to say, many applications will never need large files, so, for many programmers, 32-bit file addresses will be adequate for years to come. It is, however, a good idea to start working with 64-bit addresses from the beginning of a new development project, given the rapid pace of technical change, cost improvements, and application requirements.

Win32, despite the 64-bit file addresses, is still a 32-bit operating system because of its memory addressing, as discussed in Chapter 6; Win64 is required for 64-bit memory addresses.

File Pointers

Windows, just like UNIX, the C library, and nearly every other operating system, maintains a *file pointer* with each open file handle, indicating the current byte location in the file. The next `WriteFile` or `ReadFile` operation will start transferring data sequentially to or from that location and increment the file pointer by the number of bytes transferred. Opening the file with `CreateFile` sets the pointer to zero, indicating the start of the file, and the handle's pointer is advanced with each successive read or write. The crucial operation required for direct file access is the ability to set the file pointer to an arbitrary value, using `SetFilePointer`.

`SetFilePointer` shows, for the first time, how Windows handles the 64-bit NTFS. The techniques are not always pretty with this function, and `SetFile-Pointer` is easiest to use with small files.

```
DWORD SetFilePointer (
    HANDLE hFile,
    LONG lDistanceToMove,
    PLONG lpDistanceToMoveHigh,
    DWORD dwMoveMethod)
```

Return: The low-order DWORD (unsigned) of the new file pointer. The high-order portion of the new file pointer goes to the DWORD indicated by `lpDistanceToMoveHigh` (if non-NULL). In case of error, the return value is 0xFFFFFFFF.

Parameters

hFile is the handle of an open file with read or write access (or both).

lDistanceToMove is the LONG *signed* distance to move or *unsigned* file position, depending on the value of dwMoveMethod.

lpDistanceToMoveHigh points to the high-order portion of the move distance. If this value is NULL, the function can operate only on files whose length is limited to 2^{32}–2. This parameter is also used to receive the high-order return value of the file pointer. The low-order portion is the function's return value.

dwMoveMethod specifies one of these move modes:

- FILE_BEGIN—Position from the start of the file, interpreting DistanceToMove as *unsigned*.

- FILE_CURRENT—Move the pointer forward or backward from the current position, interpreting DistanceToMove as *signed*. Positive is forward.

- FILE_END—Position backward or forward from the end of file.

It is possible to use this function to obtain the file length by specifying a zero-length move from the end of file.

The method of representing 64-bit file positions causes complexities, because the function return can represent both a file position and an error code. For example, suppose that the actual position is location 2^{32}–1 (that is, 0xFFFFFFFF) and that the call also specifies the high-order move distance. Invoke GetLastError to determine whether the return value is a valid file position or whether the function failed, in which case the return value would not be NO_ERROR. This explains why files are limited to 2^{32}–2 when the high-order component is omitted.

Another confusing factor is the fact that the high- and low-order components are separated and treated differently. The low-order address is treated as a call by value and returned by the function, whereas the high-order address is a call by reference and is both input and output.

Fortunately, most programmers will be content with 32-bit file addresses. Nonetheless, the programming examples take the long view and "do it right" using 64-bit arithmetic.

64-Bit Arithmetic

It is not difficult to perform the 64-bit file pointer arithmetic, and our example programs use Microsoft C's LARGE_INTEGER 64-bit data type, which is a union of a LONGLONG (called QuadPart) and two 32-bit quantities (LowPart, a DWORD, and HighPart, a LONG). LONGLONG supports all the arithmetic operations. There is also a ULONGLONG, which is unsigned.

lseek (in UNIX) and fseek (in the C library) are similar to SetFilePointer. Both systems also advance the file position during read and write operations.

Specifying File Position with the Overlapped Structure

Windows 2000/NT provides another way to set the file position that does not require SetFilePointer. Recall that the final parameter to both ReadFile and WriteFile is the address of an overlapped structure, and two members of this structure are Offset and OffsetHigh. You can set the appropriate values in an offset structure, and the I/O operation can start at the specified location. The file pointer is not changed, so this provides a way, for example, to read a file header without altering a sequence of sequential reads. There is also a handle member, hEvent, that must be set to NULL. *Note*: Windows 9x requires that the overlapped pointer be NULL when processing files.

The overlapped structure is especially convenient when updating a file record, as illustrated in the following code fragment; otherwise, separate SetFilePointer calls would be required before the ReadFile and WriteFile calls. The hEvent field is the last of five fields, as is shown in the initialization statement. The LARGE_INTEGER data type is used to compute the file position.

```
OVERLAPPED ov = { 0, 0, 0, 0, NULL };
RECORD r; /* Definition not shown
      but it includes the RefCount field. */
LONGLONG n;
LARGE_INGETER FilePos;
DWORD nRead, nWrite;
...
/* Update the reference count in the n'th record. */
FilePos.QuadPart = n * sizeof (RECORD);
ov.Offset = FilePos.LowPart;
ov.OffsetHigh = FilePos.HighPart;
ReadFile (hFile, r, sizeof (RECORD), &nRead, &ov);
r.RefCount++; /* Update the record. */
WriteFile (hFile, r, sizeof (RECORD), &nWrite, &ov);
```

Overlapped structures will be used again later in this chapter to specify file lock regions and in Chapter 14 for asynchronous I/O and direct file access.

Getting the File Size

It is possible to determine a file's size by positioning zero bytes from the end and using the file pointer value returned by SetFilePointer. Alternatively, there is a specific function for this purpose.

```
DWORD GetFileSize (
    HANDLE hFile,
    LPDWORD lpdwFileSizeHigh)
```

Return: The low-order component of the file size. 0xFFFFFFFF indicates a possible error; check GetLastError.

Notice that the length is returned in much the same manner that SetFile-Pointer returns the actual file pointer.

GetFileSize and GetFileSizeEx (which returns the 64-bit size in a single data item) require that the file have an open handle. It is also possible to obtain the length by name. GetCompressedFileSize returns the size of the compressed file, and FindFirstFile, discussed in a later section, will give the exact size of a named file.

Setting the File Size and File Initialization

The SetEndOfFile function resizes the file using the current value of the file pointer to determine the length. A file can be extended or truncated. With extension, the contents of the extended region are not defined. The file will actually consume the disc space and user space quotas, because files are generally not stored sparsely, even under the NTFS on Windows 2000/NT, although Windows 2000 allows you to specify sparse files. The files can, however, be compressed to consume less space. An exercise explores this topic.

A FAT file is *not* initialized to all zeros automatically. The file contents, according to the Microsoft documentation, are not predictable; experiments confirm this. Therefore, applications must initialize the file with a series of WriteFile operations if initialization is required for correct operation. An NTFS file will be initialized, because C2 security, which Windows 2000/NT provides, requires that contents of a deleted file not be readable.

Notice that the SetEndOfFile call is not the only way to extend a file. You can also extend a file using many successive write operations, but this will result in more fragmented file allocation; `SetEndOfFile` allows the OS to allocate larger contiguous disc units.

Example: Viewing the Tail of a File

Program 3–1 shows an implementation of the UNIX `tail` command, which prints to standard output the last ten lines of a text file. The program illustrates file positioning based on the file's size. It also illustrates how to perform 64-bit arithmetic using Microsoft C's `LARGE_INTEGER` data type, and one error check is included to illustrate file pointer logic.

This implementation positions backward from the file end, assuming an average line length of less than 256. It then reads forward, recording the positions where new lines start by looking for the CR–LF sequence.

This design illustrates file pointer usage with 64-bit file positions even though it is not an optimal design for the `tail` command. An alternative is to read the file backward, one character at a time.

A Chapter 14 example, `atouMT` (on the disc only; not in the text), also illustrates direct file access.

Program 3–1   The `tail` Command

```
/* Chapter 3. tail command. */
/* Print the last 10 lines of the named file. */

#include "EvryThng.h"

#define NUM_LINES 11 /* Number of lines in tail plus 1. */
#define MAX_LINE_SIZE 256 /* Assumed max line length. */
#define MAX_CHAR NUM_LINES*MAX_LINE_SIZE

int _tmain (int argc, LPTSTR argv [])
{
    HANDLE hInFile, hStdOut = GetStdHandle (STD_OUTPUT_HANDLE);
    LARGE_INTEGER FilSiz, CurPtr, LinePos [NUM_LINES];
    DWORD LastLine, FirstLine, LineCount, nRead, FPos;
    TCHAR Buffer [MAX_CHAR + 1], c;

    /* Open the file and get its size. */
    hInFile = CreateFile (argv [1], GENERIC_READ, 0, NULL,
            OPEN_EXISTING, FILE_ATTRIBUTE_NORMAL, NULL);
    FilSiz.LowPart = GetFileSize (hInFile, &FilSiz.HighPart);
    if (FilSiz.LowPart == 0xFFFFFFFF && GetLastError () != NO_ERROR)
        ReportError (_T ("tail error: file size"), 2, TRUE);
```

```
/* Position at least 10 records from the file end. */
CurPtr.QuadPart = FilSiz.QuadPart
        - NUM_LINES * MAX_LINE_SIZE * sizeof (TCHAR);
if (CurPtr.QuadPart < 0) CurPtr.QuadPart = 0;
FPos = SetFilePointer (hInFile, CurPtr.LowPart,
        &CurPtr.HighPart, FILE_BEGIN);
LinePos [0].QuadPart = CurPtr.QuadPart;

LineCount = 1; LastLine = 1;

while (TRUE) { /* Find and retain the line start positions. */
    while (ReadFile (hInFile, &c, sizeof (TCHAR), &nRead, NULL)
            && nRead > 0 && c != CR) { }; /* Empty loop body. */
    if (nRead < sizeof (TCHAR)) break; /* End of file detected. */

    /* Look for end of line. Found a CR. Is LF next? */
    ReadFile (hInFile, &c, sizeof (TCHAR), &nRead, NULL);
    if (c != LF) continue;

    /* Obtain the current file position by moving 0 bytes
        from the current position. */
    CurPtr.QuadPart = 0;
    CurPtr.LowPart = SetFilePointer (
            hInFile, 0, &CurPtr.HighPart, FILE_CURRENT);

    /* Retain file position of the start of the current line. */
    LinePos [LastLine].QuadPart = CurPtr.QuadPart;
    LineCount++;
    LastLine = LineCount % NUM_LINES;
}

/* Print the last 10 lines. The line start positions are in the
    LinePos [] array. Position to the 10th line from the end
    and print all the lines as a single message. */
FirstLine = LastLine % NUM_LINES;
if (LineCount < NUM_LINES) FirstLine = 0;
CurPtr.QuadPart = LinePos [FirstLine].QuadPart;

/* Display the last strings. */
SetFilePointer (hInFile, CurPtr.LowPart,
        &CurPtr.HighPart, FILE_BEGIN);

ReadFile (hInFile, Buffer, sizeof (Buffer), &nRead, NULL);
Buffer [nRead] = '\0';
PrintMsg (hStdOut, Buffer);
CloseHandle (hInFile);
return 0;
}
```

File Attributes and Directory Processing

It is possible to search a directory for files and other directories that satisfy a specified name pattern and, at the same time, obtain file attributes. Searches require a *search handle* obtained by the FindFirstFile function. Obtain specific files with FindNextFile, and terminate the search with FindClose.

```
HANDLE FindFirstFile (
    LPCTSTR lpszSearchFile,
    LPWIN32_FIND_DATA lpffd)

Return: A search handle. INVALID_HANDLE_VALUE indicates
    failure.
```

FindFirstFile examines both subdirectory and file names, looking for a name match. The returned HANDLE is used in subsequent searches.

Parameters

lpszSearchFile points to a directory or pathname that can contain wildcard characters (? and *).

lpffd points to a WIN32_FIND_DATA structure that contains information about the file or directory, if it is found.

The WIN32_FIND_DATA structure is defined as follows:

```
typedef struct_WIN32_FIND_DATA {
    DWORD dwFileAttributes;
    FILETIME ftCreationTime;
    FILETIME ftLastAccessTime;
    FILETIME ftLastWriteTime;
    DWORD nFileSizeHigh;
    DWORD nFileSizeLow;
    DWORD dwReserved0;
    DWORD dwReserved1;
    TCHAR cFileName [MAX_PATH];
    TCHAR cAlternateFileName [14];
} WIN32_FIND_DATA;
```

`dwFileAttributes` can be tested for the values described with `CreateFile`. The three file times (creation, last access, and last write) are described in the next section. The file size fields, giving the current file length, are self-explanatory. `cFileName` is not the pathname; it is the file name by itself. `cAlternateFile-Name` is the DOS 8.3 (including the period) version of the file name. This is the same compaction of the file name that shows up in the Windows Explorer if you examine the file system. Both names are null-terminated strings.

Frequently, the requirement is to scan a directory for files that satisfy a name pattern containing ? and * wildcard characters. To do this, use the search handle obtained from `FindFirstFile`, which retains information about the search name, and call `FindNextFile`.

```
BOOL FindNextFile (
    HANDLE hFindFile,
    LPWIN32_FIND_DATA lpffd)
```

`FindNextFile` will return a `FALSE` in case of invalid arguments or if no more matching files can be found, in which case `GetLastError` will return `ERROR_NO_MORE_FILES`.

When the search is complete, close the search handle. Do not use `Close-Handle`. (This is a rare exception to the rule that `CloseHandle` is for all handles, and closing a search handle will cause an exception.) Instead, use the following:

```
BOOL FindClose (HANDLE hFindFile)
```

The function `GetFileInformationByHandle` obtains the same information for a specific file, specified by an open handle.[1]

This method of wildcard expansion is necessary even in programs executing from the MS-DOS prompt, because the DOS shell does not expand wildcards.

---

[1] The file information data structure for this function contains a "number of links" field that is not used by Win32 functions. (See Exercise 3–5.)

Other Methods of Obtaining File and Directory Attributes

The `FindFirstFile` and `FindNextFile` functions are capable of obtaining the following file attribute information: attribute flags, three time stamps, and file size. There are several other related functions, including one to set attributes, and they can deal directly with the open file handle rather than scan a directory or use a file name. Three such functions, `GetFileSize`, `GetFileSizeEx`, and `SetEndOfFile`, were described previously.

Distinct functions are used to obtain the other attributes. For example, to obtain the time stamps of an open file, use this function:

```
BOOL GetFileTime (
    HANDLE hFile,
    LPFILETIME lpftCreation,
    LPFILETIME lpftLastAccess,
    LPFILETIME lpftLastWrite)
```

The file times here and in the `WIN32_FIND_DATA` structure are 64-bit unsigned integers giving elapsed 100-nanosecond units (10^7 units per second) from a base time (January 1, 1601), expressed as Universal Coordinated Time (UTC). There are several convenient functions for dealing with times.

- `FileTimeToSystemTime` (not described here; see the Win32 references or Program 3–2) breaks the file time into individual units ranging from years down to seconds and milliseconds. These units are suitable, for example, when displaying or printing times.

- `SystemTimeToFileTime` reverses the process, converting time expressed in these individual units to a *file time*.

- `CompareFileTime` determines whether one file time is less than (–1), equal to (0), or greater than (+1) another.

- Change the time stamps with `SetFileTime`; times that are not to be changed are set to 0 in the function call. The NTFS supports all three file times, but the FAT gives an accurate result only for the last access time.

- `FileTimeToLocalFileTime` and `LocalFileTimeToFileTime` will convert between UTC and the local time.

`GetFileType`, not described in detail here, distinguishes among disc files, character files (actually, devices such as printers and consoles), and pipes (see Chapter 11). The file, again, is specified with a handle.

The function `GetFileAttributes` uses the file or directory name, and it returns just the `dwFileAttributes` information.

```
DWORD GetFileAttributes (LPCTSTR lpszFileName)
```

Return: The file attributes, or `0xFFFFFFFF` in case of failure.

The attributes can be tested for appropriate combinations of several mask values. Some attributes, such as the temporary file attribute, are originally set with `CreateFile`. The attribute values include the following:

`FILE_ATTRIBUTE_DIRECTORY`

`FILE_ATTRIBUTE_NORMAL`

`FILE_ATTRIBUTE_READONLY`

`FILE_ATTRIBUTE_TEMPORARY`

The function `SetFileAttributes` changes these attributes in a named file.

`opendir`, `readdir`, and `closedir` in UNIX correspond to the three `Find` functions. The function `stat` obtains file size and times, in addition to owning user and group information that relates to UNIX security. `fstat` and `lstat` are variations. These functions can also obtain type information. `utime` sets file times in UNIX. There is no UNIX equivalent to the temporary file attribute.

Temporary File Names

The next function creates names for temporary files. The name can be in any specified directory and must be unique.

`GetTempFileName` gives a unique file name, with the `.tmp` suffix, in a specified directory and optionally creates the file. This function is used extensively in later examples (Program 7–1, Program 8–1, and elsewhere).

```
UINT GetTempFileName (
    LPCTSTR lpszPath,
    LPCTSTR lpszPrefix,
    UINT uUnique,
    LPTSTR lpszTempFile)
```

Return: A unique numeric value used to create the file name. This will be uUnique if uUnique is nonzero. On failure, the return value is zero.

Parameters

lpszPath is the directory for the temporary file. "." is a typical value specifying the current directory. Alternatively, use GetTempPath, a Win32 function not described here, to give the name of a directory dedicated to temporary files.

lpszPrefix is the prefix of the temporary name. Use ANSI characters. uUnique is normally zero so that the function will generate a unique four-digit suffix and will create the file. If this value is nonzero, the file is not created; do that with CreateFile, possibly using FILE_FLAG_DELETE_ON_CLOSE.

lpszTempFile points to the buffer that receives the temporary file name. The buffer's byte length should be at least MAX_PATH. The resulting pathname is a concatenation of the path, the prefix, the four-digit hex number, and the .tmp suffix.

Example: Listing File Attributes

It is now time to illustrate the file and directory management functions. Program 3–2 shows a limited version of the UNIX ls directory listing command, which can show file modification times and the file size, although this version gives only the low order of the file size.

The program scans the directory for files that satisfy the search pattern. For each file located, the program shows the file name and, if the -l option is specified, the file attributes. This program illustrates many, but not all, Win32 directory management functions.

The bulk of Program 3–2 is concerned with directory traversal. Notice that each directory is traversed twice—once to process files and again to process subdirectories—in order to support the -R recursive option.

Program 3–2, as listed here, will properly carry out a command with a relative pathname such as

```
ls -R include\*.h
```

It will not work properly, however, with an absolute pathname such as

```
ls -R C:\Projects\rm\Debug\*.obj
```

because the program, as listed, depends on setting the directory relative to the current directory. The complete solution (on the disc) analyzes pathnames and will also carry out the second command.

Program 3–2   `ls`: File Listing and Directory Traversal

```c
/* Chapter 3. ls file list command */
/* ls [options] [files] */

#include "EvryThng.h"

BOOL TraverseDirectory (LPCTSTR, DWORD, LPBOOL);
DWORD FileType (LPWIN32_FIND_DATA);
BOOL ProcessItem (LPWIN32_FIND_DATA, DWORD, LPBOOL);

int _tmain (int argc, LPTSTR argv [])
{
    BOOL Flags [MAX_OPTIONS], ok = TRUE;
    TCHAR PathName [MAX_PATH + 1], CurrPath [MAX_PATH + 1];
    LPTSTR pSlash, pFileName;
    int i, FileIndex;

    FileIndex = Options (
            argc, argv, _T ("Rl"), &Flags [0], &Flags [1], NULL);

    /* "Parse" the search pattern into "parent" and file name */
    GetCurrentDirectory (MAX_PATH, CurrPath); /* Save current path. */
    if (argc < FileIndex + 1) /* No path specified. Current dir. */
        ok = TraverseDirectory (_T ("*"), MAX_OPTIONS, Flags);
    else for (i = FileIndex; i < argc; i++) {
        /* Process all paths on the command line. */
        ok = TraverseDirectory (pFileName, MAX_OPTIONS, Flags) && ok;
        SetCurrentDirectory (CurrPath); /* Restore directory. */
    }
    return ok ? 0 : 1;
}

static BOOL TraverseDirectory (LPCTSTR PathName, DWORD NumFlags,
        LPBOOL Flags)

/* Traverse a directory; perform ProcessItem for every match. */
```

```
/* PathName: Relative or absolute pathname to traverse. */
{
    HANDLE SearchHandle;
    WIN32_FIND_DATA FindData;
    BOOL Recursive = Flags [0];
    DWORD FType, iPass;
    TCHAR CurrPath [MAX_PATH + 1];

    GetCurrentDirectory (MAX_PATH, CurrPath);

    for (iPass = 1; iPass <= 2; iPass++) {
        /* Pass 1: List files. */
        /* Pass 2: Traverse directories (if -R specified). */
        SearchHandle = FindFirstFile (PathName, &FindData);
        do {
            FType = FileType (&FindData); /* File or directory? */
            if (iPass == 1) /* List name and attributes. */
                ProcessItem (&FindData, MAX_OPTIONS, Flags);
            if (FType == TYPE_DIR && iPass == 2 && Recursive) {
                /* Process a subdirectory. */
                _tprintf (_T ("\n%s\\%s:"), CurrPath,
                    FindData.cFileName);
                /* Prepare to traverse a directory. */
                SetCurrentDirectory (FindData.cFileName);
                TraverseDirectory (_T ("*"), NumFlags, Flags);
                /* Recursive call. */
                SetCurrentDirectory (_T (".."));
            }
        } while (FindNextFile (SearchHandle, &FindData));
        FindClose (SearchHandle);
    }
    return TRUE;
}

static BOOL ProcessItem (LPWIN32_FIND_DATA pFileData,
        DWORD NumFlags, LPBOOL Flags)
/* List file or directory attributes. */
{
    const TCHAR FileTypeChar [] = {' ', 'd'};
    DWORD FType = FileType (pFileData);
    BOOL Long = Flags [1];
    SYSTEMTIME LastWrite;

    if (FType != TYPE_FILE && FType != TYPE_DIR) return FALSE;

    _tprintf (_T ("\n"));
    if (Long) { /* Was "-l" option used on the command line? */
        _tprintf (_T ("%c"), FileTypeChar [FType - 1]);
        _tprintf (_T ("%10d"), pFileData->nFileSizeLow);
        FileTimeToSystemTime (&(pFileData->ftLastWriteTime),
```

```
                &LastWrite);
        _tprintf (_T (" %02d/%02d/%04d %02d:%02d:%02d"),
                LastWrite.wMonth, LastWrite.wDay,
                LastWrite.wYear, LastWrite.wHour,
                LastWrite.wMinute, LastWrite.wSecond);
    }
    _tprintf (_T (" %s"), pFileData->cFileName);
    return TRUE;
}

static DWORD FileType (LPWIN32_FIND_DATA pFileData)
/* Types supported - TYPE_FILE: file; TYPE_DIR: directory;
    TYPE_DOT: . or .. directory */
{
    BOOL IsDir;
    DWORD FType;
    FType = TYPE_FILE;
    IsDir = (pFileData->dwFileAttributes &
        FILE_ATTRIBUTE_DIRECTORY) != 0;
    if (IsDir)
        if (lstrcmp (pFileData->cFileName, _T (".")) == 0
                || lstrcmp (pFileData->cFileName, _T ("..")) == 0)
            FType = TYPE_DOT;
        else FType = TYPE_DIR;
    return FType;
}
```

Example: Setting File Times

Program 3–3 implements the UNIX touch command, which changes file access and modifies times to the current value of the system time. Exercise 3–12 enhances touch so that the new file time is a command line option, as with the actual UNIX command.

Program 3–3   touch: Setting File Times

```
/* Chapter 3. touch command. */
/* touch [options] files */
#include "EvryThng.h"

int _tmain (int argc, LPTSTR argv [])
{
    SYSTEMTIME SysTime;
    FILETIME NewFileTime;
    LPFILETIME pAccessTime = NULL, pModifyTime = NULL;
    HANDLE hFile;
```

```
    BOOL Flags [MAX_OPTIONS], SetAccessTime, SetModTime, CreateNew;
    DWORD CreateFlag;
    int i, FileIndex;

    FileIndex = Options (argc, argv, _T ("amc"),
            &Flags [0], &Flags [1], &Flags [2], NULL);
    SetAccessTime = !Flags [0];
    SetModTime = !Flags [1];
    CreateNew = !Flags [2];
    CreateFlag = CreateNew ? OPEN_ALWAYS : OPEN_EXISTING;
    for (i = FileIndex; i < argc; i++) {
        hFile = CreateFile (argv [i], GENERIC_READ | GENERIC_WRITE,
                0, NULL, CreateFlag, FILE_ATTRIBUTE_NORMAL, NULL);
        GetSystemTime (&SysTime);
        SystemTimeToFileTime (&SysTime, &NewFileTime);
        if (SetAccessTime) pAccessTime = &NewFileTime;
        if (SetModTime) pModifyTime = &NewFileTime;
        SetFileTime (hFile, NULL, pAccessTime, pModifyTime);
        CloseHandle (hFile);
    }
    return 0;
}
```

File Processing Strategies

An early decision in any Windows development or porting project is to select whether file processing should be done with the C library or with the Win32 functions. This is not an either/or decision, because the functions can be mixed with caution even when you're processing the same file.

The C library offers several distinct advantages, including the following:

- The code will be portable to non-Windows systems.

- Convenient line- and character-oriented functions that do not have direct Win32 equivalents simplify string processing.

- C library functions are generally easier to use than Win32 functions.

- The line and stream character-oriented functions can easily be changed to generic calls, although the portability advantage will be lost.

- The C library will operate in a multithreaded environment, as shown in Chapter 8.

Nonetheless, there are some limitations to the C library. Here are two examples:

- The C library cannot manage or traverse directories, and it cannot obtain or set most file attributes.

- Advanced features such as file security, memory-mapped files, file locking, asynchronous I/O, and interprocess communication are not available with the C library. Some of the advanced features provide performance benefits, as shown in Appendix C.

Another possibility is to port existing UNIX code using a compatibility library. Microsoft C provides such a library with many, but not all, UNIX functions. The Microsoft UNIX library includes I/O functions, but most process management and other functions are omitted. Functions are named with an underscore prefix—for example, `_read`, `_write`, and so on.

Decisions regarding the use and mix of C library, compatibility libraries, and the Win32/64 API should be driven by project requirements. Many of the Windows advantages will be shown in the following chapters, and the performance figures in Appendix C are useful when performance is a factor.

File Locking

An important issue in any system with multiple processes is coordination and synchronization of access to shared objects, such as files.

Win32 can lock files, in whole or in part, so that no other process (running program) can access the locked file region. File locks can be read-only (shared) or read-write (exclusive). Most important, the locks belong to the process. Any attempt to access part of a file (using `ReadFile` or `WriteFile`) in violation of an existing lock will fail, because the locks are mandatory at the process level. Any attempt to obtain a conflicting lock will also fail even if the process already owns the lock. File locking is a limited form of synchronization between concurrent processes and threads; synchronization is covered in much more general terms starting in Chapter 9.

The most general function, `LockFileEx`, is implemented only in Windows 2000/NT. The less general function, `LockFile`, can be used on Windows 9x. Windows CE does not support any form of file locking.

`LockFileEx` is a member of the *extended* I/O class of functions, so the *overlapped structure*, used earlier to specify file position to `ReadFile` and `WriteFile`, is required to specify the 64-bit file position and range of the file region that is to be locked.

```
BOOL LockFileEx (
    HANDLE hFile,
    DWORD dwFlags,
    DWORD dwReserved,
    DWORD nNumberOfBytesToLockLow,
    DWORD nNumberOfBytesToLockHigh,
    LPOVERLAPPED lpOverlapped)
```

LockFileEx locks a byte range in an open file for either shared (multiple readers) or exclusive (one reader-writer) access.

Parameters

hFile is the handle of an open file. The handle must have GENERIC_READ or both GENERIC_READ and GENERIC_WRITE file access.

dwFlags determines the lock mode and whether to wait for the lock to become available.

- LOCKFILE_EXCLUSIVE_LOCK, if set, indicates a request for an exclusive, read-write lock. Otherwise, it requests a shared (read-only) lock.

- LOCKFILE_FAIL_IMMEDIATELY, if set, specifies that the function should return immediately with a FALSE if the lock cannot be acquired. Otherwise, the call blocks until the lock becomes available.

dwReserved must be zero. The two parameters with the length of the byte range are self-explanatory.

lpOverlapped points to an OVERLAPPED data structure containing the start of the byte range. The OVERLAPPED structure contains three data members that must be set (the others are ignored); the first two determine the start location for the locked region.

- DWORD Offset (this is the correct name; not OffsetLow)

- DWORD OffsetHigh

- HANDLE hEvent should be set to zero.

A file lock is removed using a corresponding UnlockFileEx call; all the same parameters are used except dwFlags.

```
BOOL UnlockFileEx (
    HANDLE hFile,
    DWORD dwReserved,
    DWORD nNumberOfBytesToLockLow,
    DWORD nNumberOfBytesToLockHigh,
    LPOVERLAPPED lpOverlapped)
```

You should consider several factors when using file locks.

- The unlock must use exactly the same range as a preceding lock. It is not possible, for example, to combine two previous lock ranges or unlock a portion of a locked range. An attempt to unlock a region that does not correspond exactly with an existing lock will fail; the function returns a **FALSE** and the system error message indicates that the lock does not exist.

- Locks cannot overlap existing locked regions in a file if a conflict would result.

- It is possible to lock beyond the range of a file's length. This approach could be useful when a process or thread extends a file.

- Locks are not inherited by a newly created process.

Table 3–1 shows the lock logic when all *or* part of a range already has a lock. This logic applies even if the lock is owned by the same process that is making the new request.

Table 3–2 shows the logic when a process attempts a read or write operation on a file region with one or more locks, owned by a separate process, on all or part of the read-write region. A failed read or write may take the form of a partially completed operation if only a portion of the read or write record is locked.

Table 3–1 Lock Request Logic

	Requested Lock Type	
Existing Lock	Shared Lock	Exclusive Lock
None	Granted	Granted
Shared lock (one or more)	Granted	Refused
Exclusive lock	Refused	Refused

Table 3-2   Locks and I/O Operation

Existing Lock	I/O Operation	
	Read	Write
None	Succeeds	Succeeds
Shared lock (one or more)	Succeeds. It is not necessary for the calling process to own a lock on the file region.	Fails
Exclusive lock	Succeeds if the calling process owns the lock. Fails otherwise.	Succeeds if the calling process owns the lock. Fails otherwise.

Read and write operations are normally in the form of ReadFile and Write-File calls or their extended versions, ReadFileEx and WriteFileEx. Diagnosing a read or write failure requires calling GetLastError.

Accessing memory that is mapped to a file is another form of file I/O, as will be discussed in Chapter 6. Lock conflicts are not detected at the time of memory reference; rather, they are detected at the time that the function MapViewOfFile is called. This function makes a part of the file available to the process, so the lock must be checked at that time.

The LockFile function is a limited, special case and is a form of advisory locking. Only exclusive access is available, and LockFile returns immediately. That is, LockFile does not block. Test the return value to determine if you obtained the lock.

Releasing File Locks

Every successful LockFileEx call must be followed by a single matching call to UnlockFileEx (the same is true for LockFile and UnlockFile). If a program fails to release a lock or holds the lock longer than necessary, other programs may not be able to proceed, or, at the very least, their performance will be negatively impacted. Therefore, programs should be carefully designed and implemented so that locks are released as soon as possible, and logic that might cause the program to skip the unlock should be avoided.

Termination handlers (Chapter 4) are a useful way to ensure that the unlock is performed.

Lock Logic Consequences

Although the file lock logic shown in Tables 3–1 and 3–2 is natural, it has consequences that may be unexpected and cause unintended program defects. Here are some examples:

- Suppose that process A and process B periodically obtain shared locks on a file, and process C blocks when attempting to gain an exclusive lock on the same file after process A gets its shared lock. Process B may now gain its shared lock even though C is still blocked, and C will remain blocked even after A releases the lock. C will remain blocked until all processes release their shared locks even if they obtained them after C blocked. In this scenario, it is possible that C will be blocked forever even though all the other processes manage their shared locks properly.

- Assume that process A has a shared lock on the file and that process B attempts to read the file without obtaining a shared lock first. The read will still succeed even though the reading process does not own any lock on the file, because the read operation does not conflict with the existing shared lock.

- These statements apply both to entire files and to regions.

- A read or write may be able to complete a portion of its request before encountering a conflicting lock. The read or write will return a FALSE, and the byte transfer count will be less than the number requested.

Using File Locks

File locking examples are deferred until Chapter 4 and Chapter 7, which covers process management. Programs 4–2, 7–4, 7–5, and 7–6 use locks to ensure that only one process at a time can modify a file.

UNIX has *advisory* file locking; an attempt to obtain a lock may fail (the logic is the same as in Figure 3–1), but the process can still perform the I/O. Therefore, UNIX can achieve locking between cooperating processes, but any other process can violate the protocol.

To obtain an advisory lock, use options to the fcntl function. The commands (the second parameter) are F_SETLK, F_SETLKW (to wait), and F_GETLK. An additional block data structure contains a lock type that is one of F_RDLCK, F_WRLCK, or F_UNLCK and the range.

Mandatory locking is also available in some UNIX systems using a file's set-group-ID and group-execute, both using chmod.

UNIX file locking behavior differs in many ways. For example, locks are inherited through an exec call.

The C library does not support locking, although Visual C++ does supply non-standard extensions for locking.

The Registry

The registry is a centralized, hierarchical database for application and system configuration information. Access to the registry is through *registry keys*, which are analogous to file system directories. A key can contain other keys or name/value pairs, where the name/value pairs are analogous to file names and contents.

The user or administrator can view and edit the registry contents through the registry editor, which is accessed by the REGEDIT32 command. Alternatively, programs can manage the registry through the registry API functions described in this section.

Note: Registry programming is discussed here due to its similarity to file processing and its importance in some, but not all, applications. *Therefore, readers who are not concerned with registry programming may wish to skip this section, possibly returning at a later time.*

The registry name/value pairs contain information such as the following:

- Operating system version number, build number, and registered user.

- Similar information for every properly installed application.

- Information about the computer's processor type, number of processors, system memory, and so on.

- User-specific information, such as the home directory and application preferences.

- Security information such as user account names.

- Installed services (Chapter 13).

- Mappings from file name extensions to executable programs. These mappings are used by the user interface shell when the user clicks on a file name icon. For example, the .doc extension might be mapped to Microsoft Word.

- Mappings from network addresses to host machine names.

UNIX systems store similar information in the /etc directory and files in the user's home directory. Windows 3.1 used the .INI files for a similar purpose. The registry centralizes all this information in a uniform way. In addition, the registry is securable using the security features described in Chapter 5.

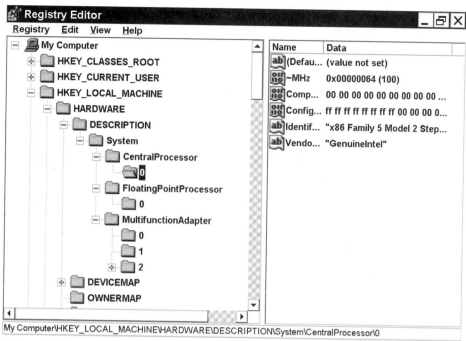

Figure 3–1   The Registry Editor

The registry management API is described here, but the detailed contents and meaning of the various registry entries are beyond the scope of this book. Nonetheless, Figure 3–1 shows a typical view from the registry editor and gives an idea of the registry structure and contents.

The specific information regarding the host machine's processor is on the right side. The bottom of the left side shows that there are numerous keys containing information about the software applications on the host system. Notice that every key must have a default value, which is listed before any of the other name/value pairs.

Registry Keys

Figure 3–1 shows the analogy between file system directories and registry keys. Each key can contain other keys or else a sequence of name/value pairs. Whereas a file system is accessed through pathnames, the registry is accessed through keys. Several predefined keys serve as entry points into the registry.

1. HKEY_LOCAL_MACHINE stores physical information about the machine, along with information about installed software. Installed software information is

created in subkeys of the form SOFTWARE*CompanyName**ProductName*\ *Version*.

2. HKEY_USERS defines user configuration information.

3. HKEY_CURRENT_CONFIG contains current settings, such as display resolution and fonts.

4. HKEY_CLASSES_ROOT contains subordinate entries to define mappings from file extension names to classes and to applications used by the shell to access objects with the specified extension. All the keys necessary for Microsoft's Component Object Model (COM) are also subordinate to this key.

5. HKEY_CURRENT_USER. User-specific information, including environment variables, printers, and application preferences, is subordinate to this key.

Registry Management

Registry management functions can query and modify name/value pairs and create new subkeys and name/value pairs. Key *handles* of type HKEY are used both to specify a key and to obtain new keys.[2] Values are typed; there are several types to select from, such as strings, double words, and expandable strings whose parameters can be replaced with environment variables.

Key Management

The first function, RegOpenKeyEx, opens a subkey. Starting from one of the predefined reserved key handles, you can traverse the registry and obtain a handle to any subordinate key.

```
LONG RegOpenKeyEx (
    HKEY hKey,
    LPCTSTR lpSubKey,
    DWORD ulOptions,
    REGSAM samDesired,
    PHKEY phkResult)
```

---

[2] It would be more convenient and consistent if the HANDLE type were used for registry management. There are several other gratuitous exceptions to standard Windows practice.

Parameters

hKey identifies a currently open key or one of the predefined reserved key handle values. phkResult points to a variable of type HKEY that is to receive the handle of the newly opened key.

lpSubKey is the name of the subkey. The subkey name can be a path, such as Microsoft\WindowsNT\CurrentVersion. A NULL value causes a new, duplicate key for hKey to be opened. ulOptions must be zero.

samDesired is the access mask describing the security for the new key. Values include KEY_ALL_ACCESS, KEY_WRITE, KEY_QUERY_VALUE, and KEY_ENUMERATE_SUBKEYS.

The return value is normally ERROR_SUCCESS. Any other value indicates an error. Close an open key handle with RegCloseKey, which takes the handle as its single parameter.

Obtain the names of subkeys by specifying a key to RegEnumKeyEx.

There is a complementary pair of functions used to obtain name/value pairs: RegEnumValue and RegQueryValueEx.[3] RegSetValueEx stores typed data in the value field of an open registry key. Here are descriptions of these functions, followed by an example.

RegEnumKeyEx enumerates subkeys of an open registry key, much as FindFirstFile and FindNextFile enumerate directory contents. This function retrieves the key name, class string, and time of last modification.

```
LONG RegEnumKeyEx (
    HKEY hKey,
    DWORD dwIndex,
    LPTSTR lpName,
    LPDWORD lpcbName,
    LPDWORD lpReserved,
    LPTSTR lpClass,
    LPDWORD lpcbClass
    PFILETIME lpftLastWriteTime)
```

dwIndex should be zero on the first call and then should be incremented on each subsequent call. The key name and its size, along with the class string and

---

[3] Notice that the Ex suffix should be used or omitted exactly as shown. When Ex is used, the function extends a function of the same name without the suffix.

its size, are returned in the normal way. The function returns ERROR_SUCCESS or an error value.

You can also create new keys using RegCreateKeyEx. Keys can be given security attributes in the same way as with directories and files (Chapter 5).

```
LONG RegCreateKeyEx (
    HKEY hKey,
    LPCTSTR lpSubKey,
    DWORD Reserved,
    LPTSTR lpClass,
    DWORD dwOptions,
    REGSAM samDesired,
    LPSECURITY_ATTRIBUTES lpSecurityAttributes,
    PHKEY phkResult,
    LPDWORD lpdwDisposition)
```

Parameters

lpSubKey is the name of the new subkey under the open key indicated by the handle hKey.

lpClass is the class, or object type, of the key describing the data represented by the key. The many possible values include REG_SZ (null-terminated string) and REG_DWORD (double word).

dwOptions is either zero or one of the mutually exclusive values: REG_OPTION_VOLATILE or REG_OPTION_NON_VOLATILE. Nonvolatile registry information is stored in a file and preserved when the system restarts. Volatile registry keys are kept in memory and will not be restored.

samDesired is the same as for RegOpenKeyEx.

lpSecurityAttributes can be NULL or else points to a security attribute. The rights can be selected from the same values as those used with samDesired.

lpdwDisposition points to a DWORD that indicates whether the key already existed (REG_OPENED_EXISTING_KEY) or was created (REG_CREATED_NEW_KEY).

To delete a key, use RegDeleteKey. The two parameters are an open key handle and a subkey name.

Value Management

You can enumerate the values for a specified open key using RegEnumValue. Specify an Index, originally zero, which is incremented in subsequent calls. On return, you get the string with the value name as well as its size. You also get the value and its type.

```
LONG RegEnumValue (
    HKEY hKey,
    DWORD dwIndex,
    LPTSTR lpValueName,
    LPDWORD lpcbValueName,
    LPDWORD lpReserved,
    LPDWORD lpType,
    LPBYTE lpData,
    LPDWORD lpcbData)
```

The actual value is returned in the buffer indicated by lpData. The size of the result can be found from lpcbData.

The data type, pointed to by lpType, has numerous possibilities, including REG_BINARY, REG_DWORD, REG_SZ (a string), and REG_EXPAND_SZ (an expandable string with parameters replaced by environment variables). See the on-line help for a list of all the value types.

Test the function's return value to determine whether you have enumerated all the keys. The value will be ERROR_SUCCESS if you have found a valid key.

RegQueryValueEx is similar except that you specify a value name rather than an index. If you know the value names, you can use this function. If you do not know the names, you can scan with RegEnumValueEx.

Set a value within an open key using RegSetValueEx, supplying the value name, value type, and actual value data.

```
LONG RegSetValueEx (
    HKEY hKey,
    LPCTSTR lpValueName,
    DWORD Reserved,
    DWORD dwType,
    CONST BYTE * lpData,
    CONST cbData)
```

Finally, delete named values using the function RegDeleteValue.

Example: Listing Registry Keys and Contents

Program 3–4, lsReg, is a modification of Program 3–2 (ls, the file and directory listing program); it processes registry keys and name/value pairs rather than directories and files.

Program 3–4   lsReg: Listing Registry Keys and Contents

```
/* Chapter 3. lsREG: Registry list command. Adapted from Prog. 3-2. */
/* lsREG [options] SubKey */

#include "EvryThng.h"

BOOL TraverseRegistry (HKEY, LPTSTR, LPTSTR, LPBOOL);
BOOL DisplayPair (LPTSTR, DWORD, LPBYTE, DWORD, LPBOOL);
BOOL DisplaySubKey (LPTSTR, LPTSTR, PFILETIME, LPBOOL);

int _tmain (int argc, LPTSTR argv [])
{
    BOOL Flags [2], ok = TRUE;
    TCHAR KeyName [MAX_PATH + 1];
    LPTSTR pScan;
    DWORD i, KeyIndex;
    HKEY hKey, hNextKey;

    /* Tables of predefined key names and keys. */
    LPTSTR PreDefKeyNames [] = {
        _T ("HKEY_LOCAL_MACHINE"), _T ("HKEY_CLASSES_ROOT"),
        _T ("HKEY_CURRENT_USER"), _T ("HKEY_CURRENT_CONFIG"), NULL };
    HKEY PreDefKeys [] = {
        HKEY_LOCAL_MACHINE, HKEY_CLASSES_ROOT,
        HKEY_CURRENT_USER, HKEY_CURRENT_CONFIG };

    KeyIndex = Options (
            argc, argv, _T ("Rl"), &Flags [0], &Flags [1], NULL);

    /* "Parse" the search pattern into "key" and "subkey". */
    /* Build the key. */
    pScan = argv [KeyIndex];
    for (i = 0; *pScan != _T ('\\') && *pScan != _T ('\0');
            pScan++, i++) KeyName [i] = *pScan;
    KeyName [i] = _T ('\0');
    if (*pScan == _T ('\\')) pScan++;

    /* Translate predefined key name to an HKEY. */
    for (i = 0; PreDefKeyNames [i] != NULL &&
        _tcscmp (PreDefKeyNames [i], KeyName) != 0; i++);
    hKey = PreDefKeys [i];
```

```
    RegOpenKeyEx (hKey, pScan, 0, KEY_READ, &hNextKey);
    hKey = hNextKey;

    ok = TraverseRegistry (hKey, argv [KeyIndex], NULL, Flags);
    return ok ? 0 : 1;
}

BOOL TraverseRegistry (HKEY hKey, LPTSTR FullKeyName, LPTSTR SubKey,
        LPBOOL Flags)

/* Traverse registry key and subkeys if the -R option is set. */
{
    HKEY hSubK;
    BOOL Recursive = Flags [0];
    LONG Result;
    DWORD ValType, Index, NumSubKs, SubKNameLen, ValNameLen, ValLen;
    DWORD MaxSubKLen, NumVals, MaxValNameLen, MaxValLen;
    FILETIME LastWriteTime;
    LPTSTR SubKName, ValName;
    LPBYTE Val;
    TCHAR FullSubKName [MAX_PATH + 1];

    /* Open up the key handle. */
    RegOpenKeyEx (hKey, SubKey, 0, KEY_READ, &hSubK);

    /* Find max size info regarding the key and allocate storage. */
    RegQueryInfoKey (hSubK, NULL, NULL, NULL, &NumSubKs,
            &MaxSubKLen, NULL, &NumVals, &MaxValNameLen,
            &MaxValLen, NULL, &LastWriteTime);
    SubKName = malloc (MaxSubKLen+1); /* Size w/o null. */
    ValName = malloc (MaxValNameLen+1); /* Allow for null. */
    Val = malloc (MaxValLen); /* Size in bytes. */

    /* First pass for name/value pairs. */
    for (Index = 0; Index < NumVals; Index++) {
        ValNameLen = MaxValNameLen + 1; /* Set each time! */
        ValLen = MaxValLen + 1;
        RegEnumValue (hSubK, Index, ValName,
                &ValNameLen, NULL, &ValType, Val, &ValLen);
        DisplayPair (ValName, ValType, Val, ValLen, Flags);
    }

    /* Second pass for subkeys. */
    for (Index = 0; Index < NumSubKs; Index++) {
        SubKNameLen = MaxSubKLen + 1;
        RegEnumKeyEx (hSubK, Index, SubKName, &SubKNameLen,
                NULL, NULL, NULL, &LastWriteTime);
        DisplaySubKey (FullKName, SubKName, &LastWriteTime, Flags);
        if (Recursive) {
```

```
                _stprintf (FullSubKName, _T ("%s\\%s"), FullKName,
                        SubKName);
                TraverseRegistry (hSubK, FullSubKName, SubKName, Flags);
            }
        }

        _tprintf (_T ("\n"));
        free (SubKName); free (ValName); free (Val);
        RegCloseKey (hSubK);
        return TRUE;
    }

BOOL DisplayPair (LPTSTR ValueName, DWORD ValueType,
            LPBYTE Value, DWORD ValueLen, LPBOOL Flags)
/* Function to display name-value pairs. */
{
    LPBYTE pV = Value;
    DWORD i;

    _tprintf (_T ("\nValue: %s = "), ValueName);
    switch (ValueType) {
    case REG_FULL_RESOURCE_DESCRIPTOR: /* 9: hardware description. */

    case REG_BINARY: /* 3: Binary data in any form. */
        for (i = 0; i < ValueLen; i++, pV++)
            _tprintf (_T (" %x"), *pV);
        break;

    case REG_DWORD: /* 4: A 32-bit number. */
        _tprintf (_T ("%x"), (DWORD)*Value);
        break;

    case REG_MULTI_SZ: /* 7: Array of null-terminated strings. */

    case REG_SZ: /* 1: A null-terminated string. */
        _tprintf (_T ("%s"), (LPTSTR) Value);
        break;
    /* ... Several other types ... */
    }
    return TRUE;
}

BOOL DisplaySubKey (LPTSTR KeyName, LPTSTR SubKeyName,
        PFILETIME pLastWrite, LPBOOL Flags)
{
    BOOL Long = Flags [1];
    SYSTEMTIME SysLastWrite;

    _tprintf (_T ("\nSubkey: %s"), KeyName);
    if (_tcslen (SubKeyName) > 0)
```

```
      _tprintf (_T ("\\%s "), SubKeyName);
   if (Long) {
      FileTimeToSystemTime (pLastWrite, &SysLastWrite);
      _tprintf (_T ("%02d/%02d/%04d %02d:%02d:%02d"),
            SysLastWrite.wMonth, SysLastWrite.wDay,
            SysLastWrite.wYear, SysLastWrite.wHour,
            SysLastWrite.wMinute, SysLastWrite.wSecond);
   }
   return TRUE;
}
```

Summary

Chapters 2 and 3 have described all the important basic functions for dealing with files, directories, and console I/O. Numerous examples show how to use these functions in building typical applications. The registry is managed in much the same way as the file system, as shown by the final example.

Later chapters will deal with advanced I/O, such as asynchronous operations and memory mapping. It is now possible to duplicate nearly any common UNIX or C library file processing.

Appendix B contains several tables showing the Win32, UNIX, and C library functions, noting how they correspond and pointing out some of the significant differences among them.

Looking Ahead

Chapter 4, Structured Exception Handling, simplifies error and exception handling and extends the `ReportError` function to handle arbitrary exceptions.

Additional Reading

See Hipson's *Expert Guide to Windows NT 4 Registry* for information on registry programming as well as registry usage.

Exercises

3–1. Use the `GetDiskFreeSpace` function to determine how the different Windows systems allocate file space sparsely. For instance, create a new file, set the file pointer to a large value, set the file size, and investigate the free space using `GetDiskFreeSpace`. The same Win32 function can also be used to determine how the disc is configured into sectors and clusters. Also, determine whether the newly allocated file space is initialized. `Free-Space.c`, on the disc, is the solution. Compare the results for Windows 2000, NT, and 9x. If you are running Windows 2000, investigate how to make a file be sparse.

3–2. What happens if you attempt to set a file's length to a size larger than the disc? Does Win32 fail gracefully?

3–3. Modify Program 3–1 (`tail`) so that it does not use `SetFilePointer`; use overlapped structures.

3–4. Write a program, `getn`, that will read a specified record number from a file; there is a solution on the disc.

3–5. Examine the "number of links" field obtained using the function `GetFile-InformationByHandle`. Is it always 1? Are the answers different for the NTFS and FAT file systems? Do the link counts appear to count links from parent directories and subdirectories, as they do in UNIX? Does Win32 open the directory as a file to get a handle before using this function? What about the shortcuts supported by the user interface?

3–6. Program 3–2 checks for "." and ".." to detect the names of the current and parent directories. What happens if there are actual files with these names? Can files have these names?

3–7. Does Program 3–2 list local times or UCTs (Universal Coordinated Times)? If necessary, modify the program to give the results in local time.

3–8. Enhance Program 3–2 so that it also lists the "." and ".." (current and parent) directories (the complete program is on the disc). Also, add options to display the file creation and last access times along with the last write time. Compare the 2000/NT and 9x results.

3–9. Create a file deletion command, `rm`, by modifying the `ProcessItem` function in Program 3–2. A solution is on the disc.

3–10. Enhance the file copy command, `cp`, from Chapter 2 so that it will copy files to a target directory. Further extensions allow for recursive copying (`-r` option) and for preserving the modification time of the copied files (`-p` option). Implementing the recursive copy option will require that you create new directories.

3–11. Write an `mv` command, similar to the UNIX command, that will move a complete directory. One significant consideration is whether the target is on a different drive from that of the source file or directory. If it is, copy the file(s); otherwise, use `MoveFile` or `MoveFileEx`.

3–12. Enhance Program 3–3 (touch) so that the new file time is specified on the command line. The UNIX command allows the time stamp to appear (optionally) after the normal options and before the file names. The format for the time is MMddhhmm [yy], where the uppercase MM is the month and mm is for minutes. A two-digit year is no longer sufficient, so require a four-digit year.

3–13. Program 3–1 is written to work with large NTFS file systems. If you have a sufficiently large disc, test this program with a very large file (length > 4GB). Verify that the 64-bit arithmetic is correct. It is not recommended that you perform this exercise on a network drive without permission from the network administrator. And don't forget to delete the test file on completion.

3–14. Write a program that locks a specified file and holds the lock for a long period of time (you may find the Sleep function useful). While the lock is held, try to access the file (use a text file) with an editor. What happens? Is the file properly locked? Alternatively, write a program that will prompt the user to specify a lock on a test file. Two instances of the program can be run in separate windows to verify that file locking works as described. TestLock.c on the disc is a solution to this exercise.

3–15. Investigate the Win32 file time representation in FILETIME. It uses 64 bits to count the elapsed number of 100-nanosecond units from January 1, 1601. When will the time expire? When will the UNIX file time representation expire?

3–16. Write an interactive utility that will prompt the user for a registry key name and a value name. Display the current value and prompt the user for a new value.

4 | Structured Exception Handling

Win32 Structured Exception Handling (SEH) provides a robust mechanism that allows applications to respond to unexpected events, such as addressing exceptions, arithmetic faults, and system errors. SEH also allows a program to exit from anywhere in a code block and automatically perform programmer-specified processing and error recovery.

SEH ensures that the program will be able to free resources and perform other cleanup processing before the block, thread, or process terminates either under program control or because of an unexpected exception. Furthermore, SEH can be added easily to existing code, often simplifying program logic.

SEH will prove to be useful in the examples and also will allow extension of the ReportError error-processing function introduced in Chapter 2.

Console control handlers, also described in this chapter, allow a program to detect external signals such as a Ctrl-c from the console or the user logging off. These signals can also be sent from one process to another.

Exceptions and Their Handlers

Without some form of exception handling, an unintended program exception, such as dereferencing a NULL pointer or division by zero, will terminate a program immediately. This could be a problem, for example, if the program has created a temporary file that should be deleted before program termination. SEH allows specification of a code block, or *exception handler*, that can delete the temporary file when an exception occurs.

SEH is supported through a combination of Win32 functions, language support provided by the compiler, and run-time support. The exact language support may vary; the examples here were all developed for Microsoft C.

Try and Except Blocks

Start by determining which code blocks to monitor and provide them with exception handlers, as described next. It is possible to monitor an entire function or to have separate exception handlers for different code blocks and functions.

A code block is a good candidate for an exception handler in situations that include:

- Detectable errors, including system call errors, might occur, and you need to recover from the error rather than terminate the program.

- Pointers are used extensively, so there is a possibility of dereferencing pointers that have not been properly initialized.

- There is extensive array manipulation, because it is possible for array indices to go out of bounds.

- The code performs floating-point arithmetic, and there is concern with zero divides, imprecise results, and overflows.

- The code calls a function that might generate an exception, either intentionally or because the function has not been well tested.

In the examples in this chapter and throughout the book, once you have decided to monitor a block, create the try and except blocks as follows:

```
__try {
   /* Block of monitored code */
}
__except (filter_expression) {
   /* Exception handling block */
}
```

Notice that __try and __except are keywords recognized by the compiler.

The try block is part of normal application code. If an exception occurs in the block, the operating system transfers control to the exception handler, which is the code in the block associated with the __except clause. The actions that follow are determined by the value of the *filter_expression*.

Notice that the exception might occur within a block embedded in the try block, in which case the run-time support "unwinds" the stack to find the exception handler and then gives control to the handler. The same thing happens when an exception occurs within a function called within a try block.

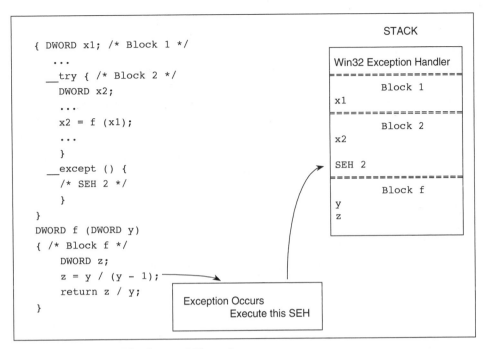

Figure 4-1 SEH, Blocks, and Functions

Figure 4–1 shows how an exception handler is located on the stack when an exception occurs. Once the exception handler block completes, control passes to the next statement after the exception block unless there is some other control flow statement in the handler.

Filter Expressions and Their Values

The *filter_expression* in the __except clause is evaluated immediately after the exception occurs. The expression is usually a literal constant, a call to a *filter function*, or a conditional expression. In all cases, the expression should return one of three values:

1. EXCEPTION_EXECUTE_HANDLER—The system executes the except block as shown in Figure 4–1. This is the normal case.

2. EXCEPTION_CONTINUE_SEARCH—The system ignores the exception handler and searches for an exception handler in the enclosing block, continuing until it finds a handler.

3. EXCEPTION_CONTINUE_EXECUTION—The system immediately returns control to the point at which the exception occurred. It is not possible to continue after some exceptions, and another exception is generated immediately if the program attempts to do so.

Here is a simple example using an exception handler to delete a temporary file if an exception occurs in the loop body. Notice that the __try clause can be applied to any block, including the block associated with a while, if, or other flow control statement. In this example, the temporary file is deleted, and the handle is closed, in the case of an exception, and then the loop iteration continues.

```
GetTempFileName (TempFile, ...);
while (...) __try {
   hFile = CreateFile (TempFile, ..., OPEN_ALWAYS, ...);
   SetFilePointer (hFile, 0, NULL, FILE_END);
   ...
   WriteFile (hFile, ...);
   i = *p; /* An addressing exception could occur. */
   ...
   CloseHandle (hFile);
}
__except (EXCEPTION_EXECUTE_HANDLER) {
   CloseHandle (hFile);
   DeleteFile (TempFile);
   /* The loop will now execute the next iteration .*/
}
/* Control passes here after normal loop termination.
   The file handle is always closed and the temp file
   will not exist if an exception occurred. */
```

The logic of this code fragment is as follows:

- Each loop iteration appends new data to the end of the temporary file.

- If an exception occurs in any loop iteration, all data accumulated in the temporary file is deleted, and the next iteration, if any, starts to accumulate data in the temporary file again.

- If an exception occurs on the last iteration, the file will not exist. In any case, the file will contain all data generated since the last exception.

- The example shows just one location where an exception could occur, although the exception could occur anywhere within the loop body.

- The file handle is assured of being closed when exiting the loop or starting a new loop iteration.

Exception Codes

The except block or the filter expression can determine the exact exception using this function:

```
DWORD GetExceptionCode (VOID)
```

The exception code must be obtained immediately after an exception. Therefore, the filter function itself cannot call `GetExceptionCode` (the compiler enforces this restriction). A common usage is to invoke it in the filter expression, as in the following example, where the exception code is the argument to a user-supplied "filter function."

```
__except (MyFilter (GetExceptionCode ())) {
}
```

In this situation, the filter function determines and returns the filter expression value, which must be one of the three values enumerated earlier. The function can use the exception code to determine the function value; for example, the filter may decide to pass floating-point exceptions to an outer handler (by returning `EXCEPTION_CONTINUE_SEARCH`) and to handle a memory access violation in the current handler (by returning `EXCEPTION_EXECUTE_HANDLER`).

A large number of possible exception code values can be returned by `GetExceptionCode`, and the codes are in several categories.

- Program violations such as the following:

  - `EXCEPTION_ACCESS_VIOLATION`—An attempt to read or write a virtual address for which the process does not have access.

  - `EXCEPTION_DATATYPE_MISALIGNMENT`—Many processors insist, for example, that DWORDs be aligned on four-byte boundaries.

  - `EXCEPTION_NONCONTINUABLE_EXECUTION`—The filter expression was `EXCEPTION_CONTINUE_EXECUTION`, but it is not possible to continue after the exception that occurred.

- Exceptions raised by the memory allocation functions—HeapAlloc and HeapCreate—if they use the HEAP_GENERATE_EXCEPTIONS flag (see Chapter 6). The value will be either STATUS_NO_MEMORY or EXCEPTION_ACCESS_VIOLATION.

- A user-defined exception code generated by the RaiseException function, which is explained in a later section.

- A large variety of arithmetic (especially floating-point) codes such as EXCEPTION_INT_DIVIDE_BY_ZERO and EXCEPTION_FLT_OVERFLOW.

- Exceptions used by debuggers, such as EXCEPTION_BREAKPOINT and EXCEPTION_SINGLE_STEP.

An alternative function, callable only from within the filter expression, which returns additional information, some of which is processor-specific, is as follows.

```
LPEXCEPTION_POINTERS GetExceptionInformation (VOID)
```

The EXCEPTION_POINTERS structure contains both processor-specific and processor-independent information organized into two other structures.

```
typedef struct _EXCEPTION_POINTERS {
    PEXCEPTION_RECORD ExceptionRecord;
    PCONTEXT ContextRecord;
} EXCEPTION_POINTERS;
```

EXCEPTION_RECORD contains a member for the ExceptionCode, with the same set of values as returned by GetExceptionCode. The ExceptionFlags member of the EXCEPTION_RECORD is either 0 or EXCEPTION_NONCONTINUABLE, which allows the filter function to determine that it should not attempt to continue execution. Other data members include a virtual memory address, ExceptionAddress, and a parameter array, ExceptionInformation. In the case of EXCEPTION_ACCESS_VIOLATION, the first element indicates whether the violation was a memory write (1) or read (0). The second element is the virtual memory address.

`ContextRecord`, the second `EXCEPTION_POINTERS` member, contains processor-specific information. There are different structures for each type of processor, and the structure can be found in `<winnt.h>`.

Summary: Exception Handling Sequence

Figure 4–2 shows the sequence of events that takes place when an exception occurs. The code is shown on the left side, and the circled numbers on the right show the steps carried out by the language run-time support. The steps are as follows:

1. The exception occurs, in this case a division by zero.

2. Control transfers to the exception handler, where the filter expression is evaluated. `GetExceptionCode` is called first, and its return value is the argument to the function `Filter`.

3. The filter function bases its actions on the exception code value.

4. The exception code is `EXCEPTION_INT_DIVIDE_BY_ZERO` in this case.

```
_try {

        ...

        i = j / 0;

        ...

}
_except (Filter (GetExceptionCode ())) {

        ...

}

        ...

DWORD Filter (DWORD ExCode)

{

        switch (ExCode) {

        ...

        case EXCEPTION_INT_DIVIDE_BY_ZERO:

        ...

        return EXCEPTION_EXECUTE_HANDLER;

        case ...

        }

}
```

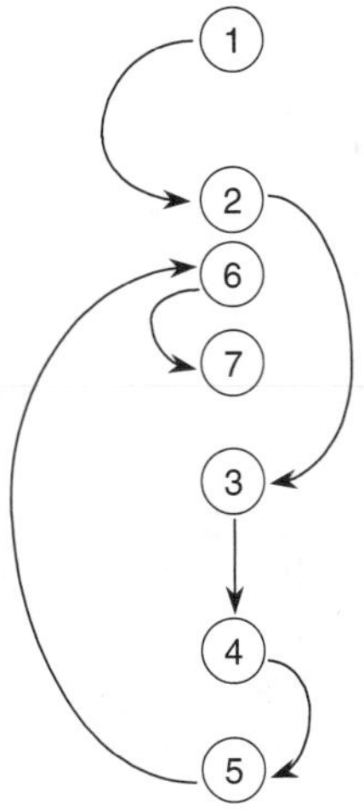

Figure 4-2   Exception Handling Sequence

5. The filter function determines that the exception handler should be executed, so the return value is EXCEPTION_EXECUTE_HANDLER.

6. The exception handler, which is the code associated with the __except clause, executes.

7. Control passes out of the try-except block.

Floating-Point Exceptions

The exception codes include seven distinct codes for floating-point exceptions. These exceptions are disabled initially and will not occur without first setting the processor-independent floating-point mask with the _controlfp function. There are specific exceptions for underflow, overflow, division by zero, inexact results, and so on, as shown in a later code fragment. Turn the mask bit *off* to enable the particular exception.

```
DWORD _controlfp (DWORD new, DWORD mask)
```

The actual value of the floating-point mask is determined by its current value (current_mask) and the two arguments as follows:

```
(current_mask & ~mask) | (new & mask)
```

The function sets the bits specified by new that are enabled by mask. All bits *not* in mask are unaltered. The floating-point mask also controls precision, rounding, and infinity values, so it is important not to alter these settings when you're enabling floating-point exceptions.

The return value will be the actual setting. Thus, if both argument values are 0, the return value is the current mask setting, which can be used later to restore the mask. Normally, to enable the floating-point exceptions, use the floating-point exception mask value, MCW_EM, as shown in the following example. Notice also that, when a floating-point exception is processed, the exception must be cleared using the _clearfp function.

```
#include <float.h>
DWORD FPOld, FPNew; /* Old and new mask values. */
   ...
FPOld = _controlfp (0, 0); /* Saved old mask. */
```

```
/* Specify six exceptions to be enabled. */
FPNew = FPOld & ~(EM_OVERFLOW | EM_UNDERFLOW
   | EM_INEXACT | EM_ZERODIVIDE | EM_DENORMAL | EM_INVALID);
/* Set new control mask. MCW_EM combines the six
   exceptions in the previous statement. */
_controlfp (FPNew, MCW_EM);
while (...) __try { /* Perform FP calculations. */
   ... /* A FP exception could occur here. */
}
__except (EXCEPTION_EXECUTE_HANDLER) {
   ... /* Process the FP exception. */
   _clearfp (); /* Clear the exception. */
   _controlfp (FPOld, 0xFFFFFFFF); /* Restore mask. */
}
```

This example enables all possible floating-point exceptions. A seventh, floating-point stack overflow EXCEPTION_FLT_STACK_CHECK, does not have a mask value indicated in the documentation or include files. Alternatively, enable specific exceptions by using only selected exception masks, such as EM_OVERFLOW.

Errors and Exceptions

An error can be thought of as a situation that could occur occasionally in known locations. System call errors, for example, should be detected and reported immediately by logic in the code. Thus, programmers normally include an explicit test to see, for instance, whether a file read operation has failed. The ReportError function was developed in Chapter 2 to diagnose and respond to errors.

An exception, on the other hand, could occur nearly anywhere, and it is not possible or practical to test for an exception. Division by zero and memory access violations are examples.

Nonetheless, the distinction is sometimes blurred. Win32 will, optionally, generate exceptions during memory allocation using the HeapAlloc and Heap-Create functions if memory is insufficient. This is described in Chapter 6. Programs can also raise their own exceptions with programmer-defined exception codes using the RaiseException function, as described next.

Exception handlers provide a convenient mechanism for exiting from inner blocks or functions under program control without resorting to a goto or longjmp to transfer control. This capability is particularly important if the block has accessed resources, such as open files, memory, or synchronization objects, because the handler can release them, and it is also possible to continue program execution after the exception handler, rather than terminating the program. Additionally, a program can restore system state, such as the floating-point mask, on exiting from a block. Many examples will use handlers in this way.

User-Generated Exceptions

It is possible to raise an exception at any point during execution of a program using the RaiseException function. In this way, your program can detect an error and treat it as an exception.

```
VOID RaiseException (
    DWORD dwExceptionCode,
    DWORD dwExceptionFlags,
    DWORD cArguments,
    LPDWORD lpArguments)
```

Parameters

dwExceptionCode is the user-defined code. Do not use bit 28, which is reserved for the system. The error code is encoded in bits 27–0 (all except the most significant hex digit). Bit 29 should be set to indicate a "customer" (not Microsoft) exception. Bits 31–30 encode the severity as follows, where the resulting lead exception code hex digit is shown with bit 29 set.

- 0—Success (lead exception code hex digit is 2)
- 1—Informational (lead exception code hex digit is 6)
- 2—Warning (lead exception code hex digit is A)
- 3—Error (lead exception code hex digit is E)

dwExceptionFlags is normally set to zero, but setting the value to EXCEPTION_NONCONTINUABLE indicates that the filter expression should not generate EXCEPTION_CONTINUE_EXECUTION; doing so will cause an immediate EXCEPTION_NONCONTINUABLE_EXCEPTION exception.

lpArguments, if not NULL, points to an array of size cArguments (the third parameter) containing 32-bit values to be passed to the filter expression. There is a maximum number, EXCEPTION_MAXIMUM_PARAMETERS, which is currently defined to be 15. This structure should be accessed using GetExceptionInformation.

Notice that it is not possible to raise an exception in another process. Under very limited circumstances, however, console control handlers, described at the end of this chapter and in Chapter 7, can be used for this purpose.

Example: Treating Errors as Exceptions

Previous examples use `ReportError` to process system call and other errors. The function terminates the process when the programmer indicates that the error is fatal. This approach, however, prevents an orderly shutdown, and it also prevents program continuation after recovering from an error. For example, the program may have created temporary files that should be deleted or the program may simply proceed to do other work after abandoning the failed task. `ReportError` has other limitations, including the following:

- A fatal error shuts down the entire process when only a single thread[1] should terminate.

- You may wish to continue program execution rather than terminate the process.

- Synchronization resources, such as mutexes, will not be released in many circumstances.[2]

Open handles will be closed by a terminating process (but not by a terminating thread), but it is necessary to address the other deficiencies.

The solution is to write a new function, `ReportException`. This function will invoke `ReportError`, which was developed in Chapter 2, with a nonfatal code in order to generate the error message. Next, on a fatal error, it will raise an exception. The system will use an exception handler from the calling try block, so the exception may not actually be fatal if the handler allows the program to recover. Essentially, `ReportException` augments normal defensive programming techniques, previously limited to `ReportError`. Once an error is detected, the exception handler allows the program to recover and continue after the error. Program 4–2 will illustrate this capability.

Program 4–1 shows the function. It is in the same source module as `Report-Error`, so the definitions and include files are omitted.

---

[1] Threads, the basic Win32 units of execution, are the topic of Chapter 8.

[2] Synchronization is described in Chapter 9.

Program 4–1   `ReportException`: Exception Reporting Function

```
/* Extension of ReportError to generate a user-exception
   code rather than terminating the process. */

VOID ReportException (LPCTSTR UserMessage, DWORD ExceptionCode)
          /* Report as a nonfatal error. */
{
    ReportError (UserMessage, 0, TRUE);
            /* If fatal, raise an exception. */
    if (ExceptionCode != 0)
        RaiseException (
            (0x0FFFFFFF & ExceptionCode) | 0xE0000000, 0, 0, NULL);
    return;
}
```

`ReportException` is used frequently in subsequent examples.

The UNIX signal model is significantly different from SEH. Signals can be missed or ignored, and the flow is different. Nonetheless, there are points of comparison.

UNIX signal handling is largely supported through the C library, which is also available in a limited implementation under Win32. In many cases, Win32 programs can use console control handlers, which are described at the end of this chapter, in place of signals.

Some signals correspond to Win32 exceptions.

Here is the limited signal-to-exception correspondence:

- `SIGILL` — `EXCEPTION_PRIV_INSTRUCTION`

- `SIGSEGV` — `EXCEPTION_ACCESS_VIOLATION`

- `SIGFPE` — Seven distinct floating-point exceptions, such as `EXCEPTION_FLT_DIVIDE_BY_ZERO`

- `SIGUSR1` — User-defined exceptions
  `SIGUSR2`

The C library `raise` function corresponds to `RaiseException`.

Win32 will not generate `SIGILL`, `SIGSEGV`, or `SIGTERM`, although `raise` can generate one of them. Win32 does not support `SIGINT`.

The UNIX `kill` function (`kill` is not in the Standard C library), which can send a signal to another process, is comparable to the Win32 function `Generate-ConsoleCtrlEvent` (Chapter 7). In the limited case of `SIGKILL`, Win32 has `TerminateProcess` and `TerminateThread`, allowing one process (or thread) to "kill" another, although these functions should be used with care (see Chapters 7 and 8).

Termination Handlers

A termination handler serves much the same purpose as an exception handler, but it is executed when a thread leaves a block as a result of normal program flow as well as when an exception occurs. On the other hand, a termination handler cannot diagnose an exception.

You construct a termination handler using the `__finally` keyword in a try-finally statement. The structure is the same as for a try-except statement, but there is no filter expression. Termination handlers, like exception handlers, are a convenient way to close handles, release resources, restore masks, and otherwise restore the process to a known state when leaving a block. For example, a program may execute `return` statements in the middle of a block, and the termination handler can perform the cleanup work. In this way, there is no need to include the cleanup code in the code block itself, nor is there a need for a `goto` statement to reach the cleanup code.

```
__try {
   /* Code block. */
}
__finally {
   /* Termination handler (finally block). */
}
```

Leaving the Try Block

The termination handler is executed whenever the control flow leaves the try block for any of the following reasons:

- Reaching the end of the try block and "falling through" to the termination handler

- Execution of one of the following statements in such a way as to leave the block:

    return
    break
    goto[3]

---

[3] It may be a matter of taste, either individual or organizational, but many programmers never use the `goto` statement and try to avoid `break`, except with the `switch` statement and sometimes in loops, and with `continue`. Reasonable people continue to differ on this subject. The termination and exception handlers can perform many of the tasks that you might want to perform with a `goto` to a labeled statement.

```
longjmp
continue
__leave⁴
```

- An exception

Abnormal Termination

Termination for any reason other than reaching the end of the try block and falling through or performing a __leave statement is considered an abnormal termination. The effect of __leave is to transfer to the end of the __try block and fall through, which is more efficient than a goto because there is no stack unwind required. Within the termination handler, use this function to determine how the try block terminated.

```
BOOL AbnormalTermination (VOID)
```

The return value will be TRUE for an abnormal termination or FALSE for a normal termination.

Note: The termination would be abnormal even if, for example, a return statement were the last statement in the try block.

Executing and Leaving the Termination Handler

The termination handler, or finally block, is executed in the context of the block or function that it monitors. Control can pass from the end of the termination handler to the next statement. Alternatively, the termination handler can execute a flow control statement (return, break, continue, goto, longjmp, or __leave). Leaving the handler because of an exception is another possibility.

Combining Finally and Except Blocks

A single try block must have a single finally or except block; it cannot have both. Therefore, the following would cause a compile error.

---

⁴ This statement is specific to the Microsoft C compiler and is an efficient way to leave a try-finally block without an abnormal termination.

```
__try {
   /* Block of monitored code. */
}
__except (filter_expression) {
   /* Except block. */
}
__finally {
   /* Do not do this! It will not compile. */
}
```

It is possible, however, to embed one block within another, a technique that is frequently useful. The following code is valid and ensures that the temporary file is deleted if the loop exits under program control or because of an exception. This technique is also useful to ensure that file locks are released, as will be shown in Program 4–2. There is also an inner try-except block where some floating-point processing is performed.

```
__try { /* Outer try-except block. */
   while (...) __try { /* Inner try-finally block. */
      hFile = CreateFile (TempFile, ...);
      if (...) __try { /* Inner try-except block. */
      /* Enable FP exceptions. Perform computations. */
         ...
      }
      __except (EXCEPTION_EXECUTE_HANDLER) {
      ... /* Process FP exception. */ _clearfp ();
      }
      ... /* Non-FP processing. /*
   }
   __finally { /* End of while loop. */
   /* Executed on EVERY loop iteration */
      CloseHandle (hFile); DeleteFile (TempFile);
   }
}
__except (filter-expression) {
   /* Exception handler. */
}
```

Global and Local Unwinds

Exceptions and abnormal terminations will cause a *global stack unwind* to search for a handler, as shown earlier in Figure 4–1.

For example, suppose an exception occurs in the monitored block of the example at the end of the preceding section before the floating-point exceptions are enabled. The termination handler will be executed first, followed by the exception handler. There might be numerous termination handlers on the stack before the exception handler is located.

Recall that the stack structure is dynamic, as shown in Figure 4–1, and that it contains, among other things, the exception and termination handlers. The actual contents at any time depend on

- The *static* structure of the program's blocks

- The *dynamic* structure of the program as reflected in the sequence of open function calls

Termination Handlers: Process and Thread Termination

Termination handlers do not execute if a process or thread terminates, whether the process or thread terminates itself by using the `ExitProcess` or `ExitThread` function, or whether the termination is external, caused by a call to `Terminate-Process` or `TerminateThread` from elsewhere. Therefore, a process or thread should not execute one of these functions inside a try-except or try-finally block.

Notice also that the C library `exit` function or a return from a `main` function will exit the process.

SEH and C++ Exception Handling

C++ exception handling uses the keywords `catch` and `throw` and is implemented using SEH. Nonetheless, C++ exception handling and SEH are distinct. They should be mixed with care, because the user-written and C++-generated exception handlers may interfere with expected operation. For example, an __except handler may be on the stack and catch a C++ exception so that the C++ handler will never receive the exception. The converse is also possible, with a C++ handler catching, for example, an SEH exception generated with `RaiseException`. The Microsoft documentation recommends that Win32 exception handlers not be used in C++ programs at all but instead that C++ exception handling be used exclusively.

Furthermore, a Win32 exception or termination handler will not call destructors to destroy C++ object instances.

Example: Using Termination Handlers to Improve Program Quality

Termination and exception handlers allow you to make your program more robust by both simplifying recovery from errors and exceptions and helping to ensure that resources and file locks are freed at critical junctures.

Program 4–2, toupper, illustrates these points, using ideas from the preceding code fragments. toupper processes multiple files, as specified on the command line, rewriting them so that all letters are in uppercase. Converted files are named by prefixing "UC_" to the original file name, and the program "specification" states that an existing file should not be overridden. File conversion is performed in memory, so a large buffer (sufficient for the entire file) is allocated for each file. Furthermore, both the input and output files are locked to ensure that no other process can modify either file during processing and that the new output file is an accurate transformation of the input file. Thus, there are multiple possible failure points for each file that is processed, but the program must defend against all such errors and then recover and attempt to process all the remaining files named on the command line. Program 4–2 achieves this and ensures that the files are unlocked in all cases without resorting to the elaborate control flow methods that would be necessary without SEH; more extensive comments are included on the disc.

Program 4–2 toupper: File Processing with Error Recovery

```
/* Chapter 4, toupper command. */
/* Convert one or more files, changing all letters to upper case.
   The output file will be the same name as the input file, except
   a "UC_" prefix will be attached to the file name. */

#include "EvryThng.h"

int _tmain (DWORD argc, LPTSTR argv [])
{
    HANDLE hIn = INVALID_HANDLE_VALUE, hOut = INVALID_HANDLE_VALUE;
    DWORD FileSize, nXfer, iFile, j;
    CHAR OutFileName [256] = "", *pBuffer = NULL;
    OVERLAPPED ov == {0, 0, 0, 0, NULL}; /* Used for file locks. */

    if (argc <= 1)
        ReportError (_T ("Usage: toupper files"), 1, FALSE);
                /* Process all files on the command line. */
    for (iFile = 1; iFile < argc; iFile++) __try { /* Excptn block. */
        /* All file handles are invalid, pBuffer == NULL, and
            OutFileName is empty. This is ensured by the handlers. */
        _stprintf (OutFileName, "UC_%s", argv [iFile]);
```

```
__try { /* Inner try-finally block. */
    /* An error at any step will raise an exception, */
    /* and the next file will be processed after cleanup */
    /* Amount of cleanup depends on where the error occurs */
    /* Create the output file (fail if file exists). */
    hIn = CreateFile (argv [iFile], GENERIC_READ, 0,
            NULL, OPEN_EXISTING, 0, NULL);
    if (hIn == INVALID_HANDLE_VALUE)
            ReportException (argv [iFile], 1);
    FileSize = GetFileSize (hIn, NULL);
    hOut = CreateFile (OutFileName,
            GENERIC_READ | GENERIC_WRITE, 0, NULL,
            CREATE_NEW, 0, NULL);
    if (hOut == INVALID_HANDLE_VALUE)
            ReportException (OutFileName, 1);;
    /* Allocate memory for the file contents. */
    pBuffer = malloc (FileSize);
    if (pBuffer == NULL)
        ReportException (_T ("Memory allocation error"), 1);;
    /* Lock both files to ensure integrity of the copy */
    if (!LockFileEx (hIn, LOCKFILE_FAIL_IMMEDIATELY, 0,
            FileSize, 0, &ov)
        ReportException (_T ("Input file lock error"), 1);
    if (!LockFileEx (hOut,
            LOCKFILE_EXCLUSIVE_LOCK | LOCKFILE_FAIL_IMMEDIATELY,
            0, FileSize, 0, &ov)
        ReportException (_T ("Output file lock error"), 1);

    /* Read data, convert, and write to the output file. */
    /* Free resources on completion or error; */
    /* process next file. */
    if (!ReadFile (hIn, pBuffer, FileSize, &nXfer, NULL))
        ReportException (_T ("ReadFile error"), 1);
    for (j = 0; j < FileSize; j++) /* Convert data. */
        if (isalpha (pBuffer [j]))
            pBuffer [j] = toupper (pBuffer [j]);
    if (!WriteFile (hOut, pBuffer, FileSize, &nXfer, NULL))
        ReportException (_T ("WriteFile error"), 1);

} __finally { /* Locks are released, file handles closed, */
    /* Memory freed, and handles and pointer reinitialized. */
    if (pBuffer != NULL) free (pBuffer); pBuffer = NULL;
    if (hIn != INVALID_HANDLE_VALUE) {
        UnlockFileEx (hIn, 0, FileSize, 0, &ov);
        CloseHandle (hIn);
        hIn = INVALID_HANDLE_VALUE;
    }
    if (hOut != INVALID_HANDLE_VALUE) {
        UnlockFileEx (hOut, 0, FileSize, 0, &ov);
        CloseHandle (hOut);
```

```
            hOut = INVALID_HANDLE_VALUE;
        }
        _tcscpy (OutFileName, _T (""));
    }
} /* End of main file processing loop and try block. */
    /* This exception handler applies to the loop body. */

__except (EXCEPTION_EXECUTE_HANDLER) {
    _tprintf (_T ("Error processing file %s\n"), argv [iFile]);
    DeleteFile (OutFileName);
}
_tprintf (_T ("All files converted, except as noted above\n"));
return 0;
}
```

Example: Using a Filter Function

Program 4–3 is a skeleton program that illustrates exception and termination handling with a filter function. This example prompts the user to specify the exception type and then proceeds to generate an exception. The filter function disposes of the different exception types in various ways; the selections here are arbitrary and are intended simply to illustrate the possibilities. In particular, the program diagnoses memory access violations, giving the virtual address of the reference.

The __finally block restores the state of the floating-point mask. Restoring state, as done here, is clearly not important when the process is about to terminate, but it is important later when a thread is terminated. In general, a process should still restore system resources by, for example, deleting temporary files and releasing synchronization resources (Chapter 9) and file locks (Chapter 7). The filter function is shown in Program 4–4.

This example does not illustrate memory allocation exceptions; they will be used extensively starting in Chapter 6.

Program 4–3   Excption: Processing Exceptions and Termination

```
#include "EvryThng.h"
#include <float.h>

DWORD Filter (LPEXCEPTION_POINTERS, LPDWORD);
double x = 1.0, y = 0.0;

int _tmain (int argc, LPTSTR argv [])
{
    DWORD ECatgry, i = 0, ix, iy = 0;
```

```
LPDWORD pNull = NULL;
BOOL Done = FALSE;
DWORD FPOld, FPNew;
FPOld = _controlfp (0, 0); /* Save old control mask. */
                /* Enable floating-point exceptions. */
FPNew = FPOld & ~(EM_OVERFLOW | EM_UNDERFLOW | EM_INEXACT
       | EM_ZERODIVIDE | EM_DENORMAL | EM_INVALID);
_controlfp (FPNew, MCW_EM);

while (!Done) _try { /* Try-Finally. */
   _tprintf (_T ("Enter exception type: "));
   _tprintf (_T
         (" 1: Mem, 2: Int, 3: Flt 4: User 5: __leave "));
   _tscanf (_T ("%d"), &i);
   __try { /* Try-Except block. */
      switch (i) {
      case 1: /* Memory reference. */
         ix = *pNull; *pNull = 5; break;
      case 2: /* Integer arithmetic. */
         ix = ix / iy; break;
      case 3: /* Floating-point exception. */
         x = x / y;
         _tprintf (_T ("x = %20e\n"), x); break;
      case 4: /* User-generated exception. */
         ReportException (_T ("User exception"), 1); break;
      case 5: /* Use the _leave statement to terminate. */
         __leave;
      default: Done = TRUE;
      }
   } /* End of inner __try. */

   __except (Filter (GetExceptionInformation (), &ECatgry))
   {
      switch (ECatgry) {
         case 0:
            _tprintf (_T ("Unknown Exception\n")); break;
         case 1:
            _tprintf (_T ("Memory Ref Exception\n")); continue;
         case 2:
            _tprintf (_T ("Integer Exception\n")); break;
         case 3:
            _tprintf (_T ("Floating-Point Exception\n"));
            _clearfp (); break;
         case 10:
            _tprintf (_T ("User Exception\n")); break;
         default:
            _tprintf ( _T ("Unknown Exception\n")); break;
      } /* End of switch statement. */

      _tprintf (_T ("End of handler\n"));
```

```
    } /* End of __try __except block. */
} /* End of While loop - the termination handler is below. */

__finally { /* This is part of the while loop. */
    _tprintf (_T ("Abnormal Termination?: %d\n"),
        AbnormalTermination ());
}
_controlfp (FPOld, 0xFFFFFFFF); /* Restore old fp mask. */
return 0;
}
```

Program 4–4 shows the filter function used in Program 4–3. This function simply checks and categorizes the various possible exception code values. The code on the disc included with the book checks every possible value; here the function tests only for a few that are relevant to the test program.

Program 4–4   The Filter Function

```
static DWORD Filter (LPEXCEPTION_POINTERS pExP, LPDWORD ECatgry)
/* Categorize the exception and decide action. */
{
    DWORD ExCode, ReadWrite, VirtAddr;
    ExCode = pExP->ExceptionRecord->ExceptionCode;
    _tprintf (_T ("Filter. ExCode: %x\n"), ExCode);
    if ((0x20000000 & ExCode) != 0) { /* User exception. */
        *ECatgry = 10;
        return EXCEPTION_EXECUTE_HANDLER;
    }

    switch (ExCode) {
        case EXCEPTION_ACCESS_VIOLATION:
            ReadWrite = /* Was it a read or a write? */
                    pExP->ExceptionRecord->ExceptionInformation [0];
            VirtAddr = /* Virtual address of the violation. */
                    pExP->ExceptionRecord->ExceptionInformation [1];
            _tprintf (
            _T ("Access Violation. Read/Write: %d. Address: %x\n"),
                    ReadWrite, VirtAddr);
            *ECatgry = 1;
            return EXCEPTION_EXECUTE_HANDLER;
        case EXCEPTION_INT_DIVIDE_BY_ZERO:
        case EXCEPTION_INT_OVERFLOW:
            *ECatgry = 2;
            return EXCEPTION_EXECUTE_HANDLER;
        case EXCEPTION_FLT_DIVIDE_BY_ZERO:
        case EXCEPTION_FLT_OVERFLOW:
            _tprintf (_T ("Flt Exception - large result.\n"));
```

```
            *ECatgry = 3;
            _clearfp ();
            return (DWORD) EXCEPTION_EXECUTE_HANDLER;

        default:
            *ECatgry = 0;
            return EXCEPTION_CONTINUE_SEARCH;
    }
}
```

Console Control Handlers

Exception handlers can respond to a variety of events, but they do not detect situations such as the user logging off or entering a Ctrl-c from the keyboard to stop a program. Console control handlers are required to detect such events, and they are available on all Windows platforms except Windows CE.

The function SetConsoleCtrlHandler allows one or more specified functions to be executed on receipt of a Ctrl-c, Ctrl-break, or one of three other console-related signals. The GenerateConsoleCtrlEvent function, described in Chapter 7, also generates these signals, and the signals can be sent to other processes that are sharing the same console. The handlers are user-specified Boolean functions that take a DWORD argument identifying the actual signal.

Multiple handlers can be associated with a signal, and handlers can be removed as well as added. Here is the function that is used to add or delete a handler.

```
BOOL SetConsoleCtrlHandler (
    PHANDLER_ROUTINE HandlerRoutine,
    BOOL Add)
```

The handler routine is added if the Add flag is TRUE; otherwise, it is deleted from the list of console control routines. Notice that the actual signal is not specified. The handler must test to see which signal was received.

The actual handler routine returns a Boolean value and takes a single DWORD parameter that identifies the actual signal. The handler name in the definition is a placeholder; the programmer specifies the name.

Here are some other considerations when using console control handlers:

- If the *HandlerRoutine* parameter is NULL and Add is TRUE, Ctrl-c signals will be ignored.

- The ENABLE_PROCESSED_INPUT flag on SetConsoleMode (Chapter 7) will cause Ctrl-c to be treated as keyboard input rather than as a signal.

- The handler routine actually executes as an *independent thread* (see Chapter 8) within the process. The normal program will continue to operate, as shown in the next example.

- Raising an exception in the handler *will not* cause an exception in the thread that was interrupted, because exceptions apply to threads, not to an entire process. If you wish to communicate with the interrupted thread, use a variable, as in the next example, or a synchronization method (Chapter 9).

There is one other important distinction between exceptions and signals. A signal applies to the entire process, whereas an exception applies only to the thread executing the code where the exception occurs. Again, processes and threads are explained in detail in Chapters 7 and 8.

```
BOOL HandlerRoutine (DWORD dwCtrlType)
```

dwCtrlType identifies the actual signal (or *event*) and can take on one of the following five values:

1. CTRL_C_EVENT indicates that the Ctrl-c sequence was entered from the keyboard.

2. CTRL_CLOSE_EVENT indicates that the console window is being closed.

3. CTRL_BREAK_EVENT indicates the Ctrl-break signal.

4. CTRL_LOGOFF_EVENT indicates that the user is logging off.

5. CTRL_SHUTDOWN_EVENT indicates that the system is shutting down.

The signal handler can perform cleanup operations just as an exception or termination handler would. The signal handler should return TRUE to indicate that the function handled the signal. If the signal handler returns FALSE, then the next handler function in the list is executed. The signal handlers are executed in the reverse order from the way they were set, so that the most recently set handler is executed first and the system handler is executed last.

Example: A Console Control Handler

Program 4–5 loops forever, calling the self-explanatory Beep function every 5 seconds. The user can terminate the program with a Ctrl-c or by closing the console. The handler routine will put out a message, wait 10 seconds, and, it would appear, return TRUE, terminating the program. The main program, however, actually detects the Exit flag and stops the process. This illustrates the concurrent operation of the handler routine; note that the timing of the signal determines the extent of the signal handler's output.

Program 4–5   Ctrlc: Signal Handling Program

```
/* Chapter 4. Cntrl.c */
/* Catch console events. */

#include "EvryThng.h"

static BOOL WINAPI Handler (DWORD CtrlEvent);
volatile static BOOL Exit = FALSE;

int _tmain (int argc, LPTSTR argv [])

/* Beep periodically until signaled to stop. */
{
    /* Add an event handler. */
    if (!SetConsoleCtrlHandler (Handler, TRUE))
        ReportError (_T ("Error setting event handler."), 1, TRUE);

    while (!Exit) {
        Sleep (5000); /* Beep every 5 seconds. */
        Beep (1000 /* Frequency. */, 250 /* Duration. */);
    }
    _tprintf (_T ("Stopping the program as requested.\n"));
    return 0;
}

BOOL WINAPI Handler (DWORD CtrlEvent)
{
    Exit = TRUE;

    switch (CntrlEvent) {
        /* Timing determines if you see the second handler message. */
        case CTRL_C_EVENT:
            _tprintf (_T ("Ctrl-c received. Leaving in 10 sec.\n"));
            Sleep (4000); /* Decrease this to get a different effect. */
            _tprintf (_T ("Leaving handler in 6 seconds.\n"));
            Sleep (6000); /* Also try decreasing this time. */
```

```
        return TRUE; /* TRUE indicates signal was handled. */
    case CTRL_CLOSE_EVENT:
        _tprintf (_T ("Leaving the handler in 10 seconds.\n"));
        Sleep (4000);
        _tprintf (_T ("Leaving handler in 6 seconds.\n"));
        Sleep (6000); /* Also try decreasing this time. */
        return TRUE; /* Try returning FALSE. Any difference? */
    default:
        _tprintf (_T ("Event: %d. Leaving in 10 seconds.\n"),
            CntrlEvent);
        Sleep (4000);
        _tprintf (_T ("Leaving handler in 6 seconds.\n"));
        Sleep (6000);
        return TRUE;
    }
}
```

Summary

Win32 Structured Exception Handling provides a robust mechanism for C programs to respond to and recover from exceptions and errors. Exception handling is efficient and can result in more understandable, maintainable, and safer code, making it an essential aid to defensive programming and higher-quality programs. Similar concepts are implemented in most languages and operating systems, although Win32's solution allows you to analyze the exact cause of an exception.

Console control handlers can respond to external events that do not generate exceptions.

Looking Ahead

ReportException and exception and termination handlers are used as convenient in subsequent examples. Chapter 6 covers memory management, and, in the process, SEH is used to detect memory allocation errors.

Exercises

4–1. Extend Program 4–2 so that every call to ReportException contains sufficient information so that the exception handler can report precisely what error occurred and also delete the output file if its contents are not meaningful.

4–2. Extend Program 4–3 by generating memory access violations, such as array index out of bounds and arithmetic faults and other types of floating-point exceptions not illustrated in Program 4–3.

4–3. Augment Program 4–3 so as to print the actual value of the floating-point mask after enabling the exceptions. Are all the exceptions actually enabled? Explain the results.

4–4. What values do you actually get after a floating-point exception, such as division by zero? Can you set the result in the filter function as Program 4–3 attempts to do?

4–5. What happens in Program 4–3 if you do not clear the floating-point exception? Explain the results. *Hint*: Request an additional exception after the floating-point exception.

4–6. Extend Program 4–5 so that the handler routine raises an exception rather than returning. Explain the results.

4–7. Extend Program 4–5 so that it can handle shutdown and log-off signals.

4–8. Confirm through experiment that Program 4–5's handler routine executes concurrently with the main program.

5 | Securing Win32 Objects

Windows 2000/NT supports a comprehensive security model that prevents unauthorized access to objects. Nearly all shareable objects can be protected, and the programmer has a fine granularity of control over access rights.

Windows 2000/NT, as a single system, is certified at the Orange Book C2 level, which requires discretionary access control with the ability to allow or deny specific rights to an object based on the identity of the user attempting to access the object. Furthermore, NT security is extended to the networked environment.

This chapter concentrates on showing how to use the Win32 security API to protect objects from unauthorized access. While access control is only a subset of Windows 2000/NT security functionality, it will be of immediate concern to anyone who needs to add security features to the programs in this book. An extended example shows how to emulate UNIX file permissions with NTFS files, and examples in later chapters apply security to several new objects as they are introduced. *Readers who are not immediately interested in security can skip this chapter, referring back as necessary.*

Applications running under Windows 9x and CE cannot use the security API.

Security Attributes

This chapter explores Win32 access control by proceeding from the top down to show how an object's security is constructed. Following an overview, the Win32 functions are described in detail. It is also possible to use the Windows Explorer to examine and manage some security attributes of NTFS objects.

First, nearly any object created with a Create system call has a security attributes parameter. Therefore, programs can secure files, processes, threads, events, semaphores, named pipes, and so on. The first step is to include a SECURITY_ATTRIBUTES structure in the Create call. Until now, our programs have always used a NULL pointer and have omitted the security structure when creating handles to shareable objects (such as files). The important element in the

SECURITY_ATTRIBUTES structure is the pointer to a *security descriptor*, which describes who owns the object and which users are allowed or denied various rights.

An individual process is identified by its *access token*, which specifies the owning user and group membership. When a process attempts to access an object, the Windows NT kernel can determine the process's identity using the token and then can decide from the information in the security descriptor whether or not the process has the required rights to access the object.

The SECURITY_ATTRIBUTES definition is as follows:

```
typedef struct _SECURITY_ATTRIBUTES {
    DWORD nLength;
    LPVOID lpSecurityDescriptor;
    BOOL bInheritHandle;
} SECURITY_ATTRIBUTES;
```

nLength should be set to sizeof (SECURITY_ATTRIBUTES). bInherit-Handle should be FALSE for now; it will be discussed in Chapter 7 along with process management.

The next section describes the security descriptor components.

Security Overview: The Security Descriptor

The security descriptor gives a good overview of essential Win32 security elements. This section mentions the various elements and the names of the functions that manage them. The security descriptor is initialized with the function InitializeSecurityDescriptor, and it contains the following:

- The owner security identifier (SID). SIDs are described in the next section, which deals with the object's owner.

- The group SID.

- A discretionary access control list (DACL)—a list of entries explicitly granting and denying access rights. ACL without a prefix will refer to DACLs.

- A system ACL (SACL), sometimes called an audit access ACL.

SetSecurityDescriptorOwner and SetSecurityDescriptorGroup associate SIDs with security descriptors, as described in the Security Identifiers section.

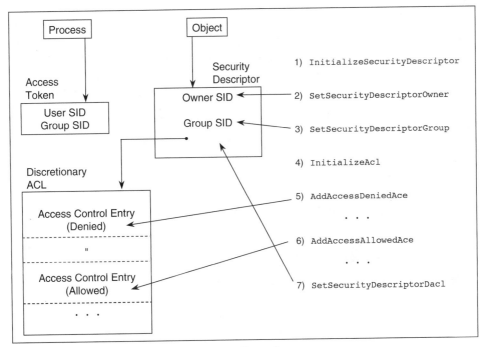

Figure 5-1 . Constructing a Security Descriptor

ACLs are initialized using the `InitializeAcl` function and are then associated with a security descriptor using `SetSecurityDescriptorDacl` or `SetSecurityDescriptorSacl`.

Security descriptors are classified as either *absolute* or *self-relative*. This distinction is ignored for now but is explained near the end of this chapter. Figure 5–1 shows the security descriptor and its components.

Access Control Lists

Each ACL is a set (list) of access control entries (ACEs). There are two types of ACEs: one for access allowed and one for access denied.

You first initialize an ACL with `InitializeAcl` and then add ACEs. Each ACE contains a SID and an *access mask*, which specifies rights to be granted or denied. `GENERIC_READ` and `DELETE` are typical access rights.

The two functions used to add ACEs to discretionary ACLs are `AddAccessAllowedAce` and `AddAccessDeniedAce`. `AddAuditAccessAce` is for adding to an SACL, causing access by the specified SID to be audited.

Finally, you remove ACEs with `DeleteAce` and retrieve them with `GetAce`.

Using Win32 Object Security

There are numerous details to be filled in, but Figure 5–1 shows the basic structure. Notice that each process also has SIDs (in an *access token*), which the kernel uses to determine whether access is allowed or is to be audited. The access token may also give the owner certain *privileges* (the inherent ability to perform operations that override the *rights* in the ACL). Thus, the administrator may have read and write privileges to all files without having specific rights in the file ACLs.

It is easy to see what happens when a process issues a call to access an object. First, the process has certain privileges by virtue of its user identity and its group membership. These privileges are encoded in the SIDs.

If the user and group IDs do not give access, the kernel scans the ACL for access rights. The first entry that specifically grants or denies the requested service is decisive. The order in which ACEs are entered into an ACL is, therefore, important. Frequently, access-denied ACEs come first so that a user who is specifically denied access will not gain access by virtue of membership in a group having such access. In a later example, however, it is essential to mix allowed and denied ACEs to obtain the desired semantics. A denied ACE for all rights can be the last ACE to ensure that no one is allowed access unless specifically mentioned in an ACE.

Object Rights and Object Access

An object, such as a file, gets its rights when it is created, although the rights can be changed at a later time. A process requests access to the object when it asks for a handle using, for example, a call to `CreateFile`. The handle request contains the desired access, such as `GENERIC_READ`, in one of the parameters. If the process has the required rights to get the requested access, the request succeeds. Different handles to the same object may have different access. The values used for access flags are the same ones used to allow or deny rights when ACLs are created.

Standard UNIX (without C2 or other extensions) provides a simpler security model. It is limited to files and based on file permissions. The example programs in this chapter will emulate the UNIX permissions.

Security Descriptor Initialization

The first step is to initialize the security descriptor. The `psd` parameter should be set to the address of a valid `SECURITY_DESCRIPTOR` structure. These structures are opaque and are managed with specific functions.

dwRevision is set to the constant `SECURITY_DESCRIPTOR_REVISION`.

```
BOOL InitializeSecurityDescriptor (
    PSECURITY_DESCRIPTOR psd,
    DWORD dwRevision)
```

Security Identifiers

Win32 uses SIDs to identify users and groups. The program can look up a SID from the account name, which can be a user, group, domain, and so on. The account can be on a remote system.

```
BOOL LookupAccountName (
    LPCTSTR lpszSystem,
    LPCTSTR lpszAccount,
    PSID psid,
    LPDWORD lpcbSid,
    LPTSTR lpszReferencedDomain,
    LPDWORD lpcchReferencedDomain,
    PSID_NAME_USE psnu)
```

Parameters

`lpszSystem` and `lpszAccount` point to the system and account names. Frequently, `lpszSystem` is `NULL` to indicate the local system.

`psid` is the returned information, which is of size `*lpcbSid`. The function will fail, returning the required size, if the buffer is not large enough.

`lpszReferencedDomain` is a string of length `*lpcchReferencedDomain` characters. The length parameter should be initialized to the buffer size (the usual protocol handles failures). The return value shows the domain where the name is found. The account name "Administrators" will return "BUILTIN," whereas a user account name will return that same user name.

```
BOOL LookupAccountSid (
    LPCTSTR lpszSystem,
    PSID psid,
    LPTSTR lpszAccount,
    LPDWORD lpcchName,
    LPTSTR lpszReferencedDomain,
    LPDWORD lpcchReferencedDomain,
    PSID_NAME_USE psnu)
```

psnu points to a SID_NAME_USE (enumerated type) variable and can be tested for values such as SidTypeWellKnownGroup, SidTypeUser, SidTypeGroup, and so on.

Given a SID, you reverse the process and obtain the account name using LookupAccountSid. Specify the SID and get the name in return. The account name can be any name available to the process. Some names, such as Everyone, are well known. Obtain the process's user account name (the logged-in user) with the function.

```
BOOL GetUserName (
    LPTSTR lpBuffer,
    LPDWORD lpcchBuffer)
```

The user name and length are returned in the conventional manner.

It is possible to create and manage SIDs using functions such as InitializeSid and AllocateAndInitializeSid. The examples confine themselves, however, to SIDs obtained from account names.

Once the SIDs are known, they can be entered into an initialized security descriptor.

```
BOOL SetSecurityDescriptorOwner (
    PSECURITY_DESCRIPTOR psd,
    PSID psidOwner,
    BOOL fOwnerDefaulted)
```

```
BOOL SetSecurityDescriptorGroup (
    PSECURITY_DESCRIPTOR psd,
    PSID psidGroup,
    BOOL fGroupDefaulted)
```

psd points to the appropriate security descriptor, and psidOwner (or psid-Group) is the address of the owner's (group's) SID. fOwnerDefaulted (or fGroupDefaulted) indicates that default information is to be used.

The functions GetSecurityDescriptorOwner and GetSecurity-DescriptorGroup return the SID (either owner or group) from a security descriptor.

Managing ACLs

This section shows how to manage ACLs, how to associate an ACL with a security descriptor, and how to add ACEs. Figure 5–1 shows the relationships between these objects and functions.

The first step is to initialize an ACL structure. The ACL should not be accessed directly, so its internal structure is not relevant. The program must, however, provide a buffer to serve as the ACL; the functions manage the contents.

```
BOOL InitializeAcl (
    PACL pAcl,
    DWORD cbAcl,
    DWORD dwAclRevision)
```

pAcl is the address of a programmer-supplied buffer of cbAcl bytes. Subsequent discussion and Program 5–4 will show how to determine the ACL size, but 1KB is more than adequate for most purposes. dwAclRevision should be ACL_REVISION.

Next, add the ACEs in the order desired. The two functions are as follows:

```
BOOL AddAccessAllowedAce (
    PACL pAcl,
    DWORD dwAclRevision
    DWORD dwAccessMask,
    PSID pSid)

BOOL AddAccessDeniedAce (
    PACL pAcl,
    DWORD dwAclRevision,
    DWORD dwAccessMask,
    PSID pSid)
```

pAcl points to the same ACL structure initialized with InitializeAcl, and dwAclRevision is ACL_REVISION again. pSid points to a SID, such as one that would be obtained from LookupAccountName.

The access mask (dwAccessMask) determines the rights to be granted or denied to the user or group specified by the SID. The predefined mask values will vary by the object type.

The final step is to associate an ACL with the security descriptor. In the case of the discretionary ACL, the function is as follows:

```
BOOL SetSecurityDescriptorDacl (
    PSECURITY_DESCRIPTOR psd,
    BOOL fDaclPresent,
    PACL pAcl,
    BOOL fDaclDefaulted)
```

fDaclPresent, if TRUE, indicates that there is an ACL in the pAcl structure. If FALSE, the function ignores anything already in pAcl.

The final flag, fDaclDefaulted, if FALSE, indicates an ACL generated by the programmer. Otherwise, it was obtained by a default mechanism, such as inheritance, and fDaclPresent should be FALSE.

Other functions delete ACEs and read ACEs from an ACL; we will discuss them in a later section. It is now time for an example.

Example: UNIX-Style Permission for NTFS Files

UNIX file permissions provide a convenient way to illustrate Windows 2000/NT security, even though this security is much more general than standard UNIX security. The implementation will create nine ACEs to grant or deny read, write, and execute permissions to the owner, group, and everyone. There will be two commands:

1. chmod is modeled after the UNIX command. The implementation has been enhanced to create the specified file if it does not already exist and to allow the user to specify the group name.

2. lsFP is an extension of the ls command in Chapter 3. When the long listing is requested, the owning user and an interpretation of the existing ACLs, which may have been set by chmod, are displayed.

These two commands are shown in Programs 5–1 and 5–2. Three supporting functions are shown in Programs 5–3, 5–4, and 5–5. These functions are as follows:

1. InitializeUnixSA, which creates a valid security attributes structure corresponding to a set of UNIX permissions. This function is general enough so that it can be used with objects other than files, such as processes (Chapter 7), named pipes (Chapter 11), and synchronization objects (Chapter 9).

2. ReadFilePermissions.

3. ChangeFilePermissions.

Program 5–1   The chmod Command

```
/* Chapter 5. chmod command. */
/* chmod [options] mode file [GroupName]
   Update access rights of the named file.
   Options:
      -f Force - do not complain if unable to change.
      -c Create the file if it does not exist.
        The optional group name is after the file name. */
/* Requires NTFS and Windows 2000/NT */

#include "EvryThng.h"

int _tmain (int argc, LPTSTR argv [])
{
    HANDLE hFile, hSecHeap;
    BOOL Force, CreateNew, Change, Exists;
```

```
    DWORD Mode, DecMode, UsrCnt = ACCT_NAME_SIZE;
    TCHAR UsrNam [ACCT_NAME_SIZE];
    int FileIndex, GrpIndex, ModeIndex;

    /* Array of file access rights settings in "UNIX order". */
    /* These rights will be different for different object types. */
    DWORD AceMasks [] =
            {GENERIC_READ, GENERIC_WRITE, GENERIC_EXECUTE};
    LPSECURITY_ATTRIBUTES pSa = NULL;
    ModeIndex = Options (argc, argv, _T ("fc"),
            &Force, &CreateNew, NULL);
    GrpIndex = ModeIndex + 2;
    FileIndex = ModeIndex + 1;
    DecMode = _ttoi (argv [ModeIndex]);

    /* The security mode is in octal (base 8). */
    Mode = ((DecMode / 100) % 10) * 64   /* Decimal conversion. */
            + ((DecMode / 10) % 10) * 8 + (DecMode % 10);
    Exists = (_taccess (argv [FileIndex], 0) == 0);
    if (!Exists && CreateNew) {
        /* File does not exist; create a new one. */
        GetUserName (UsrNam, &UsrCnt);
        pSa = InitializeUnixSA (Mode, UsrNam, argv [GrpIndex],
                AceMasks, &hSecHeap);
        hFile = CreateFile (argv [FileIndex], 0, 0, pSa,
                CREATE_ALWAYS, FILE_ATTRIBUTE_NORMAL, NULL);
        CloseHandle (hFile);
        HeapDestroy (hSecHeap); /* Release security structures. */
    }
    else if (Exists)
    {   /* File does exist; change permissions. */
        Change = ChangeFilePermissions (Mode, argv [FileIndex],
                AceMasks);
    }
    return 0;
}
```

Program 5–2 shows the relevant part of lsFP—namely, the ProcessItem function.

Program 5–2 The lsFP Command

```
static BOOL ProcessItem (LPWIN32_FIND_DATA pFileData,
        DWORD NumFlags, LPBOOL Flags)

/* List attributes, with file permissions and owner. */
/* Requires NTFS and Windows 2000/NT. */
{
```

```
    DWORD FType = FileType (pFileData), Mode, i;
    BOOL Long = Flags [1];
    TCHAR GrpNam [ACCT_NAME_SIZE], UsrNam [ACCT_NAME_SIZE];
    SYSTEMTIME LastWrite;
    TCHAR PermString [] = _T ("---------");
    const TCHAR RWX [] = {'r','w','x'}, FileTypeChar [] = {' ','d'};

    if (FType != TYPE_FILE && FType != TYPE_DIR)
        return FALSE;
    _tprintf (_T ("\n"));

    if (Long) {
        Mode = ReadFilePermissions (pFileData->cFileName,
                UsrNam, GrpNam);
        if (Mode == 0xFFFFFFFF) Mode = 0;
        for (i = 0; i < 9; i++) {
            if ((Mode / (1 << (8 - i)) % 2) == 1)
                PermString [i] = RWX [i % 3];
        }

        _tprintf (_T ("%c%s %8.7s %8.7s%10d"),
                FileTypeChar [FType - 1], PermString, UsrNam, GrpNam,
                pFileData->nFileSizeLow);

        FileTimeToSystemTime (&(pFileData->ftLastWriteTime),
                &LastWrite);

        _tprintf (_T (" %02d/%02d/%04d %02d:%02d:%02d"),
                LastWrite.wMonth, LastWrite.wDay,
                LastWrite.wYear, LastWrite.wHour,
                LastWrite.wMinute, LastWrite.wSecond);
    }
    _tprintf (_T (" %s"), pFileData->cFileName);
    return TRUE;
}
```

The next step is to show the implementation of the supporting functions.

Example: Initializing Security Attributes

Program 5–3 shows the utility function `InitializeUnixSA`. It creates a security attributes structure that contains an ACL with ACEs that emulate UNIX file permissions. There are nine ACEs granting or denying read, write, and execute permissions for the owner, the group, and everyone else. The actual array of three rights (read, write, and execute for files) can vary according to the object type being secured. This structure is not a local variable in the function but must be allocated and initialized and then returned to the calling program; notice `Ace-Masks{}` in Program 5–1.

Program 5–3   `InitUnFp`: Initializing Security Attributes

```
/* Set UNIX-style permissions as ACEs in a
   (Windows 2000/NT) SECURITY_ATTRIBUTES structure. */

#include "EvryThng.h"

#define ACL_SIZE 1024
#define INIT_EXCEPTION 0x3
#define CHANGE_EXCEPTION 0x4
#define SID_SIZE LUSIZE
#define DOM_SIZE LUSIZE

LPSECURITY_ATTRIBUTES InitializeUnixSA (DWORD UnixPerms,
        LPCTSTR UsrNam, LPCTSTR GrpNam, LPDWORD AceMasks,
        LPHANDLE pHeap)
{
    HANDLE SAHeap = HeapCreate (HEAP_GENERATE_EXCEPTIONS, 0, 0);
    LPSECURITY_ATTRIBUTES pSA = NULL;
    PSECURITY_DESCRIPTOR pSD = NULL;
    PACL pAcl = NULL;
    BOOL Success;
    DWORD iBit, iSid, UsrCnt = ACCT_NAME_SIZE;

    /* Tables of User, Group, and Everyone Names, SIDs,
       etc. for LookupAccountName and SID creation. */

    LPCTSTR pGrpNms [3] = {EMPTY, EMPTY, _T ("Everyone")};
    PSID pSidTable [3] = {NULL, NULL, NULL};
    SID_NAME_USE sNamUse [3] =
        {SidTypeUser, SidTypeGroup, SidTypeWellKnownGroup};
    TCHAR RefDomain [3] [DOM_SIZE];
    DWORD RefDomCnt [3] = {DOM_SIZE, DOM_SIZE, DOM_SIZE};
    DWORD SidCnt [3] = {SID_SIZE, SID_SIZE, SID_SIZE};

__try { /* Try-except block for memory allocation failures. */
    *pHeap = SAHeap;
    pSA = HeapAlloc (SAHeap, 0, sizeof (SECURITY_ATTRIBUTES));
    pSA->nLength = sizeof (SECURITY_ATTRIBUTES);
    pSA->bInheritHandle = FALSE;
                /* Programmer can set this later. */
    pSD = HeapAlloc (SAHeap, 0, sizeof (SECURITY_DESCRIPTOR));
    pSA->lpSecurityDescriptor = pSD;
    InitializeSecurityDescriptor (pSD,
            SECURITY_DESCRIPTOR_REVISION);
```

```
    /* Get a SID for User, Group, and Everyone. */
    pGrpNms [0] = UsrNam; pGrpNms [1] = GrpNam;
    for (iSid = 0; iSid < 3; iSid++) {
        pSidTable [iSid] = HeapAlloc (SAHeap, 0, SID_SIZE);
        LookupAccountName (NULL, pGrpNms [iSid],
                pSidTable [iSid], &SidCnt [iSid],
                RefDomain [iSid], &RefDomCnt [iSid],
                &sNamUse [iSid]);
    }
    SetSecurityDescriptorOwner (pSD, pSidTable [0], FALSE);
    SetSecurityDescriptorGroup (pSD, pSidTable [1], FALSE);
    pAcl = HeapAlloc (ProcHeap, HEAP_GENERATE_EXCEPTIONS, ACL_SIZE);
    InitializeAcl (pAcl, ACL_SIZE, ACL_REVISION);

    /* Add all the access allowed/denied ACEs. */
    for (iBit = 0; iBit < 9; iBit++) {
        if ((UnixPerms >> (8 - iBit) & 0x1) != 0 &&
                AceMasks[iBit%3] != 0)
            AddAccessAllowedAce (pAcl, ACL_REVISION,
                    AceMasks [iBit%3], pSidTable [iBit/3]);
        else if (AceMasks[iBit%3] != 0)
            AddAccessDeniedAce (pAcl, ACL_REVISION,
                    AceMasks [iBit%3], pSidTable [iBit/3]);
    }
    /* Add a final deny all to everyone ACE. */
    Success = Success && AddAccessDeniedAce (pAcl, ACL_REVISION,
            STANDARD_RIGHTS_ALL | SPECIFIC_RIGHTS_ALL, pSidTable [2]);
    /* Associate ACL with the security descriptor. */
    SetSecurityDescriptorDacl (pSD, TRUE, pAcl, FALSE);
    return pSA;
}   /* End of __try-except block. */

__except (EXCEPTION_EXECUTE_HANDLER) { /* Free all resources. */
    if (SAHeap != NULL)
        HeapDestroy (SAHeap);
    pSA = NULL;
}
    return pSA;
}
```

Comments on Program 5-3

Program 5–3 may have a straightforward structure, but its operation is hardly simple. Furthermore, it illustrates a number of points about Windows NT security that should be reviewed.

- Several memory allocations are required to hold information such as the SIDs. They are created in a dedicated heap, which is eventually destroyed by the calling program.

- The security attribute structure in this example is for files, but it will also be used with other objects such as named pipes in Chapter 11. Program 5–4 will show how to integrate the security attributes with a file.

- To emulate UNIX behavior, the order of ACE entry is critical. Notice that access-denied and access-allowed ACEs are added to the ACL as the permission bits are processed from left (Owner/Read) to right (Everyone/Execute). In this way, permission bits of, say, 460 (in octal) will deny write access to the user even though the user may be in the group.

- The ACEs' rights are access values, such as GENERIC_READ and GENERIC_WRITE, which are the same flags as those used with CreateFile. The rights are specified in the calling program (Program 5–1 in this case) so that the rights can be appropriate for the object.

- The defined constant ACL_SIZE is large enough to contain the nine ACEs. After Program 5–5, it will be apparent how to determine the required size.

- The function uses three SIDs: one each for User, Group, and Everyone. Three different techniques are employed to get the name to use as an argument to LookupAccountName. The user name comes from GetUserName. The name for everyone is Everyone in a SidTypeWellKnownGroup. The group name must be supplied as a command line argument and is looked up as a SidTypeGroup. Finding the groups that a user belongs to requires some knowledge of process handles, and solving this problem is an exercise at the end of Chapter 7.

- The program on the disc, but not the one shown here, is fastidious about error checking. It even goes to the effort to validate the generated structures using the self-explanatory IsValidSecurityDescriptor, IsValidSid, and IsValidAcl functions. This error testing proved to be extremely helpful during debugging.

Reading and Changing Security Descriptors

Now that a security descriptor is associated with a file, the next step is to determine the security of an existing file and, in turn, change it. The following functions get and set file security in terms of security descriptors:

```
BOOL GetFileSecurity (
   LPCTSTR lpszFileName,
   SECURITY_INFORMATION secInfo,
   PSECURITY_DESCRIPTOR psd,
   DWORD cbSd,
   LPDWORD lpcbLengthNeeded)

BOOL SetFileSecurity (
   LPCTSTR lpszFileName,
   SECURITY_INFORMATION secInfo,
   PSECURITY_DESCRIPTOR psd)
```

Parameters

secInfo is an enumerated type that takes on values such as OWNER_SEC-URITY_INFORMATION, GROUP_SECURITY_INFORMATION, DACL_SECURITY_IN-FORMATION, and SACL_SECURITY_INFORMATION to indicate what part of the security descriptor to get or set. These values can be combined with the bit-wise "or".

To figure out the size of the return buffer for GetFileSecurity, the best strategy is to call the function twice. The first call simply uses 0 as the cbSd value. After allocating a buffer, call the function a second time. Program 5–4 operates this way.

Needless to say, the correct file permissions are required in order to carry out these operations. For example, it is necessary to have WRITE_DAC permission or to be the object's owner to succeed with SetFileSecurity.

The functions GetSecurityDescriptorOwner and GetSecurity-DescriptorGroup can extract the SIDs from the security descriptor obtained with GetFileSecurity. Obtain the ACL with this function:

```
BOOL GetSecurityDescriptorDacl (
   PSECURITY_DESCRIPTOR psd,
   LPBOOL fDaclPresent,
   PACL *pAcl,
   LPBOOL lpfDaclDefaulted)
```

The parameters are nearly identical to those of `SetSecurityDescriptor-Dacl` except that the flags are returned to indicate whether a discretionary ACL is actually present and was set as a default or by a user.

To interpret an ACL, it is necessary to find out how many ACEs it contains.

```
BOOL GetAclInformation (
    PACL pAcl,
    LPVOID pAclInformation,
    DWORD cbAclInfo,
    ACL_INFORMATION_CLASS dwAclInfoClass)
```

In most cases, the ACL information class, `dwAclInfoClass`, is `AclSize-Information`, and the `pAclInformation` parameter is a structure of type `ACL_SIZE_INFORMATION`. `AclRevisionInformation` is the other value for the class.

An `ACL_SIZE_INFORMATION` structure has three members: the most important one is `AceCount`, which shows how many entries are in the list. To determine whether the ACL is large enough, look at the `AclBytesInUse` and `AclBytes-Free` members of the `ACL_SIZE_INFORMATION` structure.

```
BOOL GetAce (
    PACL pAcl,
    DWORD dwAceIndex,
    LPVOID *pAce)
```

Obtain the ACEs (the total number is now known) by using an index. `pAce` points to an `ACE` structure, which has a member called `Header`, which, in turn, has an `AceType` member. The type can be tested for `ACCESS_ALLOWED_ACE` and `ACCESS_DENIED_ACE`.

Example: Reading File Permissions

Program 5–4 is the function `ReadFilePermissions` that is used by Programs 5–1 and 5–2. This program methodically uses the preceding functions to extract the information. Its correct operation depends on the fact that the ACL was created by Program 5–3. The function is in the same source module as Program 5–3, so the definitions are not repeated.

Program 5–4   `ReadFilePermissions`: Reading Security Attributes

```
DWORD ReadFilePermissions (LPCTSTR lpFileName,
      LPTSTR UsrNm, LPTSTR GrpNm)

   /* Return the UNIX-style permissions for a file. */
{
   PSECURITY_DESCRIPTOR pSD = NULL;
   DWORD LenNeeded, PBits, iAce;
   BOOL DaclF, AclDefF, OwnerDefF, GroupDefF;
   BYTE DAcl [ACL_SIZE];
   PACL pAcl = (PACL) &DAcl;
   ACL_SIZE_INFORMATION ASizeInfo;
   PACCESS_ALLOWED_ACE pAce;
   BYTE AType;
   HANDLE ProcHeap = GetProcessHeap ();
   PSID pOwnerSid, pGroupSid;
   TCHAR RefDomain [2] [DOM_SIZE];
   DWORD RefDomCnt [] = {DOM_SIZE, DOM_SIZE};
   DWORD AcctSize [] = {ACCT_NAME_SIZE, ACCT_NAME_SIZE};
   SID_NAME_USE sNamUse [] = {SidTypeUser, SidTypeGroup};

   /* Get the required size for the security descriptor. */

   GetFileSecurity (lpFileName,
      OWNER_SECURITY_INFORMATION | GROUP_SECURITY_INFORMATION |
      DACL_SECURITY_INFORMATION, pSD, 0, &LenNeeded);
   pSD = HeapAlloc (ProcHeap, HEAP_GENERATE_EXCEPTIONS, LenNeeded);
   GetFileSecurity (lpFileName, OWNER_SECURITY_INFORMATION |
         GROUP_SECURITY_INFORMATION | DACL_SECURITY_INFORMATION,
         pSD, LenNeeded, &LenNeeded);
   GetSecurityDescriptorDacl (pSD, &DaclF, &pAcl, &AclDefF);
   GetAclInformation (pAcl, &ASizeInfo,
      sizeof (ACL_SIZE_INFORMATION), AclSizeInformation);
   PBits = 0; /* Compute the permissions from the ACL. */
   for (iAce = 0; iAce < ASizeInfo.AceCount; iAce++) {
      GetAce (pAcl, iAce, &pAce);
      AType = pAce->Header.AceType;
      if (AType == ACCESS_ALLOWED_ACE_TYPE)
         PBits |= (0x1 << (8-iAce));
   }
   /* Find the name of the owner and owning group. */
   GetSecurityDescriptorOwner (pSD, &pOwnerSid, &OwnerDefF);
   GetSecurityDescriptorGroup (pSD, &pGroupSid, &GroupDefF);
   LookupAccountSid (NULL, pOwnerSid, UsrNm, &AcctSize [0],
         RefDomain [0], &RefDomCnt [0], &sNamUse [0]);
```

```
        LookupAccountSid (NULL, pGroupSid, GrpNm, &AcctSize [1],
                RefDomain [1], &RefDomCnt [1], &sNamUse [1]);
        return PBits;
}
```

Example: Changing File Permissions

Program 5–5 completes the set of file security functions. This function, Change-FilePermissions, replaces the existing security descriptor with a new one, preserving the user and group SIDs but creating a new discretionary ACL.

Program 5–5   ChangeFilePermissions: Changing Security Attributes

```
BOOL ChangeFilePermissions (DWORD fPm, LPCTSTR FNm, LPDWORD AceMsk)

/* Change permissions in existing file. Group is left unchanged. */
{
    TCHAR UsrNm [ACCT_NAME_SIZE], GrpNm [ACCT_NAME_SIZE];
    DWORD OldfPerm;
    LPSECURITY_ATTRIBUTES pSA;
    PSECURITY_DESCRIPTOR pSD = NULL;
    HANDLE hSecHeap;

    if (_taccess (FNm, 0) != 0) return FALSE;
    OldfPerm = ReadFilePermissions (FNm, UsrNm, GrpNm);
    pSA = InitializeUnixSA (fPm, UsrNm, GrpNm, AceMsk, &hSecHeap);
    pSD = pSA->lpSecurityDescriptor;
    SetFileSecurity (FileName, DACL_SECURITY_INFORMATION, pSD);
    HeapDestroy (hSecHeap);
    return TRUE;
}
```

Comments on the File Permissions

When you're running these programs, it is interesting to monitor the file system using the Windows Explorer. This utility cannot interpret the access-denied ACEs and will not be able to display the permissions. The Windows NT explorer will generate an exception on encountering an access-denied ACE, and the Windows 2000 explorer says that the ACEs are out of order.

Using the access-denied ACEs is necessary, however, to emulate the UNIX semantics. If they are omitted, the Windows Explorer can view the permissions. A set of permissions set with, for example, 0446 would then allow the user and group members to write to the file because Everyone can write to the file. UNIX, however, does not act this way; it prevents the user and group members from writing to the file.

Also observe what happens when you try to create a secured file on a diskette or other FAT file system and when you run the program under Windows 95.

Overview of Additional Security Features

There is much more to Windows NT security, but this is an introduction, showing how to secure Win32 objects, such as files. The following sections give a brief overview of additional security subjects that some readers will want to explore.

Kernel and Private Object Security

The preceding sections were concerned mostly with file security, and the same techniques apply to other filelike objects, such as named pipes (Chapter 11), and to kernel objects.

Many objects, such as the file mapping objects of Chapter 6, are *kernel objects*. With each new object class, brief notes list some of the security permissions that go with that object. GENERIC_READ and GENERIC_WRITE are always useful.

To get and set kernel security descriptors, use GetKernelObjectSecurity and SetKernelObjectSecurity, which are similar to the file security functions in this chapter.

It is also possible to associate security descriptors with private, programmer-generated objects, such as Windows Sockets or a proprietary database. The appropriate functions are GetPrivateObjectSecurity and SetPrivateObject-Security. The programmer must take responsibility for enforcing access and must exchange security descriptors with CreatePrivateObjectSecurity and DestroyPrivateObjectSecurity.

Removing ACEs

The function DeleteAce will delete an ACE specified by an index, in a manner similar to that used with GetAce.

Absolute and Self-Relative Security Descriptors

Program 5–5, which changed ACLs, had the benefit of simply replacing one security descriptor (SD) with another. To change an existing SD, however, some care is required because of the distinction between absolute and self-relative SDs.

- During construction, an SD is absolute, with pointers to various structures in memory. In fact, `InitializeSecurityDescriptor` creates an absolute SD.

- When the SD is associated with a permanent object, such as the file, the operating system consolidates the SD into a compact, self-relative structure. However, changing an SD (changing an ACL, for example) causes difficulties in managing space within the absolute SD structure.

- It is possible to convert between the two forms using Win32 functions for that purpose. Use `MakeAbsoluteSD` to convert a self-relative SD, such as the one returned by `GetFileSecurity`. Modify the SD in self-relative form and then use `MakeSelfRelativeSD` to convert it back. `MakeAbsoluteSD` is one of the more formidable Win32 functions, having 11 parameters: two for each of the four SD components, one each for the input and output SDs, and one for the length of the resulting absolute SD.

System ACLs

A complete class of functions is available for managing system ACLs; it is usable only by system administrators. System ACLs specify which object accesses should be logged. The principal function is `AddAuditAccessAce`, which is similar to `AddAccessAllowedAce`. There is no concept of access denied with system ACLs.

Some other system ACL functions are `GetSecurityDescriptorSacl` and `SetSecurityDescriptorSacl`. These two functions are comparable to their discretionary ACL counterparts: `GetSecurityDescriptorDacl` and `SetSecurityDescriptorDacl`.

Access Token Information

Program 5–1 did not solve the problem of obtaining the groups associated with a process in its access token. Program 5–1 simply required the user to specify the group name. You use the function `GetTokenInformation` for this; a process handle, covered in Chapter 7, is required. Exercise 7–11 addresses this; there will be some hints. The code is also included on the disc.

Access tokens also contain security privileges so that a process will gain certain access by virtue of its identity rather than by the rights associated with the object. For example, an administrator requires access that will override those specifically granted by an object. Note, again, the distinction between a right and a privilege.

SID Management

The examples obtained SIDs from user and group names, but you can also create new SIDs with function `AllocateAndInitializeSid`. Other functions obtain SID information, and you can even copy (`CopySid`) and compare (`CompareSid`) SIDs.

Secure Sockets Layer (SSL)

Windows Sockets ("WinSock"), described in Chapter 12, provide networked communication between systems. WinSock conforms to industry standards, so it is also possible to communicate with non-Windows systems. SSL, an extension, layers a security protocol on top of the underlying transport protocol, providing message authentication, encryption, and decryption.

Summary

Windows 2000/NT implements an extensive security model that goes beyond that offered by standard UNIX. All objects, and not just files, can be secured. The example programs have shown how to emulate the UNIX permissions and ownership that are set with the `umask`, `chmod`, and `chown` functions. Programs can also set the owner (group and user). The emulation is not easy, but the functionality is much more powerful. The complexity reflects the Orange Book C2 level requirements, which specify the access control lists and object owners with access tokens.

Looking Ahead

Chapter 6 covers memory management, memory-mapped files and dynamic link libraries (DLLs). Windows memory management allows more flexibility and efficiency than that provided by the C library with `malloc` and related functions. Memory-mapped files, in turn, provide programming ease, superior performance in many cases, and memory sharing between processes.

Additional Reading

Win32

Stephen A. Sutton's *Windows NT Security* discusses NT security administration and security policies. Davis' *Windows NT Network Programming* provides security programming information and examples. Richter and Clark's *Programming*

Server-Side Applications for Microsoft Windows 2000 also describes security in depth.

Windows NT Design and Architecture

Solomon's *Inside Windows NT* book describe NT security operation in more detail.

Orange Book Security

The U.S. Department of Defense publication *DoD Trusted Computer System Evaluation Criteria* specifies the C2 and other security levels. Windows NT is C2 certified.

Exercises

5–1. Extend Program 5–1 so that multiple groups have their own unique permissions. The group name and permission pairs can be separate arguments to the function.

5–2. Extend Program 5–4 so that it can report on all the groups that have ACEs in the object's security descriptor.

5–3. Confirm that chmod has the desired effect of limiting file access.

5–4. Investigate the default security attributes you get with a file.

5–5. What are some of the other access masks that you can use with an ACE? The Microsoft documentation supplies some information.

5–6. Enhance both chmod and lsFP so that they produce an error message if asked to deal with a file on a non-NTFS file system. GetVolumeInformation is required.

5–7. Enhance the chmod command so that there is an -o option to set the owning user to be the user of the chmod program.

5–8. Determine the actual size of the ACL buffer required by Program 5–3 to store the ACEs. Program 5–3 uses 1,024 bytes. Can you determine a formula for estimating the required ACL size?

5–9. The compatibility library contains functions _open and _unmask, which manage file permissions. Investigate their emulation of UNIX file permissions and compare it with the solutions in this chapter.

5–10. Write a command, whoami, that will display your logged-in user name.

6 | Memory Management, Memory-Mapped Files, and DLLs

Most programs require some form of dynamic memory management. This need arises whenever it is necessary to create data structures whose size cannot be determined statically when the program is built. Search trees, symbol tables, and linked lists are examples of dynamic data structures.

Win32 provides flexible mechanisms for managing a program's dynamic memory segments. Win32 also provides memory-mapped files to associate a process's address space directly with a file. The operating system manages all data movement between the file and memory, and the programmer never needs to deal with `ReadFile`, `WriteFile`, `SetFilePointer`, or the other file I/O functions. With memory-mapped files, the program can maintain dynamic data structures conveniently in permanent files and memory-based algorithms can process file data. What is more, memory mapping can significantly speed up sequential file processing on Windows 2000/NT, and it provides a mechanism for memory sharing between processes.

Dynamic link libraries (DLLs) are an essential special case of file mapping and shared memory where files (primarily read-only code files) are mapped into the process address space for execution.

This chapter describes the Win32 memory management and file mapping functions, illustrates their use with several examples, and describes both implicitly and explicitly linked DLLs.

Win32 Memory Management Architecture

Win32 is an API for the Windows 32-bit OS family. The "32-bitness" manifests itself in memory addresses, and pointers (LPCTSTR, LPDWORD, and so on) are four-byte (32-bit) objects. The Win64 API provides a much larger virtual address space and 64-bit pointers, and is a natural evolution of Win32. Nonetheless, some care is required to ensure portability to Win64. The discussion here refers to Win32, and Chapter 16 discusses Win64 migration strategies and information sources.

Every Win32 process, then, has its own private virtual address space of 4GB (2^{32} bytes). The Win64 address space is, of course, much larger. Win32 makes at least half of this (2GB) available to a process. The remainder of the virtual address space is allocated to shared data and code, system code, drivers, and so on.

The details of these memory allocations, although interesting, are not discussed here; the abstractions provided by the Win32 API are used by application programs. From the programmer's perspective, the operating system provides a large address space for code, data, and other resources. This chapter concentrates on exploiting Windows memory management without being concerned with OS implementation. Nonetheless, a very short overview follows, and there are also a few explanatory comments in the text.

Memory Management Overview

The operating system manages all the details of mapping virtual to physical memory and the mechanics of page swapping, demand paging, and the like. This subject is discussed thoroughly in operating systems texts and also in Custer/Solomon. Here's a brief summary.

- The system has a relatively small amount of physical memory; 32MB is the practical minimum for all but Windows CE, and much larger physical memories are typical.[1]

- Every process—and there may be several user and system processes—has its own virtual address space, which may be much larger than the physical memory available. For example, the virtual address space of a 1GB process is 32 times larger than 32MB of physical memory, and there may be many such processes.

- The operating system maps virtual addresses to physical addresses.

---

[1] Memory prices continue to decline, and "typical" memory sizes keep increasing, so it is difficult to define typical memory size. At the time of writing, 64MB is the commonly accepted minimum for Windows 2000.

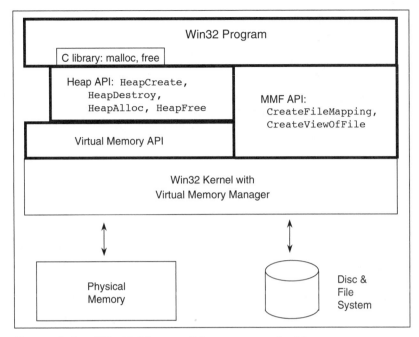

Figure 6-1   Win32 Memory Management Architecture

- Most virtual pages will not be in physical memory, so the OS responds to *page faults* (references to pages not in memory) and loads the data from disc, either from the system swap file or from a normal file. Page faults, while transparent to the programmer, have an impact on performance, and programs should be designed to minimize faults; again, many OS texts treat this important subject, which is beyond the scope of this book.

Figure 6–1 shows the Win32 memory management API layered on the Virtual Memory Manager. The Virtual Memory Win32 API (`VirtualAlloc`, `Virtual-Free`, `VirtualLock`, `VirtualUnlock`, and so on) deals with whole pages. The Win32 Heap API manages memory in user-defined units.

The layout of the virtual memory address space is also not shown, because it is not directly relevant to the API and because the Windows 9x and 2000/NT layouts are different. The Microsoft documentation provides this information.

Nonetheless, many programmers want to know more about their environment. To start to explore the memory structure, invoke the following:

```
VOID GetSystemInfo (LPSYSTEM_INFO lpSystemInfo)
```

The `LPSYSTEM_INFO` structure contains information on the system's page size and the application's physical memory address.

Heaps

Win32 maintains pools of memory in *heaps*. A process can contain several heaps, and you allocate memory from these heaps.

One heap is often sufficient, but there are good reasons, explained below, for multiple heaps. If a single heap is sufficient, just use the C library memory management functions (`malloc`, `free`, `calloc`, `realloc`).

Heaps are Win32 objects; therefore, they have handles. The heap handle is necessary when you're allocating memory. Each process has its own default heap, which is used by `malloc`, and the next function obtains its handle.

```
HANDLE GetProcessHeap (VOID)
```

Return: The handle for the process's heap; `NULL` on failure.

Notice that `NULL` is the return value to indicate failure rather than `INVALID_HANDLE_VALUE`, which is returned by `CreateFile`.

A program can also create distinct heaps. It is convenient at times to have separate heaps for allocation of separate data structures. The benefits of separate heaps include the following:

- **Fairness**. No single thread can obtain more memory than is allocated to its heap. In particular, a memory leak defect, caused by a program neglecting to free data elements that are no longer needed, will affect only one thread of a process.[2]

- **Multithreaded Performance**. By giving each thread its own heap, contention between threads is reduced, which can substantially improve performance. See Chapter 9.

---

[2] Threads are discussed in Chapter 8.

- **Allocation Efficiency**. Allocation of fixed-size data elements within a small heap can be more efficient than allocating elements of many different sizes in a single large heap. Fragmentation is also reduced. Furthermore, giving each thread a unique heap simplifies synchronization, resulting in additional efficiencies.

- **Deallocation Efficiency**. An entire heap and all the data structures it contains can be freed with a single function call. This call will also free any leaked memory allocations in the heap.

- **Locality of Reference Efficiency**. Maintaining a data structure in a small heap ensures that the elements will be confined to a relatively small number of pages, potentially reducing page faults as the data structure elements are processed.

The value of these advantages will vary depending on the application, and many programmers will use only the process heap and the C library. Such a choice, however, will prevent the program from exploiting the exception generating capability of the Win32 memory management routines (discussed later). In any case, the next two functions create and destroy heaps.

The initial heap size, which can be zero and is always rounded up to a multiple of the page size, determines how much physical storage (in a *paging file*) is *committed* to the heap initially.[3] As a program exceeds the initial size, additional pages are committed automatically up to the maximum size. Because the paging file is a limited resource, deferring commitment is a good practice unless it is known ahead of time how large the heap will become. dwMaximumSize, if nonzero, determines how large the heap can become as it expands dynamically. The process heap will also grow dynamically.

```
HANDLE HeapCreate (
    DWORD flOptions,
    SIZE_T dwInitialSize,
    SIZE_T dwMaximumSize)

Return: A heap handle, or NULL on failure.
```

---

[3] In general, create objects of type "X" with the CreateX system call. HeapCreate is an exception to this rule.

The two size fields are of type `SIZE_T` rather than `DWORD`. `SIZE_T` is defined to be either a 32-bit or 64-bit unsigned integer, depending on compiler flags (`_WIN32` and `_WIN64`). `SIZE_T` was introduced to allow for Win64 migration (see Chapter 16).

`flOptions` is a combination of two flags:

- `HEAP_GENERATE_EXCEPTIONS`—With this option, failed allocations generate an exception to be processed by a Structured Exception Handler or SEH (see Chapter 4). `HeapCreate` itself will not cause an exception; rather, functions such as `HeapAlloc`, which will be explained shortly, cause an exception on failure if this flag is set.

- `HEAP_NO_SERIALIZE`—Set this flag under certain circumstances to get a small performance improvement. This subject is discussed later.

There are several other important points regarding `dwMaximumSize`.

- If `dwMaximumSize` is nonzero, the virtual address space is allocated accordingly, even though it may not be committed in its entirety. This is the maximum size of the heap, which is said to be *nongrowable*. This option limits a heap's size, perhaps to gain the fairness advantage cited previously.

- If, on the other hand, `dwMaximumSize` is 0, then the heap is *growable* beyond the initial size. The limit is determined by the available virtual address space, some of which may be given to other heaps, and swap file space.

Notice that heaps do not have security attributes, because they are not accessible outside the process.

To destroy an entire heap, use `HeapDestroy`. This is another exception to the general rule that `CloseHandle` is the function for removing unwanted handles.

```
BOOL HeapDestroy (HANDLE hHeap)
```

`hHeap` should specify a heap generated by `HeapCreate`. Be careful not to destroy the process's heap (the one obtained from `GetProcessHeap`). Destroying a heap frees the virtual memory space and physical storage in the paging file. Naturally, well-designed programs should destroy heaps that are no longer needed.

Destroying a heap is also a quick way to free data structures without traversing them to delete one element at a time, although C++ object instances will not be destroyed inasmuch as their destructors are not called. Heap destruction has three benefits:

1. There is no need to write the data structure traversal code.

2. There is no need to deallocate each individual element.

3. The system does not spend time maintaining the heap since all data structure elements are deallocated with a single call.

The C library uses only a single heap. There is, therefore, nothing similar to Win32's heap handles.

The UNIX sbrk function can increase a process's address space, but it is not a general-purpose memory manager.

UNIX does not generate signals when memory allocation fails; explicitly test the returned pointer.

Managing Heap Memory

Obtain memory blocks from a heap by specifying the heap's handle, the block size, and several flags.

```
LPVOID HeapAlloc (
    HANDLE hHeap,
    DWORD dwFlags,
    SIZE_T dwBytes)
```

Return: A pointer to the allocated memory block, or NULL on failure (unless exception generation is specified).

HeapAlloc *Parameters*

hHeap is the handle of the heap in which the memory block is to be allocated. This handle should come from either GetProcessHeap or HeapCreate.

dwFlags is a combination of three flags:

- HEAP_GENERATE_EXCEPTIONS and HEAP_NO_SERIALIZE—These flags have the same meaning as for HeapCreate. The first flag does not need to be specified if it was set with the heap's `HeapCreate`. The second should not be used when allocating within the process heap.

- `HEAP_ZERO_MEMORY`—This flag specifies that the allocated memory will be initialized to zero; otherwise, the memory contents are not specified.

`dwSize` is the size of the block of memory to allocate. For nongrowable heaps, this is limited to `0x7FFF8` (approximately 0.5MB).

Note: Once `HeapAlloc` returns a pointer, use the pointer in the normal way; there is no need to make reference to its heap. Notice, too, that the `LPVOID` data type represents either a 32-bit or 64-bit pointer.

Deallocating memory from a heap is simple.

```
BOOL HeapFree (
    HANDLE hHeap,
    DWORD dwFlags,
    LPVOID lpMem)
```

`dwFlags` should be 0 or `HEAP_NO_SERIALIZE`. `lpMem` should be a value returned by `HeapAlloc` or `HeapReAlloc` (described next), and, of course, `hHeap` should be the heap from which `lpMem` was allocated.

Memory blocks can be reallocated to change their size.

```
LPVOID HeapReAlloc (
    HANDLE hHeap,
    DWORD dwFlags,
    LPVOID lpMem,
    SIZE_T dwBytes)
```

Return: A pointer to the reallocated block. Failure returns NULL or causes an exception.

`HeapReAlloc` *Parameters*

The first parameter, `hHeap`, was discussed previously. `dwFlags` specifies some essential control options.

- HEAP_GENERATE_EXCEPTIONS and HEAP_NO_SERIALIZE are as before.

- HEAP_ZERO_MEMORY—Only newly allocated memory (when dwBytes is larger than the original block) is initialized. The original block contents are not modified.

- HEAP_REALLOC_IN_PLACE_ONLY—This flag specifies that the block cannot be moved. When you're increasing a block's size, the new memory must be allocated at the address immediately after the existing block.

lpMem specifies the existing block in hHeap to be reallocated.

dwBytes is the new block size, which can be larger or smaller than the existing size.

Normally, the returned pointer is the same as lpMem. If, on the other hand, a block is moved (permit this by omitting the HEAP_REALLOC_IN_PLACE_ONLY flag), the returned value will be different. Be careful to update any references to the block.

Determine the size of an allocated block by calling HeapSize (this function should have been named BlockSize, because it does not obtain the size of the heap) with the heap handle and block pointer.

```
DWORD HeapSize (
    HANDLE hHeap,
    DWORD dwFlags,
    LPCVOID lpMem)
```

Return: The size of the block, or zero on failure.

The *HEAP_NO_SERIALIZE* Flag

The functions HeapCreate, HeapAlloc, and HeapReAlloc can specify the HEAP_NO_SERIALIZE flag. There can be a small performance gain with this flag, because the functions do not provide mutual exclusion to threads accessing the heap.[4] This flag is safe in a few situations, such as the following:

- The program does not use threads (Chapter 8), or, more accurately, the process (Chapter 7) has only a single thread. All examples in this chapter use the flag.

---

[4] I measured about 16 percent with some simple tests that do nothing except allocate memory blocks.

- Each thread has its own heap or set of heaps, and no other thread accesses the heap.

- The program has its own mutual exclusion mechanism (Chapter 9) to prevent concurrent access to a heap by several threads using `HeapAlloc` and `Heap-ReAlloc`. `HeapLock` and `HeapUnlock` are also available for this purpose on Windows 2000/NT.

The `HEAP_GENERATE_EXCEPTIONS` Flag

Forcing exceptions in the case of memory allocation failure avoids the need for annoying error tests after each allocation. Furthermore, the exception or termination handler can clean up memory that did get allocated. This technique is used in some examples. *Windows CE does not support heap exceptions.*

Two exception codes are possible.

1. `STATUS_NO_MEMORY`, indicating that the system could not create a block of the requested size. Causes can include fragmented memory, a nongrowable heap that has reached its limit, or even exhaustion of all memory with growable heaps.

2. `STATUS_ACCESS_VIOLATION`, indicating that the specified heap has been corrupted. For example, a program may have written memory beyond the bounds of an allocated block.

Other Heap Functions

`HeapCompact` attempts to consolidate, or *defragment*, adjacent free blocks in a heap. `HeapValidate` attempts to detect heap corruption. `HeapWalk` enumerates the blocks in a heap, and `GetProcessHeap` obtains all the heap handles that are valid in a process.

`HeapLock` and `HeapUnlock` allow a thread to serialize heap access, as described in Chapter 9.

These functions are for Windows 2000/NT only. They do not work under Windows 9x or CE.

Heap Management Summary

The normal process for using heaps is straightforward.

1. Get a heap handle with either `CreateHeap` or `GetProcessHeap`.

2. Allocate blocks within the heap using `HeapAlloc`.

3. Optionally, free some or all of the individual blocks with `HeapFree`.

4. Destroy the heap and close the handle with `HeapDestroy`.

This process is illustrated in both Figure 6–2 and Program 6–1.

Normally, programmers use the C library `<stdlib.h>` memory management functions and can continue to do so if separate heaps or exception generation are not needed. `malloc` is then equivalent to `HeapAlloc`, `realloc` to `HeapReAlloc`, and `free` to `HeapFree`. `calloc` allocates and initializes objects, and `HeapAlloc` can easily emulate this behavior. There is no C library equivalent to `HeapSize`.

Example: Sorting Files with a Binary Search Tree

A search tree is a common dynamic data structure requiring memory management. Search trees are a convenient way to maintain collections of records, and they have the additional advantage of allowing efficient sequential traversal.

Program 6–1 implements a sort (`sortBT`, a limited version of the UNIX `sort` command) by creating a binary search tree using two heaps. The keys go into the *node* heap, which represents the search tree. Each node contains left and right pointers, a key, and a pointer to the data record in the *data* heap. The complete record, a line of text from the input file, goes into the data heap. Notice that the node heap consists of fixed-size blocks, whereas the data heap contains strings with different lengths. Finally, the sorted file is output by traversing the tree.

This example arbitrarily uses the first eight bytes of a string as the key rather than using the complete string. Two other sort implementations in this chapter (Programs 6–4 and 6–5) sort keyed files, and Appendix C compares their performance.

Figure 6–2 shows the sequence of operations for creating heaps and allocating blocks. The program code on the right is *pseudocode* in that only the essential function calls and arguments are shown. The virtual address space on the left shows the three heaps along with some allocated blocks in each. The figure differs slightly from the program in that the root of the tree is allocated in the process heap in the figure but not in Program 6–1.

Note: The actual locations of the heaps and the blocks within the heaps depend on the Win32 implementation and on the process's history of previous memory use, including heap expansion beyond the original size. Furthermore, a growable heap may not occupy contiguous address space after it grows beyond the originally committed size. The best programming practice is to make no assumptions; just use the memory management functions as specified.

Program 6–1 illustrates some techniques that simplify the program and would not be possible with the C library alone or with the process heap.

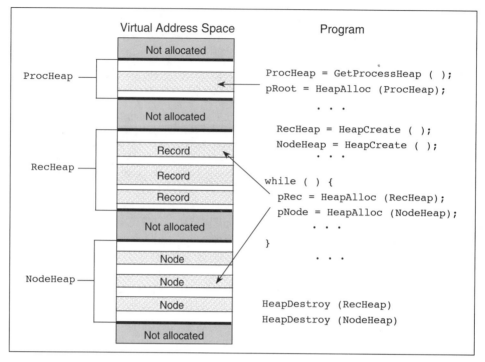

Figure 6–2   Memory Management in Multiple Heaps

- The node elements are of fixed size and go in a heap of their own, whereas the varying-length data elements are in a separate heap.

- The program prepares to sort the next file by destroying the two heaps rather than freeing individual elements.

- Allocation errors are processed as exceptions so that it is not necessary to test for NULL pointers.

An implementation such as Program 6–1 is limited to smaller files, because the complete file and a copy of the keys must reside in virtual memory. The absolute upper limit of the file length is 2GB; the practical limit is less.

Program 6–1 calls several tree management functions: FillTree, Insert-Tree, Scan, and KeyCompare. They are shown in Program 6–2.

This program uses heap exceptions; for operation under Windows CE, eliminate the exception handlers and test directly for memory allocation errors.

Program 6–1   `sortBT`: Sorting with a Binary Search Tree

```
/* Chapter 6. sortBT command. Binary Tree version. */
#include "EvryThng.h"
#define KEY_SIZE 8
typedef struct _TreeNode {/* Tree node structure definition. */
    struct _TreeNode *Left, *Right;
    TCHAR Key [KEY_SIZE];
    LPTSTR pData;
} TREENODE, *LPTNODE, **LPPTNODE;
#define NODE_SIZE sizeof (TREENODE)
#define NODE_HEAP_ISIZE 0x8000
#define DATA_HEAP_ISIZE 0x8000
#define MAX_DATA_LEN 0x1000
#define TKEY_SIZE KEY_SIZE * sizeof (TCHAR)

LPTNODE FillTree (HANDLE, HANDLE, HANDLE);
BOOL Scan (LPTNODE);
int KeyCompare (LPCTSTR, LPCTSTR); iFile; /* Excptn handler access. */
BOOL InsertTree (LPPTNODE, LPTNODE);

int _tmain (int argc, LPTSTR argv [])
{
    HANDLE hIn, hNode = NULL, hData = NULL;
    LPTNODE pRoot;
    CHAR ErrorMessage[256];
    int iFirstFile = Options (argc, argv, _T ("n"), &NoPrint, NULL);
                /* Process all files on the command line. */
    for (iFile = iFirstFile; iFile < argc; iFile++) __try {
                /* Open the input file. */
        hIn = CreateFile (argv [iFile], GENERIC_READ, 0, NULL,
            OPEN_EXISTING, 0, NULL);
        if (hIn == INVALID_HANDLE_VALUE)
            RaiseException (0, 0, 0, NULL);
        __try { /* Allocate the two heaps. */
            hNode = HeapCreate (
                HEAP_GENERATE_EXCEPTIONS | HEAP_NO_SERIALIZE,
                NODE_HEAP_ISIZE, 0);
            hData = HeapCreate (
                HEAP_GENERATE_EXCEPTIONS | HEAP_NO_SERIALIZE,
                DATA_HEAP_ISIZE, 0);
                /* Process the input file, creating the tree. */
            pRoot = FillTree (hIn, hNode, hData);
                /* Display the tree in Key order. */
            _tprintf (_T ("Sorted file: %s\n"), argv [iFile]);
            Scan (pRoot);
        } __finally { /* Heaps and file handles are always closed. */
            /* Destroy the two heaps and data structures. */
```

```
            if (hNode != NULL) HeapDestroy (hNode);
            if (hNode != NULL) HeapDestroy (hData);
            hNode = NULL; hData = NULL;
            if (hIn != INVALID_HANDLE_VALUE) CloseHandle (hIn);
        }
    } /* End of main file processing loop and try block. */

    __except (EXCEPTION_EXECUTE_HANDLER) {
        _stprintf (ErrorMessage, _T ("\n%s %s"),
            _T ("sortBT error on file:"), argv [iFile]);
        ReportError (ErrorMessage, 0, TRUE);
    }
    return 0;
}
```

Program 6–2 shows the functions that actually implement the search tree algorithms. FillTree, the first function, allocates memory in the two heaps. Key-Compare, the second function, is used in several other programs in this chapter. Notice that these functions are called by Program 6–1 and use the completion and exception handlers in that program. Thus, a memory allocation error would be handled by the main program, and the program would continue to process the next file.

Program 6–2   FillTree and Other Tree Management Functions

```
LPTNODE FillTree (HANDLE hIn, HANDLE hNode, HANDLE hData)

/* Fill the tree with records from the input file.
   Use the calling program's exception handler. */
{
    LPTNODE pRoot = NULL, pNode;
    DWORD nRead, i;
    BOOL AtCR;
    TCHAR DataHold [MAX_DATA_LEN];
    LPTSTR pString;

    while (TRUE) {
        /* Allocate and initialize a new tree node. */
        pNode = HeapAlloc (hNode, HEAP_ZERO_MEMORY, NODE_SIZE);

        /* Read the key from the next file record. */
        if (!ReadFile (hIn, pNode->Key, TKEY_SIZE,
                &nRead, NULL) || nRead != TKEY_SIZE)
            return pRoot;

        AtCR = FALSE; /* Read data until end of line. */
        for (i = 0; i < MAX_DATA_LEN; i++) {
```

```
            ReadFile (hIn, &DataHold [i], TSIZE, &nRead, NULL);
            if (AtCR && DataHold [i] == LF) break;
            AtCR = (DataHold [i] == CR);
        }
        DataHold [i - 1] = '\0';

        /* Combine Key and Data - Insert in tree. */
        pString = HeapAlloc (hData, HEAP_ZERO_MEMORY,
                (SIZE_T)(KEY_SIZE + _tcslen (DataHold) + 1) * TSIZE);
        memcpy (pString, pNode->Key, TKEY_SIZE);
        pString [KEY_SIZE] = '\0';
        _tcscat (pString, DataHold);
        pNode->pData = pString;
        InsertTree (&pRoot, pNode);
    } /* End of while (TRUE) loop. */
}

BOOL InsertTree (LPPTNODE ppRoot, LPTNODE pNode)
/* Add a single node, with data, to the tree. */
{
    if (*ppRoot == NULL) {
        *ppRoot = pNode;
        return TRUE;
    }
    /* Note the recursive calls to InsertTree. */
    if (KeyCompare (pNode->Key, (*ppRoot)->Key) < 0)
        InsertTree (&((*ppRoot)->Left), pNode);
    else
        InsertTree (&((*ppRoot)->Right), pNode);
}

static int KeyCompare (LPCTSTR pKey1, LPCTSTR pKey2)

/* Compare two records of generic characters. */
{
    return _tcsncmp (pKey1, pKey2, KEY_SIZE);
}

static BOOL Scan (LPTNODE pNode)

/* Recursively scan and print the contents of a binary tree. */
{
    if (pNode == NULL) return TRUE;
    Scan (pNode->Left);
    _tprintf (_T ("%s\n"), pNode->pData);
    Scan (pNode->Right);
    return TRUE;
}
```

Note: This search tree implementation is clearly not the most efficient, because the tree may become unbalanced. Implementing a balanced search tree would be worthwhile but would not change the program's memory management.

Memory-Mapped Files

Dynamic memory in heaps must be physically allocated in a paging file. The operating system's memory management controls page movement between physical memory and the paging file and also maps the process's virtual address space to the paging file. When the process terminates, the physical space in the file is deallocated.

Win32's memory-mapped file functionality can also map virtual memory space directly to normal files. This has several advantages:

- There is no need to perform direct file I/O (reads and writes).

- The data structures created in memory will be saved in the file for later use by the same or other programs. Be careful about pointer usage, as the last example in this chapter illustrates.

- Convenient and efficient in-memory algorithms (sorts, search trees, string processing, and so on) can process file data even though the file may be much larger than available physical memory. The performance will still be influenced by paging behavior if the file is large.

- File processing performance can be significantly improved in some cases.

- There is no need to manage buffers and the file data they contain. The operating system does this hard work and does it efficiently and reliably.

- Multiple processes (Chapter 7) can share memory by mapping their virtual address spaces to the same file or to the paging file (interprocess memory sharing is the principal reason for mapping to the paging file).

- There is no need to consume paging file space.

The operating system itself uses memory mapping to implement dynamic link libraries (DLLs) and to load and execute executable (.EXE) files. DLLs are described at the end of this chapter.

File Mapping Objects

The first step is to create a *file mapping object*, which has a handle, on an open file and then map the process's address space to all or part of the file. File mapping objects can be given names so that they are accessible to other processes for shared memory. Also, the mapping object has protection and security attributes and a size.

```
HANDLE CreateFileMapping (
    HANDLE hFile,
    LPSECURITY_ATTRIBUTES lpsa,
    DWORD fdwProtect,
    DWORD dwMaximumSizeHigh,
    DWORD dwMaximumSizeLow,
    LPCTSTR lpszMapName)
```

Return: A file mapping handle, or NULL on failure.

Parameters

hFile is the handle of an open file with protection flags compatible with fdwProtect. The value (HANDLE) 0xFFFFFFFF (equivalently, INVALID_HANDLE_VALUE) refers to the paging file, and you can use this value for interprocess memory sharing without creating a separate file.

LPSECURITY_ATTRIBUTES allows the mapping object to be secured. fdwProtect specifies the mapped file access with the following flags. Additional flags are allowed for specialized purposes. For example, the SEC_IMAGE flag specifies an executable image; see the on-line documentation for more information.

- PAGE_READONLY means that the program can only read the pages in the mapped region; it can neither write nor execute them. hFile must have GENERIC_READ access.

- PAGE_READWRITE gives full access to the object if hFile has both GENERIC_READ and GENERIC_WRITE access.

- PAGE_WRITECOPY means that when mapped memory is changed, a private (to the process) copy is written to the paging file and not to the original file. A debugger might use this flag when setting breakpoints in shared code. It has different effects under Windows 2000/NT and Windows 9x.

dwMaximumSizeHigh and dwMaximumSizeLow specify the size of the mapping object. If it is zero, the current file size is used; be sure to specify a size when using the paging file. If the file is expected to grow, use a size equal to the expected file size, and, if necessary, the file size will be set to that size immediately. Do not map to a file region beyond this specified size; the mapping object cannot grow.

lpszMapName names the mapping object, allowing other processes to share the object; the name is case-sensitive. Use NULL if you are not sharing memory.

An error is indicated by a return value of NULL (not INVALID_HANDLE_VALUE).

Obtain a file mapping handle by specifying an existing mapping object name. The name comes from a previous call to CreateFileMapping. Two processes can share memory by sharing a file mapping. The first process creates the named mapping, and subsequent processes open this mapping with the name. The open will fail if the named object does not exist. *This function is not supported by Windows CE.*

```
HANDLE OpenFileMapping (
    DWORD dwDesiredAccess,
    BOOL bInheritHandle,
    LPCTSTR lpName)

Return: A file mapping handle, or NULL on failure.
```

dwDesiredAccess uses the same set of flags as fdwProtect in CreateFileMapping. lpName is the name created by a CreateFileMapping call. Handle inheritance (bInheritHandle) is a subject for Chapter 7.

The CloseHandle function, as expected, destroys mapping handles.

Mapping Process Address Space to Mapping Objects

The next step is to allocate virtual memory space and map it to a file through the mapping object. From the programmer's perspective, this allocation is similar to HeapAlloc, although it is much coarser, with larger allocation units. A pointer to the allocated block (or file *view*) is returned; the difference lies in the fact that the allocated block is mapped to the user-specified file rather than the paging file. The file mapping object plays the same role played by the heap when HeapAlloc is used.

```
LPVOID MapViewOfFile (
    HANDLE hMapObject,
    DWORD fdwAccess,
    DWORD dwOffsetHigh,
    DWORD dwOffsetLow,
    SIZE_T cbMap)
```

Return: The starting address of the block (file view), or NULL on failure.

Parameters

hMapObject identifies a file mapping object obtained from either Create-FileMapping or OpenFileMapping.

fdwAccess must be compatible with the mapping object's access. The three possible flag values are: FILE_MAP_WRITE, FILE_MAP_READ, and FILE_MAP_ALL_ACCESS. (This is the bit-wise "or" of the previous two flags.)

dwOffsetHigh and dwOffsetLow specify the starting location of the mapped file region. The start address must be a multiple of 64K. Use a zero offset to map from the beginning of the file.

cbMap is the size, in bytes, of the mapped region. Zero indicates the entire file at the time of the MapViewOfFile Call.

MapViewOfFileEx (*unsupported by Windows CE*) is similar except that you must specify the starting memory address. This address might, for instance, be the address of an array in the program's data space. Windows 9x ensures that *all* processes will be able to use this base address if the function succeeds. This means that the virtual address space is taken from all processes. Windows 2000/NT fails if the process has already mapped the requested space.

Just as it is necessary to release memory allocated in a heap with HeapFree, it is necessary to release file views.

```
BOOL UnmapViewOfFile (LPVOID lpBaseAddress)
```

Figure 6–3 shows the relationship between process address space and a mapped file.

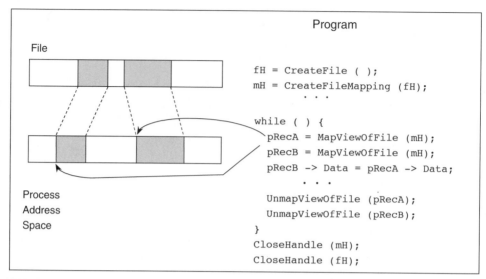

```
                                                    Program

    File
                                    fH = CreateFile ( );
                                    mH = CreateFileMapping (fH);
                                        . . .

                                    while ( ) {
                                      pRecA = MapViewOfFile (mH);
                                      pRecB = MapViewOfFile (mH);
                                      pRecB -> Data = pRecA -> Data;
                                        . . .
    Process                           UnmapViewOfFile (pRecA);
    Address                           UnmapViewOfFile (pRecB);
    Space                           }
                                    CloseHandle (mH);
                                    CloseHandle (fH);
```

Figure 6–3   Process Address Space Mapped to a File

FlushViewOfFile forces the system to write "dirty" (changed) pages to disc. Normally, a process accessing a file through mapping and another process accessing it through conventional file I/O will not have coherent views of the file. Performing the file I/O without buffering will not help, because the mapped memory will not be written to the file immediately.

Therefore, it is not a good idea to access a mapped file with ReadFile and WriteFile; coherency is not ensured. On the other hand, processes that share a file through shared memory will have a coherent view of the file. If one process changes a mapped memory location, the other process will obtain that new value when it accesses the corresponding area of the file in its mapped memory. This mechanism is illustrated in Figure 6–4, and coherency works because both processes' virtual addresses, although distinct, are in the same physical memory locations. The obvious synchronization issues are addressed in Chapters 9 and 10.[5]

UNIX, at the SVR4 and 4.3+BSD releases, supports the mmap function, which is similar to MapViewOfFile. The parameters specify the same information except that there is no mapping object.

munmap is the UnmapViewOfFile equivalent.

---

[5] Statements regarding coherency of mapped views do not apply to networked files. The files must be local.

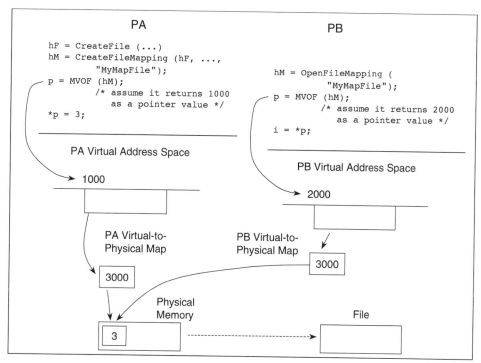

Figure 6-4 Shared Memory

There are no equivalents to the `CreateFileMapping` and `OpenFileMapping` functions. Any normal file can be mapped directly. UNIX does not use mapped files to share memory; rather, it has explicit API functions for memory sharing. The UNIX functions are `shmget`, `shmctl`, `shmat`, and `shmdt`.

File Mapping Limitations

File mapping, as mentioned previously, is a powerful and useful feature. The disparity between Win32's 64-bit file system and 32-bit addressing limits these benefits; Win64 does not have these limitations.

The principal problem is that if the file is large (greater than 2 or 3GB in this case), it is not possible to map the entire file into virtual memory space. Furthermore, the entire 2GB will not be available, because virtual address space will be allocated for other purposes and available contiguous blocks will be much smaller than the theoretical maximum. Win64 will largely remove this limitation.

When you're dealing with large files that cannot be mapped to one view, create code that carefully maps and unmaps file regions as they are needed. This technique can be as complex as managing memory buffers, although it is not necessary to perform the explicit reads and writes.

File mapping has two other notable limitations:

- A file mapping cannot be expanded. You need to know the maximum size when creating the file mapping, and it may be difficult or impossible to determine this size.

- There is no way to allocate memory within a mapped memory region without creating your own memory management functions. It would be convenient if there were a way to specify a file mapping and a pointer returned by `Map-ViewOfFile` and obtain a heap handle.

File Mapping Summary

Here is the standard sequence required by file mapping:

1. Open the file. Be certain that it has `GENERIC_READ` access.

2. If the file is new, set its length either with `CreateFileMapping` (step 3 below) or by using `SetFilePointer` followed by `SetEndOfFile`.

3. Map the file with `CreateFileMapping` or `OpenFileMapping`.

4. Create one or more views with `MapViewOfFile`.

5. Access the file through memory references. If necessary, change the mapped regions with `UnmapViewOfFile` and `MapViewOfFile`.

6. On completion, perform, in order, `UnmapViewOfFile`, `CloseHandle` for the mapping handle, and `CloseHandle` for the file handle.

Example: Sequential File Processing with Mapped Files

The `atou` program (Program 2–4) illustrates sequential file processing by converting ASCII files to Unicode, doubling the file length. This is an ideal application for memory-mapped files, because the most natural way to convert the data is to process it one character at a time without being concerned with file I/O. Program 6–3 simply maps the input file and the output file—first computing the output file length by doubling the input file length—and converts the characters one at a time.

This example clearly illustrates the trade-off between the file mapping complexity required to initialize the program and the resulting processing simplicity. This complexity may not seem worthwhile given the simplicity of a simple file I/O implementation, but there is a significant performance advantage. Appendix C shows that the memory-mapped version can be considerably faster than the file access versions for NTFS files, so the complexity is worthwhile. The disc contains additional performance studies; the highlights are:

- Memory-mapping performance improvements apply only to Windows 2000/NT and the NTFS.

- Compared with the best sequential file processing techniques, the performance improvements can be 3:1 or greater.

- The performance advantage disappears for larger files. In this example, as the input file size approaches about one-third of the physical memory size, normal sequential scanning is preferable. The mapping performance degrades at this point since the input file fills one-third of the memory and the output file, which is twice as long, fills the other two-thirds, forcing parts of the output files to be flushed to disc. Thus, on a 96MB system, mapping performance degenerates for input files longer than 30MB. Most file processing deals with smaller files and can take advantage of file mapping.

Program 6–3 shows only the function MM. The main program is the same as for Program 2–4.

Program 6–3 Asc2UnMM: File Conversion with Memory Mapping

```
/* Chapter 6. Asc2UnMM.c: Memory Mapped implementation. */

#include "EvryThng.h"
BOOL Asc2Un (LPCTSTR fIn, LPCTSTR fOut, BOOL bFailIfExists)
{
    HANDLE hIn, hOut, hInMap, hOutMap;
    LPSTR pIn, pInFile;
    LPWSTR pOut, pOutFile;
    DWORD FsLow, fdwOut;

    /* Open and map both the input and output files. */
    hIn = CreateFile (fIn, GENERIC_READ, 0, NULL,
            OPEN_EXISTING, FILE_ATTRIBUTE_NORMAL, NULL);
    hInMap = CreateFileMapping (hIn, NULL, PAGE_READONLY,
            0, 0, NULL);
    pInFile = MapViewOfFile (hInMap, FILE_MAP_READ, 0, 0, 0);

    fdwOut = bFailIfExists ? CREATE_NEW : CREATE_ALWAYS;
    hOut = CreateFile (fOut, GENERIC_READ | GENERIC_WRITE,
            0, NULL, fdwOut, FILE_ATTRIBUTE_NORMAL, NULL);
    FsLow = GetFileSize (hIn, NULL); /* Set the map size. */
```

```
hOutMap = CreateFileMapping (hOut, NULL, PAGE_READWRITE,
        0, 2 * FsLow, NULL);
pOutFile = MapViewOfFile (hOutMap, FILE_MAP_WRITE, 0, 0,
        (SIZE_T)(2 * FsLow));

/* Convert the mapped file data from ASCII to Unicode. */
pIn = pInFile;
pOut = pOutFile;
while (pIn < pInFile + FsLow)
{
    *pOut = (WCHAR) *pIn;
    pIn++;
    pOut++;
}

UnmapViewOfFile (pOutFile); UnmapViewOfFile (pInFile);
CloseHandle (hOutMap); CloseHandle (hInMap);
CloseHandle (hIn); CloseHandle (hOut);
return TRUE;
}
```

Example: Sorting a Memory-Mapped File

Another advantage of memory mapping is the ability to use convenient memory-based algorithms to process files. Sorting data in memory, for instance, is much easier than sorting records in a file.

Program 6–4 sorts a file with fixed-length records. This program, called sortFL, is similar to Program 6–1 in that it assumes an 8-byte sort key at the start of the record, but it is restricted to fixed records. Program 6–5 will rectify this shortcoming, but at the cost of increased complexity.

The sorting is performed by the <stdlib.h> C library function qsort. Notice that qsort requires a programmer-defined record comparison function, which is the same as the KeyCompare function in Program 6–2.

This program structure is straightforward. Simply create the file mapping on a temporary copy of the input file, create a single view of the file, and invoke qsort. There is no file I/O. Then the sorted file is sent to standard output using _tprintf, although a null character is appended to the file map.

Program 6–4   sortFL: Sorting a File with Memory Mapping

```
/* Chapter 6. sortFL. File sorting. Fixed length records. */
/* Usage: sortFL file */

#include "EvryThng.h"
```

```
typedef struct _RECORD {
    TCHAR Key [KEY_SIZE];
    TCHAR Data [DATALEN];
} RECORD;

#define RECSIZE sizeof (RECORD)

int _tmain (int argc, LPTSTR argv [])
{
    HANDLE hFile = INVALID_HANDLE_VALUE, hMap = NULL;
    LPVOID pFile = NULL;
    DWORD FsLow, Result = 2;
    TCHAR TempFile [MAX_PATH];
    LPTSTR pTFile;

    /* Create the name for a temporary file to hold a copy of
        the file to be sorted. Sorting is done in the temp file. */

    /* Alternatively, retain the file as a permanent sorted version. */
    _stprintf (TempFile, _T ("%s%s"), argv [1], _T (".tmp"));
    CopyFile (argv [1], TempFile, TRUE);

    Result = 1; /* tmp file is new and should be deleted. */

    /* Map the temporary file and sort it in memory. */

    hFile = CreateFile (TempFile, GENERIC_READ | GENERIC_WRITE,
            0, NULL, OPEN_EXISTING, 0, NULL);
    FsLow = GetFileSize (hFile, NULL);
    hMap = CreateFileMapping (hFile, NULL, PAGE_READWRITE,
            0, FsLow + TSIZE, NULL);
    pFile = MapViewOfFile (hMap, FILE_MAP_ALL_ACCESS, 0,
            0 /* FsLow + TSIZE */, 0);

    qsort (pFile, FsLow / RECSIZE, RECSIZE, KeyCompare);
                            /* KeyCompare is as in Program 6-1. */

    /* Print the sorted file. */

    pTFile = (LPTSTR) pFile;
    pTFile [FsLow/TSIZE] = '\0';
    _tprintf (_T ("%s"), pFile);
    UnmapViewOfFile (pFile);
    CloseHandle (hMap);
    CloseHandle (hFile);
    DeleteFile (TempFile);
    return 0;
}
```

This implementation is straightforward, but there is an alternative that does not require mapping. Just allocate memory, read the complete file, sort it in memory, and write it. Such a solution, included on the disc, would be as effective as Program 6–4 and is often faster, as shown in Appendix C.

Based Pointers

File maps are convenient, as the preceding examples demonstrate. Suppose, however, that the program creates a data structure with pointers in a mapped file and expects to access that file in the future. Pointers will all be relative to the virtual address returned from MapViewOfFile, and they will be meaningless when mapping the file the next time. The solution is to use based pointers, which are actually offsets relative to another pointer. The Microsoft C syntax, available in Visual C++ and some other systems, is:

```
type _based (base) declarator
```

Here are two examples.

```
LPTSTR pInFile = NULL;
DWORD _based (pInFile) *pSize;
TCHAR _based (pInFile) *pIn;
```

Notice that the syntax forces use of the *, a practice that is contrary to Win32 convention.

Example: Using Based Pointers

Previous programs have shown how to sort files in various situations. The object, of course, is to illustrate different ways to manage memory, not to discuss sorting techniques. Program 6–1 uses a binary search tree that is destroyed after each sort, and Program 6–4 sorts an array of fixed-size records in mapped memory. Appendix C shows performance results for different implementations, including the next one in Program 6–5.

Suppose that it is necessary to maintain a permanent index file representing the sorted keys of the original file. The apparent solution is to map a file that contains the permanent index in a search tree or sorted key form to memory. Unfortunately, there is a major difficulty with this solution. All pointers in the tree, as stored in the file, are relative to the address returned by MapViewOfFile. The next time the program runs and maps the file, the pointers will be useless.

Program 6–5, together with Program 6–6, solves this problem, which is characteristic of any mapped data structure that uses pointers. The solution uses the _based keyword available with Microsoft C. An alternative is to map the file to an array and use indexing to access records in the mapped files.

The program is written as yet another version of the sort command, this time called sortMM. There are enough new features, however, to make it interesting.

- The records are of varying lengths.

- The program uses the first field as a key but detects its length.

- There are two file mappings. One mapping is for the original file, and the other is for the file containing the sorted keys. The second file is the *index* file, and each of its records contains a key and a pointer (base address) in the original file. qsort sorts the key file, much as in Program 6–4.

- The index file is saved and can be used later, and there is an option (-I) that bypasses the sort and uses an existing index file. The index file can also be used to perform a fast key file search by performing a binary search (using, perhaps, the C library bsearch function) on the index file.

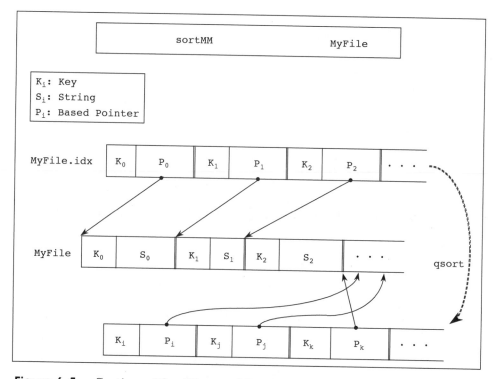

Figure 6-5   Sorting with a Memory-Mapped Index File

- This solution is limited to files that are small enough to be mapped. A more elaborate solution is feasible in which the original file is never mapped, but an intermediate mapped file (the *key file*) stores the keys and pointers, and a smaller index file consists of records with nothing but pointers to the key file.

Figure 6–5 shows the relationship of the index file to the file to be sorted. Program 6–5, sortMM, is the main program that sets up the file mapping, sorts the index file, and displays the results. It calls a function, CreateIndexFile, which is shown in Program 6–6.

Program 6–5   sortMM: Based Pointers in an Index File

```
/* Chapter 6. sortMM command.
   Memory Mapped sorting - one file only. Options:
   -r Sort in reverse order.
   -I Use existing index file to produce sorted file. */

#include "EvryThng.h"
int KeyCompare (LPCTSTR , LPCTSTR);
DWORD CreateIndexFile (DWORD, LPCTSTR, LPTSTR);
DWORD KStart, KSize; /* Key start position & size (TCHAR). */
BOOL Revrs;

int _tmain (int argc, LPTSTR argv [])
{
    HANDLE hInFile, hInMap; /* Input file handles. */
    HANDLE hXFile, hXMap; /* Index file handles. */
    HANDLE hStdOut = GetStdHandle (STD_OUTPUT_HANDLE);
    BOOL IdxExists;
    DWORD FsIn, FsX, RSize, iKey, nWrite, *pSizes;
    LPTSTR pInFile = NULL;
    LPBYTE pXFile = NULL, pX;
    TCHAR _based (pInFile) *pIn;
    TCHAR IdxFlNam [MAX_PATH], ChNewLine = TNEWLINE;
    int FlIdx =
            Options (argc, argv, _T ("rI"), &Revrs, &IdxExists, NULL);

    /* Step 1: Open and Map the Input File. */
    hInFile = CreateFile (argv [FlIdx], GENERIC_READ | GENERIC_WRITE,
            0, NULL, OPEN_EXISTING, 0, NULL);
    hInMap = CreateFileMapping (hInFile, NULL,
            PAGE_READWRITE, 0, 0, NULL);
    pInFile = MapViewOfFile (hInMap, FILE_MAP_ALL_ACCESS, 0, 0, 0);
    FsIn = GetFileSize (hInFile, NULL);

    /* Steps 2 and 3: Create the index file name. */
    _stprintf (IdxFlNam, _T ("%s%s"), argv [FlIdx], _T (".idx"));
```

```
    if (!IdxExists)
        RSize = CreateIndexFile (FsIn, IdxFlNam, pInFile);

    /* Step 4. Map the index file. */
    hXFile = CreateFile (IdxFlNam, GENERIC_READ | GENERIC_WRITE,
            0, NULL, OPEN_EXISTING, 0, NULL);
    hXMap = CreateFileMapping (hXFile, NULL, PAGE_READWRITE,
            0, 0, NULL);
    pXFile = MapViewOfFile (hXMap, FILE_MAP_ALL_ACCESS, 0, 0, 0);
    FsX = GetFileSize (hXFile, NULL);
    pSizes = (LPDWORD) pXFile; /* Size fields in .idx file. */
    KSize = *pSizes; /* Key size */
    KStart = *(pSizes + 1); /* Start position of key in record. */
    FsX -= 2 * sizeof (DWORD);

    /* Step 5. Sort the index file with qsort. */
    if (!IdxExists)
        qsort (pXFile + 2 * sizeof (DWORD), FsX / RSize,
                RSize, KeyCompare);

    /* Step 6. Output the input file in sorted order. */
    pX = pXFile + 2 * sizeof (DWORD) + RSize - sizeof (LPTSTR);
    for (iKey = 0; iKey < FsX / RSize; iKey++) {
        WriteFile (hStdOut, &ChNewLine, TSIZE, &nWrite, NULL);
                    /* The cast on pX is necessary! */
        pIn = (TCHAR _based (pInFile)*) *(LPDWORD) pX;
        while ((*pIn != CR || *(pIn + 1) != LF)
                && (DWORD) pIn < FsIn) {
            WriteFile (hStdOut, pIn, TSIZE, &nWrite, NULL);
            pIn++;
        }
        pX += RSize;
    }
    UnmapViewOfFile (pInFile);
    CloseHandle (hInMap);
    CloseHandle (hInFile);
    UnmapViewOfFile (pXFile);
    CloseHandle (hXMap);
    CloseHandle (hXFile);
    return 0;
}
```

Program 6–6 is the CreateIndexFile function, which creates the index file. It initially scans the input file to determine the key length from the first record. Subsequently, it must scan the input file to find the bound of each varying-length record to set up the structure shown in Figure 6–5.

Program 6–6 sortMM: Creating the Index File

```
DWORD CreateIndexFile (DWORD FsIn, LPCTSTR IdxFlNam, LPTSTR pInFile)
{
   HANDLE hXFile;
   TCHAR _based (pInFile) *pInScan = 0;
   DWORD nWrite;

   /* Step 2a: Create an index file. Do not map it yet. */
   hXFile = CreateFile (IdxFlNam, GENERIC_READ | GENERIC_WRITE,
         FILE_SHARE_READ, NULL, CREATE_ALWAYS, 0, NULL);

   /* Step 2b. Get first key & determine key size/start.
      Skip white space and get key length. */
   KStart = (DWORD) pInScan;
   while (*pInScan != TSPACE && *pInScan != TAB)
      pInScan++; /* Find the first key field. */
   KSize = ((DWORD) pInScan - KStart) / TSIZE;

   /* Step 3. Scan the complete file, writing keys
      and record pointers to the key file. */
   WriteFile (hXFile, &KSize, sizeof (DWORD), &nWrite, NULL);
   WriteFile (hXFile, &KStart, sizeof (DWORD),&nWrite, NULL);
   pInScan = 0;
   while ((DWORD) pInScan < FsIn) {
      WriteFile (hXFile, pInScan + KStart, KSize * TSIZE,
            &nWrite, NULL);
      WriteFile (hXFile, &pInScan, sizeof (LPTSTR),
            &nWrite, NULL);
      while ((DWORD) pInScan < FsIn && ((*pInScan != CR)
            || (*(pInScan + 1) != LF))) {
         pInScan++; /* Skip to end of line. */
      }
      pInScan += 2; /* Skip past CR, LF. */
   }
   CloseHandle (hXFile);
                  /* Size of an individual record. */
   return KSize * TSIZE + sizeof (LPTSTR);
}
```

Dynamic Link Libraries

We have now seen that memory management and file mapping are important and useful techniques in a wide class of programs. The operating system itself also uses memory management, and dynamic link libraries (DLLs) are the most visible and important use of file mapping. DLLs are used extensively by Win32 applications. DLLs are also essential to COM programs (to which Chapter 15 presents a brief introduction), and many software components are provided as DLLs.

The first step is to consider the different methods of constructing libraries of commonly used functions.

Static and Dynamic Libraries

The most direct way to construct a program is to gather the source code of all the functions, compile them, and link everything into a single executable image. Common functions, such as `ReportError`, can be put into a library to simplify the build process. This technique was used with all the sample programs presented so far, although there were only a few functions, most of them for error reporting.

This monolithic, single-image model is simple, but it has several disadvantages.

- The executable image may be large, consuming disc space, and physical memory at run time, and requiring extra effort to manage and deliver to users.

- Each program update requires a rebuild of the complete program even if the changes are small or localized.

- Every program in the system that uses the functions will have a copy of the functions, possibly different versions, in its executable image. This arrangement increases disc space usage and, perhaps more important, physical memory usage when several such programs are running simultaneously.

- Distinct versions of the program, using different techniques, might be required to get the best performance in different environments. For example, the `Asc2Un` function is implemented differently in Program 2–4 (`atou`) and Program 6–3 (`Asc2UnMM`). The only method of executing different implementations is to decide which of the two versions to run based on environmental factors.

DLLs solve these and other problems quite neatly.

- Library functions are not linked at build time. Rather, they are linked at program load time (*implicit linking*) or at run time (*explicit linking*). As a result, the program image can be much smaller because it does not include the library functions.

- DLLs can be used to create *shared libraries*. Multiple programs share a single DLL library, and only a single copy is loaded into memory. All programs map their process address space to the DLL code, although each thread will have its own copy of nonshared storage on the stack. For example, the `Report-`

Error function was used by nearly every example program; a single DLL implementation could be shared by all the programs.

- New versions or alternative implementations can be supported simply by supplying a new version of the DLL, and all programs that use the library can use the new version without modification.

- With explicit linking, a program can decide at run time which version of a library to use. The different libraries may be alternative implementations of the same function or may carry out totally different tasks, just as separate programs do. The library will run in the same process and thread as the calling program, as described in a later section.

DLLs, sometimes in limited form, are used in nearly every operating system, including UNIX and Windows 3.1. For example, UNIX uses the term "shared libraries" for the same concept. Windows (all versions, including Windows 3.1) uses DLLs to implement the OS interfaces, among other things. The entire Win32 API is supported by a DLL that invokes the executive for additional services.

Multiple Win32 processes can share DLL code, but the code, when called, runs as part of the calling process and thread. Therefore, the library will be able to use the resources of the calling process, such as file handles, and will use the calling thread's stack. DLLs should, therefore, be written to be thread-safe. (See Chapters 9 and 10 for more information on thread safety and DLLs. Programs 12–4 and 12–5 illustrate techniques for creating thread-safe DLLs.) A DLL can also export variables as well as function entry points.

Implicit Linking

Implicit, or *load-time*, linking is the easier of the two techniques. The required steps, using Microsoft Visual C++, are as follows:

- The functions in a new DLL are collected and built as a DLL, rather than, for example, a console application.

- The build process constructs a .LIB library file, which is a *stub* for the actual code. This file should be placed in a common user library directory that is specified to the project.

- The build process also constructs a .DLL file that contains the executable image. This file is typically placed in the same directory as the application that will use it, and the application loads the DLL during its initialization. The current working directory is the secondary location, and the operating system will next look in the system directory, the Windows directory, and the path specified with the PATH environment variable.

- Take care to export the function interfaces in the DLL source, as described next.

Exporting and Importing Interfaces

The most significant change required to put a function into a DLL is to declare it to be exportable (UNIX and some other systems do not require this explicit step). This is achieved either by using a .DEF file or, more simply, with Microsoft C, by using the _declspec (dllexport) storage modifier as follows:

```
_declspec (dllexport) DWORD MyFunction (...);
```

The build process will then create a .DLL file and a .LIB file. The .LIB file is the stub library that should be linked with the calling program to satisfy the external references and to create the actual links to the .DLL file at load time.

The calling program should declare that the function is to be imported by using the _declspec (dllimport) storage modifier. A standard technique is to write the include file as follows, using a preprocessor variable such as _DLLLIB.

```
#ifdef _DLLLIB
#define LIBSPEC _declspec (dllexport)
#else
#define LIBSPEC _declspec (dllimport)
#endif
LIBSPEC DWORD MyFunction (...);
```

The DLL code, then, defines _DLLLIB immediately before the #include statement (generally on the compiler command line), whereas the calling application leaves _DLLLIB undefined.

When building the calling program, specify the .LIB file. When executing the calling program, ensure that the .DLL file is available to the calling program; this is usually done by placing the .DLL file in the same directory as the executable.

It is possible to export and import variables as well as function entry points.

Explicit Linking

Explicit, or *run-time*, linking requires the program to request specifically that a DLL be loaded (LoadLibrary) or freed (FreeLibrary). Next, the program obtains the address of the required entry point and uses that address as the pointer in the function call. The function is not declared in the calling program; rather, you declare a variable as a pointer to a function. Therefore, there is no need for a library at link time. The three required functions are LoadLibrary,

GetProcAddress, and FreeLibrary. *Note*: The function definitions show their 16-bit legacy through "far pointers" and different handle types.

```
HINSTANCE LoadLibrary (LPCTSTR lpLibFileName)
```

The returned handle (HINSTANCE rather than HANDLE) will be NULL on failure. The .DLL suffix is not required on the file name. .EXE files can also be loaded with the LoadLibrary function. Since DLLs are shared, the system maintains a reference count to each DLL (incremented by LoadLibrary) so that the actual file does not need to be remapped. Even if the DLL file is found, LoadLibrary will fail if the DLL is implicitly linked to other DLLs that cannot be located.

The function LoadLibraryEx is similar but has several flags that are useful for specifying alternative search paths and loading the library as a data file.

When you're finished with this instance, possibly to load a different version, you free the library handle, thereby freeing the resources, including virtual address space, allocated to the library. The DLL will, however, remain loaded if the reference count indicates that other processes are still using it.

```
BOOL FreeLibrary (HINSTANCE hLibModule)
```

After loading a library and before freeing it, you can obtain the address of any entry point using GetProcAddress.

```
FARPROC GetProcAddress (
    HMODULE hModule,
    LPCSTR lpProcName)
```

hModule, despite the different type name (HINSTANCE is defined as HMODULE), is an instance produced by LoadLibrary or GetModuleHandle, which is not described here. lpProcName, which cannot be Unicode, is the entry point name. The return result is NULL in case of failure. FARPROC, like "long pointer," is an anachronism.

It is possible to obtain the file name associated with an hModule handle using GetModuleFileName. Conversely, given a file name (either a .dll or .exe file),

GetModuleHandle will return the handle, if any, associated with this file if the current process has loaded it.

The next example shows how to use the entry point address to invoke a function.

Example: Explicitly Linking a File Conversion Function

Program 2–4 is an ASCII to Unicode file conversion program that calls the function Asc2Un (Program 2–5) to process the file using file I/O. Program 6–3 is an alternative function that uses memory mapping to perform exactly the same operation. The circumstances under which Asc2UnMM is faster were described earlier; essentially, the file system should be NTFS and the file should not be too large.

Program 6–7 reimplements the calling program so that it can decide which implementation to load at run time. It then loads the DLL and obtains the address of the Asc2Un entry point and calls the function. There is only one entry point in this case, but it would be equally easy to locate multiple entry points. The main program is as before, except that the DLL to use is a command line parameter. Exercise 6–9 suggests that the DLL be determined on the basis of system and file characteristics. Also notice how the FARPROC address is cast to the appropriate function type using the required, but complex, C syntax.

Program 6–7   atouEL: File Conversion with Explicit Linking

```
/* Chapter 6. atou Explicit Link version. */

#include "EvryThng.h"

int _tmain (int argc, LPTSTR argv [])
{
    /* Declare variable Asc2Un to be a function. */
    BOOL (*Asc2Un)(LPCTSTR, LPCTSTR, BOOL);
    DWORD LocFileIn, LocFileOut, LocDLL, DashI;
    HINSTANCE hDLL;
    FARPROC pA2U;

    LocFileIn = Options (argc, argv, _T ("i"), &DashI, NULL);
    LocFileOut = LocFileIn + 1;
    LocDLL = LocFileOut + 1;

    /* Test for existing file && DashI is omitted. */
    /* Load the ASCII to Unicode function. */

    hDLL = LoadLibrary (argv [LocDLL]);
```

```
    if (hDLL == NULL)
        ReportError (_T ("Failed loading DLL."), 1, TRUE);

    /* Get the entry point address. */

    pA2U = GetProcAddress (hDLL, "Asc2Un");
    if (pA2U == NULL)
        ReportError (_T ("Failed to find entry point."), 2, TRUE);

    /* Cast the pointer. A typedef could be used here. */

    Asc2Un = (BOOL (*)(LPCTSTR, LPCTSTR, BOOL)) pA2U;

    /* Call the function. */
    Asc2Un (argv [LocFileIn], argv [LocFileOut], FALSE)
    FreeLibrary (hDLL);
    return 0;
}
```

Building the `Asc2Un` DLLs

This program was tested with the two file conversion functions, which must be built as DLLs with different names but identical entry points. There is only one entry point in this case. The only significant change in the source code is the addition of a storage modifier, `_declspec (dllexport)`, to export the function.

The DLL Entry Point

Optionally, you can specify an entry point for every DLL you create, and this entry point is invoked automatically every time a process attaches or detaches the DLL. For implicitly linked (load-time) DLLs, process attachment and detachment occur when the process starts and terminates. In the case of explicitly linked DLLs, LoadLibrary and FreeLibrary cause the attachment and detachment calls.

The entry point is also invoked when new threads (Chapter 8) are created or terminated by the process.

The DLL entry point is introduced here but will not be fully exploited until Chapter 12 (Program 12–4), where it provides a convenient way for threads to manage resources and so-called Thread Local Storage (TLS) in a thread-safe DLL.

```
BOOL DllMain (
    HINSTANCE hDll,
    DWORD Reason,
    LPVOID Reserved)
```

The hDll value corresponds to the instance obtained from LoadLibrary. Reserved, if NULL, indicates that the process attach was caused by Load-Library; otherwise, it was caused by implicit load-time linking. Likewise, FreeLibary gives a NULL value for process detachment.

Reason will have one of four values: DLL_PROCESS_ATTACH, DLL_THREAD_ATTACH, DLL_THREAD_DETACH, and DLL_PROCESS_DETACH. DLL entry point functions are normally written as switch statements and return TRUE to indicate correct operation.

The system serializes calls to DllMain so that only one thread at a time can execute it (threads are thoroughly discussed starting in Chapter 8). This serialization is essential, because DllMain must perform initializations that must be completed without interruption. As a consequence, however, it is recommended that there not be any blocking calls, such as I/O or wait functions (see Chapter 7) within the entry point, because they would prevent other threads from entering.

DisableThreadLibraryCalls will disable thread attach/detach calls for a specified DLL instance. Disabling the thread calls can be helpful when threads do not require any unique resources during initialization.

Summary

Win32 memory management includes the following features:

- Logic can be simplified by allowing the Win32 heap management and exception handlers to detect and process allocation errors.

- Multiple independent heaps provide several advantages over allocation from a single heap.

- Memory-mapped files, available with UNIX but not with the C library, allow files to be processed in memory, as illustrated by several examples. File mapping is independent of heap management.

- DLLs are an essential special case of mapped files, and DLLs can be loaded either explicitly or implicitly.

Appendix C shows some of the performance implications and advantages of memory-mapped files and independent heaps. Nonetheless, the C library is adequate for many file processing applications.

Looking Ahead

This completes coverage of what can be achieved within a single process. The next step is to learn how to manage concurrent processing, first with processes (Chapter 7) and then with threads (Chapter 8). Subsequent chapters will show how to synchronize and communicate between concurrent processing activities.

Additional Reading

Memory Mapping, Virtual Memory, and Page Faults

Custer/Solomon describe the important concepts, and most OS texts provide good in-depth discussion.

Data Structures and Algorithms

Search trees and sort algorithms are explained in numerous texts, including the books by Standish and Sedgewick.

Using Explicit Linking

DLLs and explicit linking are fundamental to the operation of the Component Object Model (COM; see Chapter 15 for a very brief overview), which is widely used in Windows software development. Chapter 1 of Box's *Essential COM* shows the importance of `LoadLibrary` and `GetProcAddress`.

Exercises

6–1. Design and carry out experiments to evaluate the performance gains from the `HEAP_NO_SERIALIZE` flag with `HeapCreate` and `HeapAlloc`. How are the gains affected by the heap size and by the block size? Are there differences under Windows 2000/NT and Windows 9x? The distribution disc contains a program, `HeapNoSr.c`, to help you get started on this exercise and the next one.

6–2. Modify the test in the preceding exercise to determine whether `malloc` generates exceptions or returns a null pointer when there is no memory. Is this the correct behavior? Also compare `malloc` performance with the results from the preceding exercise.

6–3. Windows 2000/NT and Windows 9x differ significantly in terms of the overhead memory in a heap. You will find that you can allocate more fixed-size memory units with Windows 9x. Design and carry out an experiment to measure how many fixed-size blocks each system will give in a single heap. Using SEH to detect when all blocks have been allocated makes the program easier. On Windows 9x, you may notice that the mapping file will grow, consuming disc space, as your program allocates large amounts of memory. This disc space will be freed a few seconds after your program terminates. A test program, `clear.c`, on the book disc will show this behavior if the explicit OS test in the code is ignored.

6–4. Modify `sortFL` (Program 6–4) to create `sortHP`, which allocates a memory buffer large enough to hold the file, and read the file into that buffer. There is no memory mapping. Compare the performance of the two programs.

6–5. Program 6–5 exploits the `_based` pointers that are specific to Microsoft C. If you have a compiler that does not support this feature (or simply for the exercise), reimplement Program 6–5 with a macro, arrays, or some other mechanism to generate the based pointer values.

6–6. Write a search program that will find a record with a specified key in a file that has been indexed by Program 6–5. The C library `bsearch` function would be convenient here.

6–7. Implement the `tail` program (Program 3–1) with memory mapping.

6–8. Put the `ReportError`, `PrintStrings`, `PrintMsg`, and `ConsolePrompt` utility functions into a DLL and rebuild some of the earlier programs. Do the same with `Options` and `GetArgs`, the command line option and argument processing functions. It is important that both the utility DLL and the calling program also use the C library in DLL form. Within Visual C++ and the Developer Studio, select, from the title bar, Project ... Settings ... C/C++ tab ... Category (Code Generation) ... Use Run-Time Library (Multi-threaded DLL). Note that DLLs must, in general, be multithreaded because they will be used by threads from several processes.

6–9. Modify Program 6–7 so that the decision as to which DLL to use is based on the file size and system configuration. The `.LIB` file is not required, so figure out how to suppress `.LIB` file generation. Use `GetVolumeInforma-tion` to determine the file system type.

6–10. Create additional DLLs for the function, each one using a different file processing technique, and extend the calling program to decide when to use each version.

CHAPTER

7 | Process Management

A process contains its own independent virtual address space with both code and data, protected from other processes. Each process, in turn, contains one or more independently executed *threads*. A process can create new threads within the processes, create new, independent processes, and manage communication and synchronization between the objects.

By creating and managing processes, applications can have multiple, concurrent tasks in processing files, performing computations, or communicating with other networked systems. It is even possible to exploit multiple processors to speed processing.

This chapter will explain the basics of process management and will also introduce the basic synchronization operations that will be used throughout the rest of the book.

Windows Processes and Threads

Every process contains one or more threads, and the Windows thread is the basic executable unit. Threads are scheduled on the basis of the usual factors: availability of resources such as CPUs and physical memory, priority, fairness, and so on. Windows 2000 and NT support symmetric multiprocessing (SMP), so threads can be allocated to individual processors.

From the programmer's perspective, each Win32 process includes the following components:

- One or more threads.

- A virtual address space that is distinct from other processes' address spaces, except where memory is explicitly shared. Note that shared memory-mapped files share physical memory, but the sharing processes will use different virtual addresses to access the mapped file.

- One or more code segments, including code in DLLs.

- One or more data segments containing global variables.

- Environment strings with environment variable information, such as the current search path.

- The process heap.

- Resources such as open handles and other heaps.

Each thread in a process shares code, global variables, environment strings, and resources. Each thread is independently scheduled, and a thread has the following elements:

- A stack for procedure calls, interrupts, exception handlers, and automatic storage.

- Thread Local Storage (TLS)—arrays of pointers giving each thread the ability to allocate storage to create its own unique data environment.

- An argument on the stack, from the creating thread, which is usually unique for each thread.

- A context structure, maintained by the kernel, with machine register values.

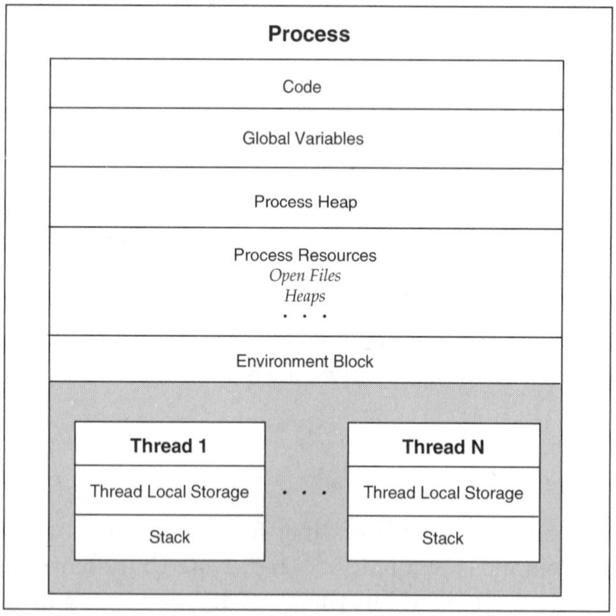

Figure 7-1   A Process and Its Threads

Figure 7–1 shows a process with several threads. This figure is schematic and does not indicate actual memory addresses, nor is it drawn to scale.

This chapter shows how to work with processes and a single thread. Chapter 8 will show how to use multiple threads.

Note: Figure 7–1 is a high-level overview from the programmer's perspective. There are numerous technical and implementation details, and the interested reader can find out more in the Custer/Solomon *Inside Windows NT* book.

A UNIX process is comparable to a Win32 process with a single thread.

Threads, in the form of POSIX Pthreads, are a recent addition to UNIX implementations and are now nearly universally used. Stevens does not discuss threads; everything is done with processes.

Needless to say, vendors and others have provided various thread implementations for many years; they are not a new concept. Pthreads is, however, the most widely used standard.

Process Creation

The fundamental Win32 process management function is `CreateProcess`, which creates a process with a single thread. Because a process requires code, it is necessary to specify the name of an executable program file as part of the `Create-Process` call.

It is common to speak of *parent* and *child* processes, but these relationships are not actually maintained by Win32. It is simply convenient to refer to the process that creates a child process as the parent.

`CreateProcess` has ten parameters to support its flexibility and power. Initially, it is simple to use default values. Just as with `CreateFile`, it is appropriate to explain all the `CreateProcess` parameters. Related functions then become easier to understand.

Notice first that the function does not return a HANDLE; rather, two separate handles, for the process and the thread, are returned in a structure specified in the call. `CreateProcess` creates a new process with a *primary* thread. The example programs are always very careful to close both of these handles when they are no longer needed in order to avoid resource leaks; a common defect is to neglect to close the thread handle. Closing a thread handle, for instance, does not terminate the thread; the `CloseHandle` function only deletes the reference to the thread.

```
BOOL CreateProcess (
    LPCTSTR lpszImageName,
    LPTSTR lpszCommandLine,
    LPSECURITY_ATTRIBUTES lpsaProcess,
    LPSECURITY_ATTRIBUTES lpsaThread,
    BOOL fInheritHandles,
    DWORD fdwCreate,
    LPVOID lpvEnvironment,
    LPCTSTR lpszCurDir,
    LPSTARTUPINFO lpsiStartInfo,
    LPPROCESS_INFORMATION lppiProcInfo)
```

Return: TRUE only if the process and thread are successfully created.

Parameters

Some parameters require extensive explanations in the following sections, and many are illustrated in the program examples.

`lpszImageName` and `lpszCommandLine` (this is an `LPTSTR` and not an `LPCTSTR`) together specify the executable program and the command line arguments, as explained in the next section.

`lpsaProcess` and `lpsaThread` point to the process and thread security attribute structures. `NULL` values imply default security.

`fInheritHandles` indicates whether the new process inherits copies of the calling process's inheritable open handles (files, mappings, and so on). Inherited handles have the same attributes as the originals and are discussed in detail in a later section.

`fdwCreate` combines several flags, including the following:

- `CREATE_SUSPENDED`—The primary thread is in a suspended state and will run only when `ResumeThread` is called.

- `DETACHED_PROCESS` and `CREATE_NEW_CONSOLE` are mutually exclusive; don't set both. The first flag creates a process without a console, and the second flag gives the new process a console. If neither flag is set, the process inherits the parent's console.

- `CREATE_NEW_PROCESS_GROUP` specifies that the new process is the root of a new process group. All processes in a group receive a console control signal

(Ctrl-c or Ctrl-break) if they all share the same console. Console control handlers were described in Chapter 4 and illustrated in Program 4–5. These process groups have similarities to UNIX process groups and are described later in this chapter.

Several of the flags control the priority of the new process's threads. The possible values are explained in more detail at the end of Chapter 8. For now, just use the parent's priority (specify nothing) or NORMAL_PRIORITY_CLASS.

lpvEnvironment points to an environment block for the new process. If NULL, the process uses the parent's environment. The environment block contains name and value strings, such as the search path.

lpszCurDir specifies the drive and directory for the new process. If NULL, the parent's working directory is used.

lpsiStartInfo specifies the main window appearance and standard device handles for the new process. Use the parent's information, which is obtained from GetStartupInfo. Alternatively, zero out the associated STARTUPINFO structure before calling CreateProcess. To specify the standard input, output, and error handles, set the standard handler fields (hStdIn, hStdOut, and hStdErr) in the STARTUPINFO structure. For this to be effective, also set another STARTUPINFO member, dwFlags, to STARTF_USESTDHANDLES, and set all the handles that the child process will require. Be certain that the handles are inheritable and that the CreateProcess fInheritHandles flag is set. The Inheritable Handles section gives more information.

lppiProcInfo specifies the structure for containing the returned process, thread handles, and identification. The PROCESS_INFORMATION structure is as follows:

```
typedef struct PROCESS_INFORMATION {
    HANDLE hProcess;
    HANDLE hThread;
    DWORD dwProcessId;
    DWORD dwThreadId;
} PROCESS_INFORMATION;
```

Why do processes and threads need handles in addition to IDs? The ID is unique to the object for its entire lifetime and in all processes, whereas a given process may have several handles, each having distinct attributes, such as security access. For this reason, some process management functions require IDs, and others require handles. Furthermore, process handles are required for the general-purpose, handle-based functions. Examples include the wait functions discussed later in this chapter, which allow waiting on handles for several different object types, including processes. *Note*: Just as with file handles, process and thread handles should be closed when no longer required.

Additional Note: The new process obtains environment, working directory, and other information from the `CreateProcess` call. Once this call is complete, any changes in the parent will not be reflected in the child process. For example, the parent might change its working directory after the `CreateProcess` call, but the child process working directory will not be affected, unless the child changes its own working directory. The two processes are entirely independent.

The UNIX and Win32 process models are considerably different. First, Win32 has no equivalent to the UNIX `fork` function, which makes a copy of the parent, including the parent's data space, heap, and stack. `fork` is difficult to emulate exactly in Win32, and, while this may seem to be a limitation, `fork` is also difficult to use in a multithreaded UNIX system, because there are numerous problems with creating an exact replica of a multithreaded system with exact copies of all threads and synchronization objects, especially on an SMP system. Therefore, `fork`, by itself, is not really appropriate in any multithreaded system.

`CreateProcess` is, however, similar to the common UNIX sequence of successive calls to `fork` and `execl` (or one of five other `exec` functions). In contrast to Win32, the search directories in UNIX are determined entirely by the `PATH` environment variable.

As previously mentioned, Win32 does not maintain parent-child relationships among processes. Thus, a child process will continue to run after the creating "parent" process terminates. Furthermore, there are no process groups in Win32. There is, however, a limited form of process group that specifies all the processes to receive a console control event.

Win32 processes are identified both by handles and by process IDs, whereas UNIX has no process handles.

Specifying the Executable Image and the Command Line

Either `lpszImageName` or `lpszCommandLine` specifies the executable image name. The rules are as follows:

- `lpszImageName`, if not NULL, is the name of the executable. Quotation marks can be used if the image name contains spaces. More detailed rules are described below.

- Otherwise, the executable is the first token in `lpszCommandLine`.

Usually, only `lpszCommandLine` is specified, with `lpszImageName` being NULL. Nonetheless, there are detailed rules for `lpszImageName`.

- If `lpszImageName` is not `NULL`, it specifies the executable module. Specify the full path and file name, or else use a partial name and the current drive and directory will be used; there is no additional searching. Include the file extension, such as `.EXE` or `.BAT`, in the name.

- If the `lpszImageName` string is `NULL`, the first white-space-delimited token in `lpszCommandLine` is the program name. If the name does not contain a full directory path, the search sequence is as follows:

  1. The directory of the current process's image.

  2. The current directory.

  3. The Windows system directory, which can be retrieved with `GetSystem-Directory`.

  4. The Windows directory, which is retrievable with `GetWindowsDirectory`.

  5. The directories as specified in the environment variable `PATH`.

The new process can obtain the command line using the usual `argv` mechanism, or it can invoke `GetCommandLine` to obtain the command line as a single string.

Notice that the command line is not a constant string. This is consistent with the fact that the `argv` parameters to the main program are not constant. A program could modify its arguments, although it is advisable to make any changes in a copy of the argument string.

The new process is not required to be built with the same `UNICODE` definition as that of the parent process. All combinations are possible. Using `_tmain` as discussed in Chapter 2 is helpful in developing portable code.

Inheritable Handles

Frequently, a child process requires access to an object referenced by a handle in the parent; if this handle is "inheritable," the child can receive a copy of the parent's open handle. The standard input and output handles are frequently shared with the child in this way. To make a handle inheritable so that a child receives and can use a copy requires several steps.

The `fInheritHandles` flag on the `CreateProcess` call determines whether the child process will inherit copies of the inheritable handles of open files, processes, and so on. The flag can be regarded as a master switch applying to all handles.

It is also necessary to make an individual handle inheritable; it is not done by default. To create an inheritable handle, use a `SECURITY_ATTRIBUTES` structure at creation time or duplicate an existing handle.

The SECURITY_ATTRIBUTES structure, introduced in Chapter 5, has a flag, bInheritHandle, that should be set to TRUE. Also, recall that nLength should be set to sizeof (SECURITY_ATTRIBUTES).

The following code segment shows how an inheritable file, or other, handle is typically created. In this example, the security descriptor within the security attributes structure is NULL, but, of course, a security descriptor could also be included.

```
HANDLE h1, h2, h3;
SECURITY_ATTRIBUTES sa =
    {sizeof(SECURITY_ATTRIBUTES), NULL, TRUE };
...
h1 = CreateFile (..., &sa, ... ); /* Inheritable. */
h2 = CreateFile (..., NULL, ... ); /* Not inheritable. */
h3 = CreateFile (..., &sa, ...);
    /* Inheritable. sa can be reused. */
```

A child process still needs to know the value of an inheritable handle, so the parent needs to communicate handle values to the child using an interprocess communication (IPC) mechanism or by assigning the handle to standard I/O in the STARTUPINFO structure, as is done in the next example (Program 7–1) and in several additional examples throughout the book. This is generally the preferred technique because it allows I/O redirection in a standard way and no changes are needed in the child program.

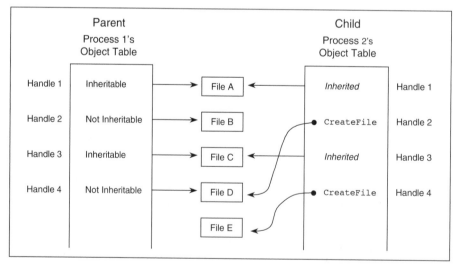

Figure 7-2   Process Handle Tables

Alternatively, nonfile handles and handles that are not used to redirect standard I/O can be converted to text and placed in a command line or in an environment variable. This approach is valid if the handle is inheritable, because both parent and child processes identify the handle with the same handle value. Exercise 7–2 suggests how to demonstrate this, and a solution is presented on the disc.

The inherited handles are distinct copies. Therefore, a parent and child might be accessing the same file using different file pointers. Furthermore, each of the two processes can, and should, close its own handle.

Figure 7–2 shows how two processes can have distinct handle tables with two distinct handles associated with the same file or other object. Process 1 is the parent, and Process 2 is the child. The handles will have identical values in both processes if the child's handle has been inherited, as is the case with Handles 1 and 3. On the other hand, the handle values may be distinct. For example, there are two handles for File D, where Process 2 obtained a handle by calling `CreateFile` rather than by inheritance. Finally, as is the case with Files B and E, one process may have a handle to an object while the other does not. This would be the case when the child process creates the handle or when a handle is duplicated from one process to another, as described in the forthcoming Duplicating Handles section.

Process Identities

A process can obtain the identity and handle of a new child process from the `PROCESS_INFORMATION` structure. Closing the child handle does not, of course, destroy the child process; it destroys only the parent's access to the child. A pair of functions is used to obtain current process identification.

```
HANDLE GetCurrentProcess (VOID)

DWORD GetCurrentProcessId (VOID)
```

`GetCurrentProcess` actually returns a *pseudohandle* and is not inheritable. This value can be used whenever a process needs its own handle. You create a real process handle from a process ID, including the one returned by `GetCurrentProcessId`, by using the `OpenProcess` function.

```
HANDLE OpenProcess (
    DWORD fdwAccess,
    BOOL fInherit,
    DWORD IDProcess)

Return: A process handle, or NULL on failure.
```

Parameters

fdwAccess determines the handle's access to the process. Some of the values are as follows:

- SYNCHRONIZE—This flag enables processes to wait for the process to terminate using the wait functions described later in this chapter.

- PROCESS_ALL_ACCESS—All the access flags are set.

- PROCESS_TERMINATE—It is possible to terminate the process with the TerminateProcess function.

- PROCESS_QUERY_INFORMATION—The handle can be used by GetExit-CodeProcess and GetPriorityClass to obtain process information.

fInherit specifies whether the new handle is inheritable. IDProcess is the identifier of the process requiring a handle.

Finally, a running process can determine the executable used to run it using GetModuleFileName, using a NULL value for the hModule parameter. A call from within a DLL will return the DLL's file name, not that of the .EXE file that uses the DLL.

Duplicating Handles

The parent and child processes may require different access to an object identified by a handle that the child inherits. A process may also need a real, inheritable process handle—rather than the pseudohandle produced by GetCurrent-Process—for use by a child process. To address this issue, the parent process can create a duplicate handle with the desired access and inheritability. Here is the function to duplicate handles:

```
BOOL DuplicateHandle (
    HANDLE hSourceProcess,
    HANDLE hSource,
    HANDLE hTargetProcess,
    LPHANDLE lphTarget,
    DWORD fdwAccess,
    BOOL fInherit,
    DWORD fdwOptions)
```

Upon completion, `lphTarget` points to a copy of the original handle, `hSource`. `hSource` is a handle in the process indicated by `hSourceProcess` and must have `PROCESS_DUP_HANDLE` access. The new handle, which is pointed to by `lphTarget`, is valid in the target process, `hTargetProcess`. Three processes are involved, including the calling process. Frequently, these target and source processes are the calling process, and the handle is obtained from `GetCurrentProcess`. Notice that it is possible to create a handle in another process; if you do this, you then need a mechanism for informing the other process of the new handle's identity.

`DuplicateHandle` can be used for any handle type.

If `fdwAccess` is not overridden by `DUPLICATE_SAME_ACCESS` in `fdwOptions`, it has many possible values (see the MSDN library on-line help).

`fdwOptions` is any combination of two flags:

- `DUPLICATE_CLOSE_SOURCE` causes the source handle to be closed.
- `DUPLICATE_SAME_ACCESS` causes `fdwAccess` to be ignored.

Next, it is necessary to learn how to determine whether a process has terminated.

Exiting and Terminating a Process

After a process is complete, it can call `ExitProcess` with an exit code.

```
VOID ExitProcess (UINT nExitCode)
```

This function does not return. Rather, the calling process and all its threads terminate. Termination handlers are ignored, but there will be detach calls to `DllMain` (see Chapter 6). The exit code is associated with the process. *Windows CE Note*: Windows CE does not support `ExitProcess`; a main program can use the `return` statement.

Another process can use `GetExitCodeProcess` to determine the exit code.

```
BOOL GetExitCodeProcess (
    HANDLE hProcess,
    LPDWORD lpdwExitCode)
```

The process identified by `hProcess` must have `PROCESS_QUERY_INFORMATION` access (see `OpenProcess`). `lpdwExitCode` points to the `DWORD` that receives the value. One possible value is `STILL_ACTIVE`, meaning that the process has not terminated.

Finally, one process can terminate another process if the handle has `PROCESS_TERMINATE` access. The terminating function also specifies the exit code.

```
BOOL TerminateProcess (
    HANDLE hProcess,
    UINT uExitCode)
```

Caution: Before exiting from a process, be certain to free all resources that might be shared with other processes. In particular, the synchronization resources of Chapter 9 (mutexes, semaphores, and events) must be handled carefully. SEH (Chapter 4) can be helpful in this regard, and the `ExitProcess` call can be in the handler. However, __finally and __except handlers are *not* executed when `ExitProcess` is called, so it is not a good idea to exit from inside a program. `TerminateProcess` is especially risky, because the terminated process will not have an opportunity to execute its SEH or DLL *DllMain* functions. Console control handlers (Chapter 4 and later in this chapter) are a limited alternative, allowing one process to send a signal to another process, which can then shut itself down cleanly.

Program 7–3 shows a technique whereby processes cooperate. One process sends a shutdown request to a second process, which proceeds to perform an orderly shutdown.

UNIX processes have a process ID, or `pid`, comparable to the Win32 process ID. `getpid` is similar to `GetCurrentProcessId`, but there are no Win32 equivalents to `getppid` and `getgpid` because Win32 has no process parents or groups.

Conversely, UNIX does not have process handles, so it has no functions comparable to `GetCurrentProcess` or `OpenProcess`.

UNIX allows open file descriptors to be used after an `exec` if the file descriptor does not have the `close-on-exec` flag set. This applies only to file descriptors, which are then comparable to inheritable file handles.

UNIX `exit`, actually in the C library, is similar to `ExitProcess`; to terminate another process, signal it with `SIGKILL`.

Waiting for a Process to Terminate

The simplest, and most limited, method of synchronizing with another process is to wait for that process to complete. The general-purpose Win32 wait functions introduced here have several interesting features.

- The functions can wait for many different types of objects; process handles are just the first use of the wait functions.

- The functions can wait for a single process, the first of several specified processes, or all processes in a group to complete.

- There is an optional time-out period.

The two general-purpose wait functions, which will get lots of future use, are as follows:

```
DWORD WaitForSingleObject (
    HANDLE hObject,
    DWORD dwTimeOut)
```

```
DWORD WaitForMultipleObjects (
    DWORD cObjects,
    LPHANDLE lphObjects,
    BOOL fWaitAll,
    DWORD dwTimeOut)
```

Return: The cause of the wait completion, or 0XFFFFFFFF for an error (use GetLastError for more information).

Specify either a single process handle (hObject) or an array of distinct objects in the array referenced by lphObjects. cObjects, the size of the array, should not exceed MAXIMUM_WAIT_OBJECTS (currently defined as 64 in WINNT.H).

dwTimeOut is in milliseconds. A value of 0 means that the function returns immediately after testing the state of the specified objects, thus allowing a program to poll for process termination. Use INFINITE for no time-out to wait until a process terminates.

fWaitAll, a parameter of the second function, specifies (if TRUE) that it is necessary to wait for all processes, rather than only one, to terminate.[1] *Windows CE Note*: Windows CE only supports FALSE for this flag.

The possible successful return values for this function are as follows:

- WAIT_OBJECT_0 means that the process terminated either in the case of WaitForSingleObject or in a special case of WaitForMultipleObjects with fWaitAll set to TRUE.

- WAIT_OBJECT_0+n, where $0 \leq n < $ cObjects. Subtract WAIT_OBJECT_0 from the return value to determine which process terminated when waiting for any of a group of processes to terminate. If several handles are signaled, the returned value is the smallest possible value of n. WAIT_ABANDONED_0 is a possible base value when using mutex handles; see Chapter 9.

- WAIT_TIMEOUT indicates that the time-out period elapsed before the wait could be satisfied.

- WAIT_FAILED indicates that the call failed; for example, the handle may not have SYNCHRONIZE access.

- WAIT_ABANDONED_0 is not possible with processes. This value is discussed in Chapter 9 along with mutex handles.

---

[1] In general, these functions wait for *synchronization objects* to become *signaled*. A process handle is set by the system to the signaled state when the process terminates.

Determine the exit code of a process using `GetExitCodeProcess`, as described in the preceding section.

Environment Blocks and Strings

Figure 7–1 includes the process environment block. The environment block contains a sequence of strings of the form

```
Name = Value
```

Each environment string, being a string, is NULL-terminated, and the entire block of strings is itself NULL-terminated. PATH is one example of a commonly used environment variable.

To pass the parent's environment to a child process, set `lpvEnvironment` to NULL in the `CreateProcess` call. Any process, in turn, can interrogate or modify its environment variables or add new environment variables to the block.

The two functions used to get and set variables are as follows:

```
DWORD GetEnvironmentVariable (
    LPCTSTR lpszName,
    LPTSTR lpszValue,
    DWORD cchValue)

BOOL SetEnvironmentVariable (
    LPCTSTR lpszName,
    LPCTSTR lpszValue)
```

`lpszName` is the variable name. On setting a value, the variable is added to the block if it does not exist and if the value is not NULL. If, on the other hand, the value is NULL, the variable is removed from the block. The "=" character cannot appear in a value string.

`GetEnvironmentVariable` returns the length of the value string, or 0 on failure. If the `lpszValue` buffer is not long enough, as indicated by `cchValue`, then the return value is the number of characters actually required to hold the complete string. Recall that `GetCurrentDirectory` (Chapter 2) uses a similar mechanism.

Process Security

Normally, `CreateProcess` gives `PROCESS_ALL_ACCESS` rights. There are, however, several specific rights, including `PROCESS_QUERY_INFORMATION`, `CREATE_PROCESS`, `PROCESS_TERMINATE`, `PROCESS_SET_INFORMATION`, `DUPLICATE_HANDLE`, and `CREATE_THREAD`. In particular, it can be useful to limit `PROCESS_TERMINATE` rights to the parent process given the frequently mentioned dangers of terminating a running process.

UNIX waits for process termination using `wait` and `waitpid`, but there are no time-outs even though `waitpid` can poll (there is a nonblocking option). These functions wait only for child processes, and there is no equivalent to the multiple wait on a collection of processes, although it is possible to wait for all processes in a process group. One slight difference is that the exit code is returned with `wait` and `waitpid`, so there is no need for a separate function equivalent to `GetExitCodeProcess`.

UNIX also supports environment strings similar to those in Win32. `getenv` (in the C library) has the same functionality as `GetEnvironmentVariable` except that the programmer must be sure to have a sufficiently large buffer. `putenv`, `setenv`, and `unsetenv` (not in the C library) are different ways to add, change, and remove variables and their values, with functionality equivalent to `SetEnvironmentVariable`.

Example: Parallel Pattern Searching

Now is the time to put Win32 processes to the test. This example, `grepMP`, creates processes to search for patterns in files, one process per search file. The pattern search program is modeled after the UNIX `grep` utility, although the technique would apply to any program that uses standard output. The search program should be regarded as a black box and is simply an executable program to be controlled by a parent process.

The command line to the program is of the form

```
grepMP pattern F1 F2 ... FN
```

The program, Program 7–1, performs the following processing:

- Each input file, `F1` to `FN`, is searched using a separate process running the same executable. The program creates a command line of the form `grep pattern FK`.

- The handle of the temporary file, specified to be inheritable, is assigned to the `hStdOut` field of the new process's start-up information structure.

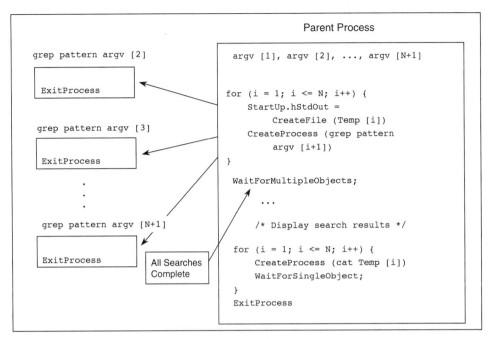

Figure 7-3　File Searching Using Multiple Processes

- Using `WaitForMultipleObjects`, the program waits for all search processes to complete.

- As soon as all searches are complete, the results (temporary files) are displayed in order, one at a time. A process to execute the `cat` utility (see Chapter 2) outputs the temporary file.

- `WaitForMultipleObjects` is limited to `MAXIMUM_WAIT_OBJECTS` (64) handles, so it is called multiple times.

- The program uses the `grep` process exit code to determine whether a specific process detected the pattern.

Figure 7–3 shows the processing performed by Program 7–1.

Program 7–1　`grepMP`: Parallel Searching

```
/* Chapter 7. grepMP. */
/* Multiple process version of grep command. */

#include "EvryThng.h"
int _tmain (DWORD argc, LPTSTR argv [])
```

```
    /* Create a separate process to search each file on the
       command line. Each process is given a temporary file,
       in the current directory, to receive the results. */
{
    HANDLE hTempFile;
    SECURITY_ATTRIBUTES StdOutSA = /* SA for inheritable handle. */
        {sizeof (SECURITY_ATTRIBUTES), NULL, TRUE};
    TCHAR CommandLine [MAX_PATH + 100];
    STARTUPINFO StartUpSearch, StartUp;
    PROCESS_INFORMATION ProcessInfo;
    DWORD iProc, ExCode;
    HANDLE *hProc; /* Pointer to an array of proc handles. */
    typedef struct {TCHAR TempFile [MAX_PATH];} PROCFILE;
    PROCFILE *ProcFile; /* Pointer to array of temp file names. */

    GetStartupInfo (&StartUpSearch);
    GetStartupInfo (&StartUp);
    ProcFile = malloc ((argc - 2) * sizeof (PROCFILE));
    hProc = malloc ((argc - 2) * sizeof (HANDLE));

    /* Create a separate "grep" process for each file. */
    for (iProc = 0; iProc < argc - 2; iProc++) {
        _stprintf (CommandLine, _T ("%s%s %s"),
            _T ("grep "), argv [1], argv [iProc + 2]);
        GetTempFileName (_T ("."), _T ("gtm"), 0,
            ProcFile [iProc].TempFile); /* For search results. */
        hTempFile = /* This handle is inheritable */
            CreateFile (ProcFile [iProc].TempFile,
                GENERIC_WRITE,
                FILE_SHARE_READ | FILE_SHARE_WRITE, &StdOutSA,
                CREATE_ALWAYS, FILE_ATTRIBUTE_NORMAL, NULL);
        StartUpSearch.dwFlags = STARTF_USESTDHANDLES;
        StartUpSearch.hStdOutput = hTempFile;
        StartUpSearch.hStdError = hTempFile;
        StartUpSearch.hStdInput = GetStdHandle (STD_INPUT_HANDLE);

        /* Create a process to execute the command line. */
        CreateProcess (NULL, CommandLine, NULL, NULL,
            TRUE, 0, NULL, NULL, &StartUpSearch, &ProcessInfo);
        /* Close unwanted handles. */
        CloseHandle (hTempFile); CloseHandle (ProcessInfo.hThread);
        hProc [iProc] = ProcessInfo.hProcess;
    }

    /* Processes are all running. Wait for them to complete. */
    for (iProc = 0; iProc < argc - 2; iProc += MAXIMUM_WAIT_OBJECTS)
        WaitForMultipleObjects ( /* Allows a large # of processes */
            min (MAXIMUM_WAIT_OBJECTS, argc - 2 - iProc),
            &hProc [iProc], TRUE, INFINITE);
    /* Result files sent to std output using "cat." */
```

```
    for (iProc = 0; iProc < argc - 2; iProc++) {
        if (GetExitCodeProcess(hProc [iProc], &ExCode) && ExCode==0) {
            /* Pattern was detected - List results. */
            if (argc > 3) _tprintf (_T ("%s:\n"), argv [iProc + 2]);
            fflush (stdout); /* Multiple processes use stdout. */
            _stprintf (CommandLine, _T ("%s%s"),
                    _T ("cat "), ProcFile [iProc].TempFile);
            CreateProcess (NULL, CommandLine, NULL, NULL,
                    TRUE, 0, NULL, NULL, &StartUp, &ProcessInfo);
            WaitForSingleObject (ProcessInfo.hProcess, INFINITE);
            CloseHandle (ProcessInfo.hProcess);
            CloseHandle (ProcessInfo.hThread);
        }

        CloseHandle (hProc [iProc]);
        DeleteFile (ProcFile [iProc].TempFile);
    }
    free (ProcFile);
    free (hProc);
    return 0;
}
```

Process Execution Times

You can determine the amount of time that a process requires (elapsed, kernel, and user times) using the GetProcessTimes function, which is available only with Windows 2000/NT.

```
BOOL GetProcessTimes (
    HANDLE hProcess,
    LPFILETIME lpCreationTime,
    LPFILETIME lpExitTime,
    LPFILETIME lpKernelTime,
    LPFILETIME lpUserTime)
```

The process handle can refer to a process that is still running or to one that has terminated. Elapsed time can be computed by subtracting the creation time from the exit time, as shown in the next example. The FILETIME type is a 64-bit item; create a union with a LARGE_INTEGER to perform the subtraction. The ls example in Chapter 3 showed how to convert and display file times.

GetThreadTimes is similar and requires a thread handle for a parameter. The next chapter covers thread management.

Example: Process Execution Times

The next example (Program 7–2) is a command called timep (time print) that is similar to the UNIX time command.[2] Elapsed, kernel, and system times can be printed, although only elapsed time is available on systems other than Windows 2000 and NT.

One use for this command is to compare the execution times and efficiencies of the various file copy and ASCII to Unicode functions implemented in previous chapters.

This program uses GetCommandLine, a Win32 function that returns the complete command line as a single string rather than individual argv strings. This function does not operate on Windows CE, so this problem would need to be modified to use the argv [ ] array if you need to run on CE.

The program also uses a utility function, SkipArg, to scan the command line and skip past the executable name. The SkipArg listing is in Appendix A.

Program 7–2 uses the GetVersionEx function to determine the OS version. With Windows 9x and CE, only the elapsed time is available.

Program 7–2   timep: Process Times

```
/* Chapter 7. timep. */

#include "EvryThng.h"
int _tmain (int argc, LPTSTR argv [])
{
    STARTUPINFO StartUp;
    PROCESS_INFORMATION ProcInfo;
    union { /* Structure required for file time arithmetic. */
        LONGLONG li;
        FILETIME ft;
    } CreateTime, ExitTime, ElapsedTime;
    FILETIME KernelTime, UserTime;
    SYSTEMTIME ElTiSys, KeTiSys, UsTiSys, StartTimeSys, ExitTimeSys;
    LPTSTR targv = SkipArg (GetCommandLine ());
    OSVERSIONINFO OSVer;
    BOOL Is2000NT;
    HANDLE hProc;
```

---

[2] time is supported by the command prompt, so a different name is required.

```
    OSVer.dwOSVersionInfoSize = sizeof(OSVERSIONINFO);
    GetVersionEx (&OSVer);
    Is2000NT = (OSVer.dwPlatformId == VER_PLATFORM_WIN32_NT);
    /* W2000 returns VER_PLATFORM_WIN32_NT. */
    GetStartupInfo (&StartUp);
    GetSystemTime (&StartTimeSys);

    /* Execute the command line; wait for process to complete. */
    CreateProcess (NULL, targv, NULL, NULL, TRUE,
            NORMAL_PRIORITY_CLASS, NULL, NULL, &StartUp, &ProcInfo);

    /* Assure that we have all REQUIRED access to the process. */
    DuplicateHandle (GetCurrentProcess (), ProcInfo.hProcess,
            GetCurrentProcess (), &hProc,
            PROCESS_QUERY_INFORMATION | SYNCHRONIZE, FALSE, 0);
    WaitForSingleObject (hProc, INFINITE);
    GetSystemTime (&ExitTimeSys);

    if (Is2000NT) { /* W 2000/NT. Elapsed, Kernel, & User times. */
        GetProcessTimes (hProc, &CreateTime.ft,
                &ExitTime.ft, &KernelTime, &UserTime);
        ElapsedTime.li = ExitTime.li - CreateTime.li;
        FileTimeToSystemTime (&ElapsedTime.ft, &ElTiSys);
        FileTimeToSystemTime (&KernelTime, &KeTiSys);
        FileTimeToSystemTime (&UserTime, &UsTiSys);
        _tprintf (_T ("Real Time: %02d:%02d:%02d:%03d\n"),
                ElTiSys.wHour, ElTiSys.wMinute, ElTiSys.wSecond,
                ElTiSys.wMilliseconds);
        _tprintf (_T ("User Time: %02d:%02d:%02d:%03d\n"),
                UsTiSys.wHour, UsTiSys.wMinute, UsTiSys.wSecond,
                UsTiSys.wMilliseconds);
        _tprintf (_T ("Sys Time: %02d:%02d:%02d:%03d\n"),
                KeTiSys.wHour, KeTiSys.wMinute, KeTiSys.wSecond,
                KeTiSys.wMilliseconds);
    } else {
        /* Windows 9x and CE. Elapsed time only. */
        SystemTimeToFileTime (&StartTimeSys, &CreateTime.ft);
        SystemTimeToFileTime (&ExitTimeSys, &ExitTime.ft);
        ElapsedTime.li = ExitTime.li - CreateTime.li;
        FileTimeToSystemTime (&ElapsedTime.ft, &ElTiSys);
        _tprintf (_T ("Real Time: %02d:%02d:%02d:%03d\n"),
                ElTiSys.wHour, ElTiSys.wMinute, ElTiSys.wSecond,
                ElTiSys.wMilliseconds);
    }
    CloseHandle (ProcInfo.hThread);
    CloseHandle (ProcInfo.hProcess);
    CloseHandle (hProc);
    return 0;
}
```

Using the `timep` Command

`timep` can now be used to compare the various ASCII to Unicode file copy and sorting utilities such as `atou` in Chapter 2 and `sortMM` in Chapter 6. Appendix C summarizes and briefly analyzes some results.

Notice that measuring a program such as `grepMP` (Program 7–1) gives kernel and user times only for the parent process. Job objects, described near the end of this chapter, allow you to collect information on a group of processes. Appendix C shows that, on an SMP system, performance can improve as the separate processes, or, more accurately, threads, run on different processors. There can also be performance gains if the files are on different physical drives.

Generating Console Control Events

Terminating a process can cause problems, because the terminated process cannot clean up. SEH does not help, because there is no way for one process to cause an exception in another. Console control events (not supported on Windows CE), however, allow one process to send a console control signal, or event, to another process. Program 4–5 illustrated how a process can set up a handler to catch such a signal. In that example, the user generated a signal from the user interface.

It is possible for a process to generate a signal event in another specified process or set of processes. Recall the `CreateProcess` creation flag value, `CREATE_NEW_PROCESS_GROUP`. If this flag is set, the new process ID identifies a group of processes, and the new process is the *root* of the group. All new processes created by the parent are in this new group until another `CreateProcess` call uses the `CREATE_NEW_PROCESS_GROUP` flag. The grouped processes are similar to UNIX process groups.

One process can generate a `CTRL_C_EVENT` or `CTRL_BREAK_EVENT` in a specified process group, identifying the group with the root process ID. The target processes must have the same console as that of the process generating the event. In particular, the calling process cannot be created with its own console (using the `CREATE_NEW_CONSOLE` or `DETACHED_PROCESS` flag).

```
BOOL GenerateConsoleCtrlEvent (
    DWORD dwCtrlEvent,
    DWORD dwProcessGroup)
```

The first parameter, then, must be one of either `CTRL_C_EVENT` or `CTRL_BREAK_EVENT`. The second parameter identifies the process group.

Example: Simple Job Management

UNIX shells provide commands to execute processes in the background and to obtain their current status. This section develops a simple "job shell" with a similar set of commands. The commands are as follows:

- `jobbg` uses the remaining part of the command line as the command line for a new process, or *job*, but the `jobbg` command returns immediately rather than waiting for the new process to complete. The new process is optionally given its own console, or is *detached*, so that it has no console at all. This approach is similar to running a UNIX command with the & option at the end.

- `jobs` lists the current active jobs, giving the job numbers and process IDs. This is similar to the UNIX command of the same name.

- `kill` terminates a job. This implementation will use the `TerminateProcess` function, which, as previously stated, does not provide a clean shutdown. There is also an option to send a console control signal.

It is straightforward to create additional commands for suspending existing jobs or moving them to the foreground.

Because the shell, which maintains the job list, may terminate, the shell employs a user-specific shared file to contain the process IDs, the command, and related information. In this way, the shell can restart and the job list will still be intact. Furthermore, several shells can run concurrently. An exercise places this information in the registry, rather than in a temporary file.

Concurrency issues will arise. Several processes, running from separate command prompts, might perform job control simultaneously. The job management functions use file locking (Chapter 3) on the job list file so that a user can invoke job management from separate shells or processes.

`JobShell` will be the basis for a more general "service shell" in Chapter 13. NT services are background processes, usually servers, that can be controlled with start, stop, pause, and other commands.

Creating a Background Job

Program 7–3 is the job shell that prompts the user for one of three commands and then carries out the command. This program uses a collection of job management functions, which are shown in Programs 7–4, 7–5, and 7–6.

Program 7–3 JobShell: Create, List, and Kill Background Jobs

```
/* Chapter 7. */
/* JobShell.c - job management commands:
    jobbg - Run a job in the background.
    jobs - List all background jobs.
    kill - Terminate a specified job of job family.
          There is an option to generate a console control signal. */

#include "EvryThng.h"
#include "JobMgt.h"

int _tmain (int argc, LPTSTR argv [])
{
    BOOL Exit = FALSE;
    TCHAR Command [MAX_COMMAND_LINE + 10], *pc;
    DWORD i, LocArgc; /* Local argc. */
    TCHAR argstr [MAX_ARG] [MAX_COMMAND_LINE];
    LPTSTR pArgs [MAX_ARG];

    for (i = 0; i < MAX_ARG; i++) pArgs [i] = argstr [i];

    /* Prompt user, read command, and execute it. */
    _tprintf (_T ("Windows Job Management\n"));
    while (!Exit) {
        _tprintf (_T ("%s"), _T ("JM$"));
        _fgetts (Command, MAX_COMMAND_LINE, stdin);
        pc = strchr (Command, '\n');
        *pc = '\0';
        /* Parse the input to obtain command line for new job. */
        GetArgs (Command, &LocArgc, pArgs); /* See Appendix A. */
        CharLower (argstr [0]);

        if (_tcscmp (argstr [0], _T ("jobbg")) == 0) {
            Jobbg (LocArgc, pArgs, Command);
        }
        else if (_tcscmp (argstr [0], _T ("jobs")) == 0) {
            Jobs (LocArgc, pArgs, Command);
        }
        else if (_tcscmp (argstr [0], _T ("kill")) == 0) {
            Kill (LocArgc, pArgs, Command);
        }
        else if (_tcscmp (argstr [0], _T ("quit")) == 0) {
            Exit = TRUE;
        }
        else _tprintf (_T ("Illegal command. Try again\n"));
    }
    return 0;
}
```

```
/* jobbg [options] command-line [Options are mutually exclusive]
      -c: Give the new process a console.
      -d: The new process is detached, with no console.
      If neither is set, the process shares console with jobbg. */

int Jobbg (int argc, LPTSTR argv [], LPTSTR Command)
{
    DWORD fCreate;
    LONG JobNo;
    BOOL Flags [2];
    STARTUPINFO StartUp;
    PROCESS_INFORMATION ProcessInfo;
    LPTSTR targv = SkipArg (Command);

    GetStartupInfo (&StartUp);
    Options (argc, argv, _T ("cd"), &Flags [0], &Flags [1], NULL);
        /* Skip over the option field as well, if it exists. */
    if (argv [1] [0] == '-') targv = SkipArg (targv);

    fCreate = Flags [0] ? CREATE_NEW_CONSOLE :
          Flags [1] ? DETACHED_PROCESS : 0;

        /* Create job/thread suspended. Resume once job entered. */
    CreateProcess (NULL, targv, NULL, NULL, TRUE,
          fCreate | CREATE_SUSPENDED | CREATE_NEW_PROCESS_GROUP,
          NULL, NULL, &StartUp, &ProcessInfo);
        /* Create a job number and enter the process ID and handle
          into the job "data base." */

    JobNo = GetJobNumber (&ProcessInfo, targv); /* See "job mgt." */
    if (JobNo >= 0)
        ResumeThread (ProcessInfo.hThread);
    else {
        TerminateProcess (ProcessInfo.hProcess, 3);
        CloseHandle (ProcessInfo.hProcess);
        ReportError (_T ("Error: No room in job list."), 0, FALSE);
        return 5;
    }
    CloseHandle (ProcessInfo.hThread);
    CloseHandle (ProcessInfo.hProcess);
    _tprintf (_T (" [%d] %d\n"), JobNo, ProcessInfo.dwProcessId);
    return 0;
}

/* jobs: List all running or stopped jobs. */
int Jobs (int argc, LPTSTR argv [], LPTSTR Command)
{
    if (!DisplayJobs ()) return 1; /* See job mgmt functions. */
    return 0;
}
```

```
/* kill [options] JobNumber
   -b Generate a Ctrl-Break
   -c Generate a Ctrl-C
      Otherwise, terminate the process. */

int Kill (int argc, LPTSTR argv [], LPTSTR Command)
{
    DWORD ProcessId, JobNumber, iJobNo;
    HANDLE hProcess;
    BOOL CntrlC, CntrlB, Killed;

    iJobNo =
        Options (argc, argv, _T ("bc"), &CntrlB, &CntrlC, NULL);

    /* Find the process ID associated with this job. */
    JobNumber = _ttoi (argv [1]);
    ProcessId = FindProcessId (JobNumber); /* See job mgmt. */
    hProcess = OpenProcess (PROCESS_ALL_ACCESS, FALSE, ProcessId);
    if (hProcess == NULL) { /* Process ID may not be in use. */
        ReportError (_T ("Process already terminated.\n"), 0, FALSE);
        return 2;
    }
    if (CntrlB)
        GenerateConsoleCtrlEvent (CTRL_BREAK_EVENT, ProcessId);
    else if (CntrlC)
        GenerateConsoleCtrlEvent (CTRL_C_EVENT, ProcessId);
    else
        TerminateProcess (hProcess, JM_EXIT_CODE);

    WaitForSingleObject (hProcess, 5000);
    CloseHandle (hProcess);
    _tprintf (_T ("Job [%d] terminated or timed out\n"), JobNumber);
    return 0;
}
```

Notice how the jobbg command creates the process in the suspended state and then calls the job management function, GetJobNumber (Program 7–4), to get a new job number and to register the job and its associated process. If the job cannot be registered for any reason, the job's process is terminated immediately. Normally, the job number is generated correctly, and the primary thread is resumed and allowed to run.

Getting a Job Number

The next three programs show three individual job management functions. These functions are all included in a single source file, JobMgt.c.

The first, Program 7–4, shows the `GetJobNumber` function. Notice the use of file locking with a completion handler to unlock the file. This technique protects against exceptions and inadvertent transfers around the unlock call. Such a transfer might be inserted accidentally during code maintenance even if the original program is correct.

Program 7–4   `JobMgt`: Creating New Job Information

```
/* Job management utility function. */
/* As implemented, these functions use LockFileEx and will not
   work under Windows 9x. Use LockFile for Windows 9x operation,
   in which case all locks will be exclusive. */

#include "EvryThng.h"
#include "JobMgt.h" /* Listed in Appendix A. */
void GetJobMgtFileName (LPTSTR);
LONG GetJobNumber (PROCESS_INFORMATION *pProcessInfo,
      LPCTSTR Command)

/* Create a job number for the new process, and enter
   the new process information into the job database. */
{
    HANDLE hJobData, hProcess;
    JM_JOB JobRecord;
    DWORD JobNumber = 0, nXfer, ExitCode, FsLow, FsHigh;
    TCHAR JobMgtFileName [MAX_PATH];
    OVERLAPPED RegionStart;

    if (!GetJobMgtFileName (JobMgtFileName)) return -1;
                /* Produces "\tmp\UserName.JobMgt" */
    hJobData = CreateFile (JobMgtFileName,
        GENERIC_READ | GENERIC_WRITE,
        FILE_SHARE_READ | FILE_SHARE_WRITE,
        NULL, OPEN_ALWAYS, FILE_ATTRIBUTE_NORMAL, NULL);
    if (hJobData == INVALID_HANDLE_VALUE) return -1;

    /* Lock the entire file plus one possible new
       record for exclusive access. */

    RegionStart.Offset = 0;
    RegionStart.OffsetHigh = 0;
    RegionStart.hEvent = (HANDLE)0;
    FsLow = GetFileSize (hJobData, &FsHigh);
    LockFileEx (hJobData, LOCKFILE_EXCLUSIVE_LOCK,
            0, FsLow + SJM_JOB, 0, &RegionStart);

    __try {
                /* Read records to find empty slot. */
```

```
        while (ReadFile (hJobData, &JobRecord, SJM_JOB, &nXfer, NULL)
                && (nXfer > 0)) {
            if (JobRecord.ProcessId == 0) break;
            hProcess = OpenProcess(PROCESS_ALL_ACCESS,
                    FALSE, JobRecord.ProcessId);
            if (hProcess == NULL) break;
            if (GetExitCodeProcess (hProcess, &ExitCode)
                    && (ExitCode != STILL_ACTIVE)) break;
            JobNumber++;
        }

        /* Either an empty slot has been found, or we are at end
            of the file and need to create a new one. */

        if (nXfer != 0) /* Not at end of file. Back up. */
            SetFilePointer (hJobData, -(LONG)SJM_JOB,
                    NULL, FILE_CURRENT);
        JobRecord.ProcessId = pProcessInfo->dwProcessId;
        _tcsnccpy (JobRecord.CommandLine, Command, MAX_PATH);
        WriteFile (hJobData, &JobRecord, SJM_JOB, &nXfer, NULL);
    } /* End try. */

    __finally {
        UnlockFileEx (hJobData, 0, FsLow + SJM_JOB, 0,
                &RegionStart);
        CloseHandle (hJobData);
    }
    return JobNumber + 1;
}
```

Listing Background Jobs

Program 7–5 shows the `DisplayJobs` job management function.

Program 7-5   `JobMgt`: Displaying Active Jobs

```
BOOL DisplayJobs (void)

/* Scan the job database file, reporting job status. */
{
    HANDLE hJobData, hProcess;
    JM_JOB JobRecord;
    DWORD JobNumber = 0, nXfer, ExitCode, FsLow, FsHigh;
    TCHAR JobMgtFileName [MAX_PATH];
    OVERLAPPED RegionStart;

    GetJobMgtFileName (JobMgtFileName);
```

```
    hJobData = CreateFile (JobMgtFileName,
            GENERIC_READ | GENERIC_WRITE,
            FILE_SHARE_READ | FILE_SHARE_WRITE,
            NULL, OPEN_EXISTING, FILE_ATTRIBUTE_NORMAL, NULL);

    RegionStart.Offset = 0;
    RegionStart.OffsetHigh = 0;
    RegionStart.hEvent = (HANDLE)0;
    FsLow = GetFileSize (hJobData, &FsHigh);
    LockFileEx (hJobData, LOCKFILE_EXCLUSIVE_LOCK,
            0, FsLow, FsHigh, &RegionStart);

    __try {
    while (ReadFile (hJobData, &JobRecord, SJM_JOB, &nXfer, NULL)
            && (nXfer > 0)){
        JobNumber++;
        if (JobRecord.ProcessId == 0)
            continue;
        hProcess = OpenProcess (PROCESS_ALL_ACCESS, FALSE,
                JobRecord.ProcessId);
        if (hProcess != NULL)
            GetExitCodeProcess (hProcess, &ExitCode);
        _tprintf (_T (" [%d] "), JobNumber);
        if (hProcess == NULL)
            _tprintf (_T (" Done"));
        else if (ExitCode != STILL_ACTIVE)
            _tprintf (_T ("+ Done"));
        else _tprintf (_T (" "));
        _tprintf (_T (" %s\n"), JobRecord.CommandLine);

        /* Remove processes that are no longer in system. */

        if (hProcess == NULL) { /* Back up one record. */
            SetFilePointer (hJobData, -(LONG)nXfer,
                    NULL, FILE_CURRENT);
            JobRecord.ProcessId = 0;
            WriteFile (hJobData, &JobRecord, SJM_JOB, &nXfer, NULL);
        }
    } /* End of while. */
    } /* End of __try. */

    __finally {
        UnlockFileEx (hJobData, 0, FsLow, FsHigh, &RegionStart);
        CloseHandle (hJobData);
    }

    return TRUE;
}
```

Finding a Job in the Job List file

Program 7–6 shows the final job management function, `FindProcessId`, which obtains the process ID of a specified job number. The process ID, in turn, can be used by the calling program to obtain a handle and other process status information.

Program 7–6   JobMgt: Getting the Process ID from a Job Number

```
DWORD FindProcessId (DWORD JobNumber)

/* Obtain the process ID of the specified job number. */
{
    HANDLE hJobData;
    JM_JOB JobRecord;
    DWORD nXfer;
    TCHAR JobMgtFileName [MAX_PATH];
    OVERLAPPED RegionStart;

    /* Open the job management file. */
    GetJobMgtFileName (JobMgtFileName);

    hJobData = CreateFile (JobMgtFileName, GENERIC_READ,
            FILE_SHARE_READ | FILE_SHARE_WRITE,
            NULL, OPEN_EXISTING, FILE_ATTRIBUTE_NORMAL, NULL);
    if (hJobData == INVALID_HANDLE_VALUE) return 0;

    /* Position to the entry for the specified job number. */

    SetFilePointer (hJobData, SJM_JOB * (JobNumber - 1),
            NULL, FILE_BEGIN);

    /* Lock and read the record. */
    RegionStart.Offset = SJM_JOB * (JobNumber - 1);
    RegionStart.OffsetHigh = 0; /* Assume a "short" file. */
    RegionStart.hEvent = (HANDLE)0;
    LockFileEx (hJobData, 0, 0, SJM_JOB, 0, &RegionStart);
    ReadFile (hJobData, &JobRecord, SJM_JOB, &nXfer, NULL);
    UnlockFileEx (hJobData, 0, SJM_JOB, 0, &RegionStart);
    CloseHandle (hJobData);
    return JobRecord.ProcessId;
}
```

Job Objects

Processes can be collected together into "job objects" so that the processes can be controlled as a group. Job objects are supported only in Windows 2000.

The first step is to create an empty job object with `CreateJobObject`, which takes two arguments, a name and security attributes, and returns a job object handle. There is also an `OpenJobObject` function to use with a named object. `CloseHandle` destroys the job object.

`AssignProcessToJobObject` simply adds a specified process handle to a job object; there are just two parameters.

Finally, you can specify control limits on the processes in a job using `SetInformationJobObject`.

```
BOOL SetInformationJobObject (
    HANDLE hJob,
    JOBOBJECTINFOCLASS JobObjectInformationClass,
    LPVOID lpJobObjectInformation,
    DWORD cbJobObjectInformationLength)
```

- `hJob` is a handle for an existing job object.

- `JobObjectInformationClass` specifies the information class for the limits you wish to set. There are five values; `JobObjectBasicLimitInformation` is one value and is used to specify information such as the total and per-process time limits, working set size limits,[3] limits on the number of active processes, priority, and processor affinity (the processors of an SMP system that can be used by threads in the job processes).

- `lpJobObjectInformation` points to the actual information required by the preceding parameter. There is a different structure for each class.

- `JOBOBJECT_BASIC_ACCOUNTING_INFORMATION` allows you to get the total time (user, kernel, and elapsed) of the processes in a job.

- The last parameter is the length of the preceding structure.

---

[3] The working set is the set of virtual address space pages that the OS determines must be loaded in memory before any thread in the process is ready to run. This subject is covered in most operating system texts.

`QueryJobInformationObject` obtains the current limits. Other information classes impose limits on the user interface, I/O completion ports (see Chapter 14), security, and job termination.

Summary

Win32 provides a straightforward mechanism for managing processes and synchronizing their execution. Examples have shown how to manage the parallel execution of multiple processes and how to obtain information about execution times. Win32 does not maintain a parent-child relationship among processes, so the programmer must manage this information if it is required.

Looking Ahead

Threads, which are independent units of execution within a process, are described in the next chapter. Thread management is similar in some ways to process management, and there will be exit codes, termination, and waiting on thread handles. To illustrate this similarity, `grepMP` (Program 7–1) will be reimplemented with threads in the first example program.

Chapter 9 will then discuss synchronization, which can be used to coordinate operation between threads in the same or different processes.

Additional Reading

Job objects are relatively new, so book coverage is limited. Richter's article in the March, 1999 *Microsoft Systems Journal* "Make Your Windows 2000 Processes Play Nice Together With Job Kernel Objects" is a good source for additional information.

Exercises

7–1.   Extend Program 7–1 (`grepMP`) so that it accepts command line options and not just the pattern.

7–2.   Rather than pass the temporary file name to the child process in Program 7–1, convert the inheritable file handle to a DWORD (a HANDLE requires four bytes) and then to a character string. Pass this string to the child process on the command line. The child process, in turn, must convert the character string back to a handle value to use for output. The `catHA.c` and `grepHA.c` programs on the disc illustrates this technique.

7–3. Program 7–1 waits for all processes to complete before listing the results. It is impossible to determine the order in which the processes actually complete within the current program. Modify the program so that it can also determine the termination order. *Hint*: Modify the call to `Wait-ForMultipleObjects` so that it returns after each individual process terminates. An alternative would be to sort by the process termination times.

7–4. The temporary files in Program 7–1 must be deleted explicitly. Can you use `FILE_FLAG_DELETE_ON_CLOSE` when creating the temporary files so that deletion is not required?

7–5. Determine any `grepMP` performance advantages (compared with sequential execution) when you have an SMP system or when the files are on separate or network drives. Appendix C presents some partial results.

7–6. Can you find a way, perhaps using job objects, to collect the user and kernel time required by `grepMP`? It may be necessary to modify `grepMP` to use job objects.

7–7. Enhance the `DisplayJobs` function (Program 7–5) so that it reports the exit code of any completed job. Also, give the times (elapsed, kernel, and user) used so far by all jobs.

7–8. The job management functions have a defect that is difficult to fix. Suppose that a job is killed and the NT executive reuses its process ID before the process ID is removed from the job management file. There could be an `OpenProcess` on the process ID that now refers to a totally different process. The fix requires creating a helper process that holds duplicated handles for every created process so that the ID will not be reused. Another technique would be to include the process start time in the job management file. This time should be the same as the process start time of the process obtained from the process ID. This technique will not work with Windows 9x, however, because the process start time is not available. *Note*: Process IDs will be reused quickly. UNIX, however, increments a counter to get a new process ID, and IDs will repeat only after the 32-bit counter wraps around. Therefore, Win32 programs cannot assume that IDs will not, for all practical purposes, be reused.

7–9. Modify `JobShell` so that job information is maintained in the registry rather than in a temporary file.

7–10. Extend `JobShell` so that the processes are associated with a job object. Impose time and other limits on the jobs, allowing the user to enter some of these limits.

7–11. Program 5–1, which created a security descriptor, required the programmer to supply the group name. Modify the function so that it creates permissions for all the user's groups. *Hint*: It is necessary to use the function Open-ProcessToken, which returns an array with the group names, although you will need to experiment to find out how group names are stored in the array. The Chapter 5 source program contains a partial solution.

7–12. Write a program, whoami, that displays your logged-in user name as well as all the groups of which you are a member. This extends an exercise from Chapter 5.

8 | Threads and Scheduling

The thread is Win32's basic unit of execution, and a process can contain multiple, independent threads sharing the process's address space and other resources. Chapter 7 limited processes to a single thread, but there are many situations in which multiple threads are desirable. This chapter describes and illustrates Win32 thread management. The example programs use threads to simplify program design and to enhance performance. Chapter 9 continues with a description of synchronization objects and the impact, positive and negative, of threads on performance. Chapter 10 describes advanced synchronization programming methods and models that greatly simplify the design and development of reliable multi-threaded programs. The techniques will then be used in the remaining chapters.

This chapter ends with a brief discussion of fibers, which allow you to create separate tasks within a thread. *Fibers are used primarily when porting some threaded legacy UNIX applications, and many readers may wish to skip the fiber section.*

Thread Overview

A thread is an independent unit of execution within a process. The multithreaded programming challenge requires organization and coordination of thread execution to simplify programs and to take advantage of the inherent parallelism of the host computer.

Traditionally, programs execute as a single thread of execution. While several processes can execute concurrently, as in the Chapter 7 examples, and even interact through mechanisms such as shared memory or pipes (Chapter 11), single-threaded processes have several disadvantages.

- It is expensive and time consuming for the operating system to switch running processes, and, in cases such as the multiprocess search (grepMP, Program 7–1), the processes are all executing the same program. Threads allow concurrent file processing within a single process, reducing overall system overhead.

- Except in the case of shared memory, processes are not tightly coupled to one another, and it is difficult to share resources, such as open files.

- It is difficult and inefficient for single-threaded processes to manage several concurrent and interacting tasks, such as waiting for and processing user input, waiting for file or network input, and performing computation.

- I/O-bound programs, such as the ASCII to Unicode conversion program in Chapter 2 (`atou`, Program 2–4) are confined to a simple read-modify-write model. When you're processing sequential files, it can be more efficient to initiate as many read operations as possible. Windows NT also allows asynchronous overlapped I/O (Chapter 14), but threads can achieve the same effect.

- The Windows executive will schedule independent threads on separate processors of an SMP system, frequently improving performance.

This chapter discusses Win32 threads and how to manage them. The examples illustrate thread usage with parallel file searching and a multithreaded sort. These two examples contrast I/O- and compute-intensive concurrent activities performed with threads. This chapter also presents an overview of Win32 process and thread scheduling.

Note: This chapter and those that follow take the point of view that not only do threads make certain programs simpler to design and implement but, with attention to a few basic rules and programming models, threaded programs also can be reliable, easy to understand, and maintainable. Thread management functions are very similar to the process management functions so that, as just one example, there is a `GetThreadExitCode` function that is comparable to `GetProcessExitCode`.

Thread Basics

Figure 7–1 shows how threads exist in a process environment. Figure 8–1 illustrates threads by showing a multithreaded server that can process simultaneous requests from multiple networked clients; a distinct thread is dedicated to each client. This model will be implemented in Chapter 11.

Threads within a process share the same data and code, so it is essential that threads also have their own unique storage. Win32 satisfies this requirement in several ways.

- Each thread has its own stack for use in function calls and other processing.

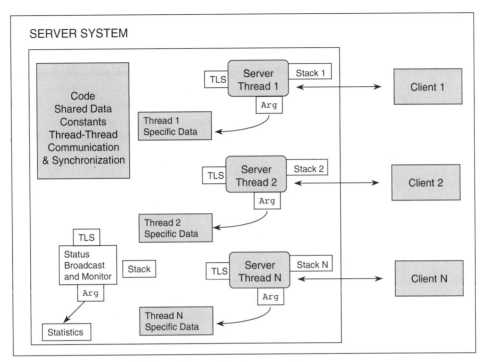

Figure 8–1   Threads in a Server Environment

- The calling process can pass an argument (`Arg` in Figure 8–1), such as a pointer, to a thread at creation time. This argument is actually on the thread's stack.

- Each thread can allocate its own Thread Local Storage (TLS) indexes and read and set TLS values. TLS, described later, provides small data arrays to threads, and a thread can access only its own array.

The thread argument—or, alternatively, TLS—can be used to point to an arbitrary data structure. In Figure 8–1's server example, this structure might contain the current request and the thread's response to that request as well as other working storage.

Windows 2000 and NT exploit symmetric multiprocessor (SMP) systems by allowing different threads, even from the same process, to run concurrently on separate processors. This capability, if used properly, can enhance performance, but without sufficient care, SMP systems can actually harm performance, as we'll see in the next chapter.

Thread Management

It should come as no surprise that threads, like any other Win32 object, have handles and that there is a `CreateThread` system call to create an executable thread in the calling process's address space. As with processes, we will sometimes speak of "parent" and "child" threads, although the operating system does not make any such distinction. `CreateThread` has several unique requirements.

- Specify the thread's start address within the process's code.

- Specify the stack size, and the stack consumes space within the process's virtual address space. The default stack size is the parent's stack size (normally 1MB). One page is initially committed to the stack (see Chapter 6). New stack pages are committed as required until the stack cannot grow anymore.

- Specify a pointer to an argument for the thread. The argument can be nearly anything and is interpreted by the thread itself.

- `CreateThread` returns a thread's ID value and its handle. A `NULL` handle value indicates a failure.

```
HANDLE CreateThread (
    LPSECURITY_ATTRIBUTES lpsa,
    DWORD cbStack,
    LPTHREAD_START_ROUTINE lpStartAddr,
    LPVOID lpThreadParm,
    DWORD fdwCreate,
    LPDWORD lpIDThread)
```

Parameters

`lpsa` is the familiar security attributes structure.

`cbStack` is the byte size of the new thread's stack. Use 0 to default to the primary thread's stack size.

`lpStartAddr` points to the function (within the calling process) to be executed. This function accepts a single pointer argument and returns a 32-bit `DWORD` exit code. The thread can interpret the argument as a `DWORD` or a pointer. The thread function signature, then, is:

```
DWORD WINAPI ThreadFunc (LPVOID)
```

lpThreadParm is the pointer passed as the thread argument and is interpreted by the thread, normally as a pointer to an argument structure.

fdwCreate, if zero, means that the thread is ready to run immediately. If fdwCreate is CREATE_SUSPENDED, the new thread will be in the suspended state, requiring a ResumeThread function call to move the thread to the ready state.

lpIDThread points to a DWORD that receives the new thread's identifier. The pointer can also be NULL, indicating that no thread ID will be returned, for Windows 2000/NT; Windows NT Version 3.51 did not allow NULL for this parameter.

All threads in a process can terminate themselves using the ExitProcess function, and the exit code returned by the thread start function will be the same as the process exit code. Alternatively, a thread can terminate itself by returning from the thread function using the exit code as the return value. The thread's stack is deallocated on termination.

```
VOID ExitThread (DWORD dwExitCode)
```

When the last thread in a process terminates, the process itself terminates.

One thread can terminate another thread with the TerminateThread function, but the thread's resources will not be deallocated, completion handlers will not be executed, and attached DLLs will not be notified. It is best if the thread terminates itself; TerminateThread usage is strongly discouraged. TerminateThread has the same disadvantages as those of TerminateProcess.

A terminated thread (again, a thread normally should terminate itself) will continue to exist until the last handle to it is closed using CloseHandle. Any other thread, perhaps one waiting for some other thread to terminate, can retrieve the exit code.

```
BOOL GetExitCodeThread (
    HANDLE hThread,
    LPDWORD lpdwExitCode)
```

lpdwExitCode will contain the thread's exit code. If the thread is still running, the value is STILL_ACTIVE.

Thread Identity

You can obtain thread IDs and handles using functions that are similar to those used with processes.

- GetCurrentThread returns a noninheritable pseudohandle to the calling thread.

- GetCurrentThreadId obtains the thread ID, rather than the handle.

- OpenThread creates a thread handle from a thread ID. OpenProcess was very useful in JobShell (Program 7–3), and OpenThread can be used in a similar fashion. OpenThread is available only with Windows 2000 and addresses an omission from the other Windows platforms.

Suspending and Resuming Threads

Every thread has a *suspend count*, and a thread can execute only if this count is zero. One thread can increment or decrement the suspend count of another thread using SuspendThread and ResumeThread. Recall that a thread can be created in the suspended state with a count of 1.

```
DWORD ResumeThread (HANDLE hThread)

DWORD SuspendThread (HANDLE hThread)
```

Both functions, if successful, return the previous suspend count. 0xFFFFFFFF indicates failure.

Waiting for Threads to Terminate

One thread can wait for another thread to terminate in the same way that threads wait for process termination, as discussed in Chapter 7. Use WaitForSingleObject or WaitForMultipleObjects using thread handles instead of process handles.

WaitForMultipleObjects can wait for only MAXIMUM_WAIT_OBJECTS (64) handles at one time, but you can perform a series of waits if you have a large number of threads. Program 7–1 already illustrated this technique; the programs in this book will perform single waits, but the full solution is on the disc.

The wait function waits for the object, indicated by the handle, to become *signaled*. In the case of threads, `ExitThread` and `TerminateThread` set the object to the signaled state, releasing all other threads waiting on the object. Note that multiple threads can wait on the same object. Similarly, the `ExitProcess` function sets the process state and the states of all its threads to signaled.

Remote Threads

The `CreateRemoteThread` function allows creation of a thread in another process. Compared with `CreateThread`, there is an additional parameter for the process handle, and the function addresses must be in the target process's address space. Windows 9x and CE do not have useful implementations of this function (older versions of the Microsoft documentation incorrectly say that Windows 98 supports this function); it is supported only in Windows NT and 2000. `CreateRemoteThread` is one of several interesting, and potentially dangerous, ways for one process to affect another directly, and it might be useful in writing, for example, a debugger.

`CreateRemoteThread` has one very interesting application. Rather than calling `TerminateProcess`, a controlling process can create a thread in a different process, and that thread can shut down the process in an orderly fashion. Exercise 8–17 gives an on-line reference to such a solution and asks that you apply it to Chapter 7's job management program. Some programmers also use `CreateRemoteProcess` to force a process to crash by executing at address 0 (or elsewhere), forcing a Dr. Watson analysis or dump file for debugging (do so at your own risk).

Threads are a well-established concept in many operating systems, and historically, many UNIX vendors and users have provided their own implementations. Some thread libraries have been implemented outside the kernel. POSIX Pthreads are now the standard. Pthreads are included as part of most commercial UNIX, as well as LINUX, implementations and are sometimes considered to be a part of UNIX. The system calls are distinguished from normal UNIX system calls by the `pthread_` prefix name. Pthreads are also supported on some non-UNIX systems such as OpenVMS.

`pthread_create` is the equivalent of `CreateThread`, and `pthread_exit` is the equivalent of `ExitThread`. One thread waits for another to exit with `pthread_join`. Pthreads provide the very useful `pthread_cancel` function, which, unlike `TerminateThread`, ensures that completion handlers and "cancellation handlers" are executed. Thread cancellation would be a welcome addition to Win32. On the other hand, Pthreads do not provide a way to suspend a thread.

Using the C Library in Threads

Most code requires the C library, even if it is just to manipulate strings. Historically, the C library was written to operate in single-threaded processes, so many functions use global storage to store intermediate results. Such libraries are not *thread-safe*, because two separate threads might, for example, be simultaneously accessing the library and modifying the library's global storage. Proper design of threaded code will be discussed again in Chapter 9, which describes Win32 synchronization.

The function strtok illustrates why some C library functions were not written to be thread-safe. strtok, which scans a string to find the next occurrence of a token, maintains *persistent state* between successive calls to the function, and this state is in static storage, shared by all the threads calling the function.

Microsoft C solves such problems by supplying a thread-safe C library implementation named LIBCMT.LIB. There is more. Do not use CreateThread; rather, use a special C function, _beginthreadex, to start a thread and create thread-specific working storage for LIBCMT.LIB. Use _endthreadex in place of Exit-Thread to terminate a thread.

Note: There is a _beginthread function, intended to be simpler to use, *but it should be avoided*. First, _beginthread does not have security attributes or flags and does not return a thread ID. More importantly, it actually closes the thread handle it creates, and the returned thread handle may be invalid by the time the parent thread stores it. Also avoid _endthread; it does not allow for a return value.

The _beginthreadex arguments are exactly the same as for the Win32 functions, but without the Win32 type definitions; therefore, it is necessary to cast the _beginthreadex return value to a HANDLE to avoid warning messages. Be certain to define _MT before any include files; this definition is included in Envirmnt.h for the sample programs. That is all there is to it. In summary, when you're using the Visual C++ development environment, be sure to do the following:

- Link with LIBCMT.LIB and override the default library.

- Include #define _MT in all source files that use the C library.

- Include <process.h> for the _beginthreadex and _endthreadex definitions.

- Create threads with _beginthreadex.

- Terminate threads with _endthreadex.

Appendix A gives instructions on how to build threaded applications. In particular, it is possible to specify the library and the _MT setting directly from the development environment.

All examples will operate this way, and the programs will never use `CreateThread` directly, allowing thread functions to use the C library.

Thread-Safe Libraries

User-developed libraries must be carefully designed to avoid thread safety issues, especially when persistent state is involved. An example in Chapter 12 (Program 12–4), where a DLL maintains state in a parameter, shows one strategy.

Another Chapter 12 example (Program 12–5) demonstrates an alternative approach that exploits the `DllMain` function and Thread Local Storage (TLS), which is described later in this chapter.

Example: Multithreaded Pattern Searching

Program 7–1, `grepMP`, used processes to search multiple files simultaneously. Program 8–1, `grepMT`, includes the `grep` pattern searching source code so that threads can perform the searching within a single process. The pattern searching code relies on the C library for file I/O. The main control program is similar to the process implementation.

`grepMP` and `grepMT` are comparable in terms of program structure and complexity, but `grepMT` has the expected advantage of better performance; it is more efficient for the kernel to switch between processes and threads. Appendix C shows that the theoretical advantage is real, especially when the files are on different disc drives. Both implementations exploit SMP systems, giving a considerable improvement in the elapsed time; threads, whether in the same process or in different processes, run in parallel on the different processors. The measured user time actually exceeds the elapsed time, because the user time is the total for all the processors.

This example also shows that asynchronous I/O can be achieved with threads without using the explicit methods described in Chapter 14. In this example, the program is managing concurrent I/O to multiple files, and the main thread, or any other thread, can perform additional processing before waiting for I/O completion. In the author's opinion, threads are a much simpler method of achieving asynchronous I/O, and Chapter 14 compares the methods, allowing the readers to form their own opinions. We will see, however, that asynchronous I/O, combined with I/O completion ports, is useful and often necessary when the number of threads is large.

grepMT, for the purposes of illustration, differs in another way from grepMP. Here, WaitForMultipleObjects waits for a *single* thread to terminate rather than waiting for all the threads. The appropriate output is displayed before waiting for another thread to complete. The completion order will, in most cases, vary from one run to the next. It is easy to modify the program to display the results in the order of the command line arguments; just imitate grepMP. This solution also works on Windows CE, which does not support a TRUE value for the fWaitAll flag.

Finally, notice that there is a limit of 64 threads due to the value of MAXI-MUM_WAIT_OBJECTS, which limits the number of handles in the WaitFor-MultipleObjects call. If more threads are required, create the appropriate logic to loop on either WaitForSingleObject or WaitForMultipleObjects.

Caution: grepMT performs asynchronous I/O in the sense that separate threads are concurrently, and synchronously, reading different files with read operations that block until the read is complete. You can also concurrently read from the same file if you have distinct handles on the file (typically, one per thread). These handles should be generated by CreateFile rather than Duplicate-Handle. Chapter 14 describes asynchronous I/O, with and without user threads, and an example on the disc (atouMT, described in Chapter14) has several threads performing I/O to the same file.

Program 8–1   grepMT: Multithreaded Pattern Searching

```
/* Chapter 8. grepMT. */
/* Parallel grep - multiple thread version. */

#include "EvryThng.h"
typedef struct { /* grep thread's data structure. */
    int argc;
    TCHAR targv [4] [MAX_PATH];
} GREP_THREAD_ARG;
typedef GREP_THREAD_ARG *PGR_ARGS;
static DWORD WINAPI ThGrep (PGR_ARGS pArgs);

int _tmain (int argc, LPTSTR argv [])
{
    GREP_THREAD_ARG * gArg;
    HANDLE * tHandle;
    DWORD ThdIdxP, ThId, ExitCode;
    TCHAR CmdLine [MAX_COMMAND_LINE];
    int iThrd, ThdCnt;
    STARTUPINFO StartUp;
    PROCESS_INFORMATION ProcessInfo;

    GetStartupInfo (&StartUp);
```

```
/* Boss thread: create separate "grep" thread for each file. */
tHandle = malloc ((argc - 2) * sizeof (HANDLE));
gArg = malloc ((argc - 2) * sizeof (GREP_THREAD_ARG));

for (iThrd = 0; iThrd < argc - 2; iThrd++) {
    _tcscpy (gArg [iThrd].targv [1], argv [1]); /* Pattern. */
    _tcscpy (gArg [iThrd].targv [2], argv [iThrd + 2]);
    GetTempFileName /* Temp file name. */
            (".", "Gre", 0, gArg [iThrd].targv [3]);
    gArg [iThrd].argc = 4;

    /* Create a worker thread to execute the command line. */
    tHandle [iThrd] = (HANDLE)_beginthreadex (
            NULL, 0, ThGrep, &gArg [iThrd], 0, &ThId);
}
/* Redirect std output for file listing process. */
StartUp.dwFlags = STARTF_USESTDHANDLES;
StartUp.hStdOutput = GetStdHandle (STD_OUTPUT_HANDLE);

/* Worker threads are all running. Wait for them to complete. */
ThdCnt = argc - 2;
while (ThdCnt > 0) {
    ThdIdxP = WaitForMultipleObjects (
            ThdCnt, tHandle, FALSE, INFINITE);
    iThrd = (int) ThdIdxP - (int) WAIT_OBJECT_0;
    GetExitCodeThread (tHandle [iThrd], &ExitCode);
    CloseHandle (tHandle [iThrd]);
    if (ExitCode == 0) { /* Pattern found. */
        if (argc > 3) { /* Print file name if more than one. */
            _tprintf (_T ("\n**Search results - file: %s\n"),
                    gArg [iThrd].targv [2]);
            fflush (stdout);
        }
        /* Use the "cat" program to list the result files. */
        _stprintf (CmdLine, _T ("%s%s"), _T ("cat "),
                gArg [iThrd].targv [3]);
        CreateProcess (NULL, CmdLine, NULL, NULL,
                TRUE, 0, NULL, NULL, &StartUp, &ProcessInfo);
        WaitForSingleObject (ProcessInfo.hProcess, INFINITE);
        CloseHandle (ProcessInfo.hProcess);
        CloseHandle (ProcessInfo.hThread);
    }
    DeleteFile (gArg [iThrd].targv [3]);

    /* Adjust thread and file name arrays. */
    tHandle [iThrd] = tHandle [ThdCnt - 1];
    _tcscpy (gArg [iThrd].targv [3], gArg [ThdCnt - 1].targv [3]);
    _tcscpy (gArg [iThrd].targv [2], gArg [ThdCnt - 1].targv [2]);
    ThdCnt--;
}
```

```
}

/* The form of the grep thread function code is:
static DWORD WINAPI ThGrep (PGR_ARGS pArgs)
{
} */
```

The Boss/Worker and Other Threading Models

grepMT illustrates the "boss/worker" threading model, and Figure 7–3 illustrates the relationship if "thread" is substituted for "process." The boss thread (the main thread in this case) assigns tasks for the worker threads to perform. Each worker thread is given a file to search, and the worker threads pass their results to the boss thread in a temporary file.

There are numerous variations, such as the "work crew" model where the workers cooperate on a single task, each performing a small piece. The next example illustrates this model (see Figure 8–2). The workers might even divide up the work themselves without direction from the boss. Nearly every management arrangement used by humans can be employed by multithreaded programs.

The two other major models are the "client/server model" (illustrated in Figure 8–1 and developed in Chapter 11) and the "pipeline model" where work moves from one thread to the next (see Chapter 10 and Figure 10–1 for an example of a multistage pipeline).

There are many advantages to using these models when designing a multi-threaded system; the advantages include:

- Most multithreaded programming problems can be solved using one of the standard models, expediting design, development, and debugging.

- Not only does using a well-understood and tested model avoid many of the mistakes that are so easy to make in a multithreaded program, but the model also helps you obtain the best performance.

- The models correspond naturally to the structures of most programming problems.

- Programmers who maintain the program will be able to understand it much more easily if documentation describes the program in terms that everyone understands.

- Troubleshooting an unfamiliar program is much easier if you analyze it in terms of models. Frequently, an underlying problem is found when the program is seen to violate the basic principles of one of the models.

- Many common defects, such as race conditions and deadlocks, are also described by simple models, as are effective methods of using the synchronization objects described in Chapters 9 and 10.

These classical thread models are used in many operating systems. The Component Object Model (COM), widely used in Windows systems, uses different terminology, and, while COM is outside the scope of this book (there is a brief overview in Chapter 15, however), the COM models are mentioned at the end of Chapter 11 and compared with program examples in this book.

Example: Merge-Sort—Divide and Conquer to Exploit SMP

This example shows how to use threads to get significant performance gains, especially on an SMP system. The basic idea is to divide the problem into component tasks, give each task to a separate thread, and then combine the results to get the complete solution. The 2000/NT executive will automatically assign the threads to separate processors, so the tasks will be performed in parallel, reducing elapsed time.

This strategy, often called the *divide and conquer* strategy or the *work crew model*, is useful both for performance and as an algorithm design method. The implementation of grepMT, Program 8–1, could be considered one example; it creates a thread for each file, or pattern matching task. Appendix C shows that there are performance gains on SMP systems, because the executive can schedule the threads on different processors.

Next, consider another example in which a single task, sorting a file, is divided into subtasks delegated to separate threads.

Merge-sort, in which the array to be sorted is divided into smaller arrays, is a classic divide and conquer algorithm. Each small array is sorted individually, and the individual sorted arrays are merged in pairs to yield larger sorted arrays. The pairwise merging continues until completion. Generally, merge-sort starts with arrays of size 1, which need no sorting. This example starts with larger arrays so that there is one array for each processor. Figure 8–2 is a sketch of the algorithm.

Program 8–2 shows the details of the implementation. The user specifies the number of tasks on the command line. Appendix C shows the results. Exercise 8–9 suggests that sortMT use GetSystemInfo to find the number of processors and then create one thread per processor.

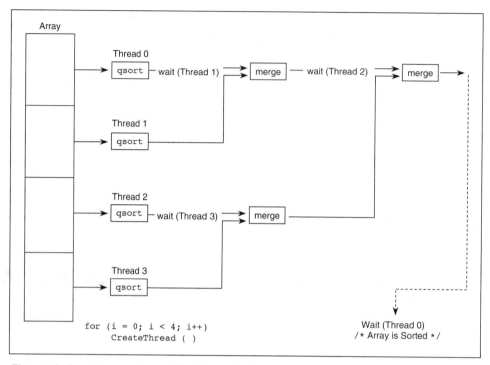

Figure 8–2   Merge-Sort with Multiple Threads

Notice that the program runs efficiently on single-processor systems with sufficient memory and gains a significant performance improvement on SMP systems. *Caution*: The algorithm as shown will work only if the number of records in the sort file is divisible by the number of threads and if the number of threads is a power of 2. Exercise 8–8 removes these limitations.

Notice that the threads are created in a suspended state and that all of them resume after all threads have been created. If the threads were created and allowed to run immediately, there would be a *race condition* defect. For example, Thread 0 might wait for Thread 1 to complete before Thread 1 is actually created. Exercise 8–14 suggests an alternative way to avoid a race condition, and other techniques are available with the synchronization objects described in Chapter 9.

Note: In understanding this program, it is important to concentrate on the thread management logic separately from the logic that determines which portion of the array a thread is to sort. Notice too that the C library qsort function is used, so there is no need to be concerned with developing an efficient sort function.

Program 8–2   `sortMT`: Merge-Sort with Multiple Threads

```
/* Chapter 8. SortMT.
   File sorting with multiple threads (a work crew).
   sortMT [options] nt file */

#include "EvryThng.h"
#define DATALEN 56 /* Key: 8 bytes; Data: 56 bytes. */
#define KEYLEN 8
typedef struct _RECORD {
        CHAR Key [KEYLEN]; TCHAR Data [DATALEN];
} RECORD;
#define RECSIZE sizeof (RECORD)
typedef RECORD * LPRECORD;

typedef struct _THREADARG {   /* Thread argument */
    DWORD iTh;                /* Thread number: 0, 1, 2, ... */
    LPRECORD LowRec;          /* Low record */
    LPRECORD HighRec;         /* High record */
} THREADARG, *PTHREADARG;

static int KeyCompare (LPCTSTR, LPCTSTR);
static DWORD WINAPI ThSort (PTHREADARG pThArg);
static DWORD nRec; /* Total number of records to be sorted. */
static HANDLE * ThreadHandle;

int _tmain (int argc, LPTSTR argv [])
{
    HANDLE hFile;
    LPRECORD pRecords = NULL;
    DWORD FsLow, nRead, LowRecNo, nRecTh, NPr, ThId, iTh;
    BOOL NoPrint;
    int iFF, iNP;
    PTHREADARG ThArg;
    LPTSTR StringEnd;

    iNP = Options (argc, argv, _T ("n"), &NoPrint, NULL);
    iFF = iNP + 1;
    NPr = _ttoi (argv [iNP]); /* Number of threads. */
    hFile = CreateFile (argv [iFF], GENERIC_READ | GENERIC_WRITE,
            0, NULL, OPEN_EXISTING, 0, NULL);
    FsLow = GetFileSize (hFile, NULL);
    nRec = FsLow / RECSIZE; /* Total number of records. */
    nRecTh = nRec / NPr; /* Records per thread. */

    /* Allocate thread args and handle array
       and space for the file. Read the complete file. */

    ThArg = malloc (NPr * sizeof (THREADARG)); /* Thread args. */
```

```
        ThreadHandle = malloc (NPr * sizeof (HANDLE));
        pRecords = malloc (FsLow + sizeof (TCHAR));
        ReadFile (hFile, pRecords, FsLow, &nRead, NULL);
        CloseHandle (hFile);

        LowRecNo = 0; /* Create the sorting threads. */
        for (iTh = 0; iTh < NPr; iTh++) {
            ThArg [iTh].iTh = iTh;
            ThArg [iTh].LowRec = pRecords + LowRecNo;
            ThArg [iTh].HighRec = pRecords + (LowRecNo + nRecTh);
            LowRecNo += nRecTh;
            ThreadHandle [iTh] = (HANDLE) _beginthreadex (NULL, 0,
                    ThSort, &ThArg [iTh], CREATE_SUSPENDED, &ThId);
        }

        for (iTh = 0; iTh < NPr; iTh++) /* Run all sort threads. */
            ResumeThread (ThreadHandle [iTh]);
        WaitForSingleObject (ThreadHandle [0], INFINITE);
        for (iTh = 0; iTh < NPr; iTh++) CloseHandle (ThreadHandle [iTh]);

        StringEnd = (LPTSTR) pRecords + FsLow;
        *StringEnd = '\0';
        if (!NoPrint) printf ("\n%s", (LPCTSTR) pRecords);
        free (pRecords);
        free (ThArg);
        free (ThreadHandle);
        return 0;
    }   /* End of _tmain. */

static VOID MergeArrays (LPRECORD, LPRECORD);
DWORD WINAPI ThSort (PTHREADARG pThArg)
{
    DWORD GrpSize = 2, RecsInGrp, MyNumber, TwoToI = 1;
    LPRECORD First;

    MyNumber = pThArg->iTh;
    First = pThArg->LowRec;
    RecsInGrp = pThArg->HighRec - First;
    qsort (First, RecsInGrp, RECSIZE, KeyCompare);
    while ((MyNumber % GrpSize) == 0 && RecsInGrp < nRec) {
                    /* Merge with the adjacent sorted array. */
        WaitForSingleObject (
                ThreadHandle [MyNumber + TwoToI], INFINITE);
        MergeArrays (First, First + RecsInGrp);
        RecsInGrp *= 2;
        GrpSize *= 2;
        TwoToI *= 2;
    }
```

```
    _endthreadex (0);
    return 0; /* Suppress a warning message. */
}

static VOID MergeArrays (LPRECORD p1, LPRECORD p2)
{
    DWORD iRec = 0, nRecs, i1 = 0, i2 = 0;
    LPRECORD pDest, p1Hold, pDestHold;

    nRecs = p2 - p1;
    pDest = pDestHold = malloc (2 * nRecs * RECSIZE);
    p1Hold = p1;
    while (i1 < nRecs && i2 < nRecs) {
        if (KeyCompare ((LPCTSTR) p1, (LPCTSTR) p2) <= 0) {
            memcpy (pDest, p1, RECSIZE);
            i1++; p1++; pDest++;
        }

        else {
            memcpy (pDest, p2, RECSIZE);
            i2++; p2++; pDest++;
        }
    }

    if (i1 >= nRecs) memcpy (pDest, p2, RECSIZE * (nRecs - i2));
    else memcpy (pDest, p1, RECSIZE * (nRecs - i1));

    memcpy (p1Hold, pDestHold, 2 * nRecs * RECSIZE);
    free (pDestHold);
    return;
}
```

Performance

Appendix C includes the results of sorting a 25.6MB file of 64-byte records using one, two, and four threads. SMP systems give significantly better results. Divide and conquer is more than just a strategy for algorithm design; it can also be the key to exploiting threads and SMP. The single-processor results can vary. On a small memory system, the use of multiple threads increases the sort time, because the threads contend for available physical memory. On the other hand, multiple threads can improve performance with a single processor when there is sufficient memory. The results are also heavily dependent on the initial data arrangement, as discussed in Appendix C.

Thread Local Storage

Threads may need to allocate and manage their own storage independently of other threads in the same process. One technique is to have the creating thread call `CreateThread` (or `_beginthreadex`) with `lpvThreadParm` pointing to a data structure that is unique for each thread. The thread can then allocate additional data structures and access them through `lpvThreadParm`. Program 8–1 used this technique.

Win32 also provides Thread Local Storage (TLS), which gives each thread its own array of pointers. Figure 8–3 shows this TLS arrangement.

Initially, no TLS indexes (rows) are allocated, but new rows can be allocated and deallocated at any time, with a maximum of `TLS_MINIMUM_AVAILABLE` (at least 64) indexes for any process. The number of columns can change as new threads are created and old ones terminate.

The first issue is TLS index management. The primary thread is a logical place to do this, but any thread can manage thread indexes.

`TlsAlloc` returns the allocated index (≥ 0), with –1 (`0xFFFFFFFF`) if no index is available.

```
DWORD TlsAlloc (VOID)

BOOL TlsFree (DWORD dwIndex)
```

An individual thread can get and set its values (void pointers) from its slot using a TLS index.

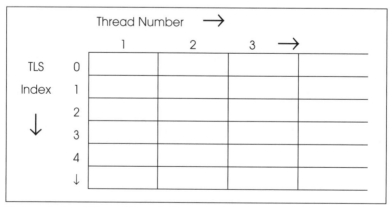

Figure 8-3   Thread Local Storage Within a Process

```
LPVOID TlsGetValue (DWORD dwTlsIndex)

BOOL TlsSetValue (DWORD dwTlsIndex,
   LPVOID lpsTlsValue)
```

The programmer must ensure that the TLS index parameter is valid—that is, that it has been allocated with `TlsAlloc` and has not been freed.

TLS provides a convenient mechanism for storage that is global within a thread but unavailable to other threads. Normal global storage is shared by all threads. Although no thread can access another thread's TLS, any thread can call `TlsFree` and destroy an index for all threads, so `TlsFree` should be used carefully. TLS is frequently used by DLLs as a replacement for global storage in a library; each thread, in effect, has its own global storage. TLS also provides a convenient way for a calling program to communicate with a DLL function, and this is the most common use of TLS. An example in Chapter 12 (Program 12–4) exploits TLS to build a thread-safe DLL; DLL thread and process attach/detach calls (Chapter 6) are another important element in the solution.

Process and Thread Priority and Scheduling

The Windows kernels always run the highest-priority thread that is ready for execution. A thread is not ready if it is waiting, suspended, or blocked for some reason.

Threads receive priority relative to their process priority classes. Four process priority classes are set initially by `CreateProcess`, as described in Chapter 7, and each has a *base priority*.

- `IDLE_PRIORITY_CLASS`, base priority 4
- `NORMAL_PRIORITY_CLASS`, base priority 9 or 7
- `HIGH_PRIORITY_CLASS`, base priority 13
- `REALTIME_PRIORITY_CLASS`, base priority 24

The two extreme classes are rarely used, and the normal class can be used most of the time. The normal base priority is 9 if the window has the focus for keyboard input; otherwise, the priority is 7.

A process can change or determine its own priority or that of another process, security permitting.

```
BOOL SetPriorityClass (HANDLE hProcess,
    DWORD fdwPriority)

DWORD GetPriorityClass (HANDLE hProcess)
```

Thread priorities are set relative to the process base priority, and, at thread creation time, the priority is set to that of the process. The thread priorities are in a range of ±2 from the process's base. The symbolic names of the resulting five thread priorities are as follows:

- THREAD_PRIORITY_LOWEST
- THREAD_PRIORITY_BELOW_NORMAL
- THREAD_PRIORITY_NORMAL
- THREAD_PRIORITY_ABOVE_NORMAL
- THREAD_PRIORITY_HIGHEST

Use these values to set and read a thread's relative priority. Note the use of signed integers rather than DWORDs.

```
BOOL SetThreadPriority (HANDLE hThread,
    int nPriority)

int GetThreadPriority (HANDLE hThread)
```

There are actually two additional thread priority values. They are absolute rather than relative and are used only in special cases.

- THREAD_PRIORITY_IDLE is a value of 1 (or 16 for real-time processes).
- THREAD_PRIORITY_TIME_CRITICAL is 15 (or 31 for real-time processes).

Thread priorities change automatically with process priority. In addition, the operating system may adjust thread priorities dynamically on the basis of thread behavior. On Windows 2000/NT, you can enable and disable this feature with the SetThreadPriorityBoost function.

Thread and Process Priority Cautions

High thread priorities and process priority classes should be used with caution. Real-time priorities should definitely be avoided for user processes. Among other dangers, user threads may preempt threads in the executive.

Furthermore, everything that we say in the following chapters about the correctness of threaded programs assumes, without comment, that thread scheduling is *fair*. Fairness ensures that all threads will, eventually, run. Without fairness, a low-priority thread could hold resources required by a high-priority thread. *Thread starvation* and *priority inversion* are terms used to describe the defects that occur when scheduling is not fair.

Thread States

Figure 8–4, which is taken from Custer's *Inside Windows NT*, page 210 (also, see Solomon's updated version of this book), shows how the executive manages threads and shows the possible thread states. This figure also shows the effect of program actions. Such state diagrams are common to all multitasking operating systems and help clarify how a thread is scheduled for execution and how a thread moves from one state to another.

Here is a quick summary of the fundamentals. See Custer/Solomon or an operating system text for more information.

- A thread is in the *running* state when it is actually running on a processor. More than one thread can be in the running state on an SMP system.

- The executive places a running thread in the *wait* state when the thread performs a wait on a nonsignaled handle, such as a thread or process handle, or on a synchronization object handle, as described in Chapter 9. I/O operations will also wait for completion of a disc or other data transfer, and numerous other functions can cause waiting. It is common to say that a thread is *blocked*, or *sleeping*, when in the wait state.

- A thread is *ready* if it could be running. The executive's scheduler could put it in the running state at any time. The scheduler will run the highest-priority ready thread when a processor becomes available, and it will run the one that has been in the ready state for the longest time if several threads have the same high priority. The thread moves through the *standby* state.

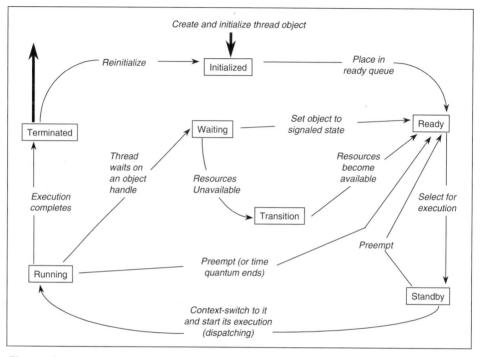

Figure 8-4 Thread States and Transitions
(From *Inside Windows NT*, Copyright © 1993, by Helen Custer. Copyright Microsoft Press. Reproduced by permission of Microsoft Press. All rights reserved.)

- Normally, as described above, the scheduler will place a ready thread on any available processor. The programmer can specify a thread's *processor affinity* by giving the processors on which a thread is to be run. In this way, the programmer can allocate processors to threads. The appropriate functions are `SetProcessorAffinityMask` and `GetProcessorAffinityMask`. `SetThreadIdealProcessor` can be used to specify a preferred processor that the scheduler will use whenever possible.

- The executive will move a running thread to the ready state if the thread's time slice expires without the thread waiting. Executing `Sleep(0)` will also move a thread from the running state to the ready state.

- The executive will place a waiting thread in the ready state as soon as the appropriate handles are signaled, although the thread actually goes through an intermediate *transition* state. It is common to say that the thread *wakes up*.

- There is no way for a program to determine the state of another thread (of course, a thread, if it is running, must be in the running state, so it would be meaningless for a thread to find its own state). Even if there were, the state might change before the inquiring thread would be able to act on the information.

- A thread, regardless of its state, can be suspended, and a ready thread will not be run if it is suspended. If a running thread is suspended, either by itself or by a thread on a different processor, it is placed in the ready state.

- A thread is in the *terminated* state after it terminates and remains there as long as there are any open handles on the thread. This arrangement allows other threads to interrogate the thread's state and exit code.

Pitfalls and Common Mistakes

There are several factors to keep in mind as you develop threaded programs; lack of attention to a few basic principles can result in serious defects, and it is best to avoid the problems in the first place rather than try to find them during testing or debugging.

The essential factor is that the threads execute asynchronously. There is no sequencing unless you create it explicitly. This asynchronous behavior is what makes threads so useful, but, without proper care, serious difficulties can occur.

Here are a few guidelines; there will be more in later chapters.

- Make no assumptions about the order in which the parent and child threads execute. It is possible for a child thread to run to completion before the parent returns from `CreateThread`, or, conversely, the child thread may not run at all for a considerable period of time. On an SMP system, the parent and one or more children may even run concurrently.

- Ensure that all initialization required by the child is complete before the `CreateThread` call, or else use thread suspension or some other technique. Failure by the parent to initialize data required by the child is a common cause of "race conditions" wherein the parent "races" the child to initialize data before the child needs it. `sortMT` illustrates this principle.

- Be certain that each distinct child has its own data structure passed through the thread function's parameter. Do not assume that one child thread will compete before another (this is another form of race condition).

- Any thread, at any time, can be preempted, and any thread, at any time, may resume execution.

- Do not use thread priority as a substitute for explicit synchronization.

- Do not use reasoning such as "that will hardly ever happen" as an argument that a program is correct. If it can happen, it will, possibly at a very embarrassing moment.

- Even more so than with single-threaded programs, testing is necessary, but not sufficient, to ensure program correctness. It is common for a program to pass extensive tests despite code defects. There is no substitute for careful design, implementation, and code inspection.

- Threaded program behavior varies widely with processor speed, number of processors, operating system version, and more. Testing on a variety of systems can isolate numerous defects, but the preceding precaution still applies.

- Be certain that threads have a sufficiently large stack, although the default 1MB will suffice in nearly all cases.

- Threads should be used only as appropriate. Thus, if there are activities that are naturally concurrent, each such activity can be represented by a thread. If, on the other hand, the activities are naturally sequential, threads only add complexity and performance overhead.

- Fortunately, correct programs are frequently the simplest and have the most elegant designs. Complexity should be avoided wherever possible.

Timed Waits

The final function, Sleep, allows a thread to give up the processor and move from the running to the wait state for a specified period of time. A thread can, for example, perform a task periodically by sleeping after carrying out the task. Once the time period is over, the scheduler moves the thread back to the ready state. A program in Chapter 11 (Program 11–4) uses this technique.

```
VOID Sleep (DWORD cMilliseconds)
```

The time period is in milliseconds and can even be INFINITE, in which case the thread will never resume. A value of zero will cause the thread to relinquish the remainder of the time slice; the kernel moves the thread from the running state to the ready state, as shown in Figure 8–4.

The function `SwitchToThread` provides another way for a thread to yield its processor to another ready thread, if there is one.

The UNIX `sleep` function is similar to `Sleep`, but time periods are measured in seconds. To obtain millisecond resolution, use the `select` or `poll` functions with no file descriptors.

Fibers

Note: Fibers are of specialized interest. See the comment after the first bulleted item below to determine if you want to skip this section.

A *fiber*, as the name implies, is a piece of a thread. More precisely, a fiber is a unit of execution within a thread that can be scheduled by the application rather than by the kernel. A thread can create numerous fibers, and the fibers themselves determine which of the thread's fibers will execute next. The fibers have independent stacks but otherwise run entirely in the context of the thread, having access, for example, to the thread's TLS and any mutexes[1] owned by the thread. Furthermore, fiber management occurs entirely in user space outside the kernel. Fibers can be thought of as lightweight threads, although there are numerous differences.

Fibers are available only under 2000/NT. They can be used for several purposes.

- Most importantly, many applications, especially some written for UNIX, are written to schedule their own threads. Fibers make it easier to port such applications to Windows 2000/NT. *Most readers will not have such requirements and may want to skip this section.*

- A thread does not need to block waiting for a file lock, mutex, named pipe input, or other resource. Rather, one fiber can poll the resource and, if the resource is not available, switch control to another specific fiber.

- Fibers operate within a thread and have access to thread and process resources. Unlike threads, fibers are not preemptively scheduled. The NT executive, in fact, is not aware of fibers; fibers are managed within the fiber DLL entirely within user space.

- Fibers allow you to implement *co-routines*, whereby an application switches among several interrelated tasks. Threads do not allow this. The programmer has no direct control over which thread will be executed next.

---

[1] A mutex, as explained in the next chapter, is a synchronization object that threads can own.

Six functions make up the fiber API. They are used in the following sequence and as shown in Figure 8–5.

1. A thread must first enable fiber operation by calling `ConvertThreadToFiber`. The thread then consists of a single fiber, which can be considered the *primary* fiber. This call provides a pointer to fiber data, which can be used in much the same way that the thread argument was used to create unique data for a thread.

2. Primary or other fibers create additional fibers using `CreateFiber`. Each fiber has a start address, a stack size, and a parameter. Each new fiber is identified by an address rather than by a handle.

3. An individual fiber can obtain its data, as received from `CreateFiber`, by calling `GetFiberData`.

4. Similarly, a fiber can obtain its identity with `GetCurrentFiber`.

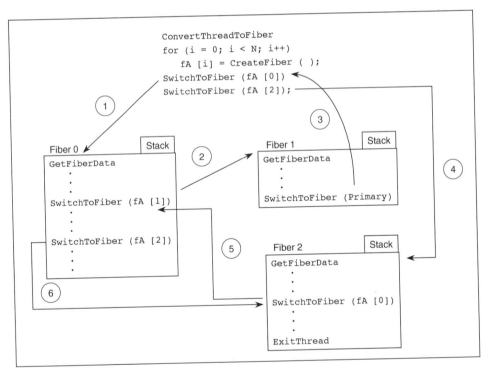

Figure 8–5 Control Flow Among Fibers in a Thread

5. A running fiber yields control to another fiber by calling `SwitchToFiber`, indicating the address of the other fiber. Fibers must explicitly indicate the next fiber that is to run within the thread.

6. The `DeleteFiber` function deletes an existing fiber and all its associated data.

Figure 8–5 shows fibers in a thread. This example shows two ways in which fibers schedule each other.

- ***Master-slave*** **scheduling**. One fiber, the primary fiber in this case, decides which fiber to run, and that fiber always yields control to the master fiber. Fiber 1 in Figure 8–5 behaves in this way.

- ***Peer-to-peer*** **scheduling**. A fiber determines the next fiber to run. The determination can be based on policies such as round-robin scheduling, priority scheduling based on a priority scheme, and so on. Co-routines would be implemented with peer-to-peer scheduling. In Figure 8–5, Fibers 0 and 2 switch control in this way.

The Fiber Functions

The first fiber function creates the primary fiber and enables the thread for fiber operation.

```
LPVOID ConvertThreadToFiber (LPVOID lpParameter)
```

The parameter is passed to the fiber as the *fiber data*. The fiber data can be similar to the thread argument in `CreateThread`, pointing to a data structure that is unique to the fiber or thread.

The return value is `NULL` on failure. On success, the result is the address of the fiber. The address plays the role of a handle and is used with other fiber functions. As always, `GetLastError` can be used to get information about a failed call.

New fibers can then be created by the primary fiber or any other fiber.

```
LPVOID CreateFiber (
    DWORD dwStackSize,
    LPFIBER_START_ROUTINE lpStateAddress,
    LPVOID lpParameter)
```

The stack size is the same as with `CreateThread`, and the parameter is as with `ConvertThreadToFiber`. The return value is the address of the new fiber, which is not to be confused with the start address. Notice that the new fiber will not run until another fiber switches to it.

The start routine is a `VOID` function, because a return would terminate the entire thread. Therefore, the prototype is as follows:

```
VOID WINAPI FiberFunction (LPVOID lpParameter)
```

One fiber switches to another by specifying the fiber address. Recall that the fiber address is returned by `CreateFiber` and `ConvertThreadToFiber`.

```
VOID SwitchToFiber (LPVOID lpFiber)
```

`lpFiber` is the address of the fiber that is to be executed. There is no specific return from this function call, so there is no return value. The next statement will, however, be executed when another fiber switches back to this one, as shown in Figure 8–5.

A fiber can get its data either directly through the fiber function argument or through a function.

```
LPVOID GetFiberData (VOID)
```

Similarly, a fiber can get its own address.

```
LPVOID GetCurrentFiber (VOID)
```

Finally, a fiber can delete another fiber.

```
VOID DeleteFiber (LPVOID lpFiber)
```

If the fiber address is the same as that of the currently running fiber, the entire thread terminates. If a fiber is deleted from another thread within the process, the results are unpredictable.

Summary

Win32 supports threads that are independently scheduled but share the same process address space and resources. Threads give the programmer an opportunity to simplify program design and to exploit multiprocessor systems for performance. Threads can even yield performance benefits on single-processor systems.

Looking Ahead

Chapter 9 describes and compares the Win32 synchronization objects, and Chapter 10 continues with more advanced synchronization topics and extended examples. Chapter 11 implements the threaded server shown in Figure 8–1. *Readers who are not interested in synchronization may want to skip Chapters 9 and 10.*

Thread pools are deferred until Chapter 14, because they require techniques introduced in that chapter.

Additional Reading

Win32

Multithreading Applications in Win32, by Jim Beveridge and Robert Wiener, is an entire book devoted to Win32 threads. *Multithreaded Programming with Win32* (Pham and Garg) and *Win32 Multithreaded Programming* (Cohen, Woodring, and Petrusha) are two additional choices.

UNIX and Pthreads

Stevens does not cover threads in UNIX, but *Programming with POSIX Threads*, by David Butenhof, is recommended. This book provides numerous guidelines for threaded program design and implementation. The information applies to Win32 as well as to Pthreads, and many of the examples can be easily ported to Win32. There is also good coverage of the boss/worker, client/server, and pipeline threading models, and Butenhof's presentation is the basis for the model descriptions in this chapter.

Exercises

8–1. Implement a set of functions that will suspend and resume threads but also allow you to obtain a thread's suspend count.

8–2. Compare the performance of the parallel search programs, one using threads (Program 8–1, grepMT) and the other using processes (Program 7–1, grepMP). Compare the results with those in Appendix C.

8–3. Perform additional performance studies with grepMT where the files are on different disc drives or are networked files. Also determine the performance gain, if any, on SMP systems.

8–4. Modify grepMT, Program 8–1, so that it puts out the results in the same order as that of the files on the command line. Does this affect the performance measurements in any way?

8–5. Further enhance grepMT, Program 8–1, so that it prints the time required by each worker thread. GetThreadTimes will be required, and this function is similar to GetProcessTimes, which was used in Chapter 7. This enhancement will work only on Windows 2000/NT.

8–6. The disc includes a multithreaded word count program, wcMT.c, that has a structure similar to that of grepMT.c. A defective version, wcMTx.c, is also included. Without referring to the correct solution, analyze and fix the defects in wcMTx.c, including any syntax errors. Also, create test cases that illustrate these defects and carry out performance experiments similar to those suggested for grepMT. There is also a single-threaded version, wcST.c, that can be used to determine whether threads give performance advantages over sequential processing.

8–7. The disc includes grepMTx.c, which is defective because it violates basic rules for thread safety. Describe the failure symptoms, identify the errors, and fix them.

8–8. `sortMT` requires that the number of records in the array to be sorted be divisible by the number of threads and that the number of threads be a power of 2. Remove these restrictions.

8–9. Enhance `sortMT` so that if the number of threads specified on the command line is zero, the program will determine the number of processors on the host system using `GetSystemInfo`. Set the number of threads to different multiples (1, 2, 4, ...) of the number of processors and determine the effect on performance.

8–10. Modify `sortMT` so that the worker threads are not suspended when they are created. What failure symptoms, if any, does the program demonstrate as a result of the race condition defect?

8–11. `sortMT` reads the entire file in the primary thread before creating the sorting threads. Modify the program so that each thread reads the portion of the file that it requires.

8–12. Modify one of the two programs in this chapter (`grepMT` or `sortMT`) so that some or all of the thread-specific information is passed through TLS rather than through a data structure.

8–13. Is there any performance benefit if you give some of the threads in `sortMT` higher priority than others? For example, it might be beneficial to give the threads that only sort and do not merge, such as Thread 3 in Figure 8–2, a higher priority. Explain the results.

8–14. `sortMT` creates all the threads in a suspended state so as to avoid a race condition. Modify the program so that it creates the threads in reverse order and in a running state. Are there any remaining race conditions? Compare performance with the original version.

8–15. Quicksort, the algorithm generally used by the C library `qsort` function, is usually fast, but it can be slow in certain cases. Most texts on algorithms show a version that is fastest when the array is reverse sorted and slowest when it is already sorted. The Microsoft C library implementation is different. Determine from the library code which sequences will produce the best and worst behavior, and study `sortMT`'s performance in these extreme cases. What is the effect of increasing or decreasing the number of threads?

8–16. The disc contains a defective `sortMTx.c` program. Demonstrate the defects with test cases and then explain and fix the defects without reference to the correct solutions. *Caution*: The defective version may have syntax errors as well as errors in the thread logic.

8–17. Read "A Safer Alternative to `TerminateProcess`" by Andrew Tucker in the *Windows Developer's Journal* at: `http://www.wdj.com/archive/1007/feature.html`. Modify `JobShell` (Chapter 7) and several processes so as to use this feature.

8–18. Read "Waiting for More than 64 Objects" by Jason Clark in the October, 1997 *Windows Developer's Journal*. Apply that solution to `grepMT`.

9 | Thread Synchronization

Threads can simplify program design and implementation and also improve performance, but thread usage requires care to ensure that shared resources are protected against simultaneous modification and that threads run only when requested or required. This chapter shows how to use Win32's synchronization objects—CRITICAL_SECTIONs, mutexes, semaphores, and events—to solve these problems and describes some of the problems that can occur when the synchronization objects are not used properly. Synchronization objects can be used to synchronize threads in the same process or in separate processes.

The examples illustrate the synchronization objects and discuss the performance impacts, both positive and negative, of different synchronization methods. Chapter 10 then shows how to use synchronization to solve additional programming problems.

Thread synchronization is a fundamental and interesting topic, and it is essential in nearly all large threaded systems. *Nonetheless, readers who are primarily interested in interprocess communication, network programming, and building threaded servers can skip to Chapter 11 and return to Chapters 9 and 10 for background material as required.*

The Need for Thread Synchronization

Chapter 8 showed how to create and manage worker threads, where each worker thread accessed its own resources. In the Chapter 8 examples, each thread processes a separate file or a separate area of storage, yet simple synchronization during thread creation and termination is still required. For example, the grepMT worker threads all run independently of one another, but the boss thread must wait for the workers to complete before reporting results. sortMT is slightly more complicated, because the workers need to synchronize by waiting for adjacent workers to complete, and the worker threads are not allowed to start until the boss thread has created all the workers.

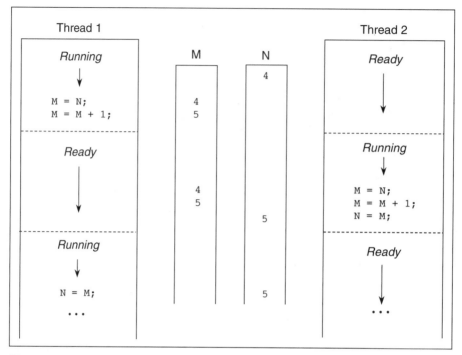

Figure 9–1   Unsynchronized Threads Sharing Memory

In many cases, however, it is necessary for two or more threads to coordinate execution throughout each thread's lifetime. For instance, several threads may access the same variable or set of variables, and this raises the issue of mutual exclusion. In other cases, a thread cannot proceed until another thread reaches a designated point. How can the programmer assume that two or more threads do not, for example, simultaneously modify the same global storage, such as the performance statistics? Furthermore, how can the programmer ensure that a thread does not attempt to remove an element from a queue before there are any elements in the queue?

Several examples will illustrate situations that can prevent code from being "thread-safe" (that is, code is thread-safe if several threads can execute the code simultaneously without any undesirable results; thread safety and reentrancy will be discussed later in this chapter and the next, as well as in Chapter 12), and later examples will show how to remedy the problem.

Figure 9–1 shows what can happen when two unsynchronized threads share a resource such as a memory location. Both threads increment variable N, but, because of the particular sequence in which the threads might execute, the final value of N is 5, whereas the correct value is 6. Notice that the particular result shown here is neither repeatable nor predictable; a different thread execution sequence could yield the correct results. Furthermore, execution on an SMP system can aggravate this problem.

Critical Code Sections

Incrementing N with a single statement such as N++ is no better, because the compiler will generate a sequence of one or more machine-level instructions that are not necessarily executed *atomically* as a single unit.

The core problem is that there is a *"critical section"* of code (the code that increments N in this example) such that, once a thread starts to execute the critical section, no other thread can be allowed to enter until the first thread exits from the code section. This critical section problem can be considered a type of race condition because the first thread "races" to complete the critical section before any other thread starts to execute the critical code section. Thus, we need to synchronize thread execution in order to ensure that only one thread at a time executes the critical section.

Defective Solutions to the Critical Section Problem

Similarly unpredictable results will occur with a code sequence that attempts to protect the increment with a polled flag.

```
while (Flag) Sleep (1000);
Flag = TRUE;
N++;
Flag = FALSE;
```

Even in this case, the thread could be preempted between the time Flag is tested and the time Flag is set to TRUE; the first two statements form a critical code section that is not properly protected from concurrent access by two or more threads.

Another attempted solution to the critical section synchronization problem might be to give each thread its own copy of the variable N, as follows:

```
DWORD WINAPI ThFunc (TH_ARGS pArgs);
{   volatile DWORD N;
    ... N++; ...
}
```

This approach is no better, however, because each thread has its own copy of the variable on its stack, where it may have been required to have N represent, for example, the total number of threads in operation. Such a solution is necessary, however, in the case in which each thread needs its own distinct copy of the variable. This technique occurs frequently in the examples.

Notice that such problems are not limited to threads within a single process. They can also occur if two processes share mapped memory or modify the same file.

volatile Storage

Yet another latent defect exists even after we solve the synchronization problem. An optimizing compiler might leave the value of N in a register rather than storing it back in N. An attempt to solve this problem by resetting compiler optimization switches would impact performance throughout the code. The correct solution is to use the ANSI C volatile storage qualifier, which ensures that the variable will be stored in memory after modification and will always be fetched from memory before use. The volatile quantifier informs the compiler that the variable can change value at any time.

Interlocked Functions

If all we need is to increment, decrement, or exchange variables, as in this simple initial example, then the *interlocked* functions will suffice. The interlocked functions are simpler and faster than any of the alternatives and will not block the thread. The two members of the interlocked function family that are important here are InterlockedIncrement and InterlockedDecrement. They apply to 32-bit signed integers. These functions are of limited utility, but they should be used wherever possible.

The task of incrementing N in Figure 9–1 could be implemented with a single line:

```
InterlockedIncrement (&N);
```

Be careful, however, not to call this function twice in succession if, for example, you need to increment the variable by 2. The thread might be preempted between the two calls. There is, however, an InterlockedExchangeAdd function, described near the end of the chapter.

Local and Global Storage

Another requirement for correct thread code is that global storage not be used for local purposes. For example, the code segment above would be necessary and appropriate if each thread required its own separate copy of N. N might hold temporary results or retain the argument. If, however, N were placed in global storage, all processes would share a single copy of N, resulting in incorrect behavior no matter how well your program synchronized access. Here is an example of such incorrect usage. N should be a local variable, allocated on the thread function's stack.

```
DWORD N;
DWORD WINAPI ThFunc (TH_ARGS pArgs);
{
    ...
    N = 2 * pArgs->Count; ...
}
```

Thread-Safe Code: Summary

Before we proceed to the synchronization objects, here are five initial guidelines to help ensure that the code will run correctly in a threaded environment.

1. Variables that are local to the thread should not be static and should be on the thread's stack or in a data structure that only the individual thread can access directly.

2. If a function is called by several threads and a thread-specific state value, such as a counter, is to persist from one function call to the next, store the state value in TLS or in a data structure dedicated to that thread, such as the data structure passed to the thread when it is created. Do not store the persistent value on the stack. Programs 12–4 and 12–5 show the required techniques when building thread-safe DLLs.

3. Avoid race conditions such as the one that would occur in Program 8–2 if the threads were not created in a suspended state. If some condition is assumed to hold at a specific point in the program, wait on a synchronization object to ensure that, for example, a handle references an existing thread.

4. Threads should not, in general, change the process environment, because that would affect all threads. Thus, a thread should not set the standard input or output handles or change environment variables.

5. Variables shared by all threads should be static or in global storage, declared `volatile`, and protected with the synchronization mechanisms that will be described next.

The next section discusses the synchronization objects. With that discussion, there will be enough to develop a simple producer/consumer example.

Thread Synchronization Objects

Two mechanisms discussed so far allow processes and threads to synchronize with one another.

1. A process can wait for another process to terminate, using `ExitProcess`, by waiting on the process handle using `WaitForSingleObject` or `WaitFor-MultipleObjects`. A thread can wait for another thread to terminate (`Exit-Thread`) in the same way.

2. File locks are specifically for synchronizing file access.

Win32 provides four other objects designed for thread and process synchronization. Three of these objects—mutexes, semaphores, and events—are kernel objects that have handles. Events are also used for other purposes, such as asynchronous I/O (Chapter 14).

The fourth object, the `CRITICAL_SECTION`, is discussed first. Because of their simplicity and performance advantages, `CRITICAL_SECTIONs` are the preferred mechanism when they are adequate for a program's requirements.

Two other synchronization objects, waitable timers and I/O completion ports, are deferred until Chapter 14. Both these objects require the Win32 asynchronous I/O techniques described in that chapter.

The `CRITICAL_SECTION` Object

A "critical section," as described above, is a section of code that only one thread can execute at a time; more than one thread executing the critical section concurrently can result in unpredictable, and incorrect, results.

Win32 provides the `CRITICAL_SECTION` object as a simple mechanism for implementing and enforcing the critical section concept.

`CRITICAL_SECTION` (CS) objects are initialized and deleted but do not have handles and are not shared by other processes. A variable should be declared to be of type `CRITICAL_SECTION`. Threads enter and leave a CS, and only one thread at a time can be in a specific CS. A thread can, however, enter and leave a specific CS at several places in the program.

To initialize and delete a `CRITICAL_SECTION` variable and its resources, use:

```
VOID InitializeCriticalSection (
    LPCRITICAL_SECTION lpcsCriticalSection)
```

```
VOID InitializeCriticalSection (
    LPCRITICAL_SECTION lpcsCriticalSection)
```

`EnterCriticalSection` blocks a thread if another thread is in the section. The waiting thread unblocks when the other thread executes `LeaveCriticalSection`. We say that a thread "owns" the CS once it returns from `EnterCriticalSection`, and `LeaveCriticalSection` relinquishes ownership. *Always be certain to relinquish a CS; failure to do so will cause other threads to wait forever, even if the owning thread terminates.*

We will often say that a CS is "locked" or "unlocked," and entering a CS is the same as locking the CS.

```
VOID EnterCriticalSection (
    LPCRITICAL_SECTION lpcsCriticalSection)

VOID LeaveCriticalSection (
    LPCRITICAL_SECTION lpcsCriticalSection)
```

If a thread already owns the CS, it can enter again without blocking. A count is maintained so that the thread must leave as many times as it enters in order to free the CS for other threads. This recursive capability can be useful in implementing recursive functions and making shared library functions thread-safe.

Leaving a CS that a thread does not own can produce unpredictable results, including thread blockage.

There is no time-out from `EnterCriticalSection`; a thread will block forever if the owning thread never leaves the CS. On Windows 2000/NT, however, you can test or poll to see whether another thread owns a CS using `TryEnterCriticalSection`.

```
BOOL TryEnterCriticalSection (
    LPCRITICAL_SECTION lpcsCriticalSection)
```

A `TRUE` return indicates that the calling thread now owns the CS, and a `FALSE` return indicates that some other thread already owns the CS.

`CRITICAL_SECTION`s have the advantage of not being kernel objects and are maintained in user space. This usually, but not always, provides performance improvements. We will discuss the performance benefit once kernel synchronization objects have been introduced.

Adjusting the Spin Count

Normally, if a thread finds that a CS is already owned when executing `EnterCriticalSection`, it enters the kernel and blocks until the `CRITICAL_SECTION` is released, which is time consuming. You can, however, require that the thread try again before blocking. This can be useful for performance when there is high contention among threads for a single `CRITICAL_SECTION`, especially on symmetric multiprocessor (SMP) systems. Performance is discussed later in this chapter.

The two functions to adjust spin count are `SetCriticalSectionSpinCount`, which allows you to adjust the count dynamically, and `InitializeCriticalSectionAndSpinCount`, which is a substitute for `InitializeCriticalSection`.

A `CRITICAL_SECTION` for Protecting Shared Variables

Using `CRITICAL_SECTION`s is simple, and one common use is to allow threads to access global shared variables. For example, consider a threaded server (as in Figure 8–1) in which there might be a need to maintain usage statistics such as:

- The total number of requests received

- The total number of responses sent

- The number of requests currently being processed by server threads

Because the count variables are global to the process, two threads must not modify the counts simultaneously. Critical section objects provide one means of ensuring this, as shown by the code sequence below and in Figure 9–2. A program example, much simpler than the server system, will illustrate this `CRITICAL_SECTION` usage.

CSs can be used to solve problems such as the one shown in Figure 9–1, in which two threads increment the same variable. The following example will do more than increment the variable, because simple incrementing is possible with the interlocked functions. Notice the use of `volatile` so that an optimizing compiler will not leave the current variable value in a register rather than store it back into the variable. This example also uses an intermediate variable; this inefficiency more clearly illustrates how the problem in Figure 9–1 is solved.

```
CRITICAL_SECTION cs1;
volatile DWORD N = 0, M;
/* N is a global variable, shared by all threads. */
IntializeCriticalSection (&cs1);
   ...
EnterCriticalSection (&cs1);
if (N < N_MAX) { M = N; M += 1; N = M; }
LeaveCriticalSection (&cs1);
   ...
DeleteCriticalSection (&cs1);
```

Figure 9–2 shows one possible execution sequence for the Figure 9–1 example and illustrates how CSs can solve synchronization problems.

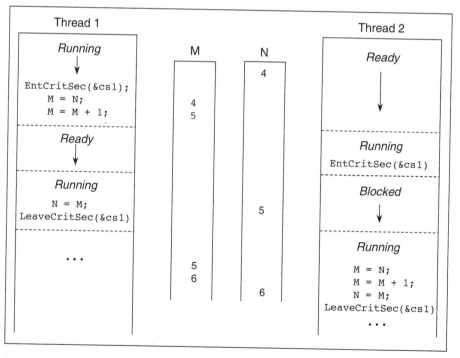

Figure 9-2   Synchronized Threads Sharing Memory

Example: A Simple Producer/Consumer System

Program 9–1 shows how CS objects can be useful. The program also shows how to build protected data structures for storing object state and introduces the concept of an "invariant," which is a property of an object's state that is guaranteed (by the proper program implementation) to be true outside a critical code section. Here is a description of the problem.

There are two threads, a "producer" and a "consumer," that act entirely asynchronously. The producer periodically creates messages containing a table of numbers, such as current stock prices, periodically updating the table. The consumer, on request from the user, displays the current data. The requirement is that the displayed data must be the *most recent complete set of data, but no data should be displayed twice.* Do not display data while the producer is updating it, and do not display old data. Note that many produced messages are never used and are "lost." This example is a special case of the pipeline model in which data moves from one thread to the next.

As an integrity check, the producer also computes a checksum of the data in the table, and the consumer validates the checksum to ensure that the data has not been corrupted in transmission from one thread to the next. If the consumer accesses the table while it is still being updated, the table will be invalid; the CS ensures that this does not happen. The two threads also maintain statistics on the total number of messages produced, consumed, and lost.

Program 9–1 `simplePC`: A Simple Producer and Consumer

```
/* Chapter 9. simplePC.c */
/* Maintain two threads, a producer and a consumer. */
/* The producer periodically creates checksummed data buffers, */
/* or "message block," that the consumer displays when prompted. */

#include "EvryThng.h"
#include <time.h>
#define DATA_SIZE 256

typedef struct msg_block_tag { /* Message block. */
    volatile DWORD f_ready, f_stop; /* Msg ready and stop flags. */
    volatile DWORD sequence; /* Message block sequence number. */
    volatile DWORD nCons, nLost;
    time_t timestamp;
    CRITICAL_SECTION mguard; /* Guard message block structure. */
    DWORD checksum; /* Message contents checksum. */
    DWORD data [DATA_SIZE]; /* Message contents. */
} MSG_BLOCK;

/* Single message block, ready to fill with a new message. */
```

```
MSG_BLOCK mblock = { 0, 0, 0, 0, 0 };

DWORD WINAPI produce (void *);
DWORD WINAPI consume (void *);
void MessageFill (MSG_BLOCK *);
void MessageDisplay (MSG_BLOCK *);

DWORD _tmain (DWORD argc, LPTSTR argv [])
{
    DWORD Status, ThId;
    HANDLE produce_h, consume_h;

    /* Initialize the message block CRITICAL SECTION. */
    InitializeCriticalSection (&mblock.mguard);

    /* Create the two threads. */
    produce_h =
        (HANDLE)_beginthreadex (NULL, 0, produce, NULL, 0, &ThId);
    consume_h =
        (HANDLE)_beginthreadex (NULL, 0, consume, NULL, 0, &ThId);

    /* Wait for the producer and consumer to complete. */
    WaitForSingleObject (consume_h, INFINITE);
    WaitForSingleObject (produce_h, INFINITE);
    DeleteCriticalSection (&mblock.mguard);

    _tprintf (_T ("Producer and consumer threads terminated\n"));
    _tprintf (_T ("Produced: %d, Consumed: %d, Known Lost: %d\n"),
            mblock.sequence, mblock.nCons, mblock.nLost);
    return 0;
}

DWORD WINAPI produce (void *arg)
/* Producer thread - create new messages at random intervals. */
{
    srand ((DWORD) time (NULL)); /* Seed the random # generator. */
    while (!mblock.f_stop) {
        /* Random delay. */
        Sleep (rand () / 100);
        /* Get the buffer, fill it. */
        EnterCriticalSection (&mblock.mguard);
        __try {
            if (!mblock.f_stop) {
                mblock.f_ready = 0;
                MessageFill (&mblock);
                mblock.f_ready = 1;
                mblock.sequence++;
            }
        }
        __finally { LeaveCriticalSection (&mblock.mguard); }
```

```
        }
        return 0;
    }


DWORD WINAPI consume (void *arg)
{
    DWORD ShutDown = 0;
    CHAR command, extra;
    /* Consume the NEXT message when prompted by the user. */
    while (!ShutDown) { /* Only thread accessing stdin, stdout. */
        _tprintf (_T ("\n**Enter 'c' for consume; 's' to stop: "));
        _tscanf ("%c%c", &command, &extra);
        if (command == 's') {
            EnterCriticalSection (&mblock.mguard);
            ShutDown = mblock.f_stop = 1;
            LeaveCriticalSection (&mblock.mguard);
        } else if (command == 'c') { /* Get new buffer to consume. */
            EnterCriticalSection (&mblock.mguard);
            __try {
                if (mblock.f_ready == 0)
                    _tprintf (_T ("No new messages. Try again.\n"));
                else {
                    MessageDisplay (&mblock);
                    mblock.nCons++;
                    mblock.nLost = mblock.sequence - mblock.nCons;
                    mblock.f_ready = 0; /* No new messages. */
                }
            }
            __finally { LeaveCriticalSection (&mblock.mguard); }
        } else {
            _tprintf (_T ("Illegal command. Try again.\n"));
        }
    }
    return 0;
}


void MessageFill (MSG_BLOCK *mblock)
{
    /* Fill the message buffer, including checksum and timestamp. */

    DWORD i;

    mblock->checksum = 0;
    for (i = 0; i < DATA_SIZE; i++) {
        mblock->data [i] = rand ();
        mblock->checksum ^= mblock->data [i];
    }
    mblock->timestamp = time (NULL);
    return;
}
```

```
void MessageDisplay (MSG_BLOCK *mblock)
{
    /* Display message buffer, timestamp, and validate checksum. */
    DWORD i, tcheck = 0;
    for (i = 0; i < DATA_SIZE; i++)
    tcheck ^= mblock->data [i];
    _tprintf (_T ("\nMessage number %d generated at: %s"),
            mblock->sequence, _tctime (&(mblock->timestamp))));
    _tprintf (_T ("First and last entries: %x %x\n"),
            mblock->data [0], mblock->data [DATA_SIZE - 1]);
    if (tcheck == mblock->checksum)
        _tprintf (_T ("GOOD ->Checksum was validated.\n"));
    else
        _tprintf (_T ("BAD ->Checksum failed. Message corrupted.\n"));
    return;
}
```

Comments on the Simple Producer/Consumer Example

This example illustrates several important points and programming conventions that will be important throughout this chapter and the next.

- The CRITICAL_SECTION object is a part of the object (the message block) that it protects.

- Every access to the message block is performed in a critical code section.

- The variables that are accessed by the different threads are volatile.

- Termination handlers are used to ensure that the CS is released. This technique, while not essential, helps to ensure that later code modifications do not inadvertently skip the LeaveCriticalSection call. Also, the termination handler is limited to C and should not be used with C++.

- The MessageFill and MessageDisplay functions are called only within critical code sections, and both functions use local, rather than global, storage for their computations. Incidentally, these two functions will be used in subsequent examples but will not be listed again.

- The producer does not have a useful way to tell the consumer that there is a new message, so the consumer simply has to wait until the ready flag, indicating a new message, is set. Event kernel objects will give us a way to eliminate this inefficiency.

- One of the "invariant" properties that this program ensures is that the message block checksum is always correct, *outside* the critical code sections. Another invariant property is:

```
0 <= nLost + nCons <= sequence
```

There will be more about this important concept in the next chapter.

- The producer thread only knows that it should stop by examining a flag in the message block, where the flag is set by the consumer. Since one thread cannot send any sort of signal to another and since `TerminateThread` has undesirable side effects, this technique is the best way to stop another thread. The threads must, of course, cooperate for this method to be effective.

The `CRITICAL_SECTION` object is a powerful synchronization mechanism, yet it does not provide all the functionality that is needed. The inability to signal another thread was noted above, and there is also no time-out capability. The Win32 kernel synchronization objects address these limitations, and more.

Mutexes

A mutex ("mutual exclusion") object provides functionality beyond that of `CRITICAL_SECTION`s. Because mutexes can be named and have handles, they can also be used for interprocess synchronization between threads in separate processes. For example, two processes that share memory by means of memory-mapped files can use mutexes to synchronize access to the shared memory.

Mutex objects are similar to CSs, but, in addition to being process-sharable, mutexes allow time-out values and become signaled when *abandoned* by a terminating process.[1] A thread gains mutex ownership (or "locks" the mutex) by waiting on the mutex handle (`WaitForSingleObject` or `WaitForMultipleObjects`), and it releases ownership with `ReleaseMutex`.

As always, threads should be careful to release resources they own as soon as possible. A thread can acquire a specific mutex several times; the thread will not block if it already has ownership. Ultimately, it must release the mutex the same number of times. This recursive ownership feature, also available with CSs, would be useful for restricting access to a recursive function or in an application that implements nested transactions.

Win32 functions are `CreateMutex`, `ReleaseMutex`, and `OpenMutex`.

---

[1] As a rule of thumb, use a `CRITICAL_SECTION` if the limitations are acceptable, and use mutexes when you have more than one process or need some other mutex capability. Also, CSs are generally, but not always, faster.

```
HANDLE CreateMutex (
    LPSECURITY_ATTRIBUTES lpsa,
    BOOL fInitialOwner,
    LPCTSTR lpszMutexName)
```

The `fInitialOwner` flag, if `TRUE`, gives the calling thread immediate owner-ship of the new mutex. This atomic operation prevents a different thread from gaining mutex ownership before the creating thread does. This flag is overridden if the mutex already exists, as determined by the name.

`lpszMutexName` indicates the mutex name; unlike files, mutex names are case-sensitive. The mutexes are unnamed if the parameter is `NULL`. Events, mu-texes, semaphores, and file mapping objects all share the same name space, which is distinct from the file system name space. Therefore, all synchronization objects should have distinct names. These names are limited to 260 characters.

A `NULL` return value indicates failure.

`OpenMutex` is for opening an existing named mutex. This function is not dis-cussed further but is used in some examples. It allows threads in different pro-cesses to synchronize just as if the threads were in the same process. The `Create` in one process must precede the `Open` in another. Semaphores and events also have `Create` and `Open` functions, as do file mappings (Chapter 6). The assump-tion always is that one process, such as a server, first performs the `Create` call to create the named object, and other processes perform the `Open` call, failing if the named object has not already been created. Alternatively, all processes can use the `Create` call with the same name if the order is not important.

`ReleaseMutex` frees a mutex that the calling thread owns. It fails if the thread does not own the mutex.

```
BOOL ReleaseMutex (HANDLE hMutex)
```

The POSIX Pthreads specification supports mutexes. The four basic functions are as follows:

- `pthread_mutex_init`
- `pthread_mutex_destroy`
- `pthread_mutex_lock`
- `pthread_mutex_unlock`

pthread_mutex_lock will block and is therefore equivalent to WaitFor-
SingleObject when used with a mutex handle. pthread_mutex_trylock is a
nonblocking, polling version that corresponds to WaitForSingleObject with a
zero time-out value. Pthreads do not provide for a time-out, nor is there anything
similar to Win32's CRITICAL_SECTION.

Abandoned Mutexes

If a thread terminates without releasing a mutex that it owns, the mutex becomes
abandoned and the handle is in the signaled state. WaitForSingleObject will
return WAIT_ABANDONED_0, and WaitForMultipleObjects will use
WAIT_ABANDONED_0 as the base value to indicate that the signaled handle(s) represents abandoned mutex(es).

The fact that abandoned mutex handles are signaled is a useful feature not
available with CSs. If an abandoned mutex is detected, there is a possibility of a
defect in the thread code, because threads should be programmed to release their
resources before terminating. It is also possible that the thread was terminated by
some other thread.

Mutexes, CRITICAL_SECTIONs, and Deadlocks

Although CSs and mutexes can solve problems such as the one in Figure 9–1, you
must use them carefully to avoid *deadlocks*, in which two threads become blocked
waiting for a resource owned by the other thread.

Deadlocks are one of the most common and insidious defects in synchronization, and they frequently occur when two or more mutexes must be locked at the
same time. Consider the following problem.

- There are two linked lists, List A and List B, each containing identical structures and maintained by worker threads.

- For one class of list element, correct operation depends on the fact that a given
  element, X, is either in both lists or neither. The invariant, stated informally,
  is: "X is either in both lists or neither."

- In other situations, an element is allowed to be in one list but not in the other.
  Motivation: The lists might be employees in Departments A and B, where
  some employees are allowed to be in both departments.

- Therefore, distinct mutexes (or CRITICAL_SECTIONs) are required for both
  lists, but both mutexes must be locked when adding or deleting a shared element. Using a single mutex would degrade performance, prohibiting concurrent independent updates to the two lists, because the mutex would be "too
  large."

Here is a possible implementation of the worker thread functions for adding and deleting shared list elements.

```
static struct {
    /* Invariant: list is a valid list. */
    HANDLE guard; /* Mutex handle. */
    struct ListStuff;
} ListA, ListB;
...
DWORD WINAPI AddSharedElement (void *arg)
/* Add a shared element to lists A and B. */
{ /* Invariant: new element is in both or neither list. */
    WaitForSingleObject (ListA.guard, INFINITE);
    WaitForSingleObject (ListB.guard, INFINITE);
    /* Add the element to both lists ... */
    ReleaseMutex (ListB.guard);
    ReleaseMutex (ListA.guard);
    return 0;
}
DWORD WINAPI DeleteSharedElement (void *arg)
/* Delete a shared element to lists A and B. */
{
    WaitForSingleObject (ListB.guard, INFINITE);
    WaitForSingleObject (ListA.guard, INFINITE);
    /* Delete the element from both lists ... */
    ReleaseMutex (ListB.guard);
    ReleaseMutex (ListA.guard);
    return 0;
}
```

The code looks correct by all the previous guidelines. However, a preemption of the AddSharedElement thread immediately after it locks List A and immediately before it tries to lock List B will deadlock if the DeleteSharedElement thread starts before the add thread resumes. Each thread owns a mutex the other requires, and neither thread can proceed to the ReleaseMutex call that would unblock the other thread.

Notice that deadlocks are really another form of race condition, as one thread races to acquire all its mutexes before the other thread starts to do so.

One way to avoid deadlock is the "try and back off" strategy whereby a thread calls WaitForSingleObject with a finite time-out value and, when detecting an owned mutex, "backs off" by yielding the processor or sleeping for a brief time before trying again. Designing for deadlock-free systems is even better and more efficient, as described next.

A far simpler method, covered in nearly all operating systems texts, is to specify a "mutex hierarchy" such that all threads acquire the mutexes in exactly the same order and release them in the opposite order. This hierarchical sequence might be arbitrary or could be natural from the structure of the problem. In this example, all that is needed is for the delete function to wait for List A and List B in order, and the threads will never deadlock as long as this hierarchical sequence is observed everywhere by all threads.

Another good way to reduce deadlock potential is to put the two mutex handles in an array and use `WaitForMultipleObjects` with the `fWaitAll` flag set to `TRUE` so that a thread either acquires both or neither of the mutexes in an atomic operation. This technique is not possible with `CRITICAL_SECTION`s.

Review: Mutexes vs. `CRITICAL_SECTIONS`

As stated several times, mutexes and `CRITICAL_SECTION`s are very similar and solve the same set of problems. In particular, both objects can be "owned" by a single thread, and other threads attempting to gain ownership will block until the object is released. Mutexes do, however, provide greater flexibility but with a performance penalty. In summary, the differences are:

- Mutexes, when abandoned by a terminated thread, are signaled so that other threads are not blocked forever.

- Mutex waits can time-out, whereas you can only poll a CS.

- Mutexes can be named and are sharable by threads in different processes.

- You can use `WaitForMultipleObjects` with mutexes, which is both a programming convenience and a way to avoid deadlocks if used properly.

- The thread that creates a mutex can specify immediate ownership. With a CS, several threads could race to acquire the CS.

- CSs are usually, but not always, considerably faster than mutexes. There will be more on this at the end of this chapter.

Heap Synchronization

A pair of functions for NT—`HeapLock` and `HeapUnlock`—is used to synchronize heap access (Chapter 6). The heap handle is the only argument. These functions are helpful when the `HEAP_NO_SERIALIZE` flag is used or when it is necessary for a thread to have exclusive access to a heap.

Semaphores

Semaphores, the second of the three kernel synchronization objects, maintain a count, and the semaphore object is signaled when the count is greater than zero. The semaphore object is unsignaled when the count is zero.

Threads or processes wait in the normal way, using one of the wait functions. When a waiting thread is released, the semaphore's count is decremented by 1.

The semaphore functions are `CreateSemaphore`, `OpenSemaphore`, and `ReleaseSemaphore`, which can increment the count by 1 or more. These functions are similar to their mutex counterparts.

```
HANDLE CreateSemaphore (
    LPSECURITY_ATTRIBUTES lpsa,
    LONG cSemInitial,
    LONG cSemMax,
    LPCTSTR lpszSemName)
```

`cSemMax`, which must be 1 or greater, is the maximum value for the semaphore. `cSemInitial`, with $0 \leq$ `cSemInitial` $\leq$ `cSemMax`, is the initial value, and the semaphore value is never allowed to go outside this range. A `NULL` return value indicates failure.

It is possible to decrease the count only by 1 with any given wait operation, but a semaphore release can increment its count by any value up to the maximum.

```
BOOL ReleaseSemaphore (
    HANDLE hSemaphore,
    LONG cReleaseCount,
    LPLONG lpPreviousCount)
```

Notice that you can find the count preceding the release, but the pointer can be `NULL` if this value is not needed.

The release count must be greater than zero, but if it would cause the semaphore count to exceed the maximum, the call will fail, returning `FALSE`, and the count will remain unchanged. Releasing a semaphore with a large count is a method used to obtain the current count atomically (of course, another thread might change the value immediately).

While it is tempting to think of a semaphore as a special case of a mutex with a maximum value of 1, this would be misleading, because there is no ownership of a semaphore. Any thread can release a semaphore, not just the one that performed the wait. Likewise, since there is no ownership, there is no concept of an abandoned semaphore.

Windows CE Note: Semaphores are not supported by Windows CE. Exercise 10–12 shows how to emulate a semaphore with a mutex and an event.

Using Semaphores

The classic semaphore application regards the semaphore count as representing the number of available resources, such as the number of messages waiting in a queue. The semaphore maximum then represents the maximum queue size. Thus, a producer would place a message in the buffer and call `ReleaseSemaphore`, usually with a release count of 1. Consumer threads would wait on the semaphore, consuming a message and decrementing the semaphore count.

Another important use is described in the discussion following Program 9–3, where a semaphore can be used to limit the number of worker threads actually running at any one time, thereby decreasing contention between threads and, in some cases, improving performance. The final example in this chapter will illustrate this technique.

The potential race condition in `sortMT` (Program 8–2) illustrates another use of a semaphore to control the exact number of threads to wake up. All the threads could be created without being suspended. All of them would immediately wait on a semaphore initialized to zero. The boss thread, rather than resuming the threads, would simply call `ReleaseSemaphore` with a count of 4 (or whatever the number of threads is), and the four threads could then proceed.

A Semaphore Limitation

There is still an important limitation with the Win32 semaphore implementation. How can a thread request that the count be decremented by 2? The thread can wait twice in succession, as shown below, but this would not be an atomic operation because the thread could be preempted between waits. A deadlock could result, as described next.

```
/* hsem is a semaphore handle.
The maximum semaphore count is 2. */
    ...
/* Decrement the semaphore by two. */
WaitForSingleObject (hSem, INFINITE);
```

```
WaitForSingleObject (hSem, INFINITE);
   ...
/* Release two semaphore counts. */
ReleaseSemaphore (hSem, 2, &PrevCount);
```

To see how a deadlock is possible in this situation, suppose that the maximum and original semaphore counts are set to 2 and that the first of two threads completes the first wait and is then preempted. A second thread could then complete the first wait, reducing the count to zero. Both threads will block forever, because neither will be able to get past the second wait. This simple deadlock situation is typical.

A possible correct solution, shown in the code fragment below, is to protect the waits with a mutex or CRITICAL_SECTION.

```
/* Decrement the semaphore by two. */
EnterCriticalSection (&csSem);
WaitForSingleObject (hSem, INFINITE);
WaitForSingleObject (hSem, INFINITE);
LeaveCriticalSection (&csSem);

   ...
ReleaseSemaphore (hSem, 2, &PrevCount);
```

Even this implementation, in general form, is limited. Suppose, for example, that the semaphore has two remaining units, Thread A needs three units, and Thread B needs just two. If Thread A arrives first, it will complete two waits and block on the third while owning the mutex. Thread B, which only needs the two remaining units, will still be blocked.

Another proposed solution would be to use WaitForMultipleObjects with the same semaphore handle used several times in the handle array. This suggestion fails for two reasons. First, Win32 will return an error if it detects two handles for the same objects. What is more, the handles would all be signaled, even if the semaphore count were only 1, which would defeat the purpose.

Exercise 10–12 provides a complete solution to this "multiple-wait" problem.

The Win32 semaphore design would be more convenient if we could perform an atomic multiple-wait operation.

Events

Events are the final kernel synchronization object. Events are used to signal other threads that some "event," such as a message being available, has occurred.

The important additional capability offered by events is that multiple threads can be released from a wait simultaneously when a single event is signaled. Events are classified as manual-reset and auto-reset, and this event property is set by the `CreateEvent` call.

- A manual-reset event can signal several threads waiting on the event simultaneously and can be reset.

- An auto-reset event signals a single thread waiting on the event, and the event is reset automatically.

Events use five new functions: `CreateEvent`, `OpenEvent`, `SetEvent`, `ResetEvent`, and `PulseEvent`.

```
HANDLE CreateEvent (
    LPSECURITY_ATTRIBUTES lpsa,
    BOOL fManualReset,
    BOOL fInitialState,
    LPTCSTR lpszEventName)
```

Specify a manual-reset event by setting `fManualReset` to TRUE. Similarly, the event is initially set to signaled if `fInitialState` is TRUE. You open a named event, possibly from another process, with `OpenEvent`.

The following three functions are used for controlling events:

```
BOOL SetEvent (HANDLE hEvent)

BOOL ResetEvent (HANDLE hEvent)

BOOL PulseEvent (HANDLE hEvent)
```

A thread can signal an event using `SetEvent`. If the event is auto-reset, a single waiting thread, possibly one of many, is released, and the event automatically returns to the nonsignaled state. If no threads are waiting on the event, the event remains in the signaled state until a thread waits on it, and the thread is immediately released. Notice that a semaphore with a maximum count of 1 would have the same effect.

If, on the other hand, the event is manual-reset, it remains signaled until a thread calls `ResetEvent` for that event. During this time, all waiting threads are released, and it is possible that other threads will wait, and be released, before the reset.

`PulseEvent` releases all threads currently waiting on a manual-reset event, but the event is then automatically reset. In the case of an auto-reset event, `PulseEvent` releases a single waiting event, if any.

Notice that `ResetEvent` is useful only after a manual-reset event is signaled with `SetEvent`. Be careful when using `WaitForMultipleObjects` to wait for *all* events to become signaled. A waiting thread will be released only when all events are simultaneously in the signaled state, and some signaled events might be reset before the thread is released.

Exercise 9–5 suggests how to modify `sortMT`, Program 8–2, to exploit events.

Pthreads' *condition variables* are somewhat comparable to events, but they are used in conjunction with a mutex. This implementation is actually very useful and will be described in the next chapter. `pthread_cond_init` and `pthread_cond_destroy` create and destroy condition variables. `pthread_cond_wait` and `pthread_cond_timedwait` are the waiting functions. `pthread_cond_signal` signals one waiting thread, as when pulsing a Win32 auto-reset event. `pthread_cond_broadcast` signals all waiting threads and is therefore similar to `PulseEvent` applied to an auto-reset event. There is no exact equivalent to `ResetEvent` and manual-reset events.

Review: The Four Event Usage Models

The combination of auto- and manual-reset events with `SetEvent` and `PulseEvent` gives four distinct ways to use events. Each combination is unique and each is useful, or even necessary, in some situations, and each model combination will be used in an example or exercise, either in this chapter or the next.

Warning: Events, if not used properly, can cause race conditions, deadlocks, and other subtle and difficult-to-diagnose errors. Chapter 10 describes techniques that are almost always required if you are using events in any but the simplest situations.

Table 9–1 describes the four situations.

An auto-reset event can be thought of as a door with a spring that slams the door shut, whereas a manual-reset event does not have a spring and will remain open. Using this metaphor, `PulseEvent` opens the door and immediately shuts it after one (auto-reset) or all (manual-reset) waiting threads go through the door. `SetEvent` opens the door and releases it.

Table 9-1   Summary of Event Behavior

	Auto-Reset Event	Manual-Reset Event
SetEvent	Exactly one thread is released. If none is currently waiting on the event, the first thread to wait on it in the future will be released immediately. The event is automatically reset.	All currently waiting threads are released. The event remains signaled until reset by some thread.
PulseEvent	Exactly one thread is released, but only if a thread is currently waiting on the event.	All currently waiting threads, if any, are released, and the event is then reset. If no thread is waiting, the event remains signaled until a thread waits on the event.

Example: A Producer/Consumer System

This example extends Program 9–1 so that the consumer can wait until there is an available message. This eliminates the problem that requires the consumer to try again if a new message is not available. The resulting program, Program 9–2, is called eventPC.

Notice that the solution uses a mutex rather than a CRITICAL_SECTION; there is no reason for this other than to illustrate mutex usage. The use of an auto-reset event and SetEvent in the producer are, however, essential for correct operation to ensure that just one thread is released.

Also notice how the mutex and event are both associated with the message block data structure. The mutex enforces the critical code section for accessing the data structure object, and the event is used to signal the fact that there is a new message. Generalizing, the mutex ensures the object's invariants, and the event signals that the object is in a specified state. This basic technique is used extensively in the next chapter.

Program 9–2   eventPC: A Signaling Producer and Consumer

```
/* Chapter 9. eventPC.c */
/* Maintain two threads, a producer and a consumer. */
/* The producer periodically creates checksummed data buffers, */
/* or "message blocks," signaling the consumer that a message */
/* is ready. The consumer displays when prompted. */

#include "EvryThng.h"
#include <time.h>
```

```
#define DATA_SIZE 256

typedef struct msg_block_tag { /* Message block. */
    volatile DWORD f_ready, f_stop;
        /* Ready state flag, stop flag. */
    volatile DWORD sequence; /* Message block sequence number. */
    volatile DWORD nCons, nLost;
    time_t timestamp;
    HANDLE mguard; /* Mutex to guard the message block structure. */
    HANDLE mready; /* "Message ready" event. */
    DWORD checksum; /* Message contents checksum. */
    DWORD data [DATA_SIZE]; /* Message contents. */
} MSG_BLOCK;

/* ... */

DWORD _tmain (DWORD argc, LPTSTR argv [])
{
    DWORD Status, ThId;
    HANDLE produce_h, consume_h;

    /* Initialize the message block mutex and event (auto-reset). */
    mblock.mguard = CreateMutex (NULL, FALSE, NULL);
    mblock.mready = CreateEvent (NULL, FALSE, FALSE, NULL);

    /* Create producer and consumer; wait until they terminate. */
    /* ... As in Program 9-1 ... */
    CloseHandle (mblock.mguard);
    CloseHandle (mblock.mready);

    _tprintf (_T ("Producer and consumer threads terminated\n"));
    _tprintf (_T ("Produced: %d, Consumed: %d, Known Lost: %d\n"),
            mblock.sequence, mblock.nCons, mblock.nLost);
    return 0;
}

DWORD WINAPI produce (void *arg)
/* Producer thread - create new messages at random intervals. */
{
    srand ((DWORD)time(NULL)); /* Seed the random # generator. */
    while (!mblock.f_stop) {
        /* Random delay. */
        Sleep (rand () / 10); /* Wait a long period for next message. */

        /* Get the buffer, fill it. */
        WaitForSingleObject (mblock.mguard, INFINITE);
        __try {
            if (!mblock.f_stop) {
                mblock.f_ready = 0;
                MessageFill (&mblock);
```

```
                    mblock.f_ready = 1;
                    mblock.sequence++;
                    SetEvent(mblock.mready); /* Signal "message ready." */
                }
            }
            __finally { ReleaseMutex (mblock.mguard); }
        }
        return 0;
}

DWORD WINAPI consume (void *arg)
{
    DWORD ShutDown = 0;
    CHAR command, extra;
    /* Consume the NEXT message when prompted by the user. */
    while (!ShutDown) { /* Only thread accessing stdin, stdout. */
        _tprintf (_T ("\n**Enter 'c' for consume; 's' to stop: "));
        _tscanf ("%c%c", &command, &extra);
        if (command == 's') {
            WaitForSingleObject (mblock.mguard, INFINITE);
            ShutDown = mblock.f_stop = 1;
            ReleaseMutex (mblock.mguard);
        } else if (command == 'c') { /* Get new buffer to consume. */
            WaitForSingleObject (mblock.mready, INFINITE);
            WaitForSingleObject (mblock.mguard, INFINITE);
            __try {
                if (!mblock.f_ready) _leave;
                /* Wait for the event indicating a message is ready. */
                MessageDisplay (&mblock);
                mblock.nCons++;
                mblock.nLost = mblock.sequence - mblock.nCons;
                mblock.f_ready = 0; /* No new messages are ready. */
            }
            __finally { ReleaseMutex (mblock.mguard); }
        } else {
            _tprintf (_T ("Illegal command. Try again.\n"));
        }
    }
    return 0;
}
```

Note: There is a possibility that the consumer, having received the message ready event, will not actually process the current message if the producer generates yet another message before the consumer acquires the mutex. This behavior could cause a consumer to process a single message twice if it were not for the test at the start of the consumer's __try block. This issue will be addressed in the next chapter.

Table 9-2 Comparison of Win32 Synchronization Objects

	`CRITICAL_SECTION`	Mutex	Semaphore	Event
Named, Securable Synchronization Object	No	Yes	Yes	Yes
Accessible from Multiple Processes	No	Yes	Yes	Yes
Synchronization	Enter	Wait	Wait	Wait
Release	Leave	Release or abandoned	Any thread can release.	Set, pulse
Ownership	One thread at a time. The owning thread can enter multiple times without blocking.	One thread at a time. The owning thread can wait multiple times without blocking.	N/A. Many threads at a time, up to the maximum count.	N/A. Any thread can set or pulse an event.
Effect of Release	One waiting thread can enter.	One waiting thread can gain ownership after last release.	Multiple threads can proceed, depending on release count.	One or several waiting threads will proceed after a set or pulse.

Review: Win32 Synchronization Objects

Table 9–2 reviews and compares the essential features of the Win32 synchronization objects.

Message and Object Waiting

The function `MsgWaitForMultipleObjects` is similar to `WaitForMultipleObjects`. Use this new function to allow a thread to process user interface events, such as mouse clicks, while waiting on synchronization objects.

Example: Synchronization Performance Impact

Synchronization can and will impact the performance of your program, and you need to be especially careful when running on SMP systems. Normally, we would expect that SMP would generally improve performance and certainly never slow down a program. However, it turns out that internal implementation mechanisms used in 2000/NT can produce unexpected effects.

The first step is to assess the performance impact of synchronization and compare CRITICAL_SECTIONs to mutexes. Program 9–3 shows statsMX.c, which uses a mutex to synchronize access to a thread-specific data structure. statsCS.c, not shown, does exactly the same thing using a CRITICAL_SECTION, and statsIN.c uses interlocked functions. Finally, statsNS.c, also not shown, uses no synchronization at all; it turns out, in this example, that synchronization is not required, because each worker accesses its own unique storage. (However, see the cautionary note after the bulleted list following the program.)

This example not only illustrates the relative performance impact of three types of synchronization but also shows the following:

- Synchronization can sometimes be avoided with careful program design.

- A common technique whereby each thread argument data structure contains state data to be maintained by the thread along with a pointer to a mutex or other synchronization object.

Program 9–3 statsMX: Maintaining Thread Statistics

```
/* Chapter 9. statsMX.c */
/* Simple boss/worker system, where each worker reports */
/* its work output back to the boss for display. */
/* MUTEX VERSION. */

#include "EvryThng.h"
#define DELAY_COUNT 20

/* Usage: statsMX nthread ntasks */
/* Start up nthread worker threads, each assigned to perform */
/* "ntasks" work units. Each thread reports its progress */
/* in its own unshared slot in a work-performed array. */
/* ntasks is limited to 64K as it's an unsigned short int. */
/* There is a reason for this, described after the program. */

DWORD WINAPI worker (void *);

typedef struct _THARG {
    int thread_number;
```

```
    HANDLE *phMutex;
    unsigned short int tasks_to_complete;
    unsigned short int *tasks_complete;
} THARG;

int _tmain (DWORD argc, LPTSTR argv [])
{
    INT tstatus, nthread, ithread;
    HANDLE *worker_t, hMutex;
    unsigned short int * task_count, tasks_per_thread;
    THARG * thread_arg;

    /* Create the mutex. */
    hMutex = CreateMutex (NULL, FALSE, NULL);

    nthread = _ttoi (argv [1]);
    tasks_per_thread = _ttoi (argv [2]);
    worker_t = malloc (nthread * sizeof (HANDLE));
    task_count = calloc (nthread, sizeof (unsigned short int));
    thread_arg = calloc (nthread, sizeof (THARG));

    for (ithread = 0; ithread < nthread; ithread++) {
        /* Fill in the thread arg. */
        thread_arg [ithread].thread_number = ithread;
        thread_arg [ithread].tasks_to_complete = tasks_per_thread;
        thread_arg [ithread].tasks_complete = &task_count [ithread];
        thread_arg [ithread].phMutex = &hMutex;
        worker_t [ithread] = (HANDLE)_beginthreadex (NULL, 0, worker,
                &thread_arg [ithread], 0, &ThId);
    }

    /* Wait for the threads to complete. */
    WaitForMultipleObjects (nthread, worker_t, TRUE, INFINITE);
    free (worker_t);
    printf ("Worker threads have terminated\n");
    for (ithread = 0; ithread < nthread; ithread++) {
        _tprintf (_T ("Tasks completed by thread %5d: %6d\n"),
             ithread, task_count [ithread]);
    }
    return 0;
    free (task_count);
    free (thread_arg);
}

DWORD WINAPI worker (void *arg)
{
    THARG * thread_arg;
    int ithread;

    thread_arg = (THARG *) arg;
```

```
        ithread = thread_arg->thread_number;

    while (*thread_arg->tasks_complete <
            thread_arg->tasks_to_complete) {
        delay_cpu (DELAY_COUNT);
        WaitForSingleObject (*(thread_arg->phMutex), INFINITE);
        (*thread_arg->tasks_complete)++;
        ReleaseMutex (*(thread_arg->phMutex));
    }
    return 0;
}
```

You can use the `timep` program from Chapter 7 to examine the behavior of the different implementations. Tests performed with 64,000 work units and 1, 2, 4, 8, 16, and 32 worker threads show:

- For a small number of theads (four or less), the NS (no synchronization), IN (interlocked functions), and CS (`CRITICAL_SECTION`) programs all require about the same amount of time, although the CS version can be marginally slower. The MX (mutex) version, however requires two to three times as long to execute.

- CS performance does not scale with the number of threads on a single processor system when the number of theads is five or more. For instance, running Windows 2000 on a 333MHz AMD processor gives elapsed times of 2.9 sec (3 threads), 3.9 sec (4 threads), 5.08 sec (5 threads), 10.52 sec (6 threads), 12.08 sec (7 threads), and 14.50 sec (8 threads). Beyond 8 threads, CS performance is nearly linear with the number of threads and, what is more, CS performance is about the same, or not as good, as MX performance.

- MX performance, while almost always slower than CS on a single processor, is nearly linear with the number of threads.

- Additional studies, suggested by the program `TimedMutualExclusion` on the disc, show that a CS can have a 10:1, or better, advantage over mutexes when the critical code section is large and the number of threads is small. Exercise 9–9 also suggests studying the effect of the spin count on performance.

- *Performance on an SMP system can be very poor*, by a factor of 10:1 or even 100:1. Intuitively, we would expect better performance with multiple processors, but the internal implementation means that the processors are contending for locks, which explains why the MX and CS results are nearly equivalent. Tuning the CS spin count can help.

- A semaphore can be used to limit the number of ready worker threads without changing the basic programming model. This technique is the subject of Exercise 9–10.

Cautionary Note: The `task_count` array deliberately uses 16-bit integers to demonstrate the potential for "word tearing" or a "cache line conflict" on SMP systems. Two separate processors, running "adjacent" worker threads, could concurrently modify adjacent task counts, making the modification in their caches (32 bits on Intel x84 systems and 64 bits for Compaq Alpha). Only one cache, however, would actually be written back to memory, producing invalid results. The solution requires that each thread's working storage be properly separated and aligned according to cache size. In this example, the task count could be grouped with the thread argument, and there is no good reason not to use a 32-bit count. Exercise 9–12 explores this subject.

More Mutex and CRITICAL_SECTION Guidelines

We are now familiar with all the Win32 synchronization objects and have shown their utility in the examples. Mutexes and CSs were the first objects described and, because events will be used extensively in the next chapter, it is worthwhile to conclude this chapter with some guidelines for using mutexes and CSs to help ensure program correctness, maintainability, and performance.

Nearly everything is stated in terms of mutexes; the statements also apply to CSs unless noted otherwise.

- If there is no time-out associated with `WaitForSingleObject` on a mutex handle, the calling thread could block forever. It is the programmer's responsibility to ensure that an owned (or "locked") mutex is eventually unlocked.

- If a thread terminates, or is terminated, before it leaves ("unlocks") a CS, the CS remains locked. Mutexes have the very useful abandonment property.

- If `WaitForSingleObject` times out waiting for a mutex, do not access the resources that the mutex is designed to protect.

- There may be multiple threads waiting on a given locked mutex. When the mutex is unlocked, *exactly one* of the waiting threads is given mutex ownership and moved to the ready state by the OS scheduler based on priority and scheduling policy. Do not assume that any particular thread will have priority; as always, program so that your application will operate correctly regardless of which waiting thread gains mutex ownership and resumes execution.

- A code "critical section" is everything between the points where the thread gains and relinquishes mutex ownership. A single mutex can be used to define several critical sections. If properly implemented, at most one thread can execute a mutex's critical section at any time.

- *Mutex granularity* affects performance and is an important consideration. *Each critical section should be just as long as necessary, and no longer, and a mutex should be owned just as long as necessary, and no longer.* Large critical sections, held for a long period of time, defeat concurrency and can impact performance.

- Associate the mutex directly with the resource it is designed to protect, possibly in a data structure. (Programs 9–1 and 9–2 use this technique.)

- Document the invariant as precisely as possible, in words or even as a logical, or Boolean, expression. The invariant is a property of the protected resource that you guarantee holds outside the critical code section. An invariant might be of the form: "the element is in both or neither list," "the checksum on the data buffer is valid," "the linked list is valid," or "0 <= nLost + nCons <= sequence." A precisely formulated invariant can be used with the ASSERT macro when debugging a program.

- Ensure that each critical section has exactly one entrance, where the thread locks the mutex, and exactly one exit, where the thread unlocks the mutex. Avoid complex conditional code and avoid premature exits, such as break, return, and goto statements, from within the critical section. Termination handlers are useful for protecting against such problems.

- If the critical section code becomes too lengthy (longer than one page, perhaps), but all the logic is required, consider putting the code in a function so that the synchronization can be easily comprehended. For example, the code to delete a node from a balanced search tree while the tree is locked might best be put in a function.

More Interlocked Functions

InterlockedIncrement and InterlockedDecrement have already been shown to be useful when all you need to do is perform very simple operations on thread-shared variables. There are several other functions that allow you to perform atomic operations to compare and exchange variable pairs.

Interlocked exchange stores one variable into another, as follows:

```
LONG InterlockedExchange (
    LPLONG Target,
    LONG Value)
```

The function returns the current value of *Target and sets *Target to Value. Target should be full-word aligned.

InterlockedExchangeAdd adds the second value to the first.

```
LONG InterlockedExchangeAdd (
    PLONG Addend,
    LONG Increment)
```

Increment is added to *Addend, and the original value of *Addend is returned. This function allows you to increment a variable by 2 (or more) atomically, which is not possible with successive calls to InterlockedIncremenet.

The final function, InterlockedCompareExchange, is similar to InterlockedExchange except that the exchange is done only if a comparison is satisfied.

```
PVOID InterlockedCompareExchange (
    PVOID *Destination,
    PVOID Exchange,
    PVOID Comparand)
```

This function atomically performs the following (the use of PVOID types for the last two parameters is confusing):

```
Temp = *Destination;
if (*Destination == Comparand) *Destination = Exchange;
return Temp;
```

One use of this function is as a lock to implement a code critical section. *Destination is the "lock variable," with 1 indicating "unlocked" and 0 indicating "locked." Exchange is 0 and Comparand is 1. A calling thread knows that it "owns" the critical section if the function returns 1. Otherwise, it should sleep or "spin"—that is, execute a meaningless loop that consumes time for a short period and try again. This spinning is essentially what EnterCriticalSection does when waiting for a CRITICAL_SECTION that has a nonzero spin count.

Memory Management Performance Considerations

Program 9–3 illustrates the potential performance impact when multiple threads contend for a shared resource. A similar effect will be seen if threads perform memory management using malloc and free from the multithreaded standard C library, because these functions use a CRITICAL_SECTION to synchronize access to a "heap" data structure (you can confirm this by examining the C library source code). Here are two possible methods of improving performance:

- Each thread that performs memory management can create a HANDLE to its own heap using HeapCreate (Chapter 6). Memory allocation is then performed using HeapAlloc and HeapFree rather than using malloc and free.

- A run-time environment variable, __MSVCRT_HEAP_SELECT, can be set to __GLOBAL_HEAP_SELECTED. This will cause malloc and free to use Win32 memory management, which uses spin locks rather than CSs and can be more efficient. This method was developed by Gerbert Orasche in a May, 2000 *Windows Developer's Journal* article, "Configuring VC++ Multithreaded Memory Management," and the article shows some favorable performance results.

Summary

Win32 supports a complete set of synchronization operations that allows threads and processes to be implemented safely. Synchronization introduces a host of program design and development issues that must be considered carefully, to ensure both program correctness and good performance.

Looking Ahead

Chapter 10 shows how to use Win32 synchronization in more general ways, and it discusses several programming models that help to ensure correctness and maintainability. Chapter 10 also creates several "compound synchronization objects" that are useful for solving a number of important problems. Chapter 12 illustrates and discusses thread safety and reentrancy in DLLs.

Additional Reading

Win32

Synchronization issues are independent of the operating system, and many operating system texts discuss the issue at length and within a more general framework.

Other books on Win32 synchronization have already been mentioned. When dealing with more general Win32 books, however, exercise caution, because some are misleading when it comes to threads and synchronization. One very popular and well-reviewed book, for instance, while consuming a large number of pages of prose, never mentions the need for `volatile` storage, does not explain the four event combinations adequately, and recommends the deadlock-prone multiple semaphore wait solution (discussed in the section on Semaphores) as a technique for obtaining more than one semaphore unit.

Also, Butenhof's *Programming with POSIX Threads* is recommended for in-depth thread and synchronization understanding, even for the Win32 programmer. The discussions and descriptions generally apply equally well to Win32, and porting the example programs can be a good exercise.

Exercises

9–1. The disc contains a defective version of `simplePC.c` (Program 9–1) called `simplePCx.c`. Test this program and describe the defect symptoms, if any. Fix the program without reference to the correct solution.

9–2. Modify `simplePC.c` so that the time period between new messages is increased. (*Suggestion*: Eliminate the division in the sleep call.) Ensure that the logic that determines if there is a new message is correct. Also experiment with the defective version, `simplePCx.c`.

9–3. Reimplement `simplePC.c` with a mutex.

9–4. Reimplement `sortMT.c` (Program 8–2) using a semaphore, rather than thread suspension, to synchronize worker thread start-up.

9–5. Reimplement `sortMT.c` (Program 8–2) using an event rather than thread suspension to synchronize worker thread start-up. The recommended solution uses `SetEvent` and a manual-reset event. Other combinations would not be assured of correct operation. Explain.

9–6. Experiment with Program 9–2 by using different combinations of auto- and manual-reset events and `SetEvent` and `PulseEvent` (the current solution uses `SetEvent` and an auto-reset event). Are the alternate implementations and the original implementation correct, given the definition of the program's intended functionality (see the note at the end of the program)? Explain the results and explain how the alternate functionality might be useful. Can you make any of the alternate implementations work by changing the program logic?

9–7. Create a worker thread pool but control the rate of worker thread operation so that only one thread is allowed to run in any 1-second interval. Modify the program so that two threads can run in the interval but the overall rate of thread operation is limited to one per second. *Hint*: The worker threads should wait on an event (what type of event?), and a controlling thread should signal the event (`SetEvent` or `PulseEvent`?) every second.

9–8. Experiment with Program 9–3 on your own system and on as many different systems (both hardware and Windows version) as are available to you. Do you obtain similar results as those reported here? What happens on an SMP system?

9–9. Experiment with `CRITICAL_SECTION` spin counts to see whether adjusting the count can improve and tune performance when you have a large number of threads.

9–10. *Recommended for Additional Performance Studies*: The program `Time-MutualExclusion.c`, included on the program disc, extends the performance studies started in Program 9–3. This program also uses a semaphore to limit the number of running threads. Understand how the semaphore is used, confirm that it can improve performance when you have numerous threads, and apply the same technique to Program 9–3 (`statsCS.c`, `statsMX.c`).

9–11. *Advanced Exercise*: Do the four variations of Program 9–3 all operate correctly, ignoring performance, on SMP systems? Experiment with a large number of worker threads. If at all possible, run on an SMP Alpha processor system running Windows NT. Can you reproduce the "word tearing" or "cache line conflict" problem described earlier and also in Butenhof's *Programming with POSIX Threads*?

9–12. *Advanced Exercise*: `CRITICAL_SECTION`s are intended to be used by threads within the same process. What happens if you create a critical section in shared, memory-mapped storage? Can both processes use the critical section? You can perform this experiment by modifying Program 9–1 so that the producer and consumer run in different processes.

10 Advanced Thread Synchronization

The preceding chapter described the Win32 synchronization objects and showed how to use them to solve several realistic, but simple, problems. This chapter will solve additional real, but more complex, problems, relying on some ideas introduced briefly in Chapter 9.

The first step is to combine two or more synchronization objects and data to create "compound objects." The most useful combination is the "condition variable model" involving a mutex and one or more events. The condition variable model is essential in numerous practical situations, and many serious program race condition defects occur when programmers do not use the Win32 synchronization objects, especially events, properly. Events are complex, and their behavior varies depending on the choices illustrated in Table 9–1, so they should be used according to well-understood models.

This chapter does not introduce any new Win32 functions; instead, the goal is to show how to use the existing functions and objects effectively and reliably. Performance considerations are also described.

Mutexes, Events, and the Condition Variable Model

Threaded programs are much easier to develop, understand, and maintain if we use well-understood and familiar techniques and models. Chapter 8 discussed this and introduced the "boss/worker" and "work crew" models to establish a useful framework for understanding many threaded programs. The "critical section" concept is essential when using mutexes, and describing the invariants of your data structure is very useful. Finally, even defects have models, as we saw with the deadlock example. *Note*: Microsoft has their own set of models, such as the "apartment model" and "free threading." These terms are most often used with COM and will be discussed at the end of Chapter 11.

Using Events and Mutexes Together

The next step is to describe how to use mutexes and events together, generalizing Program 9–2, where we had the following situation, which will occur over and over again. *Note*: This discussion applies to CRITICAL_SECTIONs as well as to mutexes.

- The mutex and event are both associated with the message block or other data structure.

- The mutex defines the critical section for accessing the data structure object.

- The event is used to signal the fact that there is a new message.

- Generalizing, the mutex ensures the object's invariants, and the event signals that the object is in a specified state.

- One thread (the producer in Program 9–2) locks the data structure, changes the object's state by creating a new message, and sets or pulses the event associated with the fact that there is a new message.

- One or more other threads (the consumer in this example) wait on the event for the object to reach the desired state. The wait must occur outside the critical section so that the producer can access the object.

- A consumer thread can also lock the mutex, test the object's state (for example, is there a new message?), and avoid the event wait if the object is already in the desired state.

The Condition Variable Model

Now, let's combine all of this into a single code fragment that represents what we will call the "condition variable model." The result is a program model that will occur many times and can be used to solve a wide variety of synchronization problems. For convenience, the example is stated in terms of a producer and a consumer.

The discussion may seem a bit abstract, but once the techniques are understood, we will be able to solve a number of synchronization problems that would be very difficult without a good model.

The code fragment has several key elements:

- There is a data structure of type STATE_TYPE that contains all the data or "state variables" such as the messages, checksums, and counters used in Program 9–2.

- A mutex and one or more events associated with, and usually a part of, the data structure.

- One or more Boolean functions to evaluate the "condition variable predicates," which are the conditions (states) on which a thread might wait. Examples include: "a new message is ready," "there is available space in the buffer," and "the queue is not empty." A distinct event is associated with each condition variable predicate. If the predicate (logical expression) is simple, there is no need for a separate function.

The code segment below shows a producer and consumer using these principles, with a single event and condition variable predicate (implemented with a function, cvp, that is assumed but not shown). When the producer signals that a desired state has been reached, this example assumes that it is appropriate to release several consumer threads—that is, the signal should be "broadcast" to all waiting consumers. For instance, the producer may have created several messages, and, in the following example, the state is changed by increasing the message count. In many situations, you want to release only a single thread, as will be discussed after the code fragment.

```
typedef struct _state_t {
    HANDLE Guard; /* Mutex to protect the object. */
    HANDLE CvpSet; /* Manual-reset event - cvp () holds. */
    ... other condition variables ...
    /* State structure with counts, checksums, etc. */
    struct STATE_VAR_TYPE StateVar;
} STATE_TYPE State;
...
/* Initialize State, creating the mutex and event. */
...
/* PRODUCER thread that modifies State. */
WaitForSingleObject (State.Guard, INFINITE);
/* Change state so that the CV predicate holds. */
/* Example: one or more messages are now ready. */
State.StateVar.MsgCount += N;
PulseEvent (State.CvpSet);
ReleaseMutex (State.Guard);
/* End of the interesting part of the producer. */

...
/* CONSUMER thread function waits for a particular state. */
WaitForSingleObject (State.Guard, INFINITE);
while (!cvp (&State)) {
```

```
        ReleaseMutex (State.Guard);
        WaitForSingleObject (State.CvpSet, TimeOut);
        WaitForSingleObject (State.Guard, INFINITE);
    }
    /* This thread now owns the mutex and cvp (&State) holds. */
    /* Take appropriate action, perhaps modifying State. */
    ...
    ReleaseMutex (State.Guard);
    /* End of the interesting part of the consumer. */
```

Comments on the Condition Variable Model

The essential feature in the segment above is the loop in the consumer. The loop body consists of three steps: 1) unlock the mutex that was locked prior to entering the loop, 2) wait on the event, and 3) lock the mutex again. *The event wait time-out is significant*, as explained later.

Pthreads, as implemented in many UNIX and other systems, combine these three steps into a single function, `pthread_cond_wait`, combining a mutex and a "condition variable" (which is similar to the Win32 event). This is the reason for using the term "condition variable model." There is also a timed version, which allows a time-out on the event wait.

Importantly, the single Pthreads function implements the first two steps (the mutex release and event wait) as an atomic operation so that no other thread can run before the calling thread waits on the event (or condition variable).

The Pthreads designers made a wise choice; the two functions (with and without a time-out) are the only ways to wait on a condition variable in Pthreads, so a condition variable must always be used with a mutex. Win32 forces you to use three separate function calls, and you need to do it in just the right way to avoid problems.

Another motivation for learning the CV model, besides the fact that it simplifies programs and is essential if you ever need to use Pthreads, is that several third parties implement OS-independent thread and synchronization classes based on the CV model. With the material here, you will be able to understand those implementations quickly.

Note: Windows 2000/NT provides a function, `SignalObjectAndWait`, that performs the first two steps atomically. In order to preserve portability to all platforms and the flexibility to use a CS in place of a mutex, however, we will not use this function in the examples; its use is left to the exercises, and Appendix C (Table C–5), where `SignalObjectAndWait` is shown to provide significant performance advantages.

Using the Condition Variable Model

The condition variable model, when implemented properly, works as follows:

- The producer locks the mutex, changes state, pulses the event when appropriate, and unlocks the mutex. For example, the producer will pulse the event when one or more messages are ready.

- The event should be pulsed with the mutex locked so that no other thread can modify the object, perhaps invalidating the condition variable predicate.

- The consumer tests the condition variable predicate *with the mutex locked*. If the predicate holds, there is no need to wait.

- If the predicate does not hold, the consumer must unlock the mutex before waiting on the event. Otherwise, no thread could ever modify the state and set the event.

- The event wait must have a time-out just in case the producer pulses the event in the interval between the mutex release (step 1) and the event wait (step 2). That is, without the *finite* time-out, there could be a "lost signal," which is another example of a race condition. The time-out value used in the producer/consumer segment is a tunable parameter. (See Appendix C for comments on optimal values.)

- The consumer always retests the predicate after the event wait. Among other things, this is necessary in case the event wait has timed out. Also, the state may have changed. For example, the producer may have produced two messages and then released three waiting consumers, and so one of the consumers will test the state, find no more messages, and wait again. Finally, the retest protects against "spurious wakeups" that might result from a thread setting or pulsing the event without the mutex locked.

- The consumer always owns the mutex when it leaves the loop, regardless of whether the loop body was executed.

Condition Variable Model Variations

Notice, first, that the example code fragment uses a manual-reset event and calls `PulseEvent` rather than `SetEvent`. Is this the correct choice, and could the event be used differently? The answer is "yes" to both questions.

Referring back to Table 9–1, we see that the example has the property that *multiple threads* will be released. This is correct in this example, where several messages are produced and there are multiple consuming threads. However, if the producer creates just one message and there are multiple consuming threads, the event should be auto-reset and the producer should call `SetEvent` to ensure that exactly one thread is released. It is still essential for the released consumer thread, which will then own the mutex, to modify the object to indicate that there is no available message (that is, the condition variable predicate will no longer hold).

Of the four combinations in Table 9–1, two are useful in the condition variable model. Considering the other two combinations, auto-reset/`PulseEvent` would have the same effect as auto-reset/`SetEvent` because of the time-out, but the dependence on the time-out would reduce responsiveness. The manual-reset/`SetEvent` combination causes "spurious signals" (the condition variable predicate test offers protection, however), because some thread must reset the event, and there will be a race among the threads before the event is reset.

Compared with Pthreads and similar synchronization models, auto-reset/`SetEvent` is the "signaling CV model," which releases a single waiting thread, while manual-reset/`PulseEvent` is the "broadcast CV model," which releases all waiting threads. The biggest difference is that Pthreads do not require the finite time-out in the event wait for the broadcast model, whereas the time-out is essential in Windows because the mutex release and event wait are not performed atomically.

An Example Condition Variable Predicate

Consider the condition variable predicate:

```
State.StateVar.Count >= K;
```

In this case, a consumer thread will wait until the count is sufficiently large, and the producer can increment the count by an arbitrary amount. This shows, for example, how to implement a multiple-wait semaphore; recall that normal semaphores do not have an atomic wait for multiple units. The consumer thread would then decrement the count by K after leaving the loop but before releasing the mutex.

Notice that the broadcast CV model is appropriate in this case because a single producer may increase the count so as to satisfy several, but not all, of the waiting consumers.

Semaphores and the Condition Variable Model

In some cases, a semaphore would be appropriate rather than an event, and semaphores have the advantage of specifying the exact number of threads to be released. For example, if each consumer were known to consume exactly one message, then the producer could call `ReleaseSemaphore` with the exact number of messages produced. In the more general case, however, the producer does not know how the individual consumers will modify the state variable structure, so the condition variable model can be used to solve a wider class of problems.

The CV model is powerful enough to implement semaphores. As described above, the basic technique is to define a predicate stating that "the semaphore count is nonzero" and create a state structure containing the count and maximum value. Exercise 10–12 shows a complete solution that allows for an atomic wait for multiple units. Pthreads do not provide semaphores, because condition variables are sufficiently powerful.

Example: A Threshold Barrier Object

Suppose that you wish to have the worker threads wait until there are enough workers to form a work crew so that work can proceed. Once the "threshold" is reached, all the workers start operation and, if any other workers arrive later, they do not wait. This problem can be solved by creating a "threshold barrier" object.

Program 10–1 and Program 10–2 show the implementation of the three functions that support the threshold barrier "compound object." Two of the functions, CreateThresholdBarrier and CloseThresholdBarrier, manage a THB_HANDLE, which is similar to the handles that we have used all along for kernel objects. The threshold number of threads is a parameter to Create-ThresholdBarrier.

Program 10–1 shows the appropriate part of the header file, SynchObj.h, while Program 10–2 shows the implementation of the three functions. Notice that the barrier object has a mutex, an event, a counter, and a threshold. The condition variable predicate is documented in the header file—that is, the event is to be set exactly when the count is greater than or equal to the threshold.

Program 10–1   SynchObj.h: Part 1—Threshold Barrier Definitions

```
/* Chapter 10. Compound synchronization objects. */

#define CV_TIMEOUT 50 /* Tunable parameter for the CV model. */

/* THRESHOLD BARRIER - TYPE DEFINITION AND FUNCTIONS. */
typedef struct THRESHOLD_BARRIER_TAG { /* Threshold barrier. */
    HANDLE b_guard; /* Mutex for the object. */
    HANDLE b_broadcast; /* Manual-reset evt: b_count >= b_threshold. */
    volatile DWORD b_destroyed; /* Set when closed. */
    volatile DWORD b_count; /* # of threads at the barrier. */
    volatile DWORD b_threshold; /* Barrier threshold. */
} THRESHOLD_BARRIER, *THB_HANDLE;
```

```
/* Error values. */
#define SYNCH_OBJ_NOMEM 1 /* Unable to allocate resources. */
#define SYNCH_OBJ_BUSY 2 /* Object is in use and cannot be closed. */
#define SYNCH_OBJ_INVALID 3 /* Object is no longer valid. */

DWORD CreateThresholdBarrier (THB_HANDLE *, DWORD /* Threshold. */);
DWORD WaitThresholdBarrier (THB_HANDLE);
DWORD CloseThresholdBarrier (THB_HANDLE);
```

Program 10–2 now shows the implementation of the three functions. A test program, `testTHB.c`, is included on the disc. Notice how the `WaitThreshold-Barrier` function contains the familiar condition variable loop. Also notice that the wait function not only waits on the event but also signals the event using `PulseEvent`. The previous producer/consumer discussion assumed that distinct thread functions were involved.

Finally, the condition variable predicate is, in this case, "persistent." Once it becomes true, it will never change, so there is no danger from signaling the event more than once.

Program 10–2 `ThbObject.c:` Implementing the Threshold Barrier

```
/* ThbObject.c. Program 10-2. */
/* Threshold barrier compound synch objects library. */

#include "EvryThng.h"
#include "synchobj.h"

/****************************/
/* THRESHOLD BARRIER OBJECTS */
/****************************/

DWORD CreateThresholdBarrier (THB_HANDLE *pthb, DWORD b_value)
{
    THB_HANDLE hthb;
    /* Initialize a barrier object. Full error testing is on disc. */
    hthb = malloc (sizeof (THRESHOLD_BARRIER));

    hthb->b_guard = CreateMutex (NULL, FALSE, NULL);

    hthb->b_broadcast = CreateEvent (NULL, FALSE /* Auto-reset */,
            FALSE, NULL);

    hthb->b_threshold = b_value;
    hthb->b_count = 0;
    hthb->b_destroyed = 0;
    *pthb = hthb;
```

```
        return 0;
}

DWORD WaitThresholdBarrier (THB_HANDLE thb)
{
    /* Wait for the specified number of threads to reach */
    /* the barrier, then set the event. */
    if (thb->b_destroyed == 1) return SYNCH_OBJ_INVALID;
    WaitForSingleObject (thb->b_guard, INFINITE);
    thb->b_count++; /* A new thread has arrived. */
    while (thb->b_count < thb->b_threshold) {
        ReleaseMutex (thb->b_guard);
        WaitForSingleObject (thb->b_broadcast, CV_TIMEOUT);
        WaitForSingleObject (thb->b_guard, INFINITE);
    }
    PulseEvent (thb->b_broadcast);
    /* SetEvent would work in this example, but not in general. */
    ReleaseMutex (thb->b_guard);
    return 0;
}

DWORD CloseThresholdBarrier (THB_HANDLE thb)
{
    /* Destroy the component mutexes and event. */
    /* Be certain that no thread is waiting on the object. */
    if (thb->b_destroyed == 1) return SYNCH_OBJ_INVALID;
    WaitForSingleObject (thb->b_guard, INFINITE);
    if (thb->b_count < thb->b_threshold) {
        ReleaseMutex (thb->b_guard);
        return SYNCH_OBJ_BUSY;
    }
    ReleaseMutex (thb->b_guard);
    CloseHandle (thb->b_guard);
    CloseHandle (thb->b_broadcast);
    free (thb);
    return 0;
}
```

Comments on the Threshold Barrier Implementation

The threshold barrier object implemented here is limited for simplicity. In general, we would want to emulate Win32 objects by:

- Allowing the object to have security attributes.

- Allowing the object to be named.

- Permitting multiple "handles" on the object and not destroying it until the reference count is zero.

- Allowing the object to be shared between processes.

The disc contains a full implementation of one such object, a multiple wait semaphore, and the techniques used there can then be used for any of the objects in this chapter.

A Queue Object

So far, we have associated a single event with each mutex, but, in general, there might be more than one condition variable predicate. For example, in implementing a first in, first out (FIFO) queue, a thread that removes an element from the queue needs to wait on an event signifying that the queue is not empty, while a thread placing an element in the queue must wait until the queue is not full. The solution is to provide two events, one for each condition.

Program 10–3 shows the definitions of a queue object and its functions. The definitions intentionally demonstrate a different naming style from the Win32 style used up to now. The original program was converted from a Pthreads implementation under UNIX, which encourages the conventions used here. In this way, the reader can sample a different style and, perhaps, determine one that is suitable for his or her own tastes and organizational requirements. Exercise 10–8 suggests making the conversion to Win32 style.

Programs 10–4 and 10–5 will show the queue functions and a program that uses them.

Program 10–3   SynchObj.h: Part 2—Queue Definitions

```
/* Definitions of synchronized, general bounded queue structure. */
/* Queues are implemented as arrays with indices to youngest */
/* and oldest messages, with wrap around. */
/* Each queue also contains a guard mutex and */
/* "not empty" and "not full" condition variables. */
/* Finally, there is a pointer to an array of messages of */
/* arbitrary type. */

typedef struct queue_tag { /* General purpose queue. */
    HANDLE q_guard; /* Guard the message block. */
    HANDLE q_ne; /* Queue is not empty. MR event
                    (AR for "signal model"). */
    HANDLE q_nf; /* Queue is not full. MR event. */
                    (AR for "signal model"). */
    volatile DWORD q_size; /* Queue max size. */
```

```
    volatile DWORD q_first; /* Index of oldest message. */
    volatile DWORD q_last; /* Index of youngest message. */
    volatile DWORD q_destroyed; /* Q receiver has terminated. */
    PVOID msg_array; /* Array of q_size messages. */
} queue_t;

/* Queue management functions. */
DWORD q_initialize (queue_t *, DWORD, DWORD);
DWORD q_destroy (queue_t *);
DWORD q_destroyed (queue_t *);
DWORD q_empty (queue_t *);
DWORD q_full (queue_t *);
DWORD q_get (queue_t *, PVOID, DWORD, DWORD);
DWORD q_put (queue_t *, PVOID, DWORD, DWORD);
DWORD q_remove (queue_t *, PVOID, DWORD);
DWORD q_insert (queue_t *, PVOID, DWORD);
```

Program 10–4 shows the functions, such as q_initialize and q_get, that are defined above. Notice that q_get and q_put provide synchronized access, while q_remove and q_insert, which the first two functions call, are not themselves synchronized and could be used in a single-threaded program. The first two functions provide for a time-out, so the normal condition variable model is extended slightly.

q_empty and q_full are two other essential functions that are used to implement condition variable predicates.

This implementation uses PulseEvent and manual-reset events (the broadcast model) so that multiple threads are notified when the queue is not empty or not full.

A nice feature of the implementation is the symmetry of the q_get and q_put functions. Note, for instance, how they use the empty and full predicates and how they use the events. This simplicity is not only pleasing in its own right, but it also has the very practical benefit of making the code easier to write, understand, and maintain. The condition variable model enables this simplicity and its benefits.

Finally, C++ programmers will notice that a synchronized queue class could be constructed from this code; Exercise 10–9 suggests doing this.

Program 10–4 QueueObj.c: The Queue Management Functions

```
/* Chapter 10. QueueObj.c. */
/* Queue function. */

#include "EvryThng.h"
#include "SynchObj.h"

/* Finite bounded queue management functions. */
```

```
DWORD q_get (queue_t *q, PVOID msg, DWORD msize, DWORD MaxWait)
{
    DWORD TotalWaitTime = 0;
    BOOL TimedOut = FALSE;

    if (q_destroyed (q)) return 1;
    WaitForSingleObject (q->q_guard, INFINITE);
    while (q_empty (q) && !TimedOut) {
        ReleaseMutex (q->q_guard);
        WaitForSingleObject (q->q_ne, CV_TIMEOUT);
        if (MaxWait != INFINITE) {
            TotalWaitTime += CV_TIMEOUT;
            TimedOut = (TotalWaitTime > MaxWait);
        }
        WaitForSingleObject (q->q_guard, INFINITE);
    }
    /* Remove the message from the queue. */
    if (!TimedOut) q_remove (q, msg, msize);
    /* Signal that queue is not full as we've removed a message. */
    PulseEvent (q->q_nf);
    ReleaseMutex (q->q_guard);
    return TimedOut ? WAIT_TIMEOUT : 0;
}

DWORD q_put (queue_t *q, PVOID msg, DWORD msize, DWORD MaxWait)
{
    DWORD TotalWaitTime = 0;
    BOOL TimedOut = FALSE;

    if (q_destroyed (q)) return 1;
    WaitForSingleObject (q->q_guard, INFINITE);
    while (q_full (q) && !TimedOut) {
        ReleaseMutex (q->q_guard);
        WaitForSingleObject (q->q_nf, CV_TIMEOUT);
        if (MaxWait != INFINITE) {
            TotalWaitTime += CV_TIMEOUT;
            TimedOut = (TotalWaitTime > MaxWait);
        }
        WaitForSingleObject (q->q_guard, INFINITE);
    }
    /* Put the message in the queue. */
    if (!TimedOut) q_insert (q, msg, msize);
    /* Signal that queue is not empty; we've inserted a message. */
    PulseEvent (q->q_ne); /* Broadcast CV model. */
    ReleaseMutex (q->q_guard);
    return TimedOut ? WAIT_TIMEOUT : 0;
}

DWORD q_initialize (queue_t *q, DWORD msize, DWORD nmsgs)
{
```

```
    /* Initialize queue, including its mutex and events. */
    /* Allocate storage for all messages. */

    q->q_first = q->q_last = 0;
    q->q_size = nmsgs;
    q->q_destroyed = 0;

    q->q_guard = CreateMutex (NULL, FALSE, NULL);
    q->q_ne = CreateEvent (NULL, TRUE, FALSE, NULL);
    q->q_nf = CreateEvent (NULL, TRUE, FALSE, NULL);

    if ((q->msg_array = calloc (nmsgs, msize)) == NULL) return 1;
    return 0; /* No error. */
}

DWORD q_destroy (queue_t *q)
{
    if (q_destroyed (q)) return 1;
    /* Free all the resources created by q_initialize. */
    WaitForSingleObject (q->q_guard, INFINITE);
    q->q_destroyed = 1;
    free (q->msg_array);
    CloseHandle (q->q_ne);
    CloseHandle (q->q_nf);
    ReleaseMutex (q->q_guard);
    CloseHandle (q->q_guard);
    return 0;
}

DWORD q_destroyed (queue_t *q)
{
    return (q->q_destroyed);
}

DWORD q_empty (queue_t *q)
{
    return (q->q_first == q->q_last);
}

DWORD q_full (queue_t *q)
{
    return ((q->q_last - q->q_first) == 1 ||
            (q->q_first == q->q_size-1 && q->q_last == 0));
}

DWORD q_remove (queue_t *q, PVOID msg, DWORD msize)
{
    char *pm;

    pm = (char *)q->msg_array;
```

```
    /* Remove oldest ("first") message. */
    memcpy (msg, pm + (q->q_first * msize), msize);
    q->q_first = ((q->q_first + 1) % q->q_size);
    return 0; /* No error. */
}

DWORD q_insert (queue_t *q, PVOID msg, DWORD msize)
{
    char *pm;
    pm = (char *) q->msg_array;
    /* Add a new youngest ("last") message. */
    if (q_full (q)) return 1; /* Error - Q is full. */
    memcpy (pm + (q->q_last * msize), msg, msize);
    q->q_last = ((q->q_last + 1) % q->q_size);
    return 0;
}
```

Comments on the Queue Management Functions and Performance

Appendix C contains performance data, based on Program 10–5, which uses the queue management functions. The comments below that refer to performance are based on that data. The disc contains code for all the implementation variations.

- This implementation uses the broadcast model (PulseEvent/MR) to allow for the general case in which multiple messages may be requested or created by a single thread. The signal model (SetEvent/AR) will work if this generality is not required, and there are significant performance advantages because there is no time-out on the event wait.

- Using a CRITICAL_SECTION, rather than a mutex, to protect the queue object also improves performance.

- SignalObjectAndWait, available in Windows NT Version 4.0 and later (not in W9x), can replace the mutex release, event wait sequences in q_get and q_put. The time-out can then be eliminated, because there is no risk of a lost signal. Again, there is another performance gain, comparable to that obtained when a CRITICAL_SECTION is used.

- Appendix C also shows the nonlinear performance impact when a large number of threads contend for a queue.

- In summary, the queue management implementation in Program 10–4 is general in that it will run on all Windows platforms. The queues can be extended to be process-sharable and to get and put multiple messages atomically.

Significant performance gains may be realized, however, by using the signal model, a `CRITICAL_SECTION`, or `SignalObjectAndWait`.

Example: Using Queues in a Multistage Pipeline

The boss/worker model, along with its variations, is one popular multithreaded programming model, and Program 9–2 is a simple producer/consumer model, a special case of the more general pipeline model.

Another important special case consists of a single boss thread that produces work items for a limited number of worker threads, placing the work items in a queue. This technique can be helpful when creating a scalable server that has a large number (perhaps thousands) of clients and it is not feasible to have a worker thread for each client. Chapter 14 discusses the scalable server problem in the context of I/O completion ports.

In the pipeline model, each thread, or group of threads, does some work on work items, such as messages, and passes the work items on to other threads for additional processing. A manufacturing assembly line is analogous to a thread pipeline. Queues are an ideal mechanism for pipeline implementations.

Program 10–5 creates multiple production and consumption stages, and each stage maintains a queue of work to perform. Each queue has a bounded, finite length. There are three pipeline stages in total connecting the four work stages. The program name is `ThreeStage.c`. The program structure is as follows:

- Producers create checksummed "unit" messages periodically, using the same message creation function as in Program 9–2, except that each message has a "destination" field indicating which consumer thread is to receive the message; each producer communicates with a single consumer. The number of producer/consumer pairs is a command line parameter. The producer then sends the unit message to the "transmitter" thread by placing the message in the "transmission queue." If the queue is full, the producer waits until the queue state changes.

- The transmitter thread gathers all the available unit messages (but no more than five at a time) and creates a "transmission message" that contains a header block with the number of unit messages. The transmitter then puts each transmission message in the "receiver queue," blocking if the queue is full. The transmitter and receiver might, in general, communicate over a network connection. The arbitrary 5:1 blocking factor is easy to adjust.

- The receiver thread processes the unit messages in each transmission message, putting each unit message in the appropriate consumer queue, if the queue is not full.

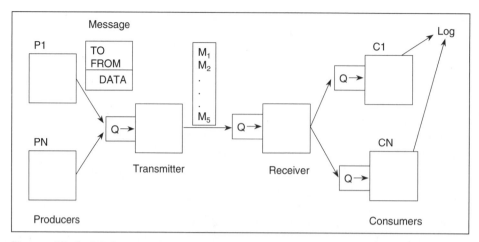

Figure 10-1 Multistage Pipeline

- Each consumer thread receives unit messages as they are available and puts the message in a log file.

Figure 10–1 shows the system. Notice how it models networking communication where messages between several sender/receiver pairs are combined and transmitted over a shared facility.

Program 10–5 shows the implementation, which uses the queue functions in Program 10–4. The message generation and display functions are not shown; they were first seen in Program 9–1. The message blocks have been augmented, however, to contain source and destination fields along with the checksum and data.

Program 10–5 ThreeStage.c: A Multistage Pipeline

```
/* Chapter 10. ThreeStage.c */
/* Three-stage producer/consumer system. */
/*                                        */
/* Usage: ThreeStage npc goal. */
/* Start up "npc" paired producer and consumer threads. */
/* Each producer must produce a total of */
/* "goal" messages, where each message is tagged */
/* with the consumer that should receive it. */
/* Messages are sent to a "transmitter thread," which performs */
/* additional processing before sending message groups to the */
/* "receiver thread." Finally, the receiver thread sends */
/* the messages to the consumer threads. */

#include "EvryThng.h"
```

```c
#include "SynchObj.h"
#include "messages.h"
#include <time.h>

#define DELAY_COUNT 1000
#define MAX_THREADS 1024

/* Q lengths and blocking factors. These are arbitrary and */
/* can be adjusted for performance tuning. The current values are */
/* not well balanced. */

#define TBLOCK_SIZE 5 /* Trsmttr combines 5 messages at a time. */
#define TBLOCK_TIMEOUT 50 /* Trsmttr time-out waiting for messages. */
#define P2T_QLEN 10 /* Producer to transmitter queue length. */
#define T2R_QLEN 4 /* Transmitter to receiver queue length. */
#define R2C_QLEN 4 /* Receiver to consumer queue length -
                      there is one such queue for each consumer. */

DWORD WINAPI producer (PVOID);
DWORD WINAPI consumer (PVOID);
DWORD WINAPI transmitter (PVOID);
DWORD WINAPI receiver (PVOID);

typedef struct _THARG {
   volatile DWORD thread_number;
   volatile DWORD work_goal; /* Used by producers. */
   volatile DWORD work_done; /* Used by producers & consumers. */
   char future [8];
} THARG;

/* Grouped messages sent by the transmitter to receiver. */
typedef struct t2r_msg_tag {
   volatile DWORD num_msgs; /* Number of messages contained. */
   msg_block_t messages [TBLOCK_SIZE];
} t2r_msg_t;

queue_t p2tq, t2rq, *r2cq_array;

static volatile DWORD ShutDown = 0;
static DWORD EventTimeout = 50;

DWORD _tmain (DWORD argc, LPTSTR * argv [])
{
   DWORD tstatus, nthread, ithread, goal, thid;
   HANDLE *producer_th, *consumer_th, transmitter_th, receiver_th;
   THARG *producer_arg, *consumer_arg;

   nthread = atoi (argv [1]);
   goal = atoi (argv [2]);
   producer_th = malloc (nthread * sizeof (HANDLE));
```

```
    producer_arg = calloc (nthread, sizeof (THARG));
    consumer_th = malloc (nthread * sizeof (HANDLE));
    consumer_arg = calloc (nthread, sizeof (THARG));

    q_initialize (&p2tq, sizeof (msg_block_t), P2T_QLEN);
    q_initialize (&t2rq, sizeof (t2r_msg_t), T2R_QLEN);
    /* Allocate, initialize Rec-Cons queue for each consumer. */
    r2cq_array = calloc (nthread, sizeof (queue_t));

    for (ithread = 0; ithread < nthread; ithread++) {
        /* Initialize r2c queue for this consumer thread. */
        q_initialize (&r2cq_array [ithread], sizeof (msg_block_t),
            R2C_QLEN);
        /* Fill in the thread arg. */
        consumer_arg [ithread].thread_number = ithread;
        consumer_arg [ithread].work_goal = goal;
        consumer_arg [ithread].work_done = 0;

        consumer_th [ithread] = (HANDLE)_beginthreadex (NULL, 0,
            consumer, (PVOID) &consumer_arg [ithread], 0, &thid);

        producer_arg [ithread].thread_number = ithread;
        producer_arg [ithread].work_goal = goal;
        producer_arg [ithread].work_done = 0;
        producer_th [ithread] = (HANDLE) _beginthreadex (NULL, 0,
            producer, (PVOID) &producer_arg [ithread], 0, &thid);
    }

    transmitter_th = (HANDLE) _beginthreadex (NULL, 0,
        transmitter, NULL, 0, &thid);
    receiver_th = (HANDLE) _beginthreadex (NULL, 0,
        receiver, NULL, 0, &thid);

    _tprintf _T ("BOSS: All threads are running\n");
    /* Wait for the producers to complete. */
    for (ithread = 0; ithread < nthread; ithread++) {
        WaitForSingleObject (producer_th [ithread], INFINITE);
        _tprintf _T ("BOSS: Producer %d produced %d work units\n",
            ithread, producer_arg [ithread].work_done);
    }
    /* Producers have completed their work. */
    _tprintf _T ("BOSS: All producers have completed their work.\n");

    /* Wait for the consumers to complete. */
    for (ithread = 0; ithread < nthread; ithread++) {
        WaitForSingleObject (consumer_th [ithread], INFINITE);
        _tprintf _T ("BOSS: consumer %d consumed %d work units\n",
            ithread, consumer_arg [ithread].work_done);
    }
```

```
    _tprintf _T ("BOSS: All consumers have completed their work.\n");
    ShutDown = 1; /* Set a shutdown flag. */

    /* Terminate, and wait for, the transmitter and receiver. */
    /* This thread termination is OK as the transmitter and */
    /* receiver cannot hold any resources other than a mutex, */
    /* which will be abandoned. Can you do this a better way? */

    TerminateThread (transmitter_th, 0);
    TerminateThread (receiver_th, 0);
    WaitForSingleObject (transmitter_th, INFINITE);
    WaitForSingleObject (receiver_th, INFINITE);

    q_destroy (&p2tq);
    q_destroy (&t2rq);
    for (ithread = 0; ithread < nthread; ithread++)
        q_destroy (&r2cq_array [ithread]);

    free (r2cq_array);
    free (producer_th); free (consumer_th);
    free (producer_arg); free (consumer_arg);
    _tprintf _T ("System has finished. Shutting down\n");
    return 0;
}

DWORD WINAPI producer (PVOID arg)
{
    THARG * parg;
    DWORD ithread, tstatus;
    msg_block_t msg;

    parg = (THARG *) arg;
    ithread = parg->thread_number;

    while (parg->work_done < parg->work_goal) {

        /* Produce work units until the goal is satisfied. */
        /* Messages receive source, destination address which are */
        /* the same here but could, in general, be different. */

        delay_cpu (DELAY_COUNT * rand () / RAND_MAX);
        message_fill (&msg, ithread, ithread, parg->work_done);

        /* Put the message in the queue. */
        tstatus = q_put (&p2tq, &msg, sizeof (msg), INFINITE);
        parg->work_done++;
    }
    return 0;
}
```

```
DWORD WINAPI transmitter (PVOID arg)
{
    /* Obtain multiple producer messages, combining into a single */
    /* compound message for the receiver. */
    DWORD tstatus, im;
    t2r_msg_t t2r_msg = {0};
    msg_block_t p2t_msg;

    while (!ShutDown) {
        t2r_msg.num_msgs = 0;
        /* Pack the messages for transmission to the receiver. */
        for (im = 0; im < TBLOCK_SIZE; im++) {
            tstatus = q_get (&p2tq, &p2t_msg,
                    sizeof (p2t_msg), INFINITE);
            if (tstatus != 0) break;
            memcpy (&t2r_msg.messages [im], &p2t_msg, sizeof (p2t_msg));
            t2r_msg.num_msgs++;
        }
        tstatus = q_put (&t2rq, &t2r_msg, sizeof (t2r_msg), INFINITE);
        if (tstatus != 0) return tstatus;
    }
    return 0;
}

DWORD WINAPI receiver (PVOID arg)
{
    /* Obtain compound messages from the transmitter; unblock */
    /* them and transmit to the designated consumer. */

    DWORD tstatus, im, ic;
    t2r_msg_t t2r_msg;
    msg_block_t r2c_msg;

    while (!ShutDown) {
        tstatus = q_get (&t2rq, &t2r_msg, sizeof (t2r_msg), INFINITE);
        if (tstatus != 0) return tstatus;

        /* Distribute the messages to the proper consumer. */
        for (im = 0; im < t2r_msg.num_msgs; im++) {
            memcpy (&r2c_msg, &t2r_msg.messages [im], sizeof (r2c_msg));
            ic = r2c_msg.destination; /* Destination consumer. */
            tstatus = q_put (&r2cq_array [ic], &r2c_msg,
                    sizeof (r2c_msg), INFINITE);
            if (tstatus != 0) return tstatus;
        }
    }
    return 0;
}
```

```
DWORD WINAPI consumer (PVOID arg)
{
    THARG * carg;
    DWORD tstatus, ithread;
    msg_block_t msg;
    queue_t *pr2cq;
    carg = (THARG *) arg;
    ithread = carg->thread_number;

    carg = (THARG *) arg;
    pr2cq = &r2cq_array [ithread];

    while (carg->work_done < carg->work_goal) {
        /* Receive and display (optionally - not shown) messages. */
        tstatus = q_get (pr2cq, &msg, sizeof (msg), INFINITE);
        if (tstatus != 0) return tstatus;
        carg->work_done++;
    }
    return 0;
}
```

Comments on the Multistage Pipeline

There are several things to notice about this implementation, some of which are mentioned in the program comments. Exercises 10–6, 10–7, 10–10, and 10–11 suggest addressing these issues.

- A significant objection could be the way that the main thread terminates the transmitter and receiver threads. A solution would be to use a time-out value in the inner transmitter and receiver loops and shut down when the global shutdown flag is detected.

- Note the symmetry between the transmitter and receiver threads. As with the queue implementation, this facilitates program design, debugging, and maintenance.

- The implementation is not well balanced in terms of the match of the message production rates, the pipeline sizes, and the transmitter-receiver blocking factor.

- This implementation (Program 10–4) uses mutexes to guard the queues. Experiments with CRITICAL_SECTIONs show an approximate 4:1 (or more) speed-up on a single processor system (see Appendix C). The CS version is included on the disc as ThreeStageCS.c. SignalObjectAndWait provides similar performance improvements.

Hints for Designing, Debugging, and Testing

At the risk of presenting advice that is contrary to that given in many other books and technical articles, which stress testing and little else, my personal advice is to balance your efforts so that you pay attention to design, implementation, and use of familiar programming models. The best debugging technique is not to create the bugs in the first place. Furthermore, when defects do occur, as they will, code inspection, balanced with debugging, often is most effective in finding, and fixing, the defects' root causes.

Overdependence on testing is not advisable, because many serious defects will elude the most extensive, and expensive, testing. Testing can only reveal defects; it cannot prove they do not exist, and testing shows only defect symptoms, not root causes. As a personal example, I ran a version of a multiple semaphore wait function that used the CV model without the finite time-out on the event variable wait. The defect, which could cause a thread to block indefinitely, did not show up in over a year of use; eventually, however, something would have failed. Simple code inspection and knowledge of the condition variable model revealed the error.

Debugging is also problematical, because debuggers change timing behavior, masking the very race conditions that you wish to expose. For example, debugging is unlikely to find a problem with an incorrect choice of event type (auto- or manual-reset) and `Set/PulseEvent`. You have to think carefully about what you wish to achieve.

Having said all that, testing on a wide variety of platforms, including SMP, is an essential part of any multithreaded software development project.

Avoiding Incorrect Code

Every bug that you don't put in your code in the first place is one more bug that you won't find in testing or production. Here are some hints, most of which are taken, although rephrased, from Butenhof's *Programming with POSIX Threads*.

- **Avoid relying on "thread inertia."** Threads are asynchronous, but we often assume, for example, that a parent thread will continue running after creating one or more child threads. The assumption is that the parent's "inertia" will keep it running before the children run. This assumption is especially dangerous on an SMP system, but it can also lead to problems on single-processor systems.

- **Never bet on a thread race.** Nearly anything can happen in terms of thread scheduling. Your program has to assume that any ready thread can start running at any time and that any running thread can be preempted at any time.

"No ordering exists between threads unless you cause ordering." (PWPT, p. 294).

- **Scheduling is not the same as synchronization.** Scheduling policy and priorities cannot ensure proper synchronization. Use synchronization objects instead.

- **Sequence races can occur even when you use mutexes to protect shared data.** Just because data is protected, there is no assurance as to the order in which different threads will access the shared data. For example, if one thread adds money to a bank account and another makes a withdrawal, there is no assurance, using a mutex guard alone, that the deposit will be made before the withdrawal.

- **Cooperate to avoid deadlocks.** You need a well-understood lock hierarchy, used by all threads, to ensure that deadlocks will not occur.

- **Never share events between predicates.** Each event used in a condition variable implementation should be associated with a distinct predicate. Furthermore, an event should always be used with the same mutex.

- **Beware of sharing stacks and related memory corrupters.** Always remember that when you return from a function or when a thread terminates, memory local to the function or thread is no longer valid. Memory on a thread's stack can be used by other threads, but you have to be sure that the first thread continues to exist.

- **Be sure to use the `volatile` storage modifier.** Whenever a shared variable can be changed in one thread and accessed in another, the variable should be `volatile` to ensure that each thread stores and fetches the variable to and from memory, rather than assuming that the variable is held in a register that is specific to the thread.

Here are some additional guidelines and rules of thumb that can be helpful.

- **Use the condition variable model properly**, being certain not to use two distinct mutexes with the same event. Understand the condition variable model on which you depend. Be certain that the invariant holds before waiting on a condition variable.

- **Understand your invariants and condition variable predicates**, even if they are stated only informally. Be certain that the invariant always holds outside the critical code section.

- **Keep it simple.** Multithreaded programming is complex enough without the burden of additional complex, poorly understood thread models and logic. If a program becomes overly complex, assess whether the complexity is really necessary or is the result of poor design. Careful use of standard threading models can simplify your program and make it easier to understand, and lack of a good model may be a symptom of a poorly designed program.

- **Test on both single and multiprocessor systems and on systems with different clock rates and other characteristics.** Some defects will never, or rarely, show up on a single-processor system but will occur immediately on an SMP system, and conversely. Likewise, a variety of system characteristics helps to ensure that a defective program has more opportunity to fail.

- **Testing is necessary but not sufficient to ensure correct behavior.** There have been a number of examples of programs, known to be defective, that seldom fail in routine, or even extensive, tests.

- **Be humble.** After all these precautions, bugs will still occur. This is true even with single-threaded programs; threads simply give us more, different, and very interesting ways to cause problems.

Summary

Multithreaded program development is much simpler if you use well-understood and familiar programming models and techniques. This chapter has shown the utility of the condition variable model and has solved several relatively complex, but important, programming problems.

Use of careful program design and implementation is the best way to improve program quality. Overdependence on testing and debugging, without attention to detail, can lead to serious problems that may be very difficult to detect and fix.

Looking Ahead

Chapter 11 shows how to use Win32 named pipes and mailslots to communicate between processes and threads in those processes. The major example is a client/server system where the server uses a pool of worker threads to service client requests. Chapter 12 then implements the same system using Windows Sockets, extending Chapter 11's client/server system to the use of standard protocols. The server also uses a DLL in-process server and creates thread-safe DLLs.

Additional Reading

Butenhof's *Programming with POSIX Threads* was the source of much of the information and programming guidelines in this chapter. The threshold barrier solution, Programs 10–1 and 10–2, was adapted from Butenhof as well.

Strategies for Implementing POSIX Condition Variables in Win32 by Douglas Schmidt and Irfan Pyarali, posted at `http://www.cs.wustl.edu/~schmidt/win32-cv-1.html`, discusses Win32 event limitations along with condition variables emulation, thoroughly analyzing and evaluating several approaches. `http://www.cs.wustl.edu/~schmidt/win32-cv-2.html`, under construction at the time of writing, builds OO wrappers around Win32 synchronization objects to achieve a platform-independent synchronization interface. Exercise 10–14 suggests that the first paper's analysis be applied to the condition variable models in this chapter. An interesting exercise would be to complete the work described in the second paper.

Exercises

10–1. Revise Program 10–1 so that it uses the `SignalObjectAndWait` function.

10–2. Modify `eventPC` (Program 9–2) so that there can be multiple consumers and so that it uses the condition variable model. Which event type is appropriate?

10–3. Experiment with different time-out values on the event waits in Programs 10–2 and 10–4 to determine the impacts on performance and responsiveness.

10–4. Change the logic in Program 10–2 so that the event is signaled only once.

10–5. Replace the mutex in the queue object used in Program 10–2 with a CS. What are the effects on performance and throughput? The solution is on the disc, and Appendix C contains experimental data.

10–6. Program 10–4 uses the broadcast CV model to indicate when the queue is either not empty or not full. Would the signal CV model work? Would the signal model even be preferable in any way? Appendix C contains experimental data.

10–7. Experiment with the queue lengths and the transmitter-receiver blocking factor in Program 10–5 to determine the effects on performance, throughput, and CPU load.

10–8. Modify Programs 10–3 through 10–5 to conform to the Win32 naming style used elsewhere in this book.

10–9. *For C++ Programmers*: The code in Programs 10–3 and 10–4 could be used to create a synchronized queue class in C++; create this class and modify Program 10–5 to test it. Which of the functions should be public and which should be private?

10–10. Study the performance behavior of Program 10–5 if CRITICAL_SECTIONs are used instead of mutexes.

10–11. Improve Program 10–5 so that it is not necessary to terminate the transmitter and receiver threads. The threads should shut themselves down.

10–12. The disc contains MultiSem.c, which implements a multiple-wait semaphore modeled after the Win32 objects (they can be named, secured, and process shared, and there are two wait models), and TestMultiSem.c is a test program. Build and test this program. How does it use the condition variable model? Is performance improved by using a CRITICAL_SECTION? What are the invariants and condition variable predicates?

10–13. Illustrate the various guidelines at the end of this chapter in terms of bugs you have encountered or in the defective versions of the programs provided on the disc.

10–14. Read *Strategies for Implementing POSIX Condition Variables in Win32* by Schmidt and Pyarali (see the Additional Reading section). Apply their fairness, correctness, serialization, and other analyses to the condition variable models (called "idioms" in their paper) in this chapter. Notice that this chapter does not directly emulate condition variables; rather, it emulates condition variable usage, whereas Schmidt and Pyarali emulate condition variables used in an arbitrary context.

CHAPTER

11 | Interprocess Communication

Chapter 7 showed how to create and manage processes, and Chapters 8, 9, and 10 showed how to manage and synchronize threads within processes. So far, however, we have not been able to perform direct process-to-process communication other than through shared memory.

The next step is to provide sequential interprocess communication (IPC) between processes[1] using filelike objects. Two primary Win32 mechanisms for IPC are the anonymous pipe and the named pipe, both of which can be accessed with the familiar `ReadFile` and `WriteFile` functions. Simple anonymous pipes are character-based and half-duplex. As such, they are well suited for redirecting the output of one program to the input of another, as is commonly done between UNIX programs. The first example shows how to do this.

Named pipes are much more powerful than anonymous pipes. They are full-duplex and message-oriented, and they allow networked communication. Furthermore, there can be multiple open handles on the same pipe. These capabilities, coupled with convenient transaction-oriented named pipe functions, make named pipes appropriate for creating client/server systems. This capability is shown in this chapter's second example, a multithreaded client/server command processor, modeled after Figure 8–1, which was used to introduce threads. Each server thread manages communication with a different client, and each thread/client pair uses a distinct handle, or named pipe instance.

Finally, mailslots allow for one-to-many message broadcasting, and this chapter's final example enhances the command processor with mailslots.

---

[1] The Windows system services also allow processes to communicate through mapped files, as demonstrated in the semaphore exercise in Chapter 10 (Exercise 10–12). Additional mechanisms for IPC include files, sockets, remote procedure calls, COM, and message posting. Sockets and remote procedure calls are described in Chapters 12 and 15, respectively.

Anonymous Pipes

The Win32 anonymous pipes allow one-way (half-duplex), character-based IPC. Each pipe has two handles: a read handle and a write handle. The `CreatePipe` function is as follows:

```
BOOL CreatePipe (
    PHANDLE phRead,
    PHANDLE phWrite,
    LPSECURITY_ATTRIBUTES lpsa,
    DWORD cbPipe)
```

As the following example shows, the pipe handles are often inheritable. `cbPipe`, the pipe byte size, is only a suggestion, and zero specifies the default value.

In order for the pipe to be used for IPC, there needs to be another process, and that process requires one of the pipe handles. Assume that the parent process, which calls `CreatePipe`, wishes to write data for a child to use. The problem, then, is to communicate the read handle (`phRead`) to the child. The parent achieves this by setting the child procedure's input handle in the start-up structure to `*phRead`.

Reading a pipe read handle will block if the pipe is empty. Otherwise, the read will accept as many bytes as are in the pipe, up to the number specified in the `ReadFile` call. A write operation to a full pipe, which is implemented in a memory buffer, will also block.

Finally, anonymous pipes are one-way. Two pipes are required for bidirectional communication.

Example: I/O Redirection Using an Anonymous Pipe

Program 11–1 shows a parent process that creates two processes from the command line and "pipes" them together. The parent process sets up the pipe and redirects standard input and output. Notice how the named pipe handles are inheritable and how standard I/O is redirected to the two child processes; these techniques were described in Chapter 7.

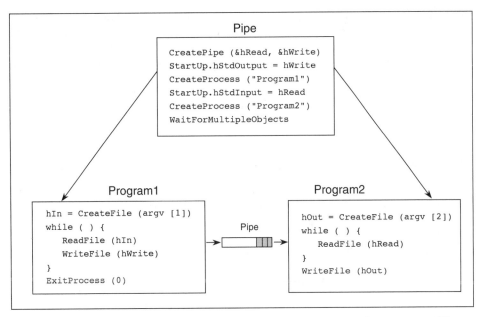

Figure 11-1   Process-to-Process Communication Using an Anonymous Pipe

Also notice how pipe and thread handles are closed at the earliest possible point. It is necessary for the parent to close the standard output handle immediately after creating the first child process so that the second process will be able to recognize an end of file when the first process terminates. If there were still an open handle, the second process might not terminate, because the system would not indicate an end of file.

Program 11–1 uses an unusual syntax; the = sign is the pipe symbol separating the two commands. The vertical bar (|) would conflict with the command processor. Figure 11–1 schematically shows the execution of the command:

```
$ pipe Program1 arguments = Program2 arguments
```

In UNIX or the Windows Command Prompt, the corresponding command would be:

```
$ Program1 arguments | Program2 arguments
```

Program 11-1   pipe: Interprocess Communication with Anonymous Pipes

```
#include "EvryThng.h"

int _tmain (int argc, LPTSTR argv [])

/* Pipe together two programs on the command line:
      pipe command1 = command2 */
{
   DWORD i = 0;
   HANDLE hReadPipe, hWritePipe;
   TCHAR Command1 [MAX_PATH];
   SECURITY_ATTRIBUTES PipeSA = /* For inheritable handles. */
         {sizeof (SECURITY_ATTRIBUTES), NULL, TRUE};
   PROCESS_INFORMATION ProcInfo1, ProcInfo2;
   STARTUPINFO StartInfoCh1, StartInfoCh2;
   LPTSTR targv = SkipArg (GetCommandLine ());

   GetStartupInfo (&StartInfoCh1);
   GetStartupInfo (&StartInfoCh2);

   /* Find the = separating the two commands. */
   while (*targv != '=' && *targv != '\0') {
      Command1 [i] = *targv;
      targv++;
      i++;
   }

   Command1 [i] = '\0';

   /* Skip to start of second command. */
   targv = SkipArg (targv);

   CreatePipe (&hReadPipe, &hWritePipe, &PipeSA, 0);

   /* Redirect standard output & create first process. */

   StartInfoCh1.hStdInput = GetStdHandle (STD_INPUT_HANDLE);
   StartInfoCh1.hStdError = GetStdHandle (STD_ERROR_HANDLE);
   StartInfoCh1.hStdOutput = hWritePipe;
   StartInfoCh1.dwFlags = STARTF_USESTDHANDLES;

   CreateProcess (NULL, (LPTSTR)Command1, NULL, NULL,
         TRUE /* Inherit handles. */, 0, NULL, NULL,
         &StartInfoCh1, &ProcInfo1);
   CloseHandle (ProcInfo1.hThread);

   /* Close the pipe's write handle as it is no longer needed
      and to ensure the second command detects a file end. */
```

```
    CloseHandle (hWritePipe);

    /* Repeat (symmetrically) for the second process. */
    StartInfoCh2.hStdInput = hReadPipe;
    StartInfoCh2.hStdOutput = GetStdHandle (STD_OUTPUT_HANDLE);
    StartInfoCh2.hStdError = GetStdHandle (STD_ERROR_HANDLE);
    StartInfoCh2.dwFlags = STARTF_USESTDHANDLES;

    CreateProcess (NULL, (LPTSTR) targv, NULL, NULL, TRUE, 0, NULL,
            NULL, &StartInfoCh2, &ProcInfo2);
    CloseHandle (ProcInfo2.hThread);

    /* Wait for the first and second processes to terminate. */
    WaitForSingleObject (ProcInfo1.hProcess, INFINITE);
    CloseHandle (ProcInfo1.hProcess);

    WaitForSingleObject (ProcInfo2.hProcess, INFINITE);
    CloseHandle (ProcInfo2.hProcess);

    CloseHandle (hReadPipe);
    return 0;
}
```

Named Pipes

Named pipes have several features that make them an appropriate mechanism for implementing IPC-based applications, including networked client/server systems.[2] Named pipe features (some are optional) include the following:

- Named pipes are message-oriented, so the reading process can read varying-length messages precisely as sent by the writing process.

- Named pipes are bidirectional, so two processes can exchange messages over the same pipe.

- There can be multiple, independent instances of a named pipe. For example, several clients can communicate with a single server using the same pipe, and the server can respond to a client using the same instance.

---

[2] This statement requires a major qualification. Windows Sockets (Chapter 12) is the preferred API for most networking applications, especially where interoperability with non-Windows systems is required. Remote procedure calls (RPCs) and COM (Chapter 15) provide other alternatives. Many developers prefer to limit named pipe usage to IPC within a single system or to communication between Windows systems.

- The pipe name can be accessed by systems on a network. Named pipe communication is the same whether the two processes are on the same machine or on different machines.

- There are several convenience and connection functions that simplify named pipe request/response interaction and client/server connection.

Using Named Pipes

CreateNamedPipe creates the first instance of a named pipe and returns a handle. The function also specifies the maximum number of pipe instances and, hence, the number of clients that can be supported simultaneously.

Normally, the creating process is regarded as the *server.* *Client* processes, possibly on other systems, open the pipe with CreateFile.

Figure 11–2 shows an illustrative client/server relationship, and the pseudocode shows one scheme for using named pipes. Notice that the server creates multiple instances of the same pipe, each of which can support a client. The server also creates a thread for each named pipe instance, so that each client has a dedicated thread and named pipe instance. Figure 11–2, then, shows how to implement the multithreaded server model, first shown in Figure 8–1.

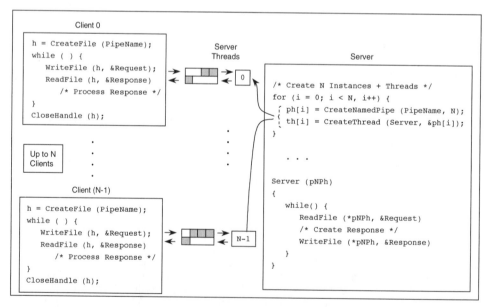

Figure 11-2   Clients and Servers Using Named Pipes

Creating Named Pipes

Only Windows 2000/NT systems can act as named pipe servers, so the following function can be used only with those two operating systems.

Here is the specification of the `CreateNamedPipe` function:

```
HANDLE CreateNamedPipe (
    LPCTSTR lpszPipeName,
    DWORD fdwOpenMode,
    DWORD fdwPipeMode,
    DWORD nMaxInstances,
    DWORD cbOutBuf,
    DWORD cbInBuf,
    DWORD dwTimeOut,
    LPSECURITY_ATTRIBUTES lpsa)
```

Parameters

`lpszPipeName` indicates the pipe name, which must be of the form:

```
\\.\pipe\[path]pipename
```

The period stands for the local machine; thus, it is not possible to create a pipe on a remote machine.

`fdwOpenMode` specifies one of the following:

- `PIPE_ACCESS_DUPLEX`—Equivalent to the combination of `GENERIC_READ` and `GENERIC_WRITE`.

- `PIPE_ACCESS_INBOUND`—Data flow is from the client to the server only, equivalent to `GENERIC_READ`.

- `PIPE_ACCESS_OUTBOUND`—Equivalent to `GENERIC_WRITE`.

The mode can also specify `FILE_FLAG_WRITE_THROUGH` (not used with message pipes) and `FILE_FLAG_OVERLAPPED` (overlapped operations are discussed in Chapter 14).

`fdwPipeMode` has three mutually exclusive flag pairs. They indicate whether writing is message-oriented or byte-oriented, whether reading is by messages or blocks, and whether read operations block.

- `PIPE_TYPE_BYTE` and `PIPE_TYPE_MESSAGE`, which are mutually exclusive, indicate whether data is written to the pipe as a stream of bytes or messages. Use the same type value for all pipe instances.

- `PIPE_READMODE_BYTE` and `PIPE_READMODE_MESSAGE` indicate whether data is read as a stream of bytes or messages. `PIPE_READMODE_MESSAGE` requires `PIPE_TYPE_MESSAGE`.

- `PIPE_WAIT` and `PIPE_NOWAIT` determine whether `ReadFile` will block. Use `PIPE_WAIT`, because there are better ways to achieve asynchronous I/O.

`nMaxInstances` determines the number of pipe instances and, therefore, the number of simultaneous clients. As Figure 11–2 shows, this same value must be used for every `CreateNamedPipe` call for a given pipe. Use the value `PIPE_UNLIMITED_INSTANCES` to have the OS base the number on available system resources.

`cbOutBuf` and `cbInBuf` give the sizes, in bytes, of the input and output buffers used for the named pipes. Specify zero to get default values.

`dwTimeOut` is a default time-out period (in milliseconds) for the `WaitNamedPipe` function, which is discussed in a later section. This situation, in which the create function specifies a time-out for a related function, is unique.

The return value in case of error is `INVALID_HANDLE_VALUE`, because pipe handles are similar to file handles. If you inadvertently attempt to create a named pipe on Windows 9x, which cannot act as a named pipe server, the return value will be `NULL`, possibly causing confusion.

`lpsa` operates as in all the other create functions.

The first `CreateNamedPipe` call actually creates the named pipe rather than just an instance. Closing the last handle to an instance will delete the instance. Deleting the last instance of a named pipe will delete the pipe itself.

Named Pipe Client Connections

Figure 11–2 shows that a client can connect to a named pipe using `CreateFile` with the named pipe name. In many cases, the client and server are on the same machine, and the name would be of the form

```
\\.\pipe\[path]pipename
```

If the server is on a different machine, the name would be

```
\\servername\pipe\[path]pipename
```

Using the name "." when the server is local—rather than using the local machine name—delivers significantly better performance.

Named Pipe Status Functions

Two functions are provided to interrogate pipe status information, and a third is provided to set state information. They are mentioned briefly but not used.

- `GetNamedPipeHandleState` returns information, given an open handle, on whether the pipe is in blocking or nonblocking mode, whether it is message-oriented or byte-oriented, the number of pipe instances, and so on.

- `SetNamedPipeHandleState` allows the program to set the same state attributes.

- `GetNamedPipeInfo` determines whether the handle is for a client or server instance, buffer sizes, and so on.

Named Pipe Connection Functions

The server, after creating a named pipe instance, can wait for a client connection (`CreateFile` or `CallNamedPipe`, described in a subsequent function) using `ConnectNamedPipe`. This last function is for 2000/NT only because it is for named pipe servers.

```
BOOL ConnectNamedPipe (
    HANDLE hNamedPipe,
    LPOVERLAPPED lpo)
```

With `lpo` set to `NULL`, `ConnectNamedPipe` will return as soon as there is a client connection. Normally, the return value is `TRUE`. However, it would be `FALSE` if the client connected between the server's `CreateNamedPipe` call and the `ConnectNamedPipe` call. In this case, `GetLastError` returns `ERROR_PIPE_CONNECTED`.

Following the return from `ConnectNamedPipe`, the server can read requests using `ReadFile` and write responses using `WriteFile`. Finally, the server should call `DisconnectNamedPipe` to free the handle (pipe instance) for connection with another client.

`WaitNamedPipe`, the final function, is for use by the client to synchronize connections to the server. The call will return as soon as the server has a pending

ConnectNamedPipe call. By using WaitNamedPipe, the client can be certain that the server is ready for a connection and the client can then call CreateFile. Furthermore, the server's ConnectNamedPipe call will not fail. Notice that there is a time-out period for WaitNamedPipe that, if specified, will override the time-out period specified with the server's CreateNamedPipe call.

Client and Server Named Pipe Connection

The proper connection sequences for the client and server are as follows. First is the server sequence, in which the server makes a client connection, communicates with the client until the client disconnects (causing ReadFile to return a FALSE), disconnects the server-side connection, and then connects to another client.

```
/* Named Pipe Server connection sequence. */
hNp = CreateNamedPipe ("\\\\.\\pipe\\my_pipe", ...);
while (... /* Continue until server shuts down. */) {
    ConnectNamedPipe (hNp, NULL);
    while (ReadFile (hNp, ...) {
        ...
        WriteFile (hNp, Response, ...);
    }
    DisconnectNamedPipe (hNp);
}
CloseHandle (hNp);
```

The client connection sequence is as follows, where the client terminates after it finishes, allowing another client to connect on the same named pipe instance. As shown, the client can connect to a networked server if it knows the server name.

```
/* Named Pipe Client connection sequence. */
WaitNamedPipe ("\\\\ServerName\\pipe\\my_pipe",
    NMPWAIT_WAIT_FOREVER);
hNp =
    CreateFile ("\\\\ServerName\\pipe\\my_pipe", ...);
while (... /* Run until there are no more requests. */ {
    WriteFile (hNp, Request, ...);
    ...
    ReadFile (hNp, Response);
}
CloseHandle (hNp); /* Disconnect from the server. */
```

Notice that there are race conditions between the client and the server. First, the client's `WaitNamedPipe` call will fail if the server has not yet created the named pipe. Next, the client may, in rare circumstances, complete its `CreateFile` call before the server calls `ConnectNamedPipe`. In that case, `ConnectNamed-Pipe` will return a `FALSE`, but the named pipe communication will still function properly.

The named pipe instance is a global resource, so once the client disconnects, another client can connect with the server.

Named Pipe Transaction Functions

Figure 11–2 shows a typical client configuration in which the client does the following:

- Opens an instance of the pipe, creating a long-lived connection to the server and consuming a pipe instance.

- Repetitively sends requests and waits for responses.

- Closes the connection.

The common `WriteFile`, `ReadFile` sequence could be regarded as a single client transaction, and Win32 provides such a function for message pipes.

```
BOOL TransactNamedPipe (
    HANDLE hNamedPipe,
    LPVOID lpvWriteBuf,
    DWORD cbWriteBuf,
    LPVOID lpvReadBuf,
    DWORD cbReadBuf,
    LPDWORD lpcbRead,
    LPOVERLAPPED lpa)
```

The parameter usage is clear, because this function combines `WriteFile` and `ReadFile` on the named pipe handle. Both the output and input buffers are specified, and `*lpcbRead` gives the message length. Overlapped operations (Chapter 14) are possible. More typically, the function waits for the response.

TransactNamedPipe is convenient, but, as in Figure 11–2, it requires a permanent connection, which limits the number of clients.[3]

CallNamedPipe, the second client convenience function, rectifies this situation by combining the complete sequence

```
CreateFile
WriteFile
ReadFile
CloseHandle
```

into a single function, and this function is used in the next example. The benefit is better pipe utilization at the cost of per-request connection overhead.

```
BOOL CallNamedPipe (
    LPCTSTR lpszPipeName,
    LPVOID lpvWriteBuf,
    DWORD cbWriteBuf,
    LPVOID lpvReadBuf,
    DWORD cbReadBuf,
    LPDWORD lpcbRead,
    DWORD dwTimeOut)
```

The parameter usage is similar to that of TransactNamedPipe except that a pipe name, rather than a handle, is used to specify the pipe. CallNamedPipe is synchronous (there is no overlapped structure—see Chapter 14). It specifies a time-out period, in milliseconds, for the connection, but not for the transaction. There are three special values for dwTimeOut:

- NMPWAIT_NOWAIT

- NMPWAIT_WAIT_FOREVER

- NMPWAIT_USE_DEFAULT_WAIT, which uses the default time-out period specified by CreateNamedPipe

---

[3] Note that TransactNamedPipe is more than a mere convenience compared with WriteFile and ReadFile and can provide some performance advantages. One experiment shows throughput enhancements ranging from 57 percent (small packets) to 24 percent (large packets).

Peeking at Named Pipe Messages

In addition to reading a named pipe using `ReadFile`, you can also determine whether there is actually a message to read using `PeekNamedPipe`. This can be used to poll the named pipe (an inefficient operation), determine the message length so as to allocate a buffer before reading, or look at the incoming data so as to prioritize its processing.

```
BOOL PeekNamedPipe (
    HANDLE hPipe,
    LPVOID lpvBuffer,
    DWORD cbBuffer,
    LPDWORD lpcbRead,
    LPDWORD lpcbAvail,
    LPDWORD lpcbMessage)
```

`PeekNamedPipe` will nondestructively read any bytes or messages in the pipe, but it does not block; it returns immediately.

Test `*lpcbAvail` to determine whether there is data in the pipe; if there is, `*lpcbAvail` will be greater than zero. In this case, `lpvBuffer` and `lpcbRead` can be NULL. If a buffer is specified with `lpvBuffer` and `cbBuffer`, then `*lpcbMessage` will tell whether there are leftover message bytes that could not fit into the buffer, allowing you to allocate a large buffer before reading from the named pipe. This value is zero for a byte mode pipe.

Again, `PeekNamedPipe` reads nondestructively, so a subsequent `ReadFile` is required to remove messages or bytes from the pipe.

Named Pipe Security

The important security rights for named pipes are:

- `GENERIC_READ`
- `GENERIC_WRITE`
- `SYNCHRONIZE` (allowing a thread to wait on the pipe)

Alternatively, simply use `STANDARD_RIGHTS_REQUIRED` as in Program 11–3, where all rights are required if the client is to connect.

You should set the appropriate rights depending on the access (duplex, inbound, or outbound). All three require SYNCHRONIZE. The server in Program 11–3 optionally secures its named pipe instances using these rights.

The UNIX FIFO is similar to a named pipe, thus allowing communication between unrelated processes. There are limitations compared with Win32 named pipes:

- FIFOs are half-duplex.

- FIFOs are limited to a single machine.

- FIFOs are still byte-oriented, so it is easiest to use fixed-size records in client/server applications. Nonetheless, individual read and write operations are atomic.

A server using FIFOs must use a separate FIFO for each client's response, although all clients can send requests to a single, well-known FIFO. A common practice is for the client to include a FIFO name in a connect request.

mkfifo is the UNIX function that is a limited version of CreateNamedPipe.

If the clients and server are to be networked, use sockets or a similar transport mechanism. Sockets are full-duplex, but there must still be one separate connection per client.

Example: A Client/Server Command Line Processor

Everything required to build a request/response client/server system is now available. The example is a command line server that executes a command on behalf of the client. Features of the system include the following:

- Multiple clients can interact with the server.

- The clients can be on different systems on the network, although the clients can also be on the server machine.

- The server is multithreaded, with a thread dedicated to each named pipe instance. That is, there is a *thread pool* of worker threads ready for use by connecting clients. Worker threads are allocated to a client on the basis of the named pipe instance that the system allocates to the client.

- The server processes a single request at a time, and so concurrency control is not an issue.

Program 11–2 shows the single-threaded client, and its server is Program 11–3. The server corresponds to the model in Figures 8–1 and 11–2. The client request is simply the command line. The server response is the resulting output, which is sent in several messages. The programs also use the include file `ClntSrvr.h`, which is included on the disc and defines the request and response data structures as well as the client and server pipe names.

The client in Program 11–2 also calls a function, `LocateServer`, which finds the name of a server's pipe. `LocateServer` uses a mailslot, as will be described in a later section and shown in Program 11–5.

The defined records have length fields that are defined as `DWORD32`; this is done so that these programs can be ported to Win64 in the future but will interoperate with servers or clients running on Win32 systems.

Program 11–2   `clientNP`: Named Pipe Connection-Oriented Client

```
/* Chapter 11. Client/Server system. CLIENT VERSION.
   clientNP - connection-oriented client. */
/* Execute a command line (on the server); display the response. */
/* The client creates a long-lived connection with the server
   (consuming a pipe instance) and prompts user for a command. */

#include "EvryThng.h"
#include "ClntSrvr.h" /* Defines the request, records. */

int _tmain (int argc, LPTSTR argv [])
{
    HANDLE hNamedPipe;
    TCHAR PromptMsg [] = _T ("\nEnter Command: ");
    TCHAR QuitMsg [] = _T ("$Quit");
    TCHAR ServerPipeName [MAX_PATH];
    REQUEST Request; /* See ClntSrvr.h. */
    RESPONSE Response; /* See ClntSrvr.h. */
    DWORD nRead, nWrite;

    LocateServer (ServerPipeName);
    WaitNamedPipe (ServerPipeName, NMPWAIT_WAIT_FOREVER);
    hNamedPipe = CreateFile (ServerPipeName,
            GENERIC_READ | GENERIC_WRITE, 0, NULL,
            OPEN_EXISTING, FILE_ATTRIBUTE_NORMAL, NULL);

    /* Prompt the user for commands. Terminate on "$quit." */
    while (ConsolePrompt (PromptMsg, Request.Record,
            MAX_RQRS_LEN, TRUE)
            && (_tcscmp (Request.Record, QuitMsg) != 0)) {
        WriteFile (hNamedPipe, &Request, RQ_SIZE, &nWrite, NULL);
        /* Read each response and send it to std out
           Response.Status == 0 indicates "end of response." */

        while (ReadFile (hNamedPipe, &Response, RS_SIZE,
            &nRead, NULL) && (Response.Status == 0))
```

```
                        _tprintf (_T ("%s"), Response.Record);
        }

        _tprintf (_T ("Quit command received. Disconnect."));
        CloseHandle (hNamedPipe);
        return 0;
}
```

Program 11–3 is the server program, including the server thread function, that processes the requests from Program 11–2. The server also creates a "server broadcast" thread (see Program 11–4) to broadcast its pipe name on a mailslot to clients that want to connect. Program 11–2 calls the LocateServer function, shown in Program 11–5, which reads the information sent by this process. Mailslots are described later in this chapter.

While the code is omitted in Program 11–4, the server (on the disc) optionally secures its named pipe to prevent access by unauthorized clients. Optionally specify the user and group name on the command line.

```
Server [UserName GroupName]
```

If the user and group names are omitted, default security is used. Note that Program 11–3 uses Program 5–3 (InitUnFp) to create the optional security attributes.

Program 11–3   serverNP: Multithreaded Named Pipe Server Program

```
/* Chapter 11. ServerNP.
 * Multithreaded command line server. Named pipe version. */

#include "EvryThng.h"
#include "ClntSrvr.h" /* Request and response message definitions. */

typedef struct { /* Argument to a server thread. */
    HANDLE hNamedPipe; /* Named pipe instance. */
    DWORD ThreadNo;
    TCHAR TmpFileName [MAX_PATH]; /* Temporary file name. */
} THREAD_ARG;
typedef THREAD_ARG *LPTHREAD_ARG;

volatile static BOOL ShutDown = FALSE;
static DWORD WINAPI Server (LPTHREAD_ARG);
static DWORD WINAPI Connect (LPTHREAD_ARG);
static DWORD WINAPI ServerBroadcast (LPLONG);
static BOOL WINAPI Handler (DWORD);
static TCHAR ShutRqst [] = _T ("$ShutDownServer");
```

```
_tmain (int argc, LPTSTR argv [])
{
    /* MAX_CLIENTS is defined in ClntSrvr.h. */

    HANDLE hNp, hMonitor, hSrvrThread [MAX_CLIENTS];
    DWORD iNp, MonitorId, ThreadId;
    LPSECURITY_ATTRIBUTES pNPSA = NULL;
    THREAD_ARG ThArgs [MAX_CLIENTS];

    /* Console control handler to permit server shutdown. */
    SetConsoleCtrlHandler (Handler, TRUE);

    /* Create a thread broadcast pipe name periodically. */
    hMonitor = (HANDLE) _beginthreadex (NULL, 0,
            ServerBroadcast, NULL, 0, &MonitorId);

    /* Create pipe instance & temp file for every server thread. */

    for (iNp = 0; iNp < MAX_CLIENTS; iNp++) {
        hNp = CreateNamedPipe ( SERVER_PIPE, PIPE_ACCESS_DUPLEX,
                PIPE_READMODE_MESSAGE | PIPE_TYPE_MESSAGE | PIPE_WAIT,
                MAX_CLIENTS, 0, 0, INFINITE, pNPSA);
        ThArgs [iNp].hNamedPipe = hNp;
        ThArgs [iNp].ThreadNo = iNp;
        GetTempFileName (_T ("."), _T ("CLP"), 0,
            ThArgs [iNp].TmpFileName);
        hSrvrThread [iNp] = (HANDLE)_beginthreadex (NULL, 0, Server,
                &ThArgs [iNp], 0, &ThreadId);
    }

    /* Wait for all the threads to terminate. */
    WaitForMultipleObjects (MAX_CLIENTS, hSrvrThread,
            TRUE, INFINITE);
    WaitForSingleObject (hMonitor, INFINITE);
    CloseHandle (hMonitor);
    for (iNp = 0; iNp < MAX_CLIENTS; iNp++) {
        /* Close pipe handles and delete temp files. */
        CloseHandle (hSrvrThread [iNp]);
        DeleteFile (ThArgs [iNp].TmpFileName);
    }

    _tprintf (_T ("Server process has shut down.\n"));
    return 0;
}

static DWORD WINAPI Server (LPTHREAD_ARG pThArg)

/* Server thread function; one for every potential client. */
{
    HANDLE hNamedPipe, hTmpFile = INVALID_HANDLE_VALUE,
```

```
                hConTh, hClient;
        DWORD nXfer, ConThId, ConThStatus;
        STARTUPINFO StartInfoCh;
        SECURITY_ATTRIBUTES TempSA =
                {sizeof (SECURITY_ATTRIBUTES), NULL, TRUE};
        PROCESS_INFORMATION ProcInfo;
        FILE *fp;
        REQUEST Request;
        RESPONSE Response;

        GetStartupInfo (&StartInfoCh);
        hNamedPipe = pThArg->hNamedPipe;

        while (!ShutDown) { /* Connection loop. */
            /* Create connection thread; wait for it to terminate. */
            hConTh = (HANDLE)_beginthreadex (NULL, 0,
                    Connect, pThArg, 0, &ConThId);

            /* Wait for a client connection & test shutdown flag. */
            while (!ShutDown && WaitForSingleObject
                    (hConTh, CS_TIMEOUT) == WAIT_TIMEOUT)
                        { /* Empty loop body. */};
            CloseHandle (hConTh);
            if (ShutDown) continue; /* Flag can be set by any thread. */
            /* A connection now exists. */
            hTmpFile = CreateFile (pThArg->TmpFileName,
                    GENERIC_READ | GENERIC_WRITE,
                    FILE_SHARE_READ | FILE_SHARE_WRITE, &TempSA,
                    CREATE_ALWAYS, FILE_ATTRIBUTE_TEMPORARY, NULL);

            while (!ShutDown && ReadFile
                    (hNamedPipe, &Request, RQ_SIZE, &nXfer, NULL)) {
                /* Receive new commands until the client disconnects. */
                ShutDown = ShutDown ||
                        (_tcscmp (Request.Record, ShutRqst) == 0);
                if (ShutDown) continue; /* Tested on each iteration. */

                /* Create a process to carry out the command. */
                StartInfoCh.hStdOutput = hTmpFile;
                StartInfoCh.hStdError = hTmpFile;
                StartInfoCh.hStdInput = GetStdHandle (STD_INPUT_HANDLE);
                StartInfoCh.dwFlags = STARTF_USESTDHANDLES;

                CreateProcess (NULL, Request.Record, NULL,
                        NULL, TRUE, /* Inherit handles. */
                        0, NULL, NULL, &StartInfoCh, &ProcInfo);

                /* Server process is running. */
                CloseHandle (ProcInfo.hThread);
                WaitForSingleObject (ProcInfo.hProcess, INFINITE);
```

```
        CloseHandle (ProcInfo.hProcess);

        /* Respond a line at a time. It is convenient to use
           C library line-oriented routines at this point. */

        fp = _tfopen (pThArg->TmpFileName, _T ("r"));
        Response.Status = 0;
        while (_fgetts (Response.Record, MAX_RQRS_LEN, fp)
                != NULL)
            WriteFile (hNamedPipe, &Response, RS_SIZE,
                    &nXfer, NULL);
        fclose (fp);

        /* Erase temp file contents. */
        SetFilePointer (hTmpFile, 0, NULL, FILE_BEGIN);
        SetEndOfFile (hTmpFile);

        /* Send an end of response indicator. */
        Response.Status = 1; strcpy (Response.Record, "");
        WriteFile (hNamedPipe, &Response, RS_SIZE, &nXfer, NULL);
    }
    /* End of main command loop. Get next command. */

    /* Force connection thread to shut down if it is still active. */
    GetExitCodeThread (hConTh, &ConThStatus);
    if (ConThStatus == STILL_ACTIVE) {
        hClient = CreateFile (SERVER_PIPE,
            GENERIC_READ | GENERIC_WRITE, 0, NULL,
            OPEN_EXISTING, FILE_ATTRIBUTE_NORMAL, NULL);
        if (hClient != INVALID_HANDLE_VALUE)
            CloseHandle (hClient);
        WaitForSingleObject (hConTh, INFINITE);
    }

    /* Client disconnected or there is a shutdown request. */
    FlushFileBuffers (hNamedPipe);
    DisconnectNamedPipe (hNamedPipe);
    CloseHandle (hTmpFile);
    hTmpFile = INVALID_HANDLE_VALUE;
    DeleteFile (pThArg->TmpFileName);
}

/* End of command loop. Free resources; exit from the thread. */
if (hTmpFile != INVALID_HANDLE_VALUE)
    CloseHandle (hTmpFile);
DeleteFile (pThArg->TmpFileName);
_tprintf (_T ("Exiting thread number %d\n"), pThArg->ThreadNo);
_endthreadex (0);
}
```

```
static DWORD WINAPI Connect (LPTHREAD_ARG pThArg)
{
    /* Connection thread allowing server to poll ShutDown flag. */
    ConnectNamedPipe (pThArg->hNamedPipe, NULL);
    _endthreadex (0);
    return 0;
}

BOOL WINAPI Handler (DWORD CtrlEvent)
{
    /* Shut down the system. */
    ShutDown = TRUE;
    return TRUE;
}
```

Comments on the Client/Server Command Line Processor

This solution includes a number of features as well as limitations that will be addressed in later chapters.

- Multiple client processes can connect with the server and perform concurrent requests; each client has a dedicated server (or "worker") thread allocated from the *thread pool*.

- The server and clients can be run from separate command prompts or can be run under control of JobShell (Program 7–3).

- If all the named pipe instances are in use when a client connects, the new client will wait until a different client disconnects on receiving a $Quit command, making a pipe instance available for another client.

- Each server thread performs synchronous I/O, but some server threads can be processing requests while others are waiting for connections or client requests.

- Extension to networked clients is straightforward, subject to the limitations of named pipes discussed earlier in this chapter. Simply change the pipe names in the header file.

- Clients that are not in the group that is used to secure the pipe cannot connect to the server.

- The clients can access exactly the same files and other objects that are available to the server on the server's machine with the server's access rights.

Exercise 11–10 suggests removing this limitation by implementing *security delegation* using the functions `ImpersonateNamedPipeClient` and `RevertToSelf`.

- Each server worker thread creates a simple "connection thread," which calls `ConnectNamedPipe` and terminates as soon as a client connects. This allows a worker thread to wait, with a time-out, on the connection thread handle and test the global shutdown flag periodically. If the worker threads blocked on `ConnectNamedPipe`, then they could not test the flag and the server could not shut down. For this reason, the server thread performs a `CreateFile` on the named pipe in order to force the connection thread to resume and shut down. An alternative would be to use asynchronous I/O (Chapter 14) so that an event could be associated with the `ConnectNamedPipe` call. The comments in the disc source file provide additional alternatives and information. *Note*: Programs 11–3 and 11–4 are total modifications of the old ones.

- Connection threads may never terminate by themselves; this situation could result in resource leaks in DLLs. This subject is discussed in the next chapter.

- There are a number of opportunities to enhance the system. For example, there could be an option to perform "in-process service" by using a DLL that implements some of the commands. This enhancement will be added in the next chapter.

- The number of server threads is limited by the `WaitForMultipleObjects` call in the main thread. While this limitation is easily overcome, the system here is not truly scalable; too many threads will impair performance, as we saw in Chapter 10. Chapter 14 will use asynchronous I/O ports to address this issue.

Mailslots

A Win32 mailslot, like a named pipe, has a name that unrelated processes can use for communication. Mailslots are a broadcast mechanism and behave differently from named pipes, making them useful in some important, but limited, situations. Here are the significant characteristics of mailslots:

- A mailslot is one-directional.

- A mailslot can have multiple writers and multiple readers, but frequently it will be one-to-many of one form or the other.

- A writer, or client, does not know for certain that all, some, or any readers, or servers, actually received the message.

- Mailslots can be located over a network domain.

- Message lengths are limited.

Using a mailslot requires the following operations:

- Each server (reader) creates a mailslot handle with `CreateMailslot`.

- The server then waits to receive a mailslot message with a `ReadFile` call.

- A write-only client should open the mailslot with `CreateFile` and write messages with `WriteFile`. The open will fail (name not found) if there are no waiting readers.

A client's message can be read by *all* servers; all of them receive the same message.

There is one further possibility. The client, in performing the `CreateFile`, can specify a name of the form:

```
\\*\mailslot\mailslotname
```

In this way, the * acts as a wildcard, and the client can locate every server in the *name domain*, a networked group of systems assigned a common name by the network administrator.

Using Mailslots

The preceding client/server command processor suggests several ways that mailslots might be useful. Here is one scenario that will solve the server location problem in the preceding client/server system (Programs 11–2 and 11–3).

The *application server*, acting as a *mailslot client*, periodically broadcasts its name and a named pipe name. Any *application client* that wants to find a server can receive this name by being a *mailslot server*. In a similar manner, the command line server can periodically broadcast its status, including information such as utilization, to the clients. This situation could be described as a single writer (the mailslot client) and multiple readers (the mailslot servers). If there were multiple mailslot clients (that is, multiple application servers), there would be a many-to-many situation.

Alternatively, a single reader could receive messages from numerous writers, perhaps giving their status—that is, there would be multiple writers and a single reader. This usage, which might be used in a bulletin board application, justifies the term *mailslot*. These first two uses—name and status broadcast—can be combined so that a client can select the most appropriate server.

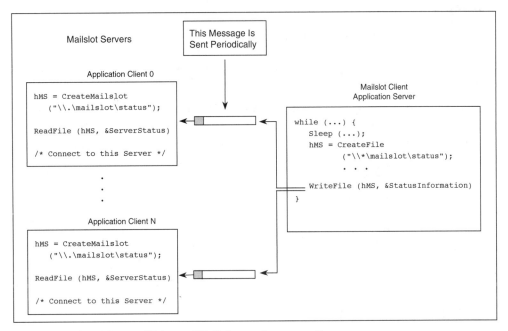

Figure 11-3   Clients Using a Mailslot to Locate a Server

The inversion of the terms *client* and *server* is confusing in this context, but notice that both named pipe and mailslot servers perform the `CreateNamedPipe` (or `CreateMailSlot`) calls, while the client (named pipe or mailslot) connects using `CreateFile`. Also, in both cases, the client performs the first `WriteFile` and the server performs the first `ReadFile`.

Figure 11–3 shows the use of mailslots for the first approach.

Creating and Opening a Mailslot

The mailslot servers (readers) use `CreateMailslot` to create a mailslot and to get a handle for use with `ReadFile`. There can be only one mailslot of a given name on a specific machine, but several systems in a network can use the same name to take advantage of mailslots in a multireader situation.

```
HANDLE CreateMailslot (LPCTSTR lpszName,
    DWORD cbMaxMsg,
    DWORD dwReadTimeout,
    LPSECURITY_ATTRIBUTES lpsa)
```

Parameters

`lpszName` points to a mailslot name of the form:

    `\\.\mailslot\`*`[path]name`*

The name must be unique. The "`.`" indicates that the mailslot is created on the current machine.

    `cbMaxMsg` is the maximum size (in bytes) for messages that a client can write. 0 means no limit.

    `dwReadTimeout` is the number of milliseconds that a read operation will wait. 0 causes an immediate return, and `MAILSLOT_WAIT_FOREVER` is an infinite wait (no time-out).

    The client (writer), when opening a mailslot with `CreateFile`, can use the following name forms:

    `\\.\mailslot\`*`[path]name`* retrieves a handle for a local mailslot.

    `\\`*`computername`*`\mailslot\`*`[path]name`* retrieves a handle for a mailslot on a specified machine.

    `\\`*`domainname`*`\mailslot\`*`[path]name`* returns a handle representing all mailslots on machines in the domain.

    `\\*\mailslot\`*`[path]name`* returns a handle representing mailslots on machines in the system's primary domain. In this case, the maximum message length is 400 bytes.

Finally, the client must specify the `FILE_SHARE_READ` flag.

    Functions `GetMailslotInfo` and `SetMailslotInfo` are similar to their named pipe counterparts.

UNIX does not have a facility comparable to mailslots. A broadcast or multicast TCP/IP datagram, however, could be used for this purpose.

Pipe and Mailslot Creation, Connection, and Naming

Table 11–1 summarizes the valid pipe names that can be used by application clients and servers. It also summarizes the functions that should be used to create and connect with named pipes.

    Table 11–2 gives similar information for mailslots. Recall that the mailslot client (or server) may not be the same process or even on the same system as the application client (or server).

Table 11-1 Named Pipes: Creating, Connecting, and Naming

	Application Client	Application Server

Named Pipe Handle or Connection	`CreateFile`
	
	`CallNamedPipe`
		`CreateNamedPipe`

Pipe Name	`\\.\`*pipename* (pipe is local) `\\`*sys_name*`\`*pipename* (pipe is local or remote)	`\\.\`*pipename* (pipe is created locally)

Table 11-2 Mailslots: Creating, Connecting, and Naming

	Mailslot Client	Mailslot Server
Mailslot Handle	`CreateFile`	`CreateMailslot`
Mailslot Name	`\\.\`*msname* (mailslot is local) `\\`*sys_name*`\`*msname* (mailslot is on a specific remote system) `\\*\`*msname* (all mailslots with this name)	`\\.\`*msname* (mailslot is created locally)

Example: A Server That Clients Can Locate

Program 11–4 shows the thread function that the command line server (Program 11–3), *acting as a mailslot client*, uses to broadcast its pipe name to waiting clients. There can be multiple servers with different characteristics and pipe names, and the clients obtain their names from the well-known mailslot name. This function is started as a thread by Program 11–3.

Note: In practice, many client/server systems invert the location logic used here. The alternative is to have the application client also act as the mailslot client and broadcast a message requesting a server to respond on a specified named pipe (the client determines the pipe name and includes that name in the message). The application server, acting as a mailslot server, then reads the request and creates a connection on the specified named pipe.

Program 11–4   SrvrBcst: Mailslot Client Thread Function

```
static DWORD WINAPI ServerBroadcast (LPLONG pNull)
{
    MS_MESSAGE MsNotify;
    DWORD nXfer;
    HANDLE hMsFile;

    /* Open the mailslot for the MS "client" writer. */
    while (!ShutDown) { /* Run as long as there are server threads. */
        /* Wait for another client to open a mailslot. */
        Sleep (CS_TIMEOUT);
        hMsFile = CreateFile (MS_CLTNAME,
                GENERIC_WRITE | GENERIC_READ,
                FILE_SHARE_READ | FILE_SHARE_WRITE,
                NULL, OPEN_EXISTING, FILE_ATTRIBUTE_NORMAL, NULL);
        if (hMsFile == INVALID_HANDLE_VALUE) continue;

        /* Send out the message to the mailslot. */

        MsNotify.msStatus = 0;
        MsNotify.msUtilization = 0;
        _tcscpy (MsNotify.msName, SERVER_PIPE);
        if (!WriteFile (hMsFile, &MsNotify, MSM_SIZE, &nXfer, NULL))
            ReportError (_T ("Server MS Write error."), 13, TRUE);
        CloseHandle (hMsFile);
    }
    _tprintf (_T ("Shutting down monitor thread.\n"));

    _endthreadex (0);
    return 0;
}
```

Program 11–5 shows the function called by the client (see Program 11–2) so that it can locate the server.

Program 11–5   LocSrver: Mailslot Server

```
/* Chapter 11. LocSrver.c */
/* Find a server by reading the mailslot that is
   used to broadcast server names. */

#include "EvryThng.h"
#include "ClntSrvr.h" /* Defines mailslot name. */

BOOL LocateServer (LPTSTR pPipeName)
{
```

```
HANDLE MsFile;
MS_MESSAGE ServerMsg;
BOOL Found = FALSE;
DWORD cbRead;

MsFile = CreateMailslot (MS_SRVNAME, 0, CS_TIMEOUT, NULL);
while (!Found) {
   _tprintf (_T ("Looking for a server.\n"));
   Found = ReadFile (MsFile, &ServerMsg, MSM_SIZE,
         &cbRead, NULL);
}
_tprintf (_T ("Server has been located.\n"));
CloseHandle (MsFile);

      /* Name of the server pipe. */
_tcscpy (pPipeName, ServerMsg.msName);
return TRUE;
}
```

Comments on Thread Models

Terms such as *thread pool*, *symmetric threads*, and *asymmetric threading* have been used to describe methods for designing threaded programs, and we have relied on the boss/worker, pipeline, and other "classical" threading models.

This section briefly describes some descriptive and helpful terms used as integral parts of Microsoft's Component Object Model (COM) object-oriented technology: *single threading*, *apartment model threading*, and *free threading*. (See Chapter 15 for a short COM overview and additional references.) Each of these models has unique performance characteristics and synchronization requirements.

- A thread pool is a collection of threads that are available for use as required. Figure 8–1 and Program 11–3 illustrate a pool of threads that can be assigned to new clients that attach by connecting to an associated named pipe. When the client disconnects, the thread is returned to the pool.

- The thread model is symmetric when a group of threads perform the same task using exactly the same thread function. grepMT, Program 8–1, used symmetric threading: all the threads execute the same pattern searching code. Note that the threads are not in a pool; all of them are created to perform specific tasks and terminate when the task is complete. Program 11–3 creates a pool of symmetric threads.

- The thread model is asymmetric when different threads perform different tasks using separate thread functions. The broadcast function shown in Figure 8–1 and Program 11–4 is an example.

- In COM terminology, an object is single-threaded when only one thread can access it. This means that access is serialized. In the case of a database server, the object would be the database itself. The examples in this chapter use a multithreaded model to access the "object," which could be considered to be the programs and files on the server machine.

- In COM terminology, apartment model threading occurs when a unique thread is assigned to each instance of an object. For example, each thread in Figure 11–1 could be assigned to a distinct database or portion of a database. Access to the object is serialized through the single thread. As always, access to global storage must be serialized.

- A free-threaded object will have a thread, generally from a thread pool, assigned to it when a request is made. The server in this chapter is free-threaded if the connection is regarded as the request. Similarly, if the threads supported a database server, the database would be free-threaded.

Some programs, such as sortMT (Program 8–2), do not fit any of these models exactly. Also, recall that we have already used other thread models—namely, the boss/worker, pipeline, and client/server models—in conformance with common non-Microsoft usage.

These threading models are also appropriate in Chapter 12, which introduces in-process servers, and the terms are used in some of the Microsoft documentation. Remember that these terms are defined specifically for COM; the preceding discussion shows how they might be used in a more general context. COM is a large and complex subject, beyond the scope of this book, other than a very brief overview in Chapter 15.

Summary

Win32 pipes and mailslots, which are accessed with file I/O operations, provide stream-oriented interprocess and networked communication. The examples show how to pipe data from one process to another and a simple, multithreaded client/server system. Pipes also provide another thread synchronization method, because a reading thread blocks until another thread writes to the pipe.

Looking Ahead

Chapter 12 shows how to use standard, rather than Win32 proprietary, interprocess and networking communication. The same client/server system, with some server enhancements, will be rewritten to use the standard methods.

Additional Reading

Win32 Network Programming

Win32 Network Programming, by Ralph Davis, shows how pipes and mailslots are implemented using networking protocols. Chapter 10 in Davis presents some useful comparisons of named pipe performance, including the performance results mentioned earlier in this chapter. Davis also discusses remote procedure calls (RPCs) and sockets (the subject of the next chapter).

Exercises

11–1. Carry out experiments to determine the accuracy of the performance advantages cited for `TransactNamedPipe`. You will need to make some changes to the code as given. Also compare the results with the current implementation.

11–2. Use the `JobShell` program from Chapter 7 to start the server and several clients, where each client is created using the "detached" option. Eventually, shut down the server by sending a console control event through the `kill` command. Can you suggest any improvements to the `serverNP` shutdown logic so that a connected server thread can test the shutdown flag while blocked waiting for a client request? *Hint*: Create a read thread similar to the connection thread.

11–3. Enhance the server so that the name of its named pipe is an argument on the command line. Bring up multiple server processes with different pipe names using the job management programs in Chapter 7. Verify that multiple clients simultaneously access this multiprocess server system. Also, confirm the correct operation of the named pipe security.

11–4. Run the client and server on different systems to confirm correct network operation. Modify `SrvrBcst` (Program 11–4) so that it includes the server machine name in the named pipe. Also, modify the mailslot name used in Program 11–4. Confirm that the named pipe security also works over the network.

11–5. Modify the system so that it applies security to the mailslots as well as to the named pipes.

11–6. Does named pipe security depend on having the NTFS? For instance, can you secure the pipes on a Windows 2000/NT system that has only a FAT file system?

11–7. Modify the server so that you measure the server's utilization. (In other words, what percentage of elapsed time is spent in the server?) Maintain performance information and report this information to the client on request. The `Request.Command` field could be used.

11–8. Enhance the server location programs so that the client will find the server with the lowest utilization rate.

11–9. Enhance the server so that the request includes a working directory. The server should set its working directory, carry out the command, and then restore the working directory to the old value. *Caution*: The server thread should not set the process working directory; instead, each thread should maintain a string representing its working directory and concatenate that string to the start of relative pathnames.

11–10. Enhance the server so that it carries out the command as if it were the client. Use `ImpersonateNamedPipeClient` and `RevertToSelf`.

11–11. serverNP is designed to run indefinitely as a server, allowing clients to connect, obtain services, and disconnect. When a client disconnects, it is important for the server to free *all* associated resources, such as memory, file handles, and thread handles. Any remaining *resource leaks* will ultimately exhaust system resources, causing the server to fail, and before failure there will be significant performance degradation. Carefully examine serverNP to ensure that there are no resource leaks, and, if you find any, fix them. (Also, please inform the author using the e-mail address in the preface.) *Note:* Resource leaks are a common and serious defect in many production systems. No "industry-strength" quality assurance effort is complete if it has not addressed this issue.

11–12. *Extended Exercise*: Synchronization objects can be used to synchronize threads in different processes on the same machine, but they cannot synchronize threads running in processes on different machines. Use named pipes and mailslots to create emulated mutexes, events, and semaphores to overcome this limitation.

12 | Network Programming with Windows Sockets

Named pipes and mailslots are suitable for interprocess communication between processes on the same system or processes on machines connected by a local or wide area network. The client/server system developed in Chapter 11, starting with Program 11–2, demonstrated these capabilities.

Named pipes and mailslots (more simply, "named pipes," unless the distinction is important) have the distinct drawback, however, of not being an industry standard. Therefore, programs such as those in Chapter 11 will not port easily to non-Windows systems, nor will they interoperate with non-Windows systems. This is the case even though named pipes are protocol-independent and can run over industry-standard protocols such as TCP/IP.

Windows provides interoperability by supporting Windows Sockets, which are nearly the same as, and interoperable with, Berkeley Sockets, a *de facto* industry standard. This chapter shows how to use the Windows Sockets (or "WinSock") API by modifying Chapter 11's client/server system. The resulting system can operate over TCP/IP-based wide area networks, and the server, for instance, can accept requests from UNIX clients.

Readers who are familiar with Berkeley Sockets may want to proceed directly to the programming examples, where not only are sockets used, but new server features are added and additional thread-safe library techniques are demonstrated.

WinSock, by enabling standards-based interoperability, allows programmers to exploit higher-level protocols, such as http, Remote Procedure Calls (RPCs), and the Component Object Model (COM), all of which provide different, and higher-level, models for standard, interoperable, networked interprocess communication.

The client/server system will be used as a vehicle for demonstrating WinSock, and, in the course of modifying the server, interesting new features will be added. In particular, *DLL entry points* (Chapter 6) and *"in-process DLL servers"* will be used for the first time. These new features could have been incorporated in the initial Chapter 11 version, but doing so would have distracted from the development and understanding of the basic system architecture. Finally, there will be additional examples of *how to create reentrant thread-safe libraries.*

WinSock, because of conformance to industry standards, has naming conventions and programming characteristics somewhat different from the Win32 functions described so far. The WinSock API is not really a part of Win32 and is available on Windows 3.1.

Windows Sockets

The WinSock API was developed as an extension of the Berkeley Sockets API into the Windows environment, and WinSock is supported in nearly all Windows systems, including, but not limited to, those supporting Win32. WinSock's benefits include:

- Porting of code already written for Berkeley Sockets is straightforward.

- Windows systems easily integrate into TCP/IP networks.

- Sockets can be used with Win32 overlapped I/O (Chapter 14), which, among other things, allows servers to scale when there is a large number of active clients.

- Sockets can be treated as file HANDLEs for use with ReadFile, WriteFile, and, with some limitations, other Win32 functions, just as UNIX allows sockets to be used as file descriptors. This capability is convenient whenever there is a need to use asynchronous I/O and I/O completion ports (Chapter 14).

- Extended, nonportable extensions are also available.

WinSock Initialization

The WinSock API is supported by a DLL (WS2_32.DLL) that can be accessed by linking WS2_32.LIB with your program. The DLL needs to be initialized with a nonstandard, WinSock-specific function, WSAStartup, which must be the first WinSock function a program calls. WSACleanup should be called when the program no longer needs to use WinSock functionality. *Note:* "WSA" denotes "Windows Sockets asynchronous..." The asynchronous capabilities will not be used here, because threads can and will be used where asynchronous operation is required.

`WSAStartup` and `WSACleanup`, while always required, may be the only non-standard functions that you will use.

```
int WSAStartup (
    WORD wVersionRequired,
    LPWSADATA lpWSAData);
```

Parameters

`wVersionRequired` indicates the highest version of the WinSock DLL that you need and can use. Version 1.1 is generally adequate and ensures the widest possible Windows interoperability. Nonetheless, Version 2.0 is available on all Win32 systems.

The return value is nonzero if the DLL cannot support the version you want.

The low byte of `wVersionRequired` specifies the major version; the high byte specifies the minor version. The `MAKEWORD` macro is usually used; thus, `MAKEWORD (1, 1)` represents Version 1.1.

`lpWSAData` points to a `WSADATA` structure that returns information on the configuration of the DLL, including the highest version available. The Visual Studio on-line help shows how to interpret the results.

`WSAGetLastError` can be used to get the error, but `GetLastError` also works, as does the `ReportError` function developed in Chapter 2.

When a program has completed or no longer needs to use sockets, it should call `WSACleanup` so that `WS2_32.DLL`, the sockets DLL, can free resources allocated for this process.

Creating a Socket

Once the WinSock DLL has been initialized, you can use the standard (i.e., Berkeley Sockets) functions to create sockets and connect for client/server or peer-to-peer communication.

A WinSock `SOCKET` data type is analogous to the Win32 `HANDLE` and can even be used with `ReadFile` and other Win32 functions requiring a `HANDLE`. The `socket` function is called in order to create (or open) a `SOCKET` where the socket is the function's return value.

```
SOCKET socket (int af, int type, int protocol);
```

Parameters

The type SOCKET is actually defined as an int, so UNIX code will port without the necessity of using the Win32 type definitions.

af denotes the address family, or "protocol"; use PF_INET (or AF_INET, which has the same value but is more properly used with the bind call) to designate IP (the Internet protocol component of TCP/IP).

type specifies connection-oriented (SOCK_STREAM) or datagram communications (SOCK_DGRAM), roughly corresponding to named pipes and mailslots, respectively.

protocol is unnecessary when af is AF_INET; use 0.

socket returns INVALID_SOCKET on failure.

You can use WinSock with protocols other than TCP/IP by specifying different protocol values; we will use only TCP/IP.

socket, like all the other standard functions, does not use uppercase letters in the function name. This is a departure from the Win32 convention and is mandated by the need to conform to industry standards.

Socket Server Functions

For convenience, a "server" is a process that accepts connections on a specified port. While sockets, like named pipes, can be used for peer-to-peer communication, this distinction is convenient and reflects the manner in which two systems connect to one another.

Unless specifically mentioned, the socket type will always be SOCK_STREAM throughout this chapter. SOCK_DGRAM will be described later in this chapter.

Binding a Socket

The next step is to "bind" the socket to its address and "service endpoint." The socket call, followed by the bind, is analogous to creating a named pipe. There is, however, no name to distinguish sockets on a given machine. A "port number" is used instead as the service endpoint. A given server can have multiple endpoints. The function is:

```
int bind (
    SOCKET s,
    const struct sockaddr *saddr,
    int namelen);
```

Parameters

s is an "unbound" SOCKET returned by socket.

saddr, filled in before the call, specifies the protocol and protocol-specific information, as described next. Among other things, the port number is included in this structure.

namelen is sizeof(sockaddr).

The return value is normally 0 or SOCKET_ERROR in case of error. The sockaddr structure is defined as follows:

```
struct sockaddr {
    u_short sa_family;
    char sa_data [14];
    };
typedef struct sockaddr SOCKADDR, *PSOCKADDR;
```

The first member, sa_family, is the protocol. The second member, sa_data, is protocol-specific. The Internet version of sockaddr is sockaddr_in.

```
struct sockaddr_in {
    short sin_family; /* AF_INET */
    u_short sin_port;
    struct in_addr sin_addr; /* 4-byte IP addr */
    char sin_zero [8];
    };
typedef struct sockaddr_in SOCKADDR_IN,
    *PSOCKADDR_IN;
```

Note the use of a short integer for the port number. The port number and other information must also be in the proper byte order, big-endian, so as to allow interoperability. The sin_addr member has a submember, s_addr, which is filled in with the familiar four-byte IP address, such as 127.0.0.1, to indicate the system from which connections will be accepted. Normally, connections from any system will be accepted, so the value INADDR_ANY is used, although this symbolic value must be converted to the correct form, as shown in the next example.

The inet_addr function can be used to convert an IP address text string into the form required, so that you can initialize the sin_addr.s_addr member of a sockaddr_in variable, as follows:

```
sa.sin_addr.s_addr = inet_addr ("192.13.12.1");
```

A bound socket, with a protocol, port number, and IP address, is sometimes said to be a *named socket*.

Putting a Bound Socket into the Listening State

listen makes a server socket available for client connection. There is no analogous named pipe function.

```
int listen (SOCKET s, int nQueueSize);
```

nQueueSize indicates the number of connection requests you are willing to have queued at the socket. There is no upper bound in WinSock Version 2.0, but Version 1.1 has a limit of SOMAXCON (which is 5).

Accepting a Client Connection

Finally, a server can wait for a client to connect, using the accept function, which returns a new "connected socket" that is used in the I/O operations. Notice that the original socket, now in the listening state, is used solely as an accept parameter and is not used directly for I/O.

accept blocks until a client connection request arrives, and then it returns the new I/O socket. It is possible, but out of scope, to make a socket be nonblocking, and the server (Program 12–2) uses a separate "accepting thread" to allow for nonblocking servers.

```
SOCKET accept (
    SOCKET s,
    LPSOCKADDR lpAddr,
    LPINT lpAddrLen);
```

Parameters

s, the first argument, is the listening socket. Preceding socket, bind, and listen calls are required to put the socket into the listening state.

lpAddr points to a sockaddr_in structure that gives the address of the client system.

lpAddrLen points to a variable that will contain the length of the returned sockaddr_in structure. It is necessary to initialize this variable to sizeof (struct sockaddr_in) before the accept call.

Disconnecting and Closing Sockets

Disconnect a socket using shutdown (s, how). The how argument is either 1 or 2 to indicate whether sending only (1) or both sending and receiving (2) are to be disconnected. shutdown does not free resources associated with the socket, but it does assure that all data is sent or received before the socket is closed. Nonetheless, an application should not reuse a socket after calling shutdown.

Once you are finished with a socket, you can close it with the closesocket (SOCKET s) function. The server first closes the socket created by accept, not the listening socket. The server should not close the listening socket until the server shuts down or will no longer accept client connections. Even if you are treating a socket as a HANDLE and using ReadFile and WriteFile, CloseHandle alone will not destroy the socket; use closesocket.

Example: Preparing for and Accepting a Client Connection

The following code fragment shows how to create a socket and then accept client connections.

This example uses two standard functions, htons ("host to network short") and htonl ("host to network long") that convert integers to big-endian form, as required by IP.

The server port can be any short integer, but user-defined services are normally in the range 1025–5000. Lower port numbers are reserved for well-known services such as `telnet` and `ftp`, while higher numbers are likely to be assigned to other standard services.

```
struct sockaddr_in SrvSAddr; /* Server address struct. */
struct sockaddr_in ConnectAddr;
SOCKET SrvSock, sockio;
...
SrvSock = socket (AF_INET, SOCK_STREAM, 0);
SrvSAddr.sin_family = AF_INET;
SrvSAddr.sin_addr.s_addr = htonl (INADDR_ANY);
SrvSAddr.sin_port = htons (SERVER_PORT);
bind (SrvSock, (struct sockaddr *) &SrvSAddr,
      sizeof SrvSAddr);
listen (SrvSock, 5);
AddrLen = sizeof (ConnectAddr);
sockio = accept (SrvSock,
      (struct sockaddr *) &ConnectAddr, &AddrLen);
... Receive requests and send responses ...
shutdown (sockio);
closesocket (sockio);
```

Socket Client Functions

A client station wishing to connect to a server must also create a socket by calling the `socket` function. The next step is to connect with a server, and it is necessary to specify a port, host address, and other information. There is just one additional function, `connect`.

Connecting to a Server

If there is a server with a listening socket, the client connects with the following function:

```
int connect (
    SOCKET s,
    LPSOCKADDR lpName,
    int nNameLen);
```

Parameters

s is a socket created with the socket function.

lpName points to a sockaddr_in structure that has been initialized with the port and IP address of a system with a socket, bound to the specified port, that is in listening mode.

Initialize nNameLen with sizeof (struct sockaddr_in).

A return value of zero indicates a successful connection, whereas SOCKET_ERROR indicates failure, possibly because there is no listening socket at the specified address.

The socket, s, does not need to be bound to a port before the connect call, although it can be. The system allocates a port if required and determines the protocol.

Example: Client Connecting to a Server

Here is the code sequence that allows a client to connect to a server. Just two function calls are required, but the address structure must be initialized before the connect call. Error testing is omitted but should be included in actual programs. In the example, it is assumed that the IP address (a text string such as "192.76.33.4") is given in argv [1] on the command line.

```
SOCKET ClientSock;
...
ClientSock = socket (AF_INET, SOCK_STREAM, 0);
memset (&ClientSAddr, sizeof (ClientSAddr), 0);
ClientSAddr.sin_family = AF_INET;
ClientSAddr.sin_addr.s_addr = inet_addr (argv [1]);
ClientSAddr.sin_port = htons (SERVER_PORT);
ConVal = connect (ClientSock,
        (struct sockaddr *) &ClientSAddr,
        sizeof (ClientSAddr));
```

Sending and Receiving Data

Socket programs exchange data using send and recv, which have identical argument forms. Only send is shown here.

```
int send (
    SOCKET s,
    LPSTR lpBuffer,
    int nBufferLen,
    int nFlags);
```

The return value is the actual number of bytes transmitted. An error is indicated by the value SOCKET_ERROR.

nFlags can be used to indicate urgency (such as "out-of-band" data), and MSG_PEEK can be used to look at incoming data without reading it.

The most important fact to remember is that send and recv *are not atomic*, and there is no assurance that all the requested data has been received or sent. "Short sends" are extremely rare, but are possible, as are "short receives." There is no concept of a message as with named pipes; therefore, you need to test the return value and resend or transmit until all data has been transmitted.

You can also use ReadFile and WriteFile with sockets by casting the socket to a HANDLE in the function call.

Comparing Named Pipes and Sockets

Named pipes, described in Chapter 11, are very similar to sockets, but there are also significant differences in how they are used and in the programming model.

- Named pipes can be message-oriented, which can simplify programs.

- Named pipes require ReadFile and WriteFile, whereas sockets can also use send and recv.

- Sockets are based on an industry standard, allowing interoperability with non-Windows systems.

There are also differences in the server and client programming models.

Comparing Named Pipe and Socket Servers

When using sockets, call accept repetitively to connect to multiple clients. Each call will return a different connected socket. Note the following differences relative to named pipes:

- Named pipes require you to create each named pipe instance and `HANDLE` with `CreateNamedPipe`, whereas socket instances are created by `accept`.

- There is no upper bound on the number of socket clients (`listen` only limits the number of queued clients), but there can be a limit on the number of named pipe instances, depending on the first call to `CreateNamedPipe`.

- Named pipes do not have explicit port numbers and are distinguished by name.

A named pipe server requires two function calls (`CreateNamedPipe` and `ConnectNamedPipe`) to obtain a usable `HANDLE`, whereas socket servers require four function calls (`socket`, `bind`, `listen`, and `accept`).

Comparing Named Pipe and Socket Clients

Named pipes use `WaitNamedPipe` followed by `CreateFile`. The socket sequence is in the opposite order, since the `socket` function can be regarded as the creation function, while `connect` is the blocking function.

An additional distinction is that "connect" is a socket client function, while a named pipe server uses `ConnectNamedPipe`.

Example: A Socket Message Receive Function

It is frequently convenient to send and receive messages as a single unit. Named pipes can do this, as shown in Chapter 11. Sockets, however, require that you create a message header with a length field, followed by the message itself. The following function receives such a message and will be used in the examples. The send message function is similar.

Notice that the message is received in two parts: the header and the contents. A user-defined `MESSAGE` type with a four-byte message length header is assumed. Even the header requires repetitive reads to ensure that it is read in its entirety. Also recall that `recv` is not atomic, so it must be called repetitively until all the requested data has been received. This is necessary even for the four-byte header.

Win64 Note: The message length variables have the fixed-precision `LONG32` type to ensure the length, which is included in messages that may be transferred to and from non-Windows systems, and have a well-defined length, even after future recompilation for Win64 (see Chapter 16).

```
DWORD ReceiveMessage (MESSAGE *pMsg, SOCKET sd)
{
    /* A message has a 4-byte length field, followed
```

```
    by the message contents. */
DWORD Disconnect = 0;
/* Set when 0 bytes are received. */
LONG32 nRemainRecv = 0, nXfer;
/* Fixed precision; helps ensure interoperability. */
LPSTR pBuffer;
/* Read message. */
/* First the length header, then contents. */
nRemainRecv = 4; /* Header field length. */
pBuffer = (LPBYTE) pMsg; /* recv may not */
/* transmit the number of bytes requested. */
while (nRemainRecv > 0 && !Disconnect) {
    nXfer = recv (sd, pBuffer, nRemainRecv, 0);
    Disconnect = (nXfer == 0);
    nRemainRecv -=nXfer; pBuffer += nXfer;
}
/* Read the message contents. */
nRemainRecv = pMsg->RqLen;
while (nRemainRecv > 0 && !Disconnect) {
    nXfer = recv (sd, pBuffer, nRemainRecv, 0);
    Disconnect = (nXfer == 0);
    nRemainRecv -=nXfer; pBuffer += nXfer;
}
return Disconnect;
}
```

Example: A Socket-Based Client

Program 12–1 reimplements the client program, which in named pipe form is Program 11–2, clientNP. The conversion is straightforward, with several small differences:

- Rather than locating a server using mailslots, the user enters the IP address on the command line. If the IP address is not specified, the default address is 127.0.0.1, which indicates the current system.

- Functions for sending and receiving messages, such as the one above, are used but are not shown here.

- The port number, SERVER_PORT, is defined in the header file, ClntSrvr.h.

Program 12–1   clientSK: Socket-Based Client

```
/* Chapter 12. clientSK.c */
/* Single-threaded command line client. */
/* WINDOWS SOCKETS VERSION. */
/* Reads a sequence of commands to send to a server process */
/* over a socket connection. Wait for and display response. */

#define _NOEXCLUSIONS /* Required to include socket definitions. */
#include "EvryThng.h"
#include "ClntSrvr.h" /* Defines request and response records. */
/* Message functions for request and response. */
static DWORD SendRequestMessage (REQUEST *, SOCKET);
static DWORD ReceiveResponseMessage (RESPONSE *, SOCKET);

struct sockaddr_in ClientSAddr; /* Clients's socket address. */

int _tmain (DWORD argc, LPTSTR argv [])
{
    SOCKET ClientSock = INVALID_SOCKET;
    REQUEST Request; /* See ClntSrvr.h. */
    RESPONSE Response; /* See ClntSrvr.h. */
    WSADATA WSStartData; /* Socket library data structure. */
    BOOL Quit = FALSE;
    DWORD ConVal, j;
    TCHAR PromptMsg [] = _T ("\nEnter Command> ");
    TCHAR Req [MAX_RQRS_LEN];
    TCHAR QuitMsg [] = _T ("$Quit");
                /* Request: shut down client. */
    TCHAR ShutMsg [] = _T ("$ShutDownServer");
                /* Stop all threads. */
    CHAR DefaultIPAddr [] = "127.0.0.1"; /* Local system. */

    /* Initialize the WS library. Ver 1.1. */
    WSAStartup (MAKEWORD (1, 1), &WSStartData);

    /* Connect to the server. */
    /* Follow the standard client socket/connect sequence. */
    ClientSock = socket (AF_INET, SOCK_STREAM, 0);
    memset (&ClientSAddr, sizeof (ClientSAddr), 0);
    ClientSAddr.sin_family = AF_INET;
    if (argc >= 2)
        ClientSAddr.sin_addr.s_addr = inet_addr (argv [1]);
    else
        ClientSAddr.sin_addr.s_addr = inet_addr (DefaultIPAddr);
    ClientSAddr.sin_port = htons (SERVER_PORT);
                /* Defined as 1070. */
    connect (ClientSock,
        (struct sockaddr *) &ClientSAddr, sizeof (ClientSAddr));
```

```
    /* Main loop to prompt user, send request, receive response. */
    while (!Quit) {
        _tprintf (_T ("%s"), PromptMsg);
        /* Generic input, but command to server must be ASCII. */
        _fgetts (Req, MAX_RQRS_LEN-1, stdin);
        for (j = 0; j <= _tcslen (Req); j++)
            Request.Record [j] = Req [j];
        /* Get rid of the new line at the end. */
        Request.Record [strlen (Request.Record) - 1] = '\0';
        if (strcmp (Request.Record, QuitMsg) == 0 ||
                strcmp (Request.Record, ShutMsg) == 0) Quit = TRUE;
        SendRequestMessage (&Request, ClientSock);
        ReceiveResponseMessage (&Response, ClientSock);
    }

    shutdown (ClientSock, 2); /* Disallow sends and receives. */
    closesocket (ClientSock);
    WSACleanup ();
    _tprintf (_T ("\n****Leaving client\n"));
    return 0;
}
```

Example: A Socket-Based Server with New Features

serverSK, Program 12–2, is similar to serverNP, Program 11–3, but there are several changes and improvements:

- Rather than creating a fixed-size *thread pool*, we now create *server threads on demand*. Every time the server accepts a client connection, it creates a server worker thread, and the thread terminates when the client quits.

- The server creates a separate *accept thread* so that the main thread can poll the global shutdown flag while the accept call is blocked. While it is possible to specify nonblocking sockets, threads provide a convenient and uniform solution. It's worth noting that a lot of the extended WinSock functionality is designed to support asynchronous operation, and Win32 threads allow you to use the much simpler, and more standard, synchronous socket functionality.

- The thread management is improved, at the cost of some complexity, so that the state of each thread is maintained.

- This server also supports *in-process services* by loading a DLL during initialization. The DLL name is a command line option, and the server thread first tries to locate an entry point in the DLL. If successful, the server thread calls the DLL entry point; otherwise, the server creates a process, as in serverNP.

A sample DLL is shown in Program 12–3. If the DLL were to generate an exception, the entire server process would be destroyed, so the DLL function call is protected by a simple exception handler.

In-process services could also have been included in `serverNP` if desired. The biggest advantage of in-process services is that no context switch to a different process is required, potentially improving performance.

Program 12–2   `serverSK`: Socket-Based Server with In-Process Services

```
/* Chapter 12. Client/Server. SERVER PROGRAM. SOCKET VERSION. */
/* Execute the command in the request and return a response. */
/* Commands will be executed in process if a shared library */
/* entry point can be located, and out of process otherwise. */
/* ADDITIONAL FEATURE: argv [1] can be name of a DLL supporting */
/* in-process services. */

#define _NOEXCLUSIONS
#include "EvryThng.h"
#include "ClntSrvr.h" /* Defines request and response records. */

struct sockaddr_in SrvSAddr;
/* Server's socket address structure. */
struct sockaddr_in ConnectSAddr; /* Connected socket. */
WSADATA WSStartData; /* Socket library data structure. */

typedef struct SERVER_ARG_TAG { /* Server thread arguments. */
    volatile DWORD number;
    volatile SOCKET sock;
    volatile DWORD status;
    /* Explained in main thread comments. */
    volatile HANDLE srv_thd;
    HINSTANCE dlhandle; /* Shared library handle. */
} SERVER_ARG;

static HANDLE srv_thd [MAX_CLIENTS];
volatile static ShutFlag = FALSE;
static SOCKET SrvSock, ConnectSock;

int _tmain (DWORD argc, LPCTSTR argv [])
{
    /* Server listening and connected sockets. */
    BOOL Done = FALSE;
    DWORD ith, tstatus, ThId;
    SERVER_ARG srv_arg [MAX_CLIENTS];
    HANDLE hAcceptTh = NULL;
    HINSTANCE hDll = NULL;
```

```
/* Initialize the WS library. Ver 1.1. */
WSAStartup (MAKEWORD (1, 1), &WSStartData);

/* Open command library DLL if specified on command line. */
if (argc > 1) hDll = LoadLibrary (argv [1]);
/* Initialize thread arg array. */
for (ith = 0; ith < MAX_CLIENTS; ith++) {
    srv_arg [ith].number = ith;
    srv_arg [ith].status = 0; srv_arg [ith].sock = 0;
    srv_arg [ith].dlhandle = hDll; srv_arg [ith].srv_thd = NULL;
}
/* Follow standard server socket/bind/listen/accept sequence. */
SrvSock = socket (AF_INET, SOCK_STREAM, 0);
SrvSAddr.sin_family = AF_INET;
SrvSAddr.sin_addr.s_addr = htonl ( INADDR_ANY );
SrvSAddr.sin_port = htons ( SERVER_PORT );
bind (SrvSock, (struct sockaddr *) &SrvSAddr,
        sizeof SrvSAddr);
listen (SrvSock, MAX_CLIENTS);

/* Main thread becomes listening/connecting/monitoring thread. */
/* Find an empty slot in the server thread arg array. */
/* status values: 0 - slot is free; 1 - thread stopped;
    2 - thread running; 3 - stop entire system. */
while (!ShutFlag) {
    for (ith = 0; ith < MAX_CLIENTS && !ShutFlag; ) {
        if (srv_arg [ith].status==1 || srv_arg [ith].status==3) {
            /* Thread stopped, normally or by shutdown request. */
            WaitForSingleObject (srv_thd [ith], INFINITE);
            CloseHandle (srv_thd [ith]);
            if (srv_arg [ith].status == 3) ShutFlag = TRUE;
            else srv_arg [ith].status = 0;
                    /* Free thread slot. */
        }
        if (srv_arg [ith].status == 0 || ShutFlag) break;
        ith = (ith + 1) % MAX_CLIENTS;
        if (ith == 0) Sleep (1000);
        /* Break the polling loop. */
        /* Alternative: use an event to signal a free slot. */
    }

    /* Wait for a connection on this socket. */
    /* Separate thread so we can poll the ShutFlag flag. */
    hAcceptTh = (HANDLE)_beginthreadex (NULL, 0, AcceptTh,
            &srv_arg [ith], 0, &ThId);
    while (!ShutFlag) {
        tstatus = WaitForSingleObject (hAcceptTh, CS_TIMEOUT);
        if (tstatus == WAIT_OBJECT_0) break;
        /* Connection made. */
    }
```

```
        CloseHandle (hAcceptTh);
        hAcceptTh = NULL; /* Prepare for next connection. */
    }

    _tprintf (_T ("Server shutdown. Wait for all srvr threads\n"));
    /* Terminate the accept thread if it is still running. */
    if (hAcceptTh != NULL) TerminateThread (hAcceptTh, 0);
    /* Wait for any active server threads to terminate. */
    shutdown (SrvSock, 2);
    closesocket (SrvSock);
    WSACleanup ();
    for (ith = 0; ith < MAX_CLIENTS; ith++)
        if (srv_arg [ith].status != 0) {
            WaitForSingleObject (srv_thd [ith], INFINITE);
            CloseHandle (srv_thd [ith]);
        }
    if (hDll != NULL) FreeLibrary (hDll);
    return 0;
}


static DWORD WINAPI AcceptTh (SERVER_ARG * pThArg)
{
    /* Accepting thread that allows the main thread to poll the */
    /* shutdown flag. This thread also creates the server thread. */
    LONG AddrLen, ThId;

    AddrLen = sizeof (ConnectSAddr);
    pThArg->sock = accept (SrvSock, /* This is a blocking call. */
        (struct sockaddr *) &ConnectSAddr, &AddrLen);
        /* A new connection. Create a server thread. */
    pThArg->status = 2;
    pThArg->srv_thd =
            (HANDLE) _beginthreadex (NULL, 0, Server, pThArg, 0, &ThId);
    return 0; /* Server thread remains running. */
}


static DWORD WINAPI Server (SERVER_ARG * pThArg)
/* Server thread function. Thread created on demand. */
{
    /* Each thread keeps its own request, response,
        and bookkeeping data structures on the stack. */
    /* ... Standard declarations from serverNP omitted ... */
    SOCKET ConnectSock;
    int Disconnect = 0, i;
    int (*dl_addr)(char *, char *);
    char *ws = " \0\t\n"; /* White space. */

    GetStartupInfo (&StartInfoCh);
    ConnectSock = pThArg->sock;
    /* Create a temp file name. */
```

```
        sprintf (TempFile, "%s%d%s", "ServerTemp",
            pThArg->number, ".tmp");

    while (!Done && !ShutFlag) { /* Main command loop. */
        Disconnect = ReceiveRequestMessage (&Request, ConnectSock);
        Done = Disconnect || (strcmp (Request.Record, "$Quit") == 0)
                || (strcmp (Request.Record, "$ShutFlagServer") == 0);
        if (Done) continue;
        /* Stop this thread on "$Quit" or "$ShutDownServer". */
        hTmpFile = CreateFile (TempFile,
                GENERIC_READ | GENERIC_WRITE,
                FILE_SHARE_READ | FILE_SHARE_WRITE, &TempSA,
                CREATE_ALWAYS, FILE_ATTRIBUTE_NORMAL, NULL);

        /* Check for a DLL command. For simplicity, shared */
        /* library commands take precedence over process
            commands. First, extract the command name. */

        i = strcspn (Request.Record, ws); /* Length of token. */
        memcpy (sys_command, Request.Record, i);
        sys_command [i] = '\0';

        dl_addr = NULL; /* Will be set if GetProcAddress succeeds. */
        if (pThArg->dlhandle != NULL) { /* Try server "in process." */
            dl_addr = (int (*)(char *, char *))
                    GetProcAddress (pThArg->dlhandle, sys_command);
            if (dl_addr != NULL) __try {
                /* Protect server process from exceptions in DLL. */
                (*dl_addr) (Request.Record, TempFile);
            } __except (EXCEPTION_EXECUTE_HANDLER {
                ReportError (_T ("Exception in DLL"), 0, FALSE);
            }
        }

        if (dl_addr == NULL) { /* No in-process support. */
        /* Create a process to carry out the command. */
        /* ... Same as in serverNP ... */
        }
        /* ... Same as in serverNP ... */

    } /* End of main command loop. Get next command. */

    /* End of command loop. Free resources; exit from the thread. */

    _tprintf (_T ("Shutting down server# %d\n"), pThArg->number);
    closesocket (ConnectSock);
    shutdown (ConnectSock, 2);
    pThArg->status = 1;
    if (strcmp (Request.Record, "$ShutDownServer") == 0) {
        pThArg->status = 3;
```

```
        ShutFlag = TRUE;
    }
    return pThArg->status;
}
```

In-Process Services

As mentioned previously, in-process services are a major enhancement in `serverSK`. Program 12–3 shows how to write a DLL to provide these services. Two familiar functions are shown, a word counting function and a "`toupper`" function.

By convention, the first parameter is the command line, while the second is the name of the output file. Beyond that, always remember that the function will execute in the same thread as the server thread, so there are strict requirements for thread safety, including, but not limited to:

- The functions should not change the process environment in any way. For example, if one of the functions changes the working directory, that change will affect the entire process.

- Similarly, the functions should not redirect standard input or output.

- Programming errors such as allowing a subscript or pointer to go out of bounds could corrupt another thread or the server process itself.

- Resource leaks, such as failing to deallocate memory or to close handles, will ultimately affect the server system.

Processes do not have such stringent requirements since a process cannot normally corrupt other processes, and resources are freed when the process terminates. A typical development methodology, then, is to develop and debug a service as a process, and when it is judged to be reliable, it can be converted to a DLL.

Program 12–3 shows a small DLL library with two functions.

Program 12–3   `command`: Sample In-Process Services

```
/* Chapter 12. commands.c. */
/* "In Process Server" commands to use with serverSK, etc. */

/* There are several commands implemented as DLLs. */
/* Each command function must be a thread-safe function */
/* and take two parameters. The first is a string: */
/* command arg1 arg2 ... argn (i.e.; a normal command line) */
/* and the second is the file name for the output. */
   ... */
```

```c
static void extract_token (int, char *, char *);

_declspec (dllexport)
int wcip (char * command, char * output_file)
/* Word count; in process. */
/* NOTE: Simple version; results may differ from wc utility. */
{
    /* ... */

    extract_token (1, command, input_file);

    fin = fopen (input_file, "r");
    /* ... */
    ch = nw = nc = nl = 0;
    while ((c = fgetc (fin)) != EOF) {
    /* ... Standard code - not important for example ... */
    }
    fclose (fin);

    /* Write the results. */
    fout = fopen (output_file, "w");
    if (fout == NULL) return 2;
    fprintf (fout, " %9d %9d %9d %s\n", nl, nw, nc, input_file);
    fclose (fout);
    return 0;
}

_declspec (dllexport)
int toupperip (char * command, char * output_file)
/* Convert input to uppercase; in process. */
/* Input file is the second token ("toupperip" is the first). */
{
    /* ... */
    extract_token (1, command, input_file);

    fin = fopen (input_file, "r");
    if (fin == NULL) return 1;
    fout = fopen (output_file, "w");
    if (fout == NULL) return 2;

    while ((c = fgetc (fin)) != EOF) {
        if (c == '\0') break;
        if (isalpha(c)) c = toupper(c);
        fputc (c, fout);
    }

    fclose (fin); fclose (fout);
    return 0;
}
```

```
static void extract_token (int it, char * command, char * token)
{
    /* Extract token number "it" (first token is number 0) */
    /* from "command." Result goes in "token." */
    /* Tokens are white space delimited.
       ... */
    return;
}
```

Line-Oriented Messages, DLL Entry Points, and TLS

`serverSK` and `clientSK` communicate using messages, where each message is composed of a four-byte length header followed by the message content. A common alternative to this approach is to have the messages delimited by end-of-line (or new-line) characters.

The difficulty with delimited messages is that there is no way of knowing the message length in advance and each incoming character must be examined. Receiving a single character at a time would be inefficient, however, so incoming characters are stored in a buffer, and the buffer contents might include one or more end-of-line characters and parts of one or more messages. *Buffer contents and state must be retained between calls to the message receive function.* In a single-threaded environment, static storage can be used, but multiple threads cannot share the same static storage.

In more general terms, we have a *multithreaded persistent state problem*. This problem occurs any time a thread-safe function must maintain information from one call to the next. The Standard C library `strtok` function, which scans a string for successive instances of a token, is a common alternative example of this problem.

Solving the Multithreaded Persistent State Problem

The solution requires a combination of:

- A dynamic link library (DLL, Chapter 6) for the message send and receive functions.

- An entry point function in the DLL.

- Thread Local Storage (TLS, Chapter 8). The DLL index is created when the process attaches, and it is destroyed when the process detaches. The index number is stored in static storage to be accessed by all the threads.

- A structure containing a buffer and its current state. A structure is allocated every time a thread attaches, and the address is stored in the TLS entry for that thread. A thread's structure is deallocated when the thread detaches.

The TLS, then, plays the role of static storage, and each thread has its own unique copy of the static storage.

Example: A Thread-Safe DLL for Socket Messages

Program 12–4 is the DLL containing two functions: `SendCSMessage` and `ReceiveCSMessage`, along with a `DllMain` entry point (see Chapter 6). These two functions are similar to, and essentially replace, `ReceiveMessage`, listed earlier in this chapter, and the functions used in Programs 12–1 and 12–2.

The `DllMain` function is a representative solution of a multithreaded persistent state problem, and it combines TLS and DLLs. The resource deallocation in the `DLL_THREAD_DETACH` case is especially important in a server environment; without it, the server would eventually exhaust resources, typically resulting in either failure or performance degradation, or both.

The disc contains client and server code, slightly modified from Programs 12–1 and 12–2, that uses this DLL.

Program 12–4   `SendReceiveSKST`: Thread-Safe DLL

```
/* SendReceiveSKST.c - Multithreaded streaming socket DLL. */
/* Messages are delimited by end-of-line characters ('\0') */
/* so the message length is not known ahead of time. Incoming */
/* data is buffered and preserved from one function call to */
/* the next. Therefore, use Thread Local Storage (TLS) */
/* so that each thread has its own private "static storage." */

#define _NOEXCLUSIONS
#include "EvryThng.h"
#include "ClntSrvr.h" /* Defines request and response records. */

typedef struct STATIC_BUF_T {
/* "static_buf" contains "static_buf_len" bytes of residual data. */
/* There may or may not be end-of-string (null) characters. */
    char static_buf [MAX_RQRS_LEN];
    LONG32 static_buf_len;
} STATIC_BUF;

static DWORD TlsIx = 0; /* TLS index - EACH PROCESS HAS ITS OWN. */
/* A single-threaded library would use the following:
    static char static_buf [MAX_RQRS_LEN];
```

```c
    static LONG32 static_buf_len; */

/* DLL main function. */
BOOL WINAPI DllMain (HINSTANCE hinstDLL,
      DWORD fdwReason, LPVOID lpvReserved)
{
    STATIC_BUF * pBuf;

    switch (fdwReason) {
        case DLL_PROCESS_ATTACH:
            TlsIx = TlsAlloc ();
    /* There is no thread attach for the primary thread, so it is
       necessary to carry out the thread attach operations as well
       during process attach. */

        case DLL_THREAD_ATTACH:
            /* Indicate that memory has not been allocated. */
            TlsSetValue (TlsIx, NULL);
            return TRUE; /* This value is actually ignored. */

        case DLL_PROCESS_DETACH:
            /* Detach the primary thread as well. */
            pBuf = TlsGetValue (TlsIx);
            if (pBuf != NULL) {
                free (pBuf);
                pBuf = NULL;
            }
            return TRUE;

        case DLL_THREAD_DETACH:
            pBuf = TlsGetValue (TlsIx);
            if (pBuf != NULL) {
                free (pBuf);
                pBuf = NULL;
            }
            return TRUE;
    }
}

_declspec (dllexport)
BOOL ReceiveCSMessage (REQUEST *pRequest, SOCKET sd)
{
    /* TRUE return indicates an error or disconnect. */
    BOOL Disconnect = FALSE;
    LONG32 nRemainRecv = 0, nXfer, k; /* Must be signed integers. */
    LPSTR pBuffer, message;
    CHAR TempBuf [MAX_RQRS_LEN + 1];
    STATIC_BUF *p;

    p = (STATIC_BUF *) TlsGetValue (TlsIx);
```

```c
if (p == NULL) { /* First time initialization. */
    /* Only threads that need this storage will allocate it. */
    /* Other thread types can use the TLS for other purposes. */
    p = malloc (sizeof (STATIC_BUF));
    TlsSetValue (TlsIx, p);
    if (p == NULL) return TRUE; /* Error. */
    p->static_buf_len = 0; /* Initialize state. */
}

message = pRequest->Record;
/* Read up to the new-line character, leaving residual data
    in the static buffer. */

for (k = 0;
    k < p->static_buf_len && p->static_buf [k] != '\0'; k++) {
        message [k] = p->static_buf [k];
} /* k is the number of characters transferred. */

if (k < p->static_buf_len) { /* A null was found in static buf. */
    message [k] = '\0';
    p->static_buf_len -= (k + 1); /* Adjust static buffer state. */
    memcpy (p->static_buf, &(p->static_buf [k + 1]),
            p->static_buf_len);
    return FALSE; /* No socket input required. */
}

/* The entire static buffer was transferred. No eol found. */
nRemainRecv = sizeof (TempBuf) - 1 - p->static_buf_len;
pBuffer = message + p->static_buf_len;
p->static_buf_len = 0;

while (nRemainRecv > 0 && !Disconnect) {
    nXfer = recv (sd, TempBuf, nRemainRecv, 0);
    if (nXfer <= 0) {
        Disconnect = TRUE;
        continue;
    }

    nRemainRecv -= nXfer;
    /* Transfer to target message up to null, if any. */
    for (k = 0; k < nXfer && TempBuf [k] != '\0'; k++) {
        *pBuffer = TempBuf [k];
        pBuffer++;
    }
    if (k >= nXfer) { /* End of line not found, read more. */
        nRemainRecv -= nXfer;
    } else { /* End of line has been found. */
        *pBuffer = '\0';
        nRemainRecv = 0;
        memcpy (p->static_buf, &TempBuf [k + 1], nXfer - k - 1);
```

```
            p->static_buf_len = nXfer - k - 1;
        }
    }
    return Disconnect;
}

_declspec (dllexport)
BOOL SendCSMessage (RESPONSE *pResponse, SOCKET sd)
{
        /* Send the request to the server on socket sd. */
    BOOL Disconnect = FALSE;
    LONG32 nRemainSend, nXfer;
    LPSTR pBuffer;

    pBuffer = pResponse->Record;
    nRemainSend = strlen (pBuffer) + 1;

    while (nRemainSend > 0 && !Disconnect) {
        /* Send does not guarantee that the entire message is sent. */
        nXfer = send (sd, pBuffer, nRemainSend, 0);
        if (nXfer <= 0) {
            fprintf (stderr,
                "\nServer disconnect before complete request sent");
            Disconnect = TRUE;
        }
        nRemainSend -=nXfer; pBuffer += nXfer;
    }

    return Disconnect;
}
```

Comments on the DLL and Thread Safety

- DllMain, with DLL_THREAD_ATTACH, is called whenever a new thread is created, but there is not a distinct DLL_THREAD_ATTACH call for the primary
  thread. The DLL_PROCESS_ATTACH case must handle the primary thread.

- In general, and even in this case (consider the accept thread), some threads
  may not require the allocated memory, but DllMain cannot distinguish the
  different thread types. Therefore, the DLL_THREAD_ATTACH case does not actually allocate any memory; it only initializes the TLS value. The Receive-
  CSMessage entry point allocates the memory the first time it is called. In this
  way, the thread-specific memory is allocated only by threads that require it,
  and different thread types can allocate exactly the resources they require.

- While this DLL is thread-safe, a given thread can use these routines with only one socket at a time, since the persistent state is associated with the thread, not the socket. The next example addresses this issue.

- The DLL source code on the disc is instrumented to print the total number of DllMain calls by type.

- There is still a resource leak risk, even with this solution. Some threads, such as the accept thread, may never terminate and therefore will never be detached from the DLL. ExitProcess will call DllMain with DLL_PROC-ESS_DETACH but not with DLL_THREAD_DETACH for threads that are still active. This does not cause a problem in this case, because the accept thread does not allocate any resources, and even memory is freed when the process terminates. There would, however, be an issue if threads allocated resources such as temporary files; the ultimate solution would be to create a globally accessible list of resources. The DLL_PROCESS_DETACH code would then have the task of scanning the list and deallocating the resources.

Example: An Alternative Thread-Safe DLL Strategy

Program 12–4, while typical of the way in which TLS and DllMain are combined to create thread-safe libraries, has a weakness that is noted in the comments above. In particular, the "state" is associated with the thread rather than with the socket, so a given thread can process only one socket at a time.

An effective alternative approach to thread-safe library functions is to create a handle-like structure that is passed to every function call. The state is then maintained in the structure. Many UNIX systems use this technique to create thread-safe C libraries; the main disadvantage is that the functions require an additional parameter for the state structure.

Program 12–5 modifies Program 12–4. Notice that DllMain is not necessary, but there are two new functions to initialize and free the state structure. The send and receive functions require only minimal changes. An associated server, serverSKHA, is included on the disc and requires only slight changes in order to create and close the socket handle.

Program 12–5   SendReceiveSKHA: Thread-Safe DLL with a State Structure

```
/* SendReceiveSKHA.c - multithreaded streaming socket. */
/* This is a modification of SendReceiveSKST.c to illustrate a */
/* different thread-safe library technique. */
/* State is preserved in a HANDLE-like state structure rather than */
/* using TLS. This allows a thread to use several sockets on once. */
/* Messages are delimited by end-of-line characters ('\0'). */
```

```
#define _NOEXCLUSIONS
#include "EvryThng.h"
#include "ClntSrvr.h " /* Defines the request and response records. */

typedef struct SOCKET_HANDLE_T {
    /* Current socket state in a "handle" structure. */
    /* Structure contains "static_buf_len" characters of
       residual data. */
    /* There may or may not be end-of-string (null) characters. */
    SOCKET sk; /* Socket associated with this "handle." */
    char static_buf [MAX_RQRS_LEN];
    LONG32 static_buf_len;
} SOCKET_HANDLE, * PSOCKET_HANDLE;

/* Functions to create and close "streaming socket handles." */
_declspec (dllexport)
PVOID CreateCSSocketHandle (SOCKET s)
{
    PVOID p;
    PSOCKET_HANDLE ps;

    p = malloc (sizeof (SOCKET_HANDLE));
    if (p == NULL) return NULL;
    ps = (PSOCKET_HANDLE) p;
    ps->sk = s;
    ps->static_buf_len = 0; /* Initialize buffer state. */
    return p;
}


_declspec (dllexport)
BOOL CloseCSSocketHandle (PVOID p)
{
    if (p == NULL) return FALSE;
    free (p);
    return TRUE;
}


_declspec (dllexport)
BOOL ReceiveCSMessage (REQUEST *pRequest, PVOID sh)
/* Use PVOID so that calling program does not need to include */
/* the SOCKET_HANDLE definition. */
{
    /* TRUE return indicates an error or disconnect.
        ... */
    PSOCKET_HANDLE p;
    SOCKET sd;

    p = (PSOCKET_HANDLE) sh;
    if (p == NULL) return FALSE;
    sd = p->sk;
```

```
    /* This is all that's changed from SendReceiveSKST!
       ... */
}

_declspec (dllexport)
BOOL SendCSMessage (RESPONSE *pResponse, PVOID sh)
{
    /* Send the request to the server on socket sd.
       ... */
    SOCKET sd;
    PSOCKET_HANDLE p;

    p = (PSOCKET_HANDLE) sh;
    if (p == NULL) return FALSE;
    sd = p->sk;

    /* That's all that's changed from SendReceiveSKST!
       ... */
}
```

Datagrams

Datagrams are similar to mailslots and are used in similar circumstances. There is no connection between the sender and receiver, and there can be multiple receivers. Delivery to the receiver is not ensured, and successive messages will not necessarily be received in the order in which they were sent.

The first step in using datagrams is to specify SOCK_DGRAM in the type field when creating the socket with the socket function.

Next, use sendto and recvfrom, which take the same arguments as send and recv, but add two arguments to designate the partner station. Thus, the sendto function is:

```
int sendto (
    SOCKET s,
    LPSTR lpBuffer,
    int nBufferLen,
    int nFlags,
    LPSOCKADDR lpAddr,
    int nAddrLen);
```

`lpAddr` points to an address structure where you can specify the name of a specific system and port, or you can specify that the datagram is to be broadcast to a specific set of systems.

When using `recvfrom`, you specify which system or systems (perhaps all) from which you are willing to accept datagrams.

Using Datagrams for Remote Procedure Calls

A common use of datagrams is in the implementation of Remote Procedure Calls (RPCs) (see Chapter 15). Essentially, in the most common situation, a client sends a request to a server using a datagram. Because delivery is not ensured, the client will retransmit the request if a response (also using a datagram) is not received from the server after a wait period. The server must be prepared to receive the same request several times.

The important point is that the RPC client and server do not require the over-head of a stream socket connection; instead, they communicate with simple requests and responses and ensure reliability through time-outs and retrans-missions. An additional advantage is that the client and server can frequently be *stateless* (they do not maintain any state information about current or pending re-quests), so that design and implementation are greatly simplified.

The commonly used Network File System (NFS) is implemented using an RPC mechanism that uses datagrams, although the RPC implementation is different from the one described in Chapter 15.

Berkeley vs. Windows Sockets

Programs that use standard Berkeley Sockets calls will port to Windows Sockets, with the following important exceptions:

- You must call `WSAStartup` to initialize the sockets DLL.

- You must use `closesocket` (which is not portable), rather than `close` (which is), to close a socket.

- You must call `WSACleanup` to shut down the DLL.

Optionally, you can use the Win32 data types such as `SOCKET` and `LONG` in place of `int`, as was done here. Programs 12–1 and 12–2 were ported from UNIX, and the effort was minimal. It was necessary, however, to modify the DLL and process management sections. Exercise 12–13 suggests that you port these two programs back to UNIX.

Overlapped I/O with Windows Sockets

Chapter 14 describes asynchronous I/O, which allows a thread to continue running while an I/O operation is in process. Sockets with Win32 asynchronous I/O will be discussed in that chapter.

Most asynchronous programming can be achieved uniformly and easily using threads. For example, serverSK used an "accept thread" rather than a nonblocking socket. Nonetheless, I/O completion ports, which are associated with asynchronous I/O, are important for scalability when there is a large number of clients. This topic is also described in Chapter 14.

Windows Sockets 2

Windows Sockets 2, available in NT 4.0, adds several areas of functionality. The examples, however, used Version 1.1 for interoperability reasons, and Version 1.1 is adequate for most purposes.

New Version 2.0 features include:

- Standardized support for overlapped I/O (see Chapter 14); this is considered to be the most important enhancement.

- Scatter/gather I/O (sending and receiving from noncontiguous buffers in memory).

- The ability to request quality of service (speed and reliability of transmission) from the Sockets support layer.

- The ability to organize sockets into groups. The quality of service of a socket group can be configured, so it does not have to be done on a socket-by-socket basis. Also, the sockets belonging to a group can be prioritized.

- Piggybacking of data onto connection requests.

- Multipoint connections (comparable to conference calls).

Summary

Windows Sockets allow the use of an industry-standard API, so that your programs can be interoperable and nearly portable in source code form. WinSock is capable of supporting nearly any network protocol, but TCP/IP is the most common.

WinSock functionality is comparable to named pipes (and mailslots) in both functionality and performance, but portability and interoperability are important reasons for considering sockets. Keep in mind that socket I/O is not atomic, so it is necessary to take care to ensure that a complete message is transmitted.

This chapter has covered the WinSock essentials, which are enough to build a workable system. There is, however, much more, including asynchronous usage, and additional information can be found in the Additional Reading references.

This chapter also provided examples of using DLLs for in-process servers and for creating thread-safe libraries.

Looking Ahead

Chapters 10 and 11 have shown how to develop "servers" that respond to client requests. Servers, in various forms, are common, especially on Windows 2000/NT systems, and so Chapter 13 describes "NT services." NT services provide a standard way to create and manage servers, in the form of services, permitting automated service start-up, shutdown, and monitoring. Chapter 13 will show how to turn a server into a manageable service.

Additional Reading

Windows Sockets

Win32 Network Programming, by Ralph Davis, describes socket programming in more detail and also provides some useful comparisons of named pipe and socket performance showing similar performance. The presentation in this book is clear and concise.

For a complete discussion of Windows Sockets, see Quinn and Shute, *Windows Sockets Network Programming*, and its supporting site, `http://www.sockets.com`.

Berkeley Sockets and TCP/IP

W. R. Stevens' *TCP/IP Illustrated, Volume 3*, covers sockets and much more, while the first two volumes in the series describe the protocols and their implementation. The same author's *UNIX Network Programming* provides comprehensive coverage that is valuable even for non-UNIX systems. Another good reference is Comer and Stevens, *Internetworking with TCP/IP, Volume III: Client-Server Programming and Applications, Windows Sockets Version*.

Exercises

12–1. Use WSAStartup to determine the highest and lowest WinSock version numbers supported on the systems accessible to you.

12–2. Use the JobShell program from Chapter 7 to start the server and several clients, where each client is created using the "detached" option. Eventually, shut down the server by sending a console control event through the kill command. Can you suggest any improvements in the serverSK shutdown logic?

12–3. Modify the client and server programs (Programs 12–1 and 12–2) so that they use datagrams to locate a server. The mailslot solution in Chapter 11 could be used as a starting point.

12–4. Modify the named pipe server in Chapter 11 so that it creates threads on demand instead of a server thread pool. Rather than predefining a fixed maximum for the number of named pipe instances, allow the system to determine the maximum.

12–5. Perform experiments to determine whether in-process services are faster than out-of-process services. For example, you can use the word count example; there is an executable wc program as well as the DLL function shown in Program 12–3.

12–6. The number of clients that serverSK can support is bounded by the array of server thread arguments. Modify the program so that there is no such bound. You will need to create a data structure that allows you to add and delete thread arguments, and you also need to be able to scan the structure for terminated server threads.

12–7. Develop additional in-process services. For example, convert the grep program (see Chapter 7).

12–8. Enhance the server (Program 12–2) so that you can specify multiple DLLs on the command line. If the DLLs do not all fit into memory, develop a strategy for loading and unloading them.

12–9. Investigate the setsockopt function and the NO_LINGER option. Apply the option to one of the server examples.

12–10. Use the scatter/gather feature of Windows Sockets 2.0 to simplify the message sending and receiving functions in Programs 12–1 and 12–2.

12–11. Ensure that serverSK is free of resource leaks (see Exercise 11–11 for more explanation). Do the same with serverSKST, which was modified to use the DLL in Program 12–4.

12–12. Extend the exception handler in Program 12–3 so that it reports the exception and exception type at the end of the temporary file used for the server results.

12–13. *Extended Exercise (requires extra equipment)*: If you have access to a UNIX system that is networked to your Windows system, port clientSK to the UNIX system and have it access serverSK to run Windows programs. You will, of course, need to convert data types such as DWORD and SOCKET to other types (unsigned long and int, respectively, in these two cases). Also, you will need to ensure that the message length is transmitted in big-endian format. Use functions such as htonl to convert the message lengths. Finally, port serverSK to UNIX so that Windows systems can execute UNIX commands. Convert the DLL calls to shared library calls.

12–14. Read about the Secure Sockets Layer (SSL) in MSDN and the Additional Reading references. Enhance the programs to use SSL for secure client/server communication.

13 | NT Services

The server programs in Chapters 11 and 12 were console applications written to run in the background. In principle, the servers could run indefinitely, serving numerous clients as they connect, send requests, receive responses, and disconnect. That is, these "servers" could provide continuous "services," but to be fully effective, the services must be manageable.

NT services, in Windows NT and 2000, provide the management capabilities required to convert our servers into services that can be initiated on command or at system boot time, paused, resumed, and terminated. NT services even make it possible to monitor the health of a service. Ultimately, any server system, such as those developed in Chapters 11 and 12, should be converted to an NT service, especially if it is to be widely used by customers or within an organization. Windows 2000/NT provides a number of services; examples include the telnet, fax, and security accounts' management services as well as device drivers. There is an administrative tool, accessible from the control panel, that will display the full set of services.

Chapter 7's `JobShell` (Program 7–3) provides rudimentary server management by allowing you to bring up a server under job control and send a termination signal. NT services, however, are much more comprehensive and robust, and the main example is a conversion of `JobShell` so that it can control NT services.

This chapter will also show how to convert an existing console application into an NT service and how to install, monitor, and control the service. Event logging, which allows a service to log its actions, will also be described.

Writing NT Services—Overview

NT services run under the control of a Service Control Manager (SCM). Converting a console application, such as `serverNP` or `serverSK`, to an NT service requires three major steps to place the program under the SCM:

1. Create a new `main ()` entry point that registers the service with the SCM, supplying the logical service entry points and names.

2. Convert the old `main ()` entry point function to *ServiceMain ()*, which registers a "service control handler" and informs the SCM of its status. The remaining code is essentially that of the existing program, although event logging commands can be added. The name *ServiceMain ()* is a placeholder for the name of a "logical service," and there can be one or more logical services.

3. Write the "service control handler" function to respond to commands from the SCM.

As these three steps are described, there will be several references to creating, starting, and controlling services. The specifics are described in later sections, and Figure 13–1 illustrates the component interactions.

The `main ()` Function

The new `main ()` function, which is called by the SCM, has the task of registering the service with the SCM and starting the service control dispatcher. This requires a call to the `StartServiceCtrlDispatcher` function with the name(s) and entry point(s) of one or more logical services.

```
BOOL StartServiceCtrlDispatcher (
    LPSERVICE_TABLE_ENTRY lpServiceStartTable)
```

The single parameter, `lpServiceStartTable`, is the address of an array of `SERVICE_TABLE_ENTRY` items, where each item is a logical service name and entry point. The end of the array is indicated by a pair of `NULL` entries.

The main thread of the service process that calls `StartServiceCtrl-Dispatcher` causes the thread to be attached to the SCM as the "service control dispatcher thread." The SCM does not return until all services have terminated. Notice, however, that the logical services are not actually started at this time.

Program 13–1 shows a typical service main program with a single logical service.

Program 13–1   `main:` The Main Service Entry Point

```
#include "EvryThng.h"

void WINAPI ServiceMain (DWORD argc, LPTSTR argv []);
```

```
static LPTSTR ServiceName = _T ("SocketCommandLineService");

/* Main routine that starts the service control dispatcher. */
VOID _tmain (int argc, LPTSTR argv [])
{
    SERVICE_TABLE_ENTRY DispatchTable [] =
    {
        { ServiceName, ServiceMain },
        { NULL, NULL }
    };

    if (!StartServiceCtrlDispatcher (DispatchTable))
        ReportError (_T ("Failed to start srvc ctrl dis."), 1, TRUE);
    /* ServiceMain () will not run until started by the SCM. */
    /* Return here only when all services have terminated. */
    return;
}
```

The *ServiceMain ()* Functions

These functions are specified in the dispatch table, as shown in Program 13–1, and represent logical services. The functions are essentially enhanced versions of the base program that is being converted to a service, and each logical service will be invoked on its own thread by the SCM. A logical service may, in turn, start up additional threads, such as the server worker threads that were used in serverSK and serverNP. Frequently, there is just one logical service within a service. In Program 13–2, the logical service is essentially the main server from Program 12–2. It would be possible, however, to run both socket and named pipe logical services under the same NT service, in which case two service main functions would be supplied.

There is, however, extra code to register the service control handler, which is a function called by the SCM to control the services.

Registering the Service Control Handler

A service control handler, called by the SCM, should be able to control the associated logical service. The console control handler in serverSK, which sets a global shutdown flag, illustrates, in limited form, what is expected of a handler. First, however, each logical service must register a handler using the Register-ServiceCtrlHandler function.

```
SERVICE_STATUS_HANDLE
    RegisterServiceCtrlHandler (
LPCTSTR lpServiceName,
LPHANDLER_FUNCTION lpHandlerProc)
```

Parameters

lpServiceName is the user-supplied service name provided in the service table entry for this logical service.

lpHandlerProc is the address of the handler function, which will be described in a later section.

The return value, which is a SERVICE_STATUS_HANDLE object, is zero if there is an error, and the usual methods can be used to analyze errors.

Setting the Service Status

Now that the handler is registered, the next task is to set the service status, which is SERVICE_START_PENDING at this point. SetServiceStatus is described here, but it will also be used in several other places and should be called periodically to inform the SCM of the service's status (the period is specified in a member field in a data structure parameter).

```
BOOL SetServiceStatus (
    SERVICE_STATUS_HANDLE hServiceStatus,
    LPSERVICE_STATUS lpServiceStatus)
```

Parameters

hServiceStatus is the SERVICE_STATUS_HANDLE returned by Register-ServiceCtrlHandler.

lpServiceStatus, pointing to a SERVICE_STATUS structure, describes service properties, status, and capabilities.

The SERVICE_STATUS Structure

The SERVICE_STATUS structure is defined as follows:

```
typedef struct _SERVICE_STATUS {
    DWORD dwServiceType;
    DWORD dwCurrentState;
    DWORD dwControlsAccepted;
    DWORD dwWin32ExitCode;
    DWORD dwServiceSpecificExitCode;
    DWORD dwCheckPoint;
    DWORD dwWaitHint;
} SERVICE_STATUS, *LPSERVICE_STATUS;
```

Parameters

dwWin32ExitCode is the normal thread exit code for the logical service. The service must set this to NO_ERROR while running and on normal termination.

dwServiceSpecificExitCode can be used to indicate an error while the service is starting or stopping, but this value will be ignored unless dwWin32-ExitCode is set to ERROR_SERVICE_SPECIFIC_ERROR.

dwCheckPoint should be incremented periodically by the service to report its progress during all steps, including initialization and shutdown. This value is invalid if the service does not have a start, stop, pause, or continue operation pending.

dwWaitHint, in milliseconds, is the elapsed time between calls to SetServiceStatus with either an incremented value of dwCheckPoint value or a change in dwCurrentState. The SCM can assume that an error has occurred if this time period passes without such a SetServiceStatus call.

The remaining SERVICE_STATUS members are now described in individual sections.

Service Type

dwServiceType must be one of the values described in Table 13–1.

For our purposes, the type is almost always SERVICE_WIN32_OWN_PROCESS, but the different values indicate that services play many different roles.

Table 13-1 Service Types

Value	Meaning
SERVICE_WIN32_OWN_PROCESS	Indicates that the Win32 service runs in its own process with its own resources. *Used in Program 13–2.*
SERVICE_WIN32_SHARE_PROCESS	Indicates a Win32 service that shares a process with other services so that several services can share resources, environment variables, etc.
SERVICE_KERNEL_DRIVER	Indicates a Windows NT device driver.
SERVICE_FILE_SYSTEM_DRIVER	A Windows NT file system driver.
SERVICE_INTERACTIVE_PROCESS	The Win32 service process that can interact with the user through the desktop.

Service State

dwCurrentState indicates the current service state. Table 13–2 shows the different possible values.

Table 13-2 Service State Values

Value	Meaning
SERVICE_STOPPED	The service is not running, generally because it has not been started.
SERVICE_START_PENDING	The service is in the process of starting but is not yet ready to respond to requests. For example, the worker threads have not yet been started.
SERVICE_STOP_PENDING	The service is stopping but has not yet completed shutdown. For example, a global shutdown flag may have been set, but the worker threads have not yet responded.
SERVICE_RUNNING	The service is running.
SERVICE_CONTINUE_PENDING	The service continue is pending after a service has been in the pause state.
SERVICE_PAUSE_PENDING	The service pause is pending, but the service is not yet safely in the pause state.
SERVICE_PAUSED	The service is paused.

Table 13-3 Controls That a Service Accepts

Value	Meaning
SERVICE_ACCEPT_STOP	Enables the SERVICE_CONTROL_STOP.
SERVICE_ACCEPT_PAUSE_CONTINUE	Enables SERVICE_CONTROL_PAUSE and SERVICE_CONTROL_CONTINUE.
SERVICE_ACCEPT_SHUTDOWN (The ControlService function cannot send this control code.)	The service is notified when system shutdown occurs. This enables the system to send a SERVICE_CONTROL_SHUTDOWN value to the service.

Controls Accepted

dwControlsAccepted specifies the control codes that the service will accept and process through its service control handler (see the next section). Table 13–3 enumerates the possible values, and the appropriate values should be combined by bit-wise "or" (|). The service version of serverSK, developed later, will accept all three values. Additional values are described in the MSDN documentation.

Service-Specific Code

Once the handler has been registered and the service status has been set to SERVICE_START_PENDING, the service can initialize itself and set its status again. In the case of converting serverSK, once the sockets are initialized and the server is ready to accept clients, the status should be set to SERVICE_RUNNING.

The Service Control Handler

The service control handler, specified in RegisterServiceCtrlHandler, has the form

```
VOID WINAPI ServerCtrlHandler (DWORD fdwControl)
```

The single parameter, fdwControl, indicates the actual control signal sent by the SCM that should be processed. Thus, the control handler is a general form of the console control handlers introduced in Chapters 4 and 7.

The five possible values for `fdwControl` are:

`SERVICE_CONTROL_STOP`

`SERVICE_CONTROL_PAUSE`

`SERVICE_CONTROL_CONTINUE`

`SERVICE_CONTROL_INTERROGATE`

`SERVICE_CONTROL_SHUTDOWN`

User-defined values in the range 128–255 are also permitted but will not be used here.

The handler is invoked by the SCM in the same thread as the main program, and the function is usually written as a `switch` statement.

Example: A Service "Wrapper"

Program 13–2 carries out the `serverSK` conversion discussed previously. The conversion to a service depends on carrying out all the tasks described above. The existing server code, with some very minor modifications, is placed in a function, `ServiceSpecific`. Therefore, the code shown here is essentially a wrapper around an existing server program whose entry point has been changed from `main` to `ServiceSpecific`.

Another addition, not shown here but included on the disc, is the use of a log file, because services frequently run "headless" without a console. When a log file is specified on the command to `ServiceMain`, significant events will be logged to that file.

Program 13–2   `SimpleService`: A Service Wrapper

```
/* Chapter 13. serviceSK.c
   serverSK modified to be an NT service.
   This is, however, a general purpose wrapper. */

#include "EvryThng.h"
#include "ClntSrvr.h"
#define UPDATE_TIME 1000 /* One second between updates. */

VOID LogEvent (LPCTSTR, DWORD, BOOL);
void WINAPI ServiceMain (DWORD argc, LPTSTR argv []);
VOID WINAPI ServerCtrlHandler(DWORD);
void UpdateStatus (int, int); /* Calls SetServiceStatus. */
int ServiceSpecific (int, LPTSTR *); /* Former main program. */
```

```
volatile static BOOL ShutDown = FALSE, PauseFlag = FALSE;
static SERVICE_STATUS hServStatus;
static SERVICE_STATUS_HANDLE hSStat; /* Handle to set status. */

static LPTSTR ServiceName = _T ("SocketCommandLineService");
static LPTSTR LogFileName = _T ("CommandLineServiceLog.txt");

/* Main routine that starts the service control dispatcher. */
VOID _tmain (int argc, LPTSTR argv [])
{
    SERVICE_TABLE_ENTRY DispatchTable [] =
    {
        { ServiceName, ServiceMain },
        { NULL, NULL }
    };

    StartServiceCtrlDispatcher (DispatchTable);
    return;
}

/* ServiceMain entry point, called when the service is created. */
void WINAPI ServiceMain (DWORD argc, LPTSTR argv [])
{
    DWORD i;

    /* Set the current directory and open a log file, appending to
       an existing file. */

    /* Set all server status data members. */
    hServStatus.dwServiceType = SERVICE_WIN32_OWN_PROCESS;
    hServStatus.dwCurrentState = SERVICE_START_PENDING;
    hServStatus.dwControlsAccepted = SERVICE_ACCEPT_STOP |
            SERVICE_ACCEPT_SHUTDOWN | SERVICE_ACCEPT_PAUSE_CONTINUE;
    hServStatus.dwWin32ExitCode = ERROR_SERVICE_SPECIFIC_ERROR;
    hServStatus.dwServiceSpecificExitCode = 0;
    hServStatus.dwCheckPoint = 0;
    hServStatus.dwWaitHint = 2 * CS_TIMEOUT;

    hSStat = RegisterServiceCtrlHandler (ServiceName,
        ServerCtrlHandler);
    SetServiceStatus (hSStat, &hServStatus);

    /* Start service-specific work; generic work is complete. */
    if (ServiceSpecific (argc, argv) != 0) {
        hServStatus.dwCurrentState = SERVICE_STOPPED;
        hServStatus.dwServiceSpecificExitCode = 1;
                /* Server initialization failed. */
        SetServiceStatus (hSStat, &hServStatus);
        return;
    }
```

```
        /* We will only return here when the ServiceSpecific function
           completes, indicating system shutdown. */
        UpdateStatus (SERVICE_STOPPED, 0);
        return;
    }


    void UpdateStatus (int NewStatus, int Check)
    /* Set a new service status and checkpoint -
       either specific value or increment. */
    {
        if (Check < 0) hServStatus.dwCheckPoint++;
        else hServStatus.dwCheckPoint = Check;
        if (NewStatus >= 0) hServStatus.dwCurrentState = NewStatus;
        SetServiceStatus (hSStat, &hServStatus);
        return;
    }


    /* Control handler function, invoked by the SCM to run */
    /* in the same thread as the main program. */
    VOID WINAPI ServerCtrlHandler (DWORD Control)
    {
        switch (Control) {
            case SERVICE_CONTROL_SHUTDOWN:
            case SERVICE_CONTROL_STOP:
                ShutDown = TRUE; /* Set the global shutdown flag. */
                UpdateStatus (SERVICE_STOP_PENDING, -1);
                break;
            case SERVICE_CONTROL_PAUSE:
                PauseFlag = TRUE; /* Interrogated periodically. */
                break;
            case SERVICE_CONTROL_CONTINUE:
                PauseFlag = FALSE;
                break;
            case SERVICE_CONTROL_INTERROGATE:
                break;
            default:
                if (Control > 127 && Control < 256) /* User defined. */
                break;
        }
        UpdateStatus (-1, -1); /* Increment checkpoint. */
        return;
    }


    /* This is the service-specific function, or "main," and is
       called from the more generic ServiceMain.
       In general, you can take any server, such as ServerNP.c, and
       rename "main" as "ServiceSpecific"; putting code right here.
       But some changes are required to update status. */
```

```
int ServiceSpecific (int argc, LPTSTR argv [])
{
    UpdateStatus (-1, -1); /* Increment the checkpoint. */
    /* ... Initialize system ... */
    /* Be sure to update the checkpoint periodically. */

    return 0;
}
```

Managing Windows NT Services

Once a service has been written, the next task is to put the service under the control of the SCM so that it can be started, stopped, and otherwise controlled.

Several steps are required to open the SCM, create a service under SCM control, and then start the service. These steps do not directly control the service; they are directives to the SCM, which in turn controls the specified service.

Opening the SCM

A separate process, running as "Administrator," is required to create the service, much as JobShell was used in Chapter 7 to start jobs. The first step is to open the SCM, obtaining a handle that then allows the service to be created.

```
SC_HANDLE OpenSCManager (
    LPCTSTR lpMachineName,
    LPCTSTR lpDatabaseName,
    DWORD dwDesiredAccess)
```

Parameters

lpMachineName is NULL if the SCM is on the local system, but you can also access the SCM on networked machines.

lpDatabaseName is also normally NULL.

dwDesiredAccess is normally SC_MANAGER_ALL_ACCESS, but you can specify more limited access rights, as described in the on-line documentation.

Creating and Deleting a Service

New services are entered into the registry under:

```
HKEY_LOCAL_MACHINE\SYSTEM\CurrentControlSet\Services
```

It is necessary to call `CreateService`, using the `SC_HANDLE` returned from `OpenSCManager`.

```
SC_HANDLE CreateService (
    SC_HANDLE hSCManager,
    LPCTSTR lpServiceName,
    LPCTSTR lpDisplayName,
    DWORD dwDesiredAccess,
    DWORD dwServiceType,
    DWORD dwStartType,
    DWORD dwErrorControl,
    LPCTSTR lpBinaryPathName,
    LPCTSTR lpLoadOrderGroup,
    LPDWORD lpdwTagId,
    LPCTSTR lpDependencies,
    LPCTSTR lpServiceStartName,
    LPCTSTR lpPassword);
```

Parameters

`hSCManager` is the `SC_HANDLE` obtained from `OpenSCManager`.

`lpServiceName` is the name that you use in future references to the service and is one of the logical service names specified in the dispatch table in the `StartServiceCtrlDispatcher` call. Notice that there is a separate `Create-Service` call for each logical service.

`lpDisplayName` is the name that will show up as a registry key and in the "Services" administrative tool (accessed from the control panel under "Administrative Tools"). You will see this name entered immediately after a successful `CreateService` call.

`dwDesiredAccess` can be `SERVICE_ALL_ACCESS` or combinations of `GENERIC_READ`, `GENERIC_WRITE`, and `GENERIC_EXECUTE`. See the on-line documentation for additional details.

dwServiceType has values as in Table 13–1.

dwStartType specifies how the service is started. SERVICE_DEMAND_START is used in our examples, but other values (SERVICE_BOOT_START and SERVICE_SYSTEM_START) allow device driver services to be started during bootup or at system start time, and SERVICE_AUTO_START specifies that a service is to be started at system start-up.

lpBinaryPathName gives the service's executable; the .exe extension is not required.

Other parameters specify account name and password, groups for combining services, and dependencies when there are several interdependent services.

There is also an OpenService function to obtain a handle to a named service. Use DeleteService to remove a service from the registry and CloseService-Handle to close SC_HANDLEs.

Starting a Service

A service, once created, is not running. Start the *ServiceMain ()* function by specifying the handle obtained from CreateService along with the argc, argv command line parameters expected by the service's "main" function (that is, the function specified in the dispatch table).

```
BOOL StartService (
    SC_HANDLE hService,
    DWORD argc,
    LPTSTR argv [])
```

Controlling a Service

Control a service by telling the SCM to invoke the service's control handler with the specified control.

```
BOOL ControlService (
    SC_HANDLE hService,
    DWORD ControlCode,
    LPSERVICE_STATUS pServStat)
```

ControlCode, if access permits, is one of:

SERVICE_CONTROL_STOP

SERVICE_CONTROL_PAUSE

SERVICE_CONTROL_CONTINUE

SERVICE_CONTROL_INTERROGATE

SERVICE_CONTROL_SHUTDOWN

or a user-specified value in the range 128–255. These are the same values as those used with the fdwControl flag in the ServerCtrlHandler function.

pServStat points to a SERVICE_STATUS structure that receives the current status. This is the same structure as that used by the SetServiceStatus function.

Querying Service Status

Obtain a service's current status in a SERVICE_STATUS structure with:

```
BOOL QueryServiceStatus (
    SC_HANDLE hService,
    LPSERVICE_STATUS lpServiceStatus)
```

Summary: Service Operation and Management

Figure 13–1 shows the Service Control Manager (SCM) and its relation to the services and to a service control program, such as the one in Program 13–3 in the next section. In particular, a service must register with the SCM, and all commands to the service pass through the SCM.

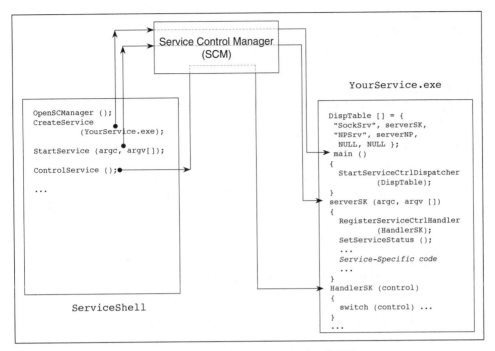

Figure 13-1   Controlling NT Services Through the SCM

Example: A Service Control Shell

Services can be controlled from the administrative tools, or, alternatively, you can control user-developed services using ServiceShell (Program 13–3) which was developed by modifying Chapter 7's JobShell (Program 7–3).

Program 13–3   ServiceShell: A Service Control Program

```
/* Chapter 13. */
/* ServiceShell.c NT Service Management shell program.
   This program modifies Chapter 7's job management program,
   managing services rather than jobs. */
/* Commands supported are:
     create - create a service
     delete - delete a service
     start - start a service
     control - control a service */

#include "EvryThng.h"
```

```
    static SC_HANDLE hScm;
    static BOOL Debug;

    int _tmain (int argc, LPTSTR argv [])
    {
        BOOL Exit = FALSE;
        TCHAR Command [MAX_COMMAND_LINE + 10], *pc;
        DWORD i, LocArgc; /* Local argc. */
        TCHAR argstr [MAX_ARG] [MAX_COMMAND_LINE];
        LPTSTR pArgs [MAX_ARG];

        /* Prepare the local "argv" array as pointers to strings. */
        for (i = 0; i < MAX_ARG; i++) pArgs [i] = argstr [i];

        /* Open the SC Control Manager on the local machine. */
        hScm = OpenSCManager (NULL, NULL, SC_MANAGER_ALL_ACCESS);

        /* Main command processing loop. */
        _tprintf (_T ("\nNT Service Management"));
        while (!Exit) {
            _tprintf (_T ("\nSM$"));
            _fgetts (Command, MAX_COMMAND_LINE, stdin);
            ... Similar to JobShell ...
            if (_tcscmp (argstr [0], _T ("create")) == 0) {
                Create (LocArgc, pArgs, Command);
            }
            ... Similarly for all commands ...
        }
        CloseServiceHandle (hScm);
        return 0;
    }

    int Create (int argc, LPTSTR argv [], LPTSTR Command)
    {
        /* Create a new service as a "demand start" service:
            argv [1]: service Name
            argv [2]: display Name
            argv [3]: binary executable */
        SC_HANDLE hSc;
        TCHAR CurrentDir [MAX_PATH + 1], Executable [MAX_PATH + 1];

        hSc = CreateService (hScm, argv [1], argv [2],
                SERVICE_ALL_ACCESS, SERVICE_WIN32_OWN_PROCESS,
                SERVICE_DEMAND_START, SERVICE_ERROR_NORMAL,
                Executable, NULL, NULL, NULL, NULL, NULL);
        return 0;
    }

    /* Delete a service - argv [1]: ServiceName to delete. */
```

```
int Delete (int argc, LPTSTR argv [], LPTSTR Command)
{
    SC_HANDLE hSc;
    hSc = OpenService (hScm, argv [1], DELETE);
    DeleteService (hSc);
    CloseServiceHandle (hSc);
    return 0;
}

/* Start a named service - argv [1]: service name to start. */
int Start (int argc, LPTSTR argv [], LPTSTR Command)
{
    SC_HANDLE hSc;
    TCHAR WorkingDir [MAX_PATH + 1];
    LPTSTR pWorkingDir = WorkingDir;
    LPTSTR argvStart [] = {argv [1], WorkingDir, NULL};

    GetCurrentDirectory (MAX_PATH + 1, WorkingDir);
    hSc = OpenService(hScm, argv [1], SERVICE_ALL_ACCESS);
    /* Start the service with one arg, the working directory. */
    StartService (hSc, 2, argvStart);
    CloseServiceHandle (hSc);
    return 0;
}

/* Control a named service. argv [1]: service name to control.
   argv [2]: Control command: stop, pause, resume, interrogate. */
static LPCTSTR Commands [] =
    {"stop," "pause," "resume," "interrogate," "user"};
static DWORD Controls [] = {
    SERVICE_CONTROL_STOP, SERVICE_CONTROL_PAUSE,
    SERVICE_CONTROL_CONTINUE, SERVICE_CONTROL_INTERROGATE, 128};

int Control (int argc, LPTSTR argv [], LPTSTR Command)
{
    SC_HANDLE hSc;
    SERVICE_STATUS ServiceStatus;
    DWORD dwControl, i;
    BOOL Found = FALSE;

    for (i= 0; i < sizeof (Controls)/sizeof (DWORD) && !Found; i++)
        Found = (_tcscmp (Commands [i], argv [2]) == 0);
    if (!Found) {
        _tprintf (_T ("\nIllegal Control Command %s"), argv [1]);
        return 1;
    }
    dwControl = Controls [i - 1];
    hSc = OpenService(hScm, argv [1],
        SERVICE_INTERROGATE | SERVICE_PAUSE_CONTINUE |
        SERVICE_STOP | SERVICE_USER_DEFINED_CONTROL |
```

```
        SERVICE_QUERY_STATUS);
    ControlService (hSc, dwControl, &ServiceStatus);

    if (dwControl == SERVICE_CONTROL_INTERROGATE) {
        QueryServiceStatus (hSc, &ServiceStatus);
        printf (_T ("Status from QueryServiceStatus\n"));
        printf (_T ("Service Status\n"));
            ... Print all other status information ...
    }
    if (hSc != NULL) CloseServiceHandle (hSc);
    return 0;
}
```

Sharing Kernel Objects with a Service

There can be situations in which a service and applications share a kernel object. For example, the service might use a named mutex to protect a shared memory region that is used to communicate with applications. Furthermore, in this example, the file mapping would also be a shared kernel object.

There is a difficulty caused by the fact that applications run in a security context separate from that of services, which run under the system account. Even if no protection is required, it is not adequate to create and/or open the shared kernel objects with a NULL security attribute pointer (see Chapter 5). Instead, a NULL DACL is required—that is, the applications and the service need to use a security attribute structure with a NULL security descriptor pointer.

Also notice that since a service runs under the system account, there can be difficulties in accessing resources on other machines, such as shared files, from within a service.

Event Logging

Services frequently run "headless" without a display, so it is not generally appropriate for a service to display status messages directly. Some services will create a console, message box,[1] or window for user interaction, but the best technique is to log events to a log file or use the event logging functionality provided with Windows 2000 and NT. Such events are maintained in the registry and can be viewed from the event viewer provided in the Administrative Tools.

---

[1] If a service calls MessageBox, it must specify MB_SERVICE_NOTIFICATION for the message box type. The message is then displayed on the active desktop, even if no user is logged on to the computer.

The `serviceSK.c` and `SimpleService.c` programs on the disc show how to log significant service events and errors to a log file, and commented code shows how to use event logging. There are three functions, all described in the on-line documentation:

1. `RegisterEventSource`—obtains a handle to the log file.

2. `ReportEvent`—used to register a record in the log file.

3. `DeregisterEventSource`—closes the handle to the log file.

Notes on Debugging a Service

A service is expected to run continuously, so it must be reliable and as defect-free as possible. While a service can be attached to the debugger and event logs can be used to trace service operation, these techniques are most appropriate once a service has been deployed.

During initial development and debugging, however, it is often easier to take advantage of the service wrapper presented in Program 13–2.

- Develop the "preservice" version as a stand-alone program. `serverSK`, for example, was developed in this way.

- Instrument the program with event logging or a log file.

- Once the program is judged to be ready for deployment as a service, rename the main entry point and link it with the service wrapper code shown in Program 13–2 (and included on the disc with two programs: `SimpleService.c` and `serviceSK.c`).

- Additional testing on a service is essential to detect both additional logic errors and security issues. Services run under the system account and do not, for instance, necessarily have access to user objects, and the preservice version may not detect such problems.

- Normal events and minor maintenance debugging can be performed using information in the log file or event log. Even the status information can help to determine server health and defect symptoms.

- If extensive maintenance is required, the service code can be removed from the wrapper and converted back to a stand-alone program.

It is also possible to attach the Visual C++ debugger to a service, and there is publicly available software. For an example of the latter, see `DBWin32` at `http://www.halcyon.com/ast/swdev.htm`.

Summary

NT services provide standardized capabilities to add user-developed services to Windows 2000/NT systems. An existing stand-alone program can be converted to a service using the methods discussed in this chapter.

Services are controlled and monitored through the Service Control Manager, and all services are entered in registry.

A service can be created, controlled, and monitored using the administrative tool or the `ServiceShell` program presented in this chapter.

Looking Ahead

Chapter 14 describes asynchronous I/O, which provides two techniques that allow multiple read and write operations to take place concurrently with other processing. It is not necessary to use threads; only one user thread is required.

In most cases, multiple threads are easier to program than asynchronous I/O, and thread performance is generally superior. However, asynchronous I/O is essential to the use of I/O completion ports, which are extremely useful when building scalable servers that can handle large numbers of clients; thus, an additional improvement to a system such as Program 13–2 would be to use I/O completion ports.

Waitable timers are also described in Chapter 14, and they use techniques introduced earlier.

Additional Reading

Kevin Miller's *Professional NT Services* thoroughly covers the subject.

Exercises

13–1. Extend `serviceSK` so that it can accept pause controls in a meaningful way.

13–2. `ServiceShell`, when interrogating service status, simply prints out the numbers. Extend the program so that status is presented in a more readable form.

13–3. Convert `serverNP` (from Chapter 11) into a service.

13–4. Modify `serviceSK` so that it uses event logging.

14 Asynchronous Input/Output and Completion Ports

Input and output are inherently slow compared with other processing. This slowness is due to factors such as:

- Delays caused by track and sector seek time on random access devices (such as discs and CD-ROMs).

- Delays caused by the relatively slow data transfer rate between a physical device and system memory.

- Delays in network data transfer.

All I/O in previous examples has been *thread-synchronous*. That is, the entire thread waits until the I/O operation completes.

This chapter shows how a thread can continue without waiting for an operation to complete—that is, threads can perform *asynchronous* I/O. Examples illustrate the different techniques available in Win32, primarily on Windows 2000/NT.

Waitable timers, which require some of the same techniques, are also described here.

Finally, and more importantly, once standard asynchronous I/O is understood, we are in a position to use *I/O Completion Ports*, which are extremely useful when building scalable servers that must be able to support large numbers of clients. Program 14–4 will modify an earlier server to exploit I/O completion ports.

Overview of Win32 Asynchronous I/O

There are three techniques for achieving asynchronous I/O in Win32, but Windows 9x and CE do not support all of them completely.

- **Multithreaded I/O.** Each thread within a process or set of processes performs normal synchronous I/O, but other threads can continue execution.

- **Overlapped I/O.** A thread continues execution after issuing a read, write, or other I/O operation. When the thread requires the I/O results before continuing, it waits on either the handle or a specified event. Windows 9x supports overlapped I/O only for serial devices such as named pipes.

- **Completion Routines (or Extended I/O).** The system invokes a specified *completion routine* within the thread when the I/O operation completes. Windows 9x does not support extended I/O for disc files.

The threaded server in Chapter 11 performs asynchronous I/O on named pipes, although, within a given thread, the I/O is synchronous. `grepMT` (Program 8–1) manages concurrent I/O to several files. Thus, we have already written programs that perform asynchronous I/O, but the individual threads still perform synchronous I/O.

Overlapped I/O is the subject of the next section, and the examples implement file conversion (ASCII to Unicode) using this technique in order to illustrate sequential file processing.

Following overlapped I/O, extended I/O with completion routines is explained. Additional possibilities, such as file merging with extended I/O, are left for Exercise 14–2.

Note: Overlapped and extended I/O can be complex, seldom yield performance benefits and may even harm performance, and, for file I/O, work only on Windows 2000/NT. Threads overcome these problems, *so some readers might wish to skip ahead to the sections on Waitable Timers and I/O Completion Ports*, referring back as necessary. On the other hand, the asynchronous I/O concepts can be found in both old and very new technology, so it can be worthwhile to learn the techniques. For example, COM on Windows 2000 supports the "asynchronous method call," and many readers who are using or will be using COM may find this feature useful. Also, the asynchronous procedure call operation is very similar to extended I/O, and, while my personal preference is to use threads, others like to use this mechanism.

Overlapped I/O

The first requirement for asynchronous I/O, whether overlapped or extended, is to set the overlapped attribute of the file or other handle. This is done by specifying the `FILE_FLAG_OVERLAPPED` flag on the `CreateFile` or other call that creates the file, named pipe, or other handle.

Sockets (Chapter 12), whether created by `socket` or `accept`, have the overlapped attribute set by default in WinSock 1.1, but the attribute must be set explicitly in WinSock 2.0. An overlapped socket can be used asynchronously in Windows 9x as well as in Windows 2000/NT.

Until now, overlapped structures have been used with `LockFileEx` (Chapter 7) as an alternative to `SetFilePointer` (Chapter 3), but they are essential for overlapped I/O. These structures are optional parameters on four I/O functions that can potentially block while the operation completes:

> `ReadFile`
>
> `WriteFile`
>
> `TransactNamedPipe`
>
> `ConnectNamedPipe`

Recall that when you're specifying `FILE_FLAG_OVERLAPPED` as part of `fdwAttrsAndFlags` (for `CreateFile`) or as part of `fdwOpenMode` (for `CreateNamedPipe`), the pipe or file is to be used only in overlapped mode. Overlapped I/O does not work with anonymous pipes. *Note*: The `CreateFile` documentation suggests that using the `FILE_FLAG_NO_BUFFERING` flag will enhance overlapped I/O performance. Experiments show a small improvement (about 15 percent, as can be verified by experimenting with Program 14–1), but you must ensure that the read length of every `ReadFile` and `WriteFile` operation is a multiple of the disc sector size.

Overlapped Sockets

One of the most important additions to Windows Sockets 2.0 (Chapter 12) is the standardization of overlapped I/O. In particular, sockets are no longer created automatically as overlapped file handles. `socket` will create a nonoverlapped handle. To create an overlapped socket, call `WSASocket` and explicitly ask for one by setting the `dwFlags` parameter of `WSASocket` to `WSA_FLAG_OVERLAPPED`.

```
SOCKET WSAAPI WSASocket (
    int iAddressFamily,
    int iSocketType,
    int iProtocol,
    LPWSAPROTOCOL_INFO lpProtocolInfo,
    GROUP g,
    DWORD dwFlags);
```

Use WSASocket, rather than socket, to create the socket. Any socket returned by accept will have the same properties as the argument.

Consequences of Overlapped I/O

Overlapped I/O is asynchronous. There are several consequences.

- I/O operations do not block. The system returns immediately from a call to ReadFile, WriteFile, TransactNamedPipe, or ConnectNamedPipe.

- The returned function value is not useful for indicating success or failure, because the I/O operation is most likely not yet complete. A different mechanism for indicating status is required.

- The returned number of bytes transferred is also not useful, because the transfer may not be complete. Win32 must provide another means of obtaining this information.

- The program may issue multiple reads or writes on a single overlapped file handle. Therefore, the handle's file pointer is meaningless. There must be another method of specifying file position with each read or write. This is not a problem with named pipes, which are inherently sequential.

- The program must be able to wait (synchronize) on I/O completion. In case of multiple outstanding operations on a single handle, it must be able to determine which operation has completed. I/O operations do not necessarily complete in the same order in which they were issued.

The last two issues listed above—file position and synchronization—are addressed by the overlapped structures.

Overlapped Structures

The overlapped structure (specified, for example, by the `lpOverlapped` parameter of `ReadFile`) indicates the following:

- The file position (64 bits) where the read or write is to start, as previously discussed in Chapter 3.

- The event (manual reset) that will be signaled when the operation completes.

The `OVERLAPPED` structure is as follows:

```
typedef struct_OVERLAPPED {
    DWORD Internal;
    DWORD InternalHigh;
    DWORD Offset;
    DWORD OffsetHigh;
    HANDLE hEvent;
} OVERLAPPED
```

The file position (pointer) must be set in both `Offset` and `OffsetHigh`, although the high-order portion is frequently zero. Do not use `Internal` and `InternalHigh`, which are reserved for the system.

`hEvent` is an event handle (created with `CreateEvent`). The event can be named or unnamed, but it *must* be a manually reset event (see Chapter 9). `hEvent` can be `NULL`, in which case the program can wait on the file handle, which is also a synchronization object (see the list of cautions below). The system signals completion on the file handle when `hEvent` is `NULL`; that is, the file handle becomes the synchronization object. *Note*: For convenience. the term "file handle" is used to describe the handle with `ReadFile`, `WriteFile`, and so on, even though this handle could refer to a pipe or device rather than to a file.

This event is immediately reset (set to the nonsignaled state) by the system when the program makes an I/O call. When the I/O operation completes, the event is signaled.

Even if the file handle is synchronous (it was created without `FILE_FLAG_OVERLAPPED`), the overlapped structure is an alternative to `SetFilePointer` for specifying file position. In this case, the `ReadFile` or other call does not return until the operation is complete. This feature was discussed in Chapter 3.

Notice also that an outstanding I/O operation is uniquely identified by the combination of file handle and overlapped structure.

Here are a few cautions to be aware of.

- Do not reuse an OVERLAPPED structure while its associated I/O operation, if any, is outstanding.

- Similarly, do not reuse an event while it is part of an OVERLAPPED structure.

- If there is more than one outstanding request on an overlapped handle, use events, rather than the file handle, for synchronization.

- If the OVERLAPPED structure or event is an automatic variable in a block, be certain not to exit the block before synchronizing with the I/O operation.

Overlapped I/O States

An overlapped ReadFile or WriteFile operation—or, for that matter, one of the two named pipe operations—returns immediately. In most cases, the I/O will not be complete, and the read or write returns a FALSE. GetLastError will return ERROR_IO_PENDING.

After waiting on a synchronization object (an event or, perhaps, the file handle) for the operation to complete, you need to determine how many bytes were transferred. This is the primary purpose of GetOverlappedResult.

```
BOOL GetOverlappedResult (
    HANDLE hFile,
    LPOVERLAPPED lpOverlapped,
    LPWORD lpcbTransfer,
    BOOL fWait)
```

The handle and overlapped structure combine to indicate the specific I/O operation. fWait, if TRUE, specifies that GetOverlappedResult will wait until the specified operation is complete; otherwise, it returns immediately. In either case, the function returns TRUE only if the operation has completed successfully. GetLastError will return ERROR_IO_INCOMPLETE in case of a FALSE return from GetOverlappedResult, so it is possible to poll for I/O completion with this function.

The number of bytes transferred is in `*lpcbTransfer`. Be certain that the overlapped structure is unchanged from when it was used with the overlapped I/O operation.

Canceling Overlapped I/O Operations

The Boolean function, `CancelIO`, will cancel outstanding overlapped I/O operations on the specified handle (there is just one parameter). All operations issued by the calling thread using the handle will be canceled. Operations initiated by other threads will not be affected. The canceled operations will complete with `ERROR_OPERATION_ABORTED`.

Example: Synchronizing on a File Handle

Overlapped I/O can be useful and relatively simple when there is only one outstanding operation. The program can synchronize on the file handle rather than on an event.

The following code fragment shows how a program can initiate a read operation to read a portion of a file, continue to perform other processing, and then wait on the handle.

```
OVERLAPPED ov = { 0, 0, 0, 0, NULL /* No event. */ };
HANDLE hF;
DWORD nRead;
BYTE Buffer [BUF_SIZE];
...
hF = CreateFile ( ..., FILE_FLAG_OVERLAPPED, ... );
ReadFile (hF, Buffer, sizeof (Buffer), &nRead, &ov);
/* Perform other processing. nRead is not valid. */
/* Wait for the read to complete. */
WaitForSingleObject (hF, INFINITE);
GetOverlappedResult (hF, &ov, &nRead, FALSE);
```

Example: File Conversion with Overlapped I/O and Multiple Buffers

Program 2–4 (`atou`) converted an ASCII file to Unicode, processing the file sequentially, and Chapter 6 showed how to perform the same sequential file processing with memory-mapped files. Program 14–1 (`atouOV`) performs the same task using overlapped I/O and multiple buffers holding fixed-size records.

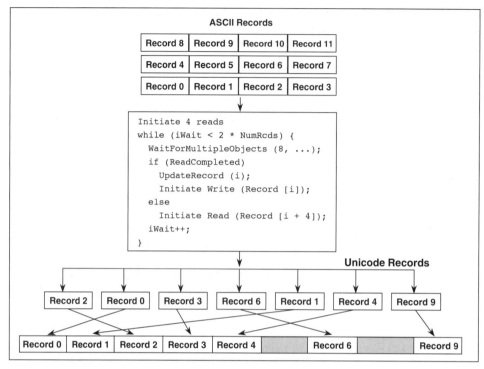

Figure 14-1 An Asynchronous File Update Model

Figure 14–1 shows the program organization with four fixed-size buffers. The program is implemented so that the number of buffers is defined in a preprocessor variable, but the following discussion assumes four buffers.

First, the program initializes all the overlapped structures with events and file positions. There is a separate overlapped structure for each input and each output buffer. Next, an overlapped read is issued for each of the four input buffers. The program then uses `WaitForMultipleObjects` to wait for a single event, indicating either a read or a write completed. When a read is completed, the buffer is copied and converted into the corresponding output buffer and the write is initiated. When a write completes, the next read is initiated. Notice that the events associated with the input and output buffers are arranged in a single array to be used as an argument to `WaitForMultipleObjects`.

Program 14–1 `atouOV`: File Conversion with Overlapped I/O

```
/* Chapter 14. atouOV
   OVERLAPPED I/O ASCII to Unicode file conversion.
   Windows 2000 and NT only. */
```

```
#include "EvryThng.h"

#define MAX_OVRLP 4 /* Number of overlapped I/O operations. */
#define REC_SIZE 0x8000 /* 32K: Minimum size for good performance. */
#define UREC_SIZE 2 * REC_SIZE
int _tmain (int argc, LPTSTR argv [])
{
    HANDLE hInputFile, hOutputFile;
    /* There is a copy of each of the following variables and */
    /* structures for each outstanding overlapped I/O operation. */
    DWORD nin [MAX_OVRLP], nout [MAX_OVRLP], ic, i;
    OVERLAPPED OverLapIn [MAX_OVRLP], OverLapOut [MAX_OVRLP];
    /* The first event index is 0 for read, 1 for write. */
    /* WaitForMultipleObjects requires a contiguous array. */
    HANDLE hEvents [2] [MAX_OVRLP];
    /* The first index on these two buffers is the I/O operation. */
    CHAR AsRec [MAX_OVRLP] [REC_SIZE];
    WCHAR UnRec [MAX_OVRLP] [REC_SIZE];
    LARGE_INTEGER CurPosIn, CurPosOut, FileSize;
    LONGLONG nRecord, iWaits;

    hInputFile = CreateFile (argv [1], GENERIC_READ,
            0, NULL, OPEN_EXISTING, FILE_FLAG_OVERLAPPED, NULL);
    hOutputFile = CreateFile (argv [2], GENERIC_WRITE,
            0, NULL, CREATE_ALWAYS, FILE_FLAG_OVERLAPPED, NULL);

    /* Total number of records to process based on input file size. */
    /* There may be a partial record at the end. */
    FileSize.LowPart = GetFileSize (hInputFile, &FileSize.HighPart);
    nRecord = FileSize.QuadPart / REC_SIZE;
    if ((FileSize.QuadPart % REC_SIZE) != 0) nRecord++;

    CurPosIn.QuadPart = 0;
    for (ic = 0; ic < MAX_OVRLP; ic++) {
        /* Create read and write events for each overlapped struct. */
        hEvents [0] [ic] = OverLapIn [ic].hEvent /* Read event/strct. */
                = CreateEvent (NULL, TRUE, FALSE, NULL);
        hEvents [1] [ic] = OverLapOut [ic].hEvent /* Write. */
                = CreateEvent (NULL, TRUE, FALSE, NULL);
        /* Initial file positions for each overlapped structure. */
        OverLapIn [ic].Offset = CurPosIn.LowPart;
        OverLapIn [ic].OffsetHigh = CurPosIn.HighPart;
        /* Initiate an overlapped read for this overlapped struct. */
        if (CurPosIn.QuadPart < FileSize.QuadPart)
            ReadFile (hInputFile, AsRec [ic], REC_SIZE,
                    &nin [ic], &OverLapIn [ic]);
        CurPosIn.QuadPart += (LONGLONG) REC_SIZE;
    }

    /* All read operations are running. Wait for an event to complete
```

and reset it immediately. Read and write events are stored contiguously in the event array. */

```
iWaits = 0; /* Number of I/O operations completed so far. */
while (iWaits < 2 * nRecord) {
    ic = WaitForMultipleObjects (2 * MAX_OVRLP,
            hEvents [0], FALSE, INFINITE) - WAIT_OBJECT_0;
    iWaits++; /* Increment # of complete I/O operations. */
    ResetEvent (hEvents [ic / MAX_OVRLP] [ic % MAX_OVRLP]);

    if (ic < MAX_OVRLP) { /* A read completed. */
        GetOverlappedResult (hInputFile,
                &OverLapIn [ic], &nin [ic], FALSE);

        /* Process the record and initiate the write. */
        CurPosIn.LowPart = OverLapIn [ic].Offset;
        CurPosIn.HighPart = OverLapIn [ic].OffsetHigh;
        CurPosOut.QuadPart =
                (CurPosIn.QuadPart / REC_SIZE) * UREC_SIZE;
        OverLapOut [ic].Offset = CurPosOut.LowPart;
        OverLapOut [ic].OffsetHigh = CurPosOut.HighPart;

        /* Convert an ASCII record to Unicode. */
        for (i = 0; i < REC_SIZE; i++)
            UnRec [ic] [i] = AsRec [ic] [i];
        WriteFile (hOutputFile, UnRec [ic], nin [ic] * 2,
                &nout [ic], &OverLapOut [ic]);

        /* Prepare for the next read, which will be initiated
           after the write, issued above, completes. */
        CurPosIn.QuadPart +=
                REC_SIZE * (LONGLONG) (MAX_OVRLP);
        OverLapIn [ic].Offset = CurPosIn.LowPart;
        OverLapIn [ic].OffsetHigh = CurPosIn.HighPart;

    } else if (ic < 2 * MAX_OVRLP) { /* A write completed. */
        /* Start the read. */
        ic -= MAX_OVRLP; /* Set the output buffer index. */
        if (!GetOverlappedResult (hOutputFile,
                &OverLapOut [ic], &nout [ic], FALSE))
            ReportError (_T ("Read failed."), 0, TRUE);
        CurPosIn.LowPart = OverLapIn [ic].Offset;
        CurPosIn.HighPart = OverLapIn [ic].OffsetHigh;
        if (CurPosIn.QuadPart < FileSize.QuadPart) {
            /* Start a new read. */
            ReadFile (hInputFile, AsRec [ic], REC_SIZE,
                    &nin [ic], &OverLapIn [ic]);
        }
    }
}
```

```
    /* Close all events. */
    for (ic = 0; ic < MAX_OVRLP; ic++) {
        CloseHandle (hEvents [0] [ic]);
        CloseHandle (hEvents [1] [ic]);
    }
    CloseHandle (hInputFile);
    CloseHandle (hOutputFile);
    return 0;
}
```

Program 14–1 works only under Windows 2000/NT. Windows 9x asynchronous I/O cannot use disc files. Appendix C shows that `atouOV` has relatively poor performance and comments on the results. Experiments show that the buffer should be at least 32KB for good performance, but, even then, normal synchronous I/O is faster. Furthermore, the program does not benefit from SMP, because the CPU is not the bottleneck in this example, which processes just two files.

Extended I/O with Completion Routines

There is an alternative to the use of synchronization objects. Rather than requiring a thread to wait for a completion signal on an event or handle, the system can invoke a user-specified completion routine when an I/O operation completes. The completion routine can then start the next I/O operation and perform any other bookkeeping.

How can the program specify the completion routine? There are no remaining `ReadFile` or `WriteFile` parameters or data structures to hold the routine's address. There is, however, a family of extended I/O functions, which are identifiable by the `Ex` suffix, containing an extra parameter for the completion routine address. The read and write functions are `ReadFileEx` and `WriteFileEx`. Additionally, it is necessary to use one of five *alertable wait* functions:

- `WaitForSingleObjectEx`

- `WaitForMultipleObjectsEx`

- `SleepEx`

- `SignalObjectAndWait`

- `MsgWaitForMultipleObjectsEx`

Extended I/O is sometimes called *alertable I/O*. The following sections show how to use the extended functions.

Note: Extended I/O will not work with disc files or communications ports under Windows 9x. Windows 9x extended I/O, however, will work with named pipes, mailslots, sockets, and sequential devices.

ReadFileEx, WriteFileEx, and Completion Routines

The extended read and write functions can be used with open file, named pipe, and mailslot handles if FILE_FLAG_OVERLAPPED was used at open (create) time. Notice that the flag sets a handle attribute and, while overlapped I/O and extended I/O are distinguished, a single overlapped flag is used to enable both types of asynchronous I/O on a handle.

Overlapped sockets (Chapter 12) can be used with ReadFileEx and WriteFileEx in Windows 9x as well as Windows 2000/NT.

```
BOOL ReadFileEx (
    HANDLE hFile,
    LPVOID lpBuffer,
    DWORD nNumberOfBytesToRead,
    LPOVERLAPPED lpOverlapped,
    LPOVERLAPPED_COMPLETION_ROUTINE lpcr)

BOOL WriteFileEx (
    HANDLE hFile,
    LPVOID lpBuffer,
    DWORD nNumberOfBytesToWrite,
    LPOVERLAPPED lpOverlapped,
    LPOVERLAPPED_COMPLETION_ROUTINE lpcr)
```

The two functions are familiar but have an extra parameter to specify the completion routine.

The overlapped structures must be supplied, but there is no need to specify the hEvent member; the system ignores it. It turns out, however, that this member is useful for carrying identifying information, as will be shown in the next example program.

In comparison to ReadFile and WriteFile, notice that the extended functions do not require the parameters for the number of bytes transferred. That information is conveyed to the completion routine, which must be included in the program.

The completion routine has parameters for the byte count, an error code, and the overlapped structure. The last parameter is required so that the completion routine can determine which of several outstanding operations has completed. Notice that the same cautions regarding reuse or destruction of overlapped structures apply here as they did for overlapped I/O.

```
VOID WINAPI FileIOCompletionRoutine (
    DWORD fdwError,
    DWORD cbTransferred,
    LPOVERLAPPED lpo)
```

As was the case with `CreateThread`, which also specified a function name, `FileIOCompletionRoutine` is a placeholder and not an actual function name.

`fdwError` is limited to 0 (success) and `ERROR_HANDLE_EOF` (when a read tries to go past the end of file). The overlapped structure is the one used by the completed `ReadFileEx` or `WriteFileEx` call.

Two things must happen before the completion routine is invoked by the system:

1. The I/O operation must complete.

2. The calling thread must be in an *alertable wait state*, notifying the system that it should execute any queued completion routines.

How does a thread get into an alertable wait state? It must make an explicit call to one of three alertable wait functions. In this way, the thread can ensure that the completion routine does not execute prematurely.

Once these two conditions have been met, completion routines that have been queued as the result of I/O completion are executed. *Completion routines are executed in the same thread that made the original I/O call and is in the alertable wait state.* Therefore, the thread should enter an alertable wait state only when it is safe for completion routines to execute.

Alertable Wait Functions

There are five alertable wait functions, and the three that relate directly to our current needs are described here. Each has an `fAlertable` flag that must be set to TRUE. The functions are extensions of the familiar `wait` and `Sleep` functions.

```
DWORD WaitForSingleObjectEx (
    HANDLE hObject,
    DWORD dwTimeOut,
    BOOL fAlertable)

DWORD WaitForMultipleObjectsEx (
    DWORD cObjects,
    LPHANDLE lphObjects,
    BOOL fWaitAll,
    DWORD dwTimeOut,
    BOOL fAlertable)

DWORD SleepEx (
    DWORD dwTimeOut,
    BOOL fAlertable)
```

Time-outs, as always, are in milliseconds. These three functions will return as soon as *any one* of the following situations occurs.

- Handle(s) are signaled so as to satisfy one of the two wait functions in the normal way.

- The time-out period expires.

- All queued completion routines in the thread finish, and `fAlertable` is set.

Notice that no events are associated with the `ReadFileEx` and `WriteFileEx` overlapped structures, so any handles in the wait call will have no direct relation to the I/O operations. `SleepEx`, on the other hand, is not associated with a synchronization object and is the easiest of the three functions to use. `SleepEx` is usually used with an `INFINITE` time-out so that the function will return only after the queued completion routines have all finished.

Execution of Completion Routines and the Alertable Wait Return

As soon as an extended I/O operation is complete, its associated completion routine, with the overlapped structure, byte count, and error status arguments, is queued for execution.

All of a thread's queued completion routines are executed when the thread enters an alertable wait state. They are executed sequentially but not necessarily in the same order as I/O completion. The alertable wait function returns only after the completion routines return. This property is essential to the proper operation of most programs, because it assumes that the completion routines can prepare for the next use of the overlapped structure and perform related operations to get the program to a known state before the alertable wait return.

`SleepEx` will return `WAIT_IO_COMPLETION` if one or more queued completion routines were executed, and `GetLastError` will return this same value after one of the wait functions returns.

Here are three final points.

1. Use an `INFINITE` time-out value with any alertable wait function. Without the possibility of a time-out, you will return only after all queued completion routines have been executed or the handles have been signaled.

2. It is common practice to use the `hEvent` data member of the overlapped structure to convey information to the completion routine, because this field is ignored by the OS.

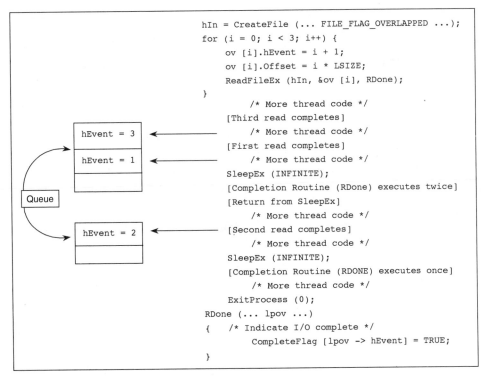

Figure 14-2 Asynchronous I/O with Completion Routines

3. You can create your own asynchronous procedure calls using `QueueUserAPC`. See the MSDN for additional information.

Figure 14–2 illustrates the interaction among the main thread, the completion routines, and the alertable waits. In this example, three concurrent read operations are started, and two are completed by the time the alertable wait is performed.

Example: File Conversion with Extended I/O

Program 14–2, atouEX, reimplements Program 14–1. These programs show how the two asynchronous I/O techniques differ. atouEX is similar to Program 14–1 but moves most of the bookkeeping code to the completion routines, and many variables are made global so as to be accessible to the completion routines. Appendix C shows, however, that atouEX performs competitively with other non-memory mapped techniques, whereas atouOV is consistently slower.

Program 14–2   atouEX: File Conversion with Extended I/O

```
/* Chapter 14. atouEX
   EXTENDED I/O ASCII to Unicode file conversion. */
/* atouEX file1 file2 */

#include "EvryThng.h"

#define MAX_OVRLP 4
#define REC_SIZE 8096 /* Block size is not as important for
        performance as with atouOV. */
#define UREC_SIZE 2 * REC_SIZE

static VOID WINAPI ReadDone (DWORD, DWORD, LPOVERLAPPED);
static VOID WINAPI WriteDone (DWORD, DWORD, LPOVERLAPPED);

/* The first overlapped structure is for reading,
    and the second is for writing. Structures and buffers are
    allocated for each outstanding operation. */
OVERLAPPED OverLapIn [MAX_OVRLP], OverLapOut [MAX_OVRLP];
CHAR AsRec [MAX_OVRLP] [REC_SIZE];
WCHAR UnRec [MAX_OVRLP] [REC_SIZE];
HANDLE hInputFile, hOutputFile;
LONGLONG nRecord, nDone;
LARGE_INTEGER FileSize;

int _tmain (int argc, LPSTR argv [])
{
```

```
        DWORD ic;
        LARGE_INTEGER CurPosIn;
        hInputFile = CreateFile (argv [1], GENERIC_READ,
                0, NULL, OPEN_EXISTING, FILE_FLAG_OVERLAPPED, NULL);
        hOutputFile = CreateFile (argv [2], GENERIC_WRITE,
                0, NULL, CREATE_ALWAYS, FILE_FLAG_OVERLAPPED, NULL);
        FileSize.LowPart = GetFileSize (hInputFile, &FileSize.HighPart);
        nRecord = FileSize.QuadPart / REC_SIZE;
        if ((FileSize.QuadPart % REC_SIZE) != 0) nRecord++;
        CurPosIn.QuadPart = 0;
        for (ic = 0; ic < MAX_OVRLP; ic++) {
            OverLapIn [ic].hEvent = (HANDLE) ic; /* Overload the event. */
            OverLapOut [ic].hEvent = (HANDLE) ic; /* Fields. */
            OverLapIn [ic].Offset = CurPosIn.LowPart;
            OverLapIn [ic].OffsetHigh = CurPosIn.HighPart;
            if (CurPosIn.QuadPart < FileSize.QuadPart)
                ReadFileEx (hInputFile, AsRec [ic], REC_SIZE,
                        &OverLapIn [ic], ReadDone);
            CurPosIn.QuadPart += (LONGLONG) REC_SIZE;
        }
        /* All read operations are running. Enter an alertable wait
           state and continue until all records have been processed. */
        nDone = 0;
        while (nDone < 2 * nRecord)
            SleepEx (INFINITE, TRUE);
        CloseHandle (hInputFile);
        CloseHandle (hOutputFile);
        _tprintf (_T ("ASCII to Unicode conversion completed.\n"));
        return 0;
    }

    static VOID WINAPI ReadDone (DWORD Code, DWORD nBytes,
            LPOVERLAPPED pOv)
    {
        /* A read completed. Convert the data and initiate a write. */
        LARGE_INTEGER CurPosIn, CurPosOut;
        DWORD ic, i;
        nDone++;
        /* Process the record and initiate the write. */
        ic = (DWORD) (pOv->hEvent);
        CurPosIn.LowPart = OverLapIn [ic].Offset;
        CurPosIn.HighPart = OverLapIn [ic].OffsetHigh;
        CurPosOut.QuadPart =
                (CurPosIn.QuadPart / REC_SIZE) * UREC_SIZE;
        OverLapOut [ic].Offset = CurPosOut.LowPart;
        OverLapOut [ic].OffsetHigh = CurPosOut.HighPart;
        /* Convert an ASCII record to Unicode. */
        for (i = 0; i < nBytes; i++)
            UnRec [ic] [i] = AsRec [ic] [i];
        WriteFileEx (hOutputFile, UnRec [ic], nBytes*2,
```

```
                &OverLapOut [ic], WriteDone);
       /* Prepare the overlapped structure for the next read. */
       CurPosIn.QuadPart += REC_SIZE * (LONGLONG) (MAX_OVRLP);
       OverLapIn [ic].Offset = CurPosIn.LowPart;
       OverLapIn [ic].OffsetHigh = CurPosIn.HighPart;
       return;
   }

   static VOID WINAPI WriteDone (DWORD Code, DWORD nBytes,
           LPOVERLAPPED pOv)
   {
       /* A write completed. Initiate the next read. */
       LARGE_INTEGER CurPosIn;
       DWORD ic;
       nDone++;
       ic = (DWORD) (pOv->hEvent);
       CurPosIn.LowPart = OverLapIn [ic].Offset;
       CurPosIn.HighPart = OverLapIn [ic].OffsetHigh;
       if (CurPosIn.QuadPart < FileSize.QuadPart) {
           ReadFileEx (hInputFile, AsRec [ic], REC_SIZE,
                   &OverLapIn [ic], ReadDone);
       }
       return;
   }
```

Asynchronous I/O with Threads

Overlapped and extended I/O achieves asynchronous I/O within a single thread, although the operating system creates its own threads to support the functionality. These techniques are common, in one form or another, in many older operating systems for supporting limited forms of asynchronous operation in single-threaded systems.

Win32, however, supports threads, so the same effect is possible by performing synchronous I/O operations in separate threads. The multithreaded servers and Chapter 8's grepMT have already illustrated this. Threads also provide a uniform and, arguably, much simpler way to perform asynchronous I/O. In the current example, each thread could be given its own handle to the file and could synchronously process every fourth record.

The program atouMT, not listed here but included on the disc, illustrates how to use threads in this way. Not only does atouMT work under Windows 9x and Windows CE, but it is also simpler than the two asynchronous I/O programs because the bookkeeping is less complex. Each thread simply maintains its own buffers on its own stack and performs the read, convert, write sequence synchronously in a loop. The performance is also competitive. *Note*: The atouMT.c program on the disc contains some comments about several pitfalls that can occur when a single file is accessed concurrently from several threads. In particular, the distinct file handles should all be created with `CreateFile` rather than with `DuplicateHandle`.

The author's personal preference is to use threads rather than asynchronous I/O for file processing. Threads are easier to program, they work under Windows 9x, and they provide the best performance in most cases.

There are two exceptions to this generalization. The first exception, as shown earlier in this chapter, is a situation in which there is only a single outstanding operation and the file handle can be used for synchronization. The second, and more important, exception occurs with asynchronous I/O completion ports, as will be described at the end of this chapter.

Waitable Timers

Waitable timers, a type of waitable kernel object, are supported by Windows 2000/NT, but they are not available in Windows 9x and CE.

You can always create your own timing signal by creating a timing thread that sets an event after waking from a `Sleep` call. `serverNP` also uses a timing thread to broadcast its pipe name periodically. Therefore, waitable timers are a redundant, but useful, way to perform tasks periodically or at specified times. In particular, a waitable timer can be set to signal at a specified absolute time.

A waitable timer can be either a "synchronization timer" or a "manual reset notification timer." A synchronization timer is associated with a callback function, similar to an extended I/O completion routine, whereas a wait function is used to synchronize on a manual reset notification timer.

The first step is to create a timer handle with `CreateWaitableTimer`.

```
HANDLE CreateWaitableTimer (
    LPSECURITY_ATTRIBUTES lpTimerAttributes,
    BOOL bManualReset,
    LPCTSTR lpTimerName);
```

The second parameter determines whether the timer is a synchronization timer or a manual reset notification timer. Program 14–3 uses a synchronization timer, but you can change the comment to obtain a notification timer. Notice that there is also an `OpenWaitableTimer` function that can use the optional name supplied in the third argument.

The timer is initially inactive, but `SetWaitableTimer` activates it and specifies the initial signal time and the time between periodic signals.

```
BOOL SetWaitableTimer (
    HANDLE hTimer,
    const LARGE_INTEGER *pDueTime,
    LONG lPeriod,
    PTIMERAPCROUTINE pfnCompletionRoutine,
    LPVOID lpArgToCompletionRoutine,
    BOOL fResume);
```

The second parameter is either a positive absolute time or a negative relative time and is actually expressed as a `FILETIME` with a resolution of 100 ns. `FILETIME` variables were introduced in Chapter 3 and were used in Chapter 7's `timep` program.

The interval between signals is specified in the third parameter, but in ms units. If this value is zero, the timer is only signaled once. A positive value indicates that the timer is a periodic timer and continues signaling periodically until you call `CancelWaitableTimer`. Negative interval values are not allowed.

The fourth parameter specifies the time-out function (completion routine) to be called when the timer is signaled *and* the thread enters an alertable wait state. The routine is called with the pointer specified in the fifth parameter.

Having set a synchronization timer, you can now call `SleepEx` to enter an alertable wait state. In the case of a manual reset notification timer, wait on the timer handle. The handle will remain signaled until another call to `SetWaitableTimer`.

The final parameter, `fResume`, is concerned with power conservation. See the documentation for more information.

Use `CancelWaitableTimer` to cancel the last effect of a previous `SetWaitableTimer`, although it will not change the signaled state of the timer. Use another `SetWaitableTimer` call to do that.

Example: Using a Waitable Timer

Program 14–3 shows how to use a waitable timer to signal the user periodically.

Program 14–3   TimeBeep.c: A Periodic Signal

```
/* Chapter 14. TimeBeep.c. Periodic alarm.
/* Usage: TimeBeep Period (in ms). */
#define _WIN32_WINNT 0x0400 /* Required in <winbase.h> to define
       waitable timer functions by setting the OS version number.
       This is not explained in the documentation. */
#include "EvryThng.h"

static BOOL WINAPI Handler (DWORD CntrlEvent);
static VOID APIENTRY Beeper (LPVOID, DWORD, DWORD);
volatile static BOOL Exit = FALSE;
HANDLE hTimer;

int _tmain (int argc, LPTSTR argv [])
{
    DWORD Count = 0, Period;
    LARGE_INTEGER DueTime;

    /* Catch cntrl-c to terminate operation. See Chapter 4. */
    SetConsoleCtrlHandler (Handler, TRUE);
    Period = _ttoi (argv [1]) * 1000;

    DueTime.QuadPart = -(LONGLONG)Period * 10000;
            /* Due time is negative for first time-out relative to
                current time. Period is in ms (10**-3 sec) whereas
                the due time is in 100 ns (10**-7 sec) units to be
                consistent with a FILETIME. */

    hTimer = CreateWaitableTimer (NULL,
        FALSE /* "Synchronization timer" */, NULL);
    SetWaitableTimer (hTimer, &DueTime, Period,
            Beeper, &Count, TRUE);

    while (!Exit) {
        _tprintf (_T ("Count = %d\n"), Count);
        /* Count is increased in the timer routine. */
        /* Enter an alertable wait state. */
        SleepEx (INFINITE, TRUE);
    }

    _tprintf (_T ("Shut down. Count = %d"), Count);
    CancelWaitableTimer (hTimer);
    CloseHandle (hTimer);
    return 0;
}

static VOID APIENTRY Beeper (LPVOID lpCount,
        DWORD dwTimerLowValue, DWORD dwTimerHighValue)
```

```
    {
        *(LPDWORD) lpCount = *(LPDWORD) lpCount + 1;

        _tprintf (_T ("Perform beep number: %d\n"), *(LPDWORD) lpCount);
        Beep (1000 /* Frequency. */, 250 /* Duration (ms). */);
        return;
    }

    BOOL WINAPI Handler (DWORD CntrlEvent)
    {
        Exit = TRUE;
        _tprintf (_T ("Shutting Down\n"));
        CloseHandle (hTimer);
        return TRUE;
    }
```

Comments on the Waitable Timer Example

There are four combinations based on timer type and whether you wait on the handle or use a completion routine. Program 14–3 illustrates using a completion routine and a synchronization timer. The four combinations can be tested using the version of `TimeBeep.c` on the disc by changing some comments.

I/O Completion Ports

I/O completion ports, supported only on Windows 2000/NT, combine features of both overlapped I/O and independent threads and are most useful in server programs. To see the requirement for this, consider the servers that we built in Chapters 11 and 12, where each client is supported by a distinct worker thread associated with a socket or named pipe instance. This solution works very well when the number of clients is not large.

Consider what would happen, however, if there were 1,000 clients. The current model would then require 1,000 threads, each with a substantial amount of virtual memory space. For example, by default, each thread will consume 1MB of stack space, so 1,000 threads would require 1GB of virtual address space, and thread context switches could increase page fault delays.[1] Furthermore, the threads would contend for shared resources both in the executive and in the process, and the timing data in Chapter 9 showed the performance degradation that can result. Therefore, there is a requirement to allow a small pool of worker threads to serve a large number of clients.

---

[1]This problem may become less severe in the future with Win64 and larger physical memories.

I/O completion ports provide a solution by allowing you to create a limited number of server threads in a thread pool while having a very large number of named pipe handles (or sockets). Handles are not paired with individual worker server threads; rather, a server thread can process data on any handle that has available data.

An I/O completion port, then, is a set of overlapped handles, and threads wait on the port. When a read or write on one of the handles is complete, one thread is awakened and given the data and the results of the I/O operation. The thread can then process the data and wait on the port again.

The first task is to create an I/O completion port and add overlapped handles to the port.

Managing I/O Completion Ports

A single function, `CreateIoCompletionPort`, is used both to create the port and to add handles. Since this one function must perform two tasks, the parameter usage is correspondingly complex.

```
HANDLE CreateIoCompletionPort (
    HANDLE FileHandle,
    HANDLE ExistingCompletionPort,
    DWORD CompletionKey,
    DWORD NumberOfConcurrentThreads);
```

Parameters

An I/O completion port is a collection of file handles opened in OVERLAPPED mode. `FileHandle` is an overlapped handle to add to the port. If the value is INVALID_HANDLE_VALUE, a new I/O completion port is created and returned by the function. The next parameter, `ExistingCompletionPort`, must be NULL in this case.

`ExistingCompletionPort` is the port created on the first call, and it indicates the port to which the handle in the first parameter is to be added. The function also returns the port handle when the function is successful; NULL indicates failure.

`CompletionKey` specifies the key that will be included in the "completion packet" for `FileHandle`. The key is usually an index to an array of data structures containing an operation type, a handle, and a pointer to the data buffer.

`NumberOfConcurrentThreads` indicates the maximum number of threads allowed to execute concurrently. Any threads in excess of this number that are waiting on the port will remain blocked even if there is a handle with available data. If this parameter is zero, the number of processors in the system is used as the limit.

An unlimited number of overlapped handles can be associated with an I/O completion port. Call `CreateIoCompletionPort` initially to create the port and to specify the maximum number of threads. Call the function again for every overlapped handle that is to be associated with the port. Unfortunately, there is no way to remove a handle from a completion port, and this omission limits program flexibility.

The handles associated with a port should not be used with `ReadFileEx` or `WriteFileEx` functions. The Microsoft documentation suggests that the files or other objects not be shared using other open HANDLEs.

Waiting on an I/O Completion Port

Use `ReadFile` and `WriteFile`, along with overlapped structures (no event handle is necessary), to perform I/O on the handles associated with a port. The I/O operation is then queued on the completion port.

A thread waits for a queued overlapped completion not by waiting on an event but by calling `GetQueuedCompletionStatus`, specifying the completion port. When the calling thread wakes up, the function returns a key that was specified when the handle, whose operation has completed, was initially added to the port, and this key can specify the number of bytes transferred and the identity of the actual handle for the completed operation.

Notice that the thread that initiated the read or write is not necessarily the thread that will receive the completion notification. Any waiting thread can receive completion notification. Therefore, the key must be able to identify the handle of the completed operation.

There is also a time-out associated with the wait.

```
BOOL GetQueuedCompletionStatus (
    HANDLE CompletionPort,
    LPDWORD lpNumberOfBytesTransferred,
    LPDWORD lpCompletionKey,
    LPOVERLAPPED *lpOverlapped,
    DWORD dwMilliseconds);
```

It is sometimes convenient to have an operation not be queued on the I/O completion port. In such a case, a thread can wait on the overlapped event, as shown in Program 14–4 and in an additional example, atouMTCP, on the disc. In order to specify that an overlapped operation should *not* be queued on the completion port, you must set the low-order bit in the overlapped structure's event handle; then you can wait on the event for that specific operation. This is a strange design, but it is documented, although not prominently.

Posting to an I/O Completion Port

A thread can post a completion event to a port satisfying an outstanding call to GetQueuedCompletionStatus. The PostQueuedCompletionStatus function supplies all the required information.

```
BOOL PostQueuedCompletionStatus (
    HANDLE CompletionPort,
    DWORD dwNumberOfBytesTransferred,
    DWORD dwCompletionKey,
    LPOVERLAPPED lpOverlapped);
```

Alternatives to I/O Completion Ports

Chapter 9 showed how a semaphore can be used to limit the number of ready threads, and this technique is effective in maintaining throughput when a large number of threads compete for limited resources.

We could use the same technique with serverSK and serverNP. All that is required is to wait on the semaphore after the read request completes, perform the request, create the response, and release the semaphore before writing the response. This solution is much simpler than the I/O completion port example in the next section. The only problem is that there may be a large number of threads, each with its own stack space, which will consume virtual memory. Exercise 14–7 involves experimentation with this alternative solution, and there is an example implementation on the disc.

There is yet another possibility when creating scalable servers. A limited number of worker threads can take work item packets from a queue (see Chapter 10). The incoming work items can be placed in the queue by one or more boss threads, such as in Program 10–5.

Example: A Server Using I/O Completion Ports

Program 14–4 modifies `serverNP` (Chapter 11) to allow use of I/O completion ports. This server creates a small server thread pool and a larger pool of overlapped pipe handles along with a completion key for each handle. The overlapped handles are added to the completion port and a `ConnectNamedPipe` is issued. The server threads wait for completions associated with both client connections and read operations. After a read is detected, the associated client request is processed and the results are returned without using the completion port. Rather, the server thread waits on the event after the write, and the event in the overlapped structure has its low-order bit set.

An alternative and more flexible design would close a handle every time a client disconnected and would create a new handle for each new connection. This would be similar to the way that sockets were used in Chapter 12. The difficulty, however, is that handles cannot be removed from the competition port, so these short-lived handles would cause a resource leak.

Much of the code is familiar from previous examples and is omitted here.

Program 14–4   `serverCP.c`: A Server Using a Completion Port

```
/* Chapter 14. ServerNPCP. Multithreaded server.
   Named pipe version, COMPLETION PORT example.
   Usage: Server [UserName GroupName] */

#include "EvryThng.h"
#include "ClntSrvr.h"

/* Request and response messages defined here. */
typedef struct { /* Completion port keys point to these structures, */
    HANDLE hNp; /* which represent outstanding ReadFile */
    REQUEST Req; /* and ConnectNamedPipe operations. */
    DWORD Type; /* 0 for ConnectNamedPipe; 1 for ReadFile. */
    OVERLAPPED Ov;
} CP_KEY;
static CP_KEY Key [MAX_CLIENTS_CP]; /* Available to all threads. */
/* ... */
_tmain (int argc, LPTSTR argv [])
{
    HANDLE hCp, hMonitor, hSrvrThread [MAX_CLIENTS];
    DWORD iNp, iTh, MonitorId, ThreadId;
    THREAD_ARG ThArgs [MAX_SERVER_TH];

    /* ... */

    hCp = CreateIoCompletionPort (INVALID_HANDLE_VALUE, NULL, 0,
        MAX_SERVER_TH);
```

```c
    /* Create an overlapped named pipe for every potential client, */
    /* add to the completion port, and wait for a connection. */
    /* Assume that the maximum number of clients far exceeds */
    /* the number of server threads. */

    for (iNp = 0; iNp < MAX_CLIENTS_CP; iNp++) {
        memset (&Key [iNp], 0, sizeof (CP_KEY));
        Key [iNp].hNp = CreateNamedPipe (SERVER_PIPE,
            PIPE_ACCESS_DUPLEX | FILE_FLAG_OVERLAPPED,
            PIPE_READMODE_MESSAGE | PIPE_TYPE_MESSAGE | PIPE_WAIT,
            MAX_CLIENTS_CP, 0, 0, INFINITE, pNPSA);
        CreateIoCompletionPort (Key [iNp].hNp, hCp, iNp,
            MAX_SERVER_TH + 2);
        Key [iNp].Ov.hEvent = CreateEvent (NULL, TRUE, FALSE, NULL);
        ConnectNamedPipe (Key [iNp].hNp, &Key [iNp].Ov);
    }

    /* Create server worker threads and a temp file name for each. */
    for (iTh = 0; iTh < MAX_SERVER_TH; iTh++) {
        ThArgs [iTh].hCompPort = hCp;
        ThArgs [iTh].ThreadNo = iTh;
        GetTempFileName (_T ("."), _T ("CLP"), 0,
            ThArgs [iTh].TmpFileName);
        hSrvrThread [iTh] = (HANDLE)_beginthreadex (NULL, 0, Server,
            &ThArgs [iTh], 0, &ThreadId);
    }

    /* Wait for all the threads to terminate and clean up. */
    /* ... */
    return 0;
}

static DWORD WINAPI Server (LPTHREAD_ARG pThArg)

/* Server thread function.
   There is a thread for every potential client. */
{
    HANDLE hCp, hTmpFile = INVALID_HANDLE_VALUE;
    HANDLE hWrEvent = CreateEvent (NULL, TRUE, FALSE, NULL);
    DWORD nXfer, KeyIndex, ServerNumber;
    /* ... */
    BOOL Success, Disconnect, Exit = FALSE;
    LPOVERLAPPED pOv;
    OVERLAPPED ovResp = {0, 0, 0, 0, hWrEvent}; /* For responses. */

    /* To prevent an overlapped operation from being queued on the
       CP, the event must have the low-order bit set. This is strange,
       but it's the documented way to do it. */
    ovResp.hEvent = (HANDLE) ((DWORD) hWrEvent | 0x1);
    GetStartupInfo (&StartInfoCh);
```

```
hCp = pThArg->hCompPort;
ServerNumber = pThArg->ThreadNo;

while (!ShutDown && !Exit) __try {
    Success = FALSE; /* Set only when everything has succeeded. */
    Disconnect = FALSE;
    GetQueuedCompletionStatus (hCp, &nXfer, &KeyIndex, &pOv,
            INFINITE);
    if (Key [KeyIndex].Type == 0) {
        /* A connection has completed. */
        /* Open the temporary results file for this connection. */
        hTmpFile = CreateFile (pThArg->TmpFileName, /* ... */);
        Key [KeyIndex].Type = 1;
        Disconnect = !ReadFile (Key [KeyIndex].hNp,
            &Key [KeyIndex].Req, RQ_SIZE, &nXfer, &Key [KeyIndex].Ov)
            && GetLastError () == ERROR_HANDLE_EOF; /* First read. */
        if (Disconnect) continue;
        Success = TRUE;
    } else { /* A read has completed. process the request. */
        ShutDown = ShutDown ||
            (_tcscmp (Key [KeyIndex].Req.Record, ShutRqst) == 0);
        if (ShutDown) continue;

        /* Create a process to carry out the command. */
        /* ... */

        /* Respond a line at a time. It is convenient to use
            C library line-oriented routines at this point. */

        fp = _tfopen (pThArg->TmpFileName, _T ("r"));
        Response.Status = 0;
        /* Responses are not queued on the completion port as the
            low-order bit of the event is set. */
        while (_fgetts(Response.Record, MAX_RQRS_LEN, fp) != NULL) {
            WriteFile (Key [KeyIndex].hNp, &Response, RS_SIZE,
                    &nXfer, &ovResp);
            WaitForSingleObject (hWrEvent, INFINITE);
        }
        fclose (fp);

        /* Erase temp file contents. */
        SetFilePointer (hTmpFile, 0, NULL, FILE_BEGIN);
        SetEndOfFile (hTmpFile);
        /* Send an end of response indicator. */
        Response.Status = 1; strcpy (Response.Record, "");
        WriteFile (Key [KeyIndex].hNp, &Response, RS_SIZE,
                &nXfer, &ovResp);
        WaitForSingleObject (hWrEvent, INFINITE);
        /* End of main command loop. Get next command. */
        Disconnect = !ReadFile (Key [KeyIndex].hNp,
```

```
                &Key [KeyIndex].Req, RQ_SIZE, &nXfer, &Key [KeyIndex].Ov)
                && GetLastError () == ERROR_HANDLE_EOF; /* Next read. */

            if (Disconnect) continue;
            Success = TRUE;
        }

    } __finally {
        if (Disconnect) { /* Issue another connect on this pipe. */
            Key [KeyIndex].Type = 0;
            DisconnectNamedPipe (Key [KeyIndex].hNp);
            ConnectNamedPipe (Key [KeyIndex].hNp, &Key [KeyIndex].Ov);
        }
        if (!Success) {
            ReportError (_T ("Server failure"), 0, TRUE);
            Exit = TRUE;
        }
    }
    FlushFileBuffers (Key [KeyIndex].hNp);
    DisconnectNamedPipe (Key [KeyIndex].hNp);
    CloseHandle (hTmpFile);
    /* ... */
    _endthreadex (0);
    return 0; /* Suppress a compiler warning message. */
}
```

Summary

Win32 has three methods for performing asynchronous I/O. Using threads is the
most general technique and, unlike the other two, will work with Windows 9x.
Each thread is responsible for a sequence of one or more sequential, blocking I/O
operations. Furthermore, each thread should have its own file or pipe handle.

Overlapped I/O allows a single thread to perform asynchronous operations on
a single file handle, but there must be an event handle, rather than a thread and
file handle pair, for each operation. Wait specifically for each I/O operation to complete and then perform any required cleanup or sequencing operations.

Extended I/O, on the other hand, automatically invokes the completion code,
and it does not require additional events.

The one indispensable advantage provided by overlapped I/O is the ability to
create I/O completion ports, but, as mentioned previously and illustrated by a program on the disc, even that advantage is somewhat limited by the ability to use
semaphores to limit the number of active threads in a worker thread pool. The inability to remove handles from a completion port is an additional limitation.

UNIX supports threads through Pthreads, as discussed previously.

System V UNIX limits asynchronous I/O to streams and cannot be used for file or pipe operations.

4.3+ BSD uses a combination of signals (SIGIO) to indicate an event on a file descriptor and select a function to determine the ready state of file descriptors. The file descriptors must be set in the O_ASYNC mode. This approach works only with terminals and network communication.

Looking Ahead

Chapter 15 completes our discussion of Win32 and looks ahead by surveying two advanced topics that extend subjects we have covered here. The two new topics are:

- Remote Procedure Calls (RPCs), which allow distributed systems to communicate as if they were programs calling procedures (functions) rather than using pipes or sockets to send messages.

- The Component Object Model (COM), which allows functions to be grouped into an interface so that realizations of the interface are available both locally and on remote systems. Object-oriented concepts are required.

Exercises

14–1. Reimplement Program 14–1 (multibuffered file update) with synchronous I/O and multiple threads. *Hint*: Create a thread and a separate file handle for each input buffer. Compare with atouOV and atouEX in terms of program simplicity and performance. Then compare your program with the atouMT program on the disc. See the comment regarding some pitfalls. Next, replace the SetFilePosition calls with overlapped structures in the ReadFile and WriteFile calls.

14–2. Use asynchronous I/O to merge several sorted files into a larger sorted file.

14–3. Does the FILE_FLAG_NO_BUFFERING flag improve atouOV or atouEX performance, as suggested by the CreateFile documentation? Are there any restrictions on file size?

14–4. Modify TimeBeep (Program 14-3) so that it uses a manual reset notification timer.

14–5. Modify the named pipe client in Chapter 11, `clientNP`, to use overlapped I/O so that the client can continue operation after sending the request. In this way, it can have several outstanding requests.

14–6. Rewrite the socket server, `serverSK` in Chapter 12, so that it uses I/O completion ports.

14–7. Rewrite either `serverSK` or `serverNP` so that the number of ready worker threads is limited by a semaphore. Experiment with a large thread pool to determine the effectiveness of this alternative. `serverSM` on the disc is a modification of `serverNP`. As Win64 implementations and large physical memories become available, the trade-offs between this solution and completion ports may shift.

14–8. Use `JobShell` (Chapter 7's job management program) to bring up a large number of clients and compare the responsiveness of `serverNP` and `serverCP`. Networked clients can provide additional load. Determine an optimal range for the number of active threads.

15 | Remote Procedure Calls and COM Overview

The description of the principal Windows system service functions is now complete. With this background, it is possible to go beyond the core system services and explore other technologies that leverage what we have learned so far.

The technologies introduced here are Remote Procedure Calls (RPCs) and, briefly, the Component Object Model (COM) and the closely related Distributed Component Object Model (DCOM). These technologies extend the distributed computing techniques used in Chapter 11 (named pipes) and Chapter 12 (sockets), and they can be used to create NT services. What is more, many RPC and COM programs include logic that is implemented using techniques described in the previous chapters.

RPCs are frequently not used directly, but they are used by DCOM to communicate between systems, and RPC concepts, such as interfaces and Globally Unique Identifiers (GUIDs), are fundamental to COM as well, so it is helpful to describe RPCs as a step on the path from C-based procedural programming to COM.

This chapter is only an overview, and a brief one at that. The intent of this chapter is simply to introduce these concepts, indicate how they extend the core system services described in this book, and perhaps motivate interested readers to explore additional interesting and important topics. A short RPC example is included, however.

Remote Procedure Calls

RPCs are an alternative to message-based interprocess communication using pipes or sockets, and RPCs extend the familiar procedure-based programming model to distributed systems. For example, RPCs could be used to implement the client/server systems in Chapters 11 and 12. Rather than using messages for client/server communication, the RPC client would call a function (procedure) as if it were on the local system, but the RPC mechanism would invoke a procedure on a remote system and return the results transparently to the calling program.

RPCs are used as an implementation mechanism for Windows 2000/NT distributed services as well as for COM, as will be discussed at the end of this chapter. Despite their utility, however, RPCs are less popular than named pipes and sockets for user-developed distributed applications.

Threads, DLLs, and NT services are important underlying capabilities for RPC-based applications.

Remote Procedure Calls and Interoperability

The Windows RPC implementation is modeled after, and is compatible with, the Distributed Computing Environment (DCE) RPC implementations available on nearly all major platforms. Therefore, Windows 2000/NT RPC-based applications can interoperate with UNIX and other systems much as Windows Sockets applications can interoperate with compatible applications on non-Windows platforms.

One prerequisite for this interoperability is that TCP/IP must be available as an underlying transport and network protocol, and, in fact, this is the case. Windows RPC applications can use TCP/IP, named pipes, and other protocols.

Other RPC implementations are in use; Sun RPC is the best known. While the concepts are the same, Sun RPC applications do not interoperate with DCE RPC applications.

Basic RPC Architecture

Procedures are basic programming tools, and every programmer learns to use them when building nontrivial programs. Normally, however, both the calling program and the procedure itself are on the same system running as part of the same process. A remote procedure, however, is on a different system and does not have direct access to the memory and other resources available to the calling program. What is more, the client (calling) and server (remote procedure) systems may differ in terms of features such as host operating systems, byte ordering, data types (for example, a `long` integer may be 32 bits on one system and 64 bits on another), and file systems.

The RPC system must make the network and system differences transparent so that the client and server programs differ as little as possible from what would be written on a single system.

In order to address these issues, an RPC application is constructed from the following components in several steps.

- An interface definition, which describes the *interface* that the server exports to clients. The interface consists of one or more functions, and the functions, along with required data types, are defined using the *interface definition language*, or IDL. An IDL definition is similar to a header (`.h`) file, but there are extensions and restrictions to account for the fact that data must be communicated between systems and to allow for uniform data types.

- The Microsoft IDL (MIDL) compiler, which compiles the IDL program producing client and server *stub* source programs and a header file.

- The client stub, whose source code is produced by MIDL, is a proxy for the remote procedure, and its source should be included in the client project. The client stub *marshals* procedure arguments, including strings and structures, into messages suitable for network communications. Likewise, incoming results from the server must be *unmarshaled* and put into the correct byte order for the client system.[1]

- Likewise, the server stub is a proxy for the calling program (client) and is included in the project for the server. The server stub also performs marshaling and unmarshaling.

- Finally, MIDL produces a header `.h` file that is used by both the client and the server projects.

- The RPC run-time library (`rpcrt4.lib`) and network services library (`rpcns4.lib`) provide reliable network communication between clients and servers and locate and bind to servers with requested interfaces.

- The developer must program actual client and server code to use the RPC services.

Figure 15–1 shows the RPC components.

---

[1] DCE RPC uses the "receiver makes it right" strategy whereby the data is tagged by the system type that sends the data, and the receiver adjusts the data if necessary.

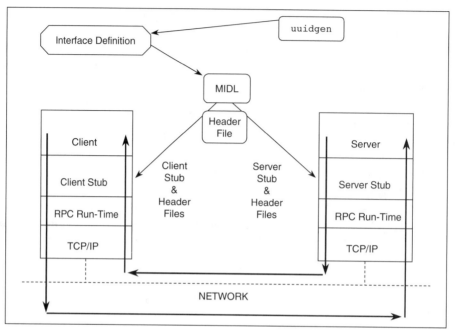

Figure 15-1 RPC Architecture

RPC Interface Definitions

An interface definition, written in IDL, not only defines the required data types and function prototypes but also specifies whether function parameters are used for input, output, or both.

The IDL program names the interface, which contains the defined functions, and it also assigns a "Unique Universal Identifier" (UUID) to the interface. This UUID, 128 bits long, is composed of a high-resolution time stamp and the unique Media Access Control (MAC) address of a network card. The UUID then provides a unique key allowing instances of the interface, in the form of servers that export it, to be identified by clients using RPC's network services. Once a UUID has been generated, you can use it to identify the interface, regardless of the servers that export the interface and regardless of changes to the actual server code and design; the interface, defined by the functions it provides, is what is being identified. The term "Globally Unique Identifier" (GUID) is also commonly used, especially with COM.

Generating a UUID

UUIDs are used for many purposes other than identifying RPC interfaces. For example, UUIDs are frequently used as "cookies" in network browsers, and they are also used by COM.

Generate a UUID when you first define the interface. The uuidgen utility is provided for this purpose and can be run from the command prompt. For example, here is one instance of using uuidgen:

```
$ uuidgen > uuid.txt
$ type uuid.txt
526d8629-98e7-4b5d-9d43-b8656ca0186f
```

Typically, the UUID can be cut and pasted into the IDL file, as shown next.

Example: An Interface Definition

Program 15–1 shows an interface definition named AboutRemoteSystem. The functions allow you to obtain disc and operating system information from a remote system.

Important features are as follows:

- The UUID is associated with the interface name and a version number. The "unique" pointer type allows null values and prevents aliasing.

- All functions are void.

- Data types are standard. Thus, an IDL long is 32 bits.

- All function parameters have tagged modifiers such as [in] and [out] to indicate whether they are input (to the remote procedure), output, or both.

- Strings contain a maximum size.

- Structures and arrays, while not shown here, can also be defined.

- Standard, rather than Windows, types are used. For example, integer parameters are long rather than DWORD.

Program 15–1   `SysCommands.IDL`: An Interface Definition File

```
/* Chapter 15. SysCommands.IDL */
/* Interface definition language for commands implemented as
   remote procedures to obtain system information.
   Process this file with the MIDL compiler to produce
   the client and server source files and the common header file.
   The command is:
       midl SysCommands.idl
   Note: You need the .idl extension on the file name. */

[   uuid (526d8629-98e7-4b5d-9d43-b8656ca0186f),
    version (1.0),
    pointer_default (unique)]
interface AboutRemoteSystem
{
    /* Obtain the information returned by GetDiskFreeSpaceEx. */
    void get_disk_free_space ([in, string, size_is (256)]
        char *RootPathName,
        [out] long *SecPerClus, [out] long *BytesPerSec,
        [out] long *NumFreeClus);

    /* Obtain the information returned by GetDriveType. */
    void get_drive_type ([in, string, size_is (256)]
            char *RootPathName, [out] int *Type);

    /* Obtain the information returned by GetVersionEx. */
    void get_os_version ([out] long *pOSVerInfoSize,
        [out] long *pMajorVersion,
        [out] long *pMinorVersion, [out] long *pBuildNum,
        [out] long *pPlatId,
        [out, string, size_is (64)] char *ServicePack);
}
```

Running the MIDL Compiler

The next step is to run the MIDL compiler on `SysCommands.idl` as follows:

```
$ midl SysCommands.IDL
Microsoft (R) MIDL Compiler Version 5.01.0164
Copyright (c) Microsoft Corp 1991-1997. All rights reserved.
Processing .\Syscommands.idl
Syscommands.idl
```

Three files are produced:

1. SysCommand.h is a header file to be used by both the client and the server programs. This file contains proper C definitions for the three functions.

2. SysCommands_c.c is the client stub source file to be included with the client project. The client stub name is formed by adding the _c.c suffix to the interface name.

3. Similarly, SysCommands_s.c is the server stub.

Example: An RPC Client

The RPC client program, as shown in Program 15–2, is very similar to what you would write for local procedures. All that is required in this simple example is the SysCommands.h header file and SysCommands_c.c in the project.

Program 15–2   SysCommandClient.c: RPC Client Program

```
/* Chapter 15. SysCommandClient.c */
/* Server to call remote procedures to obtain system information. */

#include "EvryThng.h"
#include <stdio.h>
#include <rpc.h>
#include "SysCommands.h"

int _tmain (DWORD argc, LPCTSTR argv [])
{
    /* Use the RPC try-except mechanism, which is similar to SEH. */
    /* (Chapter 6). */
    char Drive [] = "C:\\";
    int SecPerClus, BytesPerSec, NumFreeClus, Type;
    int VerInfoSize, MajVer, MinVer, BuildNum, PlatId;
    char ServicePack [128];

    RpcTryExcept {
        /* Get remote GetDiskFreeSpace information. */
        get_disk_free_space ((unsigned char __RPC_FAR *) Drive,
                &SecPerClus, &BytesPerSec, &NumFreeClus);
        printf _T (("Remote drive %s SecPerClus = %d.\
            BytesPerSec = %d. NumFreeClus = %d\n"),
            Drive, SecPerClus, BytesPerSec, NumFreeClus);

        /* Get remote GetDriveType information. */
        get_drive_type ((unsigned char __RPC_FAR *) Drive, &Type);
        _tprintf ("Remote drive type is: %d\n", Type);

        /* Get remote GetVersionEx information. */
```

```
    get_os_version (&VerInfoSize, &MajVer, &MinVer,
            &BuildNum, &PlatId, ServicePack);
    _tprintf ("Remote Version %d.%d. BuildNum: %d.\
            PlatId: %d\n", MajVer, MinVer, BuildNum, PlatId);
}

RpcExcept (1) {
    /* 1 is similar to EXCEPTION_EXECUTE_HANDLER. */
    /* 0 is similar to EXCEPTION_CONTINUE_SEARCH. */
    _tprintf (_T ("RPC run-time exception code = %d\n"),
            RpcExceptionCode ());
}
RpcEndExcept
return 0;
}

/* System-specific memory allocation and deallocation functions. */

void __RPC_FAR* __RPC_API MIDL_user_allocate (size_t len)
{
    return ((void __RPC_FAR*) malloc (len));
}

void __RPC_API MIDL_user_free (void __RPC_FAR* ptr)
{
    free (ptr);
}
```

Comments on the RPC Client

There are several interesting features in Program 15–2.

- The actual function calls are identical to local calls.

- RPC errors, such as a time-out due to network delays or the inability to locate a server with the requested interface, are handled with an exception handling mechanism that is similar to Windows SEH.

- The user must provide two simple system-specific memory allocation and deallocation functions. They are at the end of the program listing and, in general, could be provided in a DLL.

- rpc.h must be included, along with the MIDL-generated SysCommands.h.

- The interface and its UUID are never explicitly mentioned in the client. All the relevant information is contained in the stub and header files.

- Advanced options allow the programmer to specify the "reliability semantics." For example, you can specify whether the server is stateless or stateful and whether or not the server is "idempotent" (that is, whether it is all right for the server to execute a given request more than once). Normally, as in this example, the RPC run-time library uses datagrams to send requests to the server, and, if the server does not respond in a timely way, the RPC run time sends the request again. In case there are multiple unsuccessful retries, the run-time library will generate an RPC exception (the required number of retries is one of several adjustable parameters that have default values).

- The client/server binding is very simple in this example. The RPC library simply locates an instance of a server exporting the interface. (The next section shows how servers export interfaces.) In general, you can locate specific servers, bind to a different server on each RPC call, or specify that the binding should change only on request. Binding is beyond the scope of this introduction, but several references are given in the Additional Reading section at the end of the chapter.

Example: An RPC Server

The actual server function implementations are straightforward. The server, however, must also specify the protocols (such as TCP/IP and named pipes) that it supports, provide several other parameters such as the "endpoint" (a port number or a pipe name), and announce the fact that it supports the interface. Finally, the server listens for requests from clients.

Program 15–3, with its comments, illustrates a typical server. The code at the beginning is boilerplate and would be used by any server; the actual function implementations are at the end of the program.

Program 15–3   `SysCommandServer.c`: RPC Server Program

```
/* Chapter 15. SysCommandServer.c */
/* Server to implement remote procedures to obtain
   system information. */

#include "EvryThng.h"
#include <rpc.h>
#include "SysCommands.h"
      /* Shared header file created by MIDL compiler. */

void _tmain (DWORD argc, LPCTSTR argv [])
{
    RPC_BINDING_VECTOR *pBindVector;
```

```
    LPTSTR Endpoint = "1071";
        /* Port number: Use \\pipe\pipename for named pipe. */
    LPTSTR ProtocolSequence = "ncacn_ip_tcp";
        /* ncacn_np for named pipes. */
    DWORD MaxCalls = RPC_C_PROTSEQ_MAX_REQS_DEFAULT;

    /* Establish the RPC network protocol. */
    if (RpcServerUseProtseqEp (ProtocolSequence, MaxCalls,
            Endpoint, NULL) != 0)
        ReportError (_T ("Error specifying protocol"), 1, TRUE);

    /* Register interface for location by clients. */
    if (RpcServerRegisterIf (AboutRemoteSystem_v1_0_s_ifspec,
            NULL, NULL) != 0)
        ReportError (_T ("Error registering i/f"), 2, TRUE);

    /* Register server with locator program. Two steps:
        1) Place function information in a binding vector. */
    if (RpcServerInqBindings (&pBindVector) != 0)
        ReportError (_T ("Error: binding handle"), 3, TRUE);

    /* 2) Export binding info to locator's name service
            database; clients can import this binding info. */
    if (RpcNsBindingExport (RPC_C_NS_SYNTAX_DEFAULT,
            "/.:/AboutRemoteSystem",
            AboutRemoteSystem_v1_0_s_ifspec,
            pBindVector, /* Set by RpcServerInqBindings. */
            NULL) != 0)
        ReportError (_T ("Error exporting binding"), 4, TRUE);

    /* Server registered; listen for incoming requests. */
    printf ("Server is now ready for client requests\n");
    if (RpcServerListen ((long)1, MaxCalls, FALSE) != 0)
        ReportError (_T ("Err: RpcServerListen"), 5, TRUE);
}


/* System-specific memory allocation and deallocation functions. */
/* Alternatively, you could allocate from heaps (see Chapter 6). */

void __RPC_FAR* __RPC_API MIDL_user_allocate (size_t len)
{
    return ((void __RPC_FAR*) malloc (len));
}

void __RPC_API MIDL_user_free (void __RPC_FAR* ptr)
{
    free (ptr);
}
```

```
/* End of boilerplate code. Server-specific implementations. */

/* Obtain the information returned by GetDiskFreeSpaceEx. */
void get_disk_free_space (char *Drive, long *pSecPerClus,
        long *pBytesPerSec, long *pNumFreeClus)
{
    DWORD TotalNumClusters;
    GetDiskFreeSpace (Drive, pSecPerClus, pBytesPerSec,
            pNumFreeClus, &TotalNumClusters);
    return;
}

/* Obtain the information returned by GetDriveType. */
void get_drive_type (char *Drive, int *pType)
{
    *pType = GetDriveType (Drive);
    return;
}

/* Obtain the information returned by GetVersionEx. */
void get_os_version (long *pOSVerInfoSize, long *pMajVer,
        long *pMinVer, long *pBuildNum, long *pPlatId,
        unsigned char __RPC_FAR *ServicePack)
{
    OSVERSIONINFO VerInfo = {sizeof (OSVERSIONINFO)};

    GetVersionEx (&VerInfo);
    *pOSVerInfoSize = VerInfo.dwOSVersionInfoSize;
    *pMajVer = VerInfo.dwMajorVersion;
    *pMinVer = VerInfo.dwMinorVersion;
    *pBuildNum = VerInfo.dwBuildNumber;
    *pPlatId = VerInfo.dwPlatformId;
    strcpy (ServicePack, VerInfo.szCSDVersion);
    return;
}
```

A Brief COM and DCOM Overview

As the name "Component Object Model" implies, COM groups functions, or "methods," into interfaces and registers the interfaces in the registry for use by clients. Distributed Component Object Model (DCOM) is the distributed version of COM, and RPCs are used to communicate between systems. COM+ is an evolutionary extension with additional tools and integrated extensions, such as database access and transactions.

Among other advantages, COM interfaces are designed to be language-independent, whereas RPC interfaces are defined in a C-like language. COM also supports object-oriented languages.

COM, like RPC, uses IDL files, stubs, and GUIDs, and the interface definition uses the IDL syntax. Furthermore, Microsoft's Developer Studio facilitates the conversion of RPC systems into COM, as will be described in a subsequent section.

This overview unavoidably makes references to subjects that are beyond the scope of this discussion; this is only an overview, and more detail can be found online or in the suggestions in the Additional Reading section.

COM Elements

COM integrates a number of concepts that have been used throughout this book and, in addition, puts them in an object-oriented context, which is well beyond our scope. Here are the essential elements.

- A COM component is an explicitly linked DLL (see Chapter 6).

- A COM object can support several interfaces, where interfaces are similar to those used with RPCs.

- A class can have several distinct interfaces, each associated with a GUID. This is different from C++, where a class has a single interface and there is no need for a distinction.

- There is a strict distinction between interfaces and implementations, where an implementation is represented by a DLL.

- Methods within an interface implementation, other than a small collection of standard interfaces, are located by `GetProcAddress`.

Detailed explanations can be found in MSDN (look under "COM" and then go to "class factory"); additional references are given at the end. The next section describes how you can create a COM project, and the result, together with the suggested reading, will also show many COM features.

Converting an RPC Server to COM

The Visual C++ Developer Studio contains an "ATL COM AppWizard" that can be used when creating a new project, and this wizard is helpful when converting an RPC server to COM. *Note*: ATL is the Active Template Library, on which the online help has several useful articles.

Here are the major server creation steps, illustrated with the `SysCommand` system presented in the preceding section.

- Create a new workspace of type `ATL COM AppWizard`. Most projects up to now have been console applications. Give the project a suggestive name such as "`COMSysCommand`." In the appropriate dialog box, specify "`Executable (.EXE)`" and press OK. These steps have generated a skeleton stand-alone executable.

- The next step is to create a COM class written in C++ but using the C code from the existing RPC server. From the command bar, select "`Insert`" – "`New ATL Object`." In the resulting window, select the "`Object`" category and then select "`Simple Object`."

- The next dialog box asks you to provide a short name ("`SysCommands`" in this example), which is the base for naming the class (`CSysCommands`), header file, C++ source file, and interface (`ISysCommands` in this case). The dialog box also requests attributes on a separate tab and the apartment threading model (see the discussion at the end of Chapter 11). A custom interface and no aggregation should be selected for this example. We now have a C++ class that can be invoked remotely. The actual methods have not yet been usefully implemented, however.

- Implementing the methods involves pasting code from `SysCommandServer.c` into generated templates. First, use the class view tab in the workspace window, and expand the classes.

- For each method (three in this case), select `ISysCommands`, right click, and select "`Add Method`."

  - On the resulting dialog box, the default `HRESULT` return type is correct, and the method name should be `get_drive_type` (or one of the other two function names in `SysCommand.IDL`). The parameters line should be exactly as in the IDL file (do not include the parentheses).

  - On expanding `CSysCommands` and then, under it, `ISysCommands`, you will see a skeleton of the method with a "to do" comment. The source code of your original server function implementation, without the return statement, can be pasted below the "to do" comment.

  - Repeat the two steps above for the other two entry points. Also, be sure to include any necessary header files, such as `windows.h`, required by your code.

You can now build the project and obtain an executable server. On execution, it will be registered in the registry, but there will be no other direct evidence that the server is running.

Finding and Connecting to Servers

The client, described in the next section, must be able to locate an interface and then bind to it. Two functions are necessary. The first, CLSIDFromProgID, locates a server as a "CLSID" (class identifier) in the registry corresponding to a program identifier. The program identifier is expressed as project name (COMSysCommand) and class name (SysCommands), as specified when creating the server. The program identifier is a "pointer to an OLE string" (LPCOLESTR), which is actually a Unicode string.

After a server has been located, a specific instance is created and can be used to invoke the server. CoCreateInstance is the function used in the representative client code shown below.

```
ISysCommand isc; // A system command interface.
CLSID clsId;
CLSIDFromProgID (OLESTR ("COMSysCommand.SysCommands"),
        &clsId );
CoCreateInstance (clsId, NULL, CLSCTX_SERVER,
        ISysCommand, &isc);
/* "isc" can now be used to access the interface. */
isc->get_drive_type (...);
...
```

Creating the Client

The client can be created as a console application in the usual way, but select "An application that supports MFC" in the final wizard dialog box.

Then, assuming that the client project was named COMSysCommandClient, there will be a source file, COMSysCommandClient.cpp, which should be extended to contain code such as that in the preceding section. Furthermore, you will need to import a "table file" located in the project directory. The statement at the top of the source file should be:

```
#import project_path_name/COMSysCommandClient/
        COMSysCommandClient.tab
```

With that, the client project can be built to created a client program that can communicate with the COM server.

Summary

RPCs and COM are advanced interprocess communication and distributed computation capabilities that are built on, and leverage, the system services that have been discussed throughout this book. RPCs constitute an intermediate step and are used by the COM implementation.

Additional Reading

This chapter is only a simple introduction to RPCs and COM. More detailed information is available from books and other sources.

Remote Procedure Calls

Davis (*Win32 Network Programming*) provides a good treatment of RPCs and also discusses sockets and pipes. He also compares the performance of the different mechanisms. For a general overview, see *Understanding DCE* (Rosenberry et al.), and for a platform-independent technical discussion, see *Guide to Writing DCE Applications* (Shirley). *Distributing Applications Across DCE and Windows NT* (Rosenberry and Teague) discusses the Windows specifics and interoperability considerations.

COM

Box's *Essential Com* is a well-regarded introduction and gives a very good explanation of COM's important role in Windows programming. *Inside Distributed COM* by Eddon and Eddon is also well reviewed.

Looking Ahead

Chapter 16 describes Win64. The appendixes describe the sample program disc contents (Appendix A); the comparisons of Win32/64, UNIX, and C library functions (Appendix B); and the results of performance tests of several programs running on representative Windows systems (Appendix C).

Exercises

15–1. Modify Program 15–2 (the RPC client) and the IDL file (Program 15–1) so that the client can locate and interrogate more than one server.

15–2. Modify Program 15–3 (the RPC server) so that it is an NT service.

15–3. Examine the stub source files and the header file produced by MIDL.

15–4. If you have the required equipment, port the RPC client and server to UNIX (or other system) and ensure that you can interoperate with the Windows versions.

15–5. Build the COM client and server following the guidelines given in this chapter and make the necessary changes. Examine the source files generated by the wizard to help gain understanding of COM architecture and principles.

16 | Win64 Programming

The most significant advance in PC functionality since the introduction of Windows NT and 95 will be the advent and adoption of 64-bit programming, enabled by:

- Intel's IA-64 architecture, available on the Itanium (formerly code named "Merced") processor in mid-2000, and

- Microsoft's Win64 API designed to support the IA-64 architecture with minimal impact on existing source and binary code.

This chapter describes Win64 benefits, the programming model, and portability and migration issues.

Note: At the time of writing (May, 2000), Win64 and Itanium systems are not available. There will undoubtedly be rapid progress over the next few years, and updates to the material in this chapter will be posted on the author's site (see the Preface).

64-Bit Architecture Overview

From a programmer's perspective, the major issue in migrating from 32- to 64-bit programming models is that pointers can now be 64 bits long. Therefore, process virtual address space is no longer limited to 4GB (actually, only 2GB is directly available to applications). Thus, Win32 to Win64 migration can be regarded essentially as a "pointer stretch" and, within the Windows model, there is very little effect on data.

The Need for 64-Bit Addressing

Many applications require the ability to access large address spaces. Examples are numerous and include:

- **Imaging Applications**. 4GB yields only about 20 seconds of high definition television (HDTV) with true color.

- **Mechanical and Electronic Computer Aided Design (MCAD and ECAD)**. Part assemblies for complex components require more than 2GB to be represented, and chip design simulations are extremely memory-intensive.

- **Databases and Data Warehousing**. It is not uncommon to use files of hundreds of gigabytes, and similar amounts of virtual address space simplify the file processing.

Not only is there a need for large address spaces, but the physical systems can now support this demand. 64-bit microprocessors have been available for some time, and many systems support large physical memories at reasonable cost.

The same factors that make very large files (4GB or more in size) desirable and necessary also drive the need for 64-bit addressing, and now that sufficiently powerful IA-64 microprocessors are available, it is only natural that Windows should evolve to meet this need. A 64-bit operating system is essential if Windows is to play a significant role in enterprise and high-end computing.

Nonetheless, many 32-bit applications will continue to work well and will not require early migration. Personal productivity applications, such as Microsoft Office and Frame, will probably not require 64-bit migration for some time. Consequently, Windows 2000 will support backward compatibility.

The Intel Itanium processors (and compatibles) also provide performance gains, as would be expected, but these gains do not directly impact programming at the source level.

The UNIX Experience

PC systems have always lagged behind mainframe and UNIX systems in terms of core functionality and scalability. The same is true of 64-bit architectures.

- 48- and 64-bit microprocessors have been available from the major UNIX vendors since the early 1990s.

- The same major UNIX vendors have supported 64-bit APIs during the same time period.

- The UNIX community has standardized on the so-called LP64 model, which is different from Win64's P64 model, as will be described later.

- Migrations from 32 to 64 bits have been relatively painless, and the same can be expected of Win32 to Win64 migration.

The Windows 16- to 32-Bit Experience

The Windows 16- to 32-bit migration started in the early 1990s with the introduction of Windows NT, and the migration picked up momentum when Windows 95 became commonplace. Although it is tempting to say that we will see a replay of the same history, there are differences.

- Windows NT and 95 were the first widely used "real" PC operating systems—that is, these two systems supported demand paging, threads, preemptive scheduling, synchronization, and many other features previously described in Chapter 1.

- While Win32 greatly expanded the useful address space, as does Win64, the advance was more than that. Obsolete and awkward, but popular, extended memory models were replaced. Although Windows 2000 has one similar extended memory model (not described in this book), the overall change is not as significant.

- Win32 introduced extensive new functionality, whereas Win64 does not.

Are 64 Bits Enough?

Within the PC world, one could argue that the old 16-bit Intel x86 model (which actually provided 20 bits of address space) lasted for more than a decade and that the 32-bit architecture will last about that long before 64-bit programming starts to dominate.

We could, only half seriously, invoke the oft-quoted Moore's Law to the effect that cost/performance is halved every 18 months. In turn, speed and capacity approximately double every 18 months. Applying this argument to address space, we need one extra bit of address space every 18 months, implying that the 64-bit model should be good for 48 years (nearly as long as the history of modern computing). Whether or not this informal argument, which I have seen in a formal presentation, will hold, remains to be seen. However, PC resource requirements in the past have grown faster than this argument would predict.

The Win64 Programming Model

There are several possible programming model choices depending on how the standard C data types, such as pointers and integers (`long`, `int`, and `short`) are represented, and on whether or not nonstandard data types are added. Recall that ANSI Standard C does not strictly define the data type sizes, although it does require that a `long int` have at least as many bits as an `int`, which, in turn, must have at least as many as a `short int`.

The Goal

The objective is to have a single API definition for both Win32 and Win64, therefore allowing for a single source code base. Some source code changes may be required to use this single definition, but the changes should be minimized.

Microsoft selected the "LLP64" model (long long data type and 64-bit pointer), which is usually referred to simply as the "P64" model. In particular, for both signed and unsigned data, we have the following for the *standard* data types:

- A `char` is 8 bits, and a `wchar_t` data item is 16 bits.

- A `short int` requires 16 bits.

- An `int` is 32 bits.

- A `long int` is also 32 bits.

- A pointer of any type, such as `PVOID`, is 64 bits.

Additional data types are provided when you need to specify the length. Thus, `_int16`, `_int32`, and `_int64` are all data types recognized by the Microsoft compiler.

The Data Types

The Windows 2000 Software Development Kit (SDK), which is available to MSDN subscribers and is freely downloadable (there is more information at the end), provides additional types for fixed precision arithmetic and pointers of specific size. The tables below are taken directly from the on-line help and represent the Windows Uniform Data Model. The type definitions can be found in `BASETSD.H` (part of the Visual C++ system).

Fixed-Precision Types

The fixed-precision types provide a length suffix to familiar Win32 types such as `DWORD` and `LONG`, as shown in Table 16–1.

Table 16-1 The Fixed-Precision Data Types

Type	Definition
DWORD32	32-bit unsigned integer
DWORD64	64-bit unsigned integer
INT32	32-bit signed integer
INT64	64-bit signed integer
LONG32	32-bit signed integer
LONG64	64-bit signed integer
UINT32	Unsigned INT32
UINT64	Unsigned INT64
ULONG32	Unsigned LONG32
ULONG64	Unsigned LONG64

Pointer Precision Data Types

Quoting from the Microsoft paper, "The New Data Types," "As the pointer precision changes (that is, as it becomes 32 bits with Win32 code and 64 bits with Win64 code), these data types reflect the precision accordingly. Therefore, it is safe to cast a pointer to one of these types when performing pointer arithmetic; if the pointer precision is 64 bits, the type is 64 bits. The count types also reflect the maximum size to which a pointer can refer." These types, then, allow integer sizes to track pointer sizes and are sometimes called "polymorphic data types" or "platform scaled types." Table 16–2 shows the pointer precision data type.

SIZE_T is the most important of these data types and is used in Chapter 6 to describe memory block sizes.

Table 16-2 The Pointer Precision Data Types

Type	Definition
DWORD_PTR	Unsigned long type for pointer precision
HALF_PTR	Half the size of a pointer. Use within a structure that contains a pointer and two small fields.

Table 16-2   The Pointer Precision Data Types (cont.)

INT_PTR	Signed integral type for pointer precision
LONG_PTR	Signed long type for pointer precision
SIZE_T	The maximum number of bytes to which a pointer can refer. Use for a count that must span the full range of a pointer.
SSIZE_T	Signed SIZE_T
UHALF_PTR	Unsigned HALF_PTR
UINT_PTR	Unsigned INT_PTR
ULONG_PTR	Unsigned LONG_PTR

Example: Using Pointer Precision Data Types

The thread argument passed to a thread function by CreateThread and
_beginthreadex (see Chapter 8) is a PVOID pointer. In some situations, the pro-
grammer may wish only to pass an integer value indicating, for example, the
thread's number or an index to a global table. The thread function, which interprets the parameter as an unsigned integer, might be written as follows:

```
DWORD WINAPI MyThreadFunc (PVOID Index_PTR)
{
    DWORD_PTR Index;
    ...
    Index = (DWORD_PTR) Index_PTR;
    ...
}
```

Similarly, knowing that the actual argument is an integer, you might write the
main "parent" thread as:

```
    ...
    DWORD_PTR Ix;
    ...
    for (Ix = 0; Ix < NumThreads; Ix++) {
        hTh [Ix] = _beginthreadex (NULL, 0, MyThreadFunc,
            (PVOID) Ix, 0, NULL);
        ...
    }
```

Notice that existing code should be changed as required. There will be more about this later.

A Caution

Do not expect to have the full virtual address space, at least in initial implementations. Intel documentation shows a virtual address space of 512GB, indicating a limitation of 39 bits. Over time, this upper bound can be expected to change.

Windows and UNIX Divergence

Windows and UNIX have selected different strategies. Most UNIX vendors implement the "LP64 model," which means that both long and pointer data types are 64 bits. This is sometimes called the "I32, LP64" model to emphasize that int data types are still 32 bits. The divergence, then, is simply the length of long integers. What is more, the data types in Tables 16–1 and 16–2 are unique to Windows.

Both models represent reasonable solutions, and the UNIX choice is justified in the "Aspen" white paper given in the Additional Reading section. It would be convenient, however, if both operating systems used the same conventions.

The Three Win64 Programming Models

There are actually three programming models supported by Win64 running on IA-64 systems. Three models are required by backward compatibility considerations. Both binary and source compatibility are required.

The programming model is a property of a running process. Processes running different models can communicate using any appropriate interprocess communication mechanism, but the processes must be written carefully to ensure that communicated data is used and interpreted properly.

IA-64 with Constrained 64-Bit Pointers

This mode is appropriate when the full IA-64 power is required with a large application. Both source code changes and a recompile are required to use this model. This is necessary and possible because, while all pointers are 64 bits, the system calls never generate pointers that use the high-order 32 address bits. Program executable size will expand slightly.

The changes required in order to migrate a legacy application to the 64-bit pointer model are described in the next section.

Note that 32-bit DLLs cannot be used with 64-bit programs.

IA-64 with 32-Bit Pointers

This mode will yield the full performance advantages and is for applications with "small" virtual address spaces. These applications can (and must) use 64-bit DLLs and the 64-bit APIs. This is possible because pointers are truncated when system and other calls are made to 64-bit DLLs. The system loads the application into the lower 2GB of virtual address space.

This model requires a recompile and minimal source code changes. The changes are required primarily to deal with OS structures that contain 64-bit pointers.

IA-32 Binary Compatibility

Existing IA-32, Win32 binaries will run under Win64 without change. The application and Win32 libraries are hosted on the Win64 kernel.

For example, personal productivity applications (word processors, spread sheets, and the like) will most likely not be ported to Win64 in the immediate future.

Future development will also be supported, because compiler switches (_WIN32 and _WIN64) will allow the programmer to select between Win32 and Win64. Full performance is not ensured. Programs running in IA-32 binary compatibility mode must use 32-bit DLLs, including system DLLs.

IA-32 binary compatibility is simply a convenience ensuring that existing programs will run properly without recompilation.

Legacy Code Migration

The Windows Uniform Data Model is designed to minimize source code changes, but it is impossible to avoid modification altogether. For example, functions that deal directly with memory allocation and memory block sizes, such as Heap-Create and HeapAlloc (Chapter 6), must use either a 32- or 64-bit size field, depending on the model. Similarly, you need to examine code carefully to ensure that there are no hidden assumptions about the sizes of pointers and size fields.

API changes, primarily to the memory management functions, are described first.

API Changes

The most significant API changes are in the memory management functions introduced in Chapter 6. The new definitions use the SIZE_T data type (Table 16–2) in the count field. For example, the definition of HeapAlloc is:

```
LPVOID HeapAlloc (
    HANDLE hHeap,
    DWORD dwFlags,
    SIZE_T dwBytes);
```

The third field, the number of bytes requested, is of type `SIZE_T` and is therefore either a 64-bit or 32-bit unsigned integer. Previously, this field was defined to be a `DWORD` (always 32 bits).

`SIZE_T` is used as required in Chapter 6. Notice that the `HeapSize` function returns a `DWORD` according to the MSDN documentation at the time of writing.

Changes to Remove Data Item Size Assumptions

There are numerous potential problems based on data size assumptions. Here are a few examples.

- A `DWORD` is no longer appropriate for a memory block size. Use `SIZE_T` or `DWORD64` instead.

- Communicating processes, whether on the same system or on different systems, must be careful about field lengths. For instance, the Chapter 12 socket messages were defined with `LONG32` length fields to ensure that a port to UNIX would not result in a 64-bit field. Memory block sizes should be limited to 2GB during communication between Windows processes that use different models.

- Use `sizeof` to compute data structure lengths; literal constants should be removed (this, of course, is always good advice).

- Unions that mix pointers with arithmetic data types should be examined.

- Any cast or other conversion between a pointer and an arithmetic type should be examined carefully. For instance, see the code fragments in the example following Table 16–2.

- Additional structure padding caused by 64-bit pointers and integers can increase data structure size more than necessary. Moving such items to the beginning of a structure will minimize this "bloat."

- Use the format specifier "`%p`" rather than "`%x`" to print a pointer, and use a specifier such as "`%ld`" when printing a "platform scaled type" such as `SIZE_T`.

- `setjmp` and `longjmp` should use the `<setjmp.h>` ANSI C header rather than assuming anything about `jmp_buf`, which must contain a pointer.

Additional Reading

The best additional information sources are the MSDN library and information posted by Microsoft and Intel. Here are some suggestions.

- The Microsoft "New Data Types" article is available at: `http://msdn.microsoft.com//library/psdk/buildapp/64bitwin_7zg3.htm`. Tables 16–1 and 16–2 are from this article.

- The UNIX "Aspen" rationale, which makes a strong case for the LP64 model, is `http://www.opengroup.org/public/tech/aspen/lp64_wp.htm`

- The Intel developer's page at `http://developer.intel.com/design/ia64` provides extensive information regarding the IA-64 architecture, developer's manual, and much more.

APPENDIX

A | Using the Sample Programs

The CD-ROM included with this book contains the source code for all the sample programs as well as the include files, utility functions, and projects. A number of programs illustrate additional features and solve specific exercises, although the disc does not include solutions for all exercises or show every alternative implementation.

- All programs have been tested while running under Windows 2000 and NT on Intel and Digital Alpha systems. Where appropriate, they have also been tested under Windows 95 and Windows 98.

- The programs have been built and run with and without UNICODE defined under 2000/NT. Under Windows 9x, only the non-Unicode versions will operate.

- Nearly all programs compile without warning messages under Microsoft Visual C++ Version 6.0 using warning level 3. There are a few exceptions, such as warnings about "no return from main program" when ExitProcess is used.

- The Visual C++ generic C library functions are used extensively, as are compiler-specific keywords such as __try, __except, and __leave. The multithreaded C run-time library, _beginthreadex, and _endthreadex are essential starting with Chapter 8.

- The projects (in release, not debug, form) and make files are included. The projects are all very simple, with minimal dependencies, and can also be created quickly with the desired configuration and as either debug or release versions.

- Build all programs, with the exception of static or dynamic libraries, as *console* applications; projects are included.

Disc Organization

The primary directory is named `Win32Smp` ("Win32 Sample Programs"), and this directory can be copied directly to the hard disc. There is a subdirectory for each chapter. All include files are in the `Include` directory, and the `Utility` directory contains the commonly used functions such as `ReportError` and `PrintStrings`. Complete projects are in the `Projects` directory. Executables and DLLs for all projects are in the `Run` directory. The `TimeTest` directory contains files required to run the performance tests described in Appendix C.

The `Utility` Directory

The `Utility` directory contains six source files for utility functions required by the sample programs.

1. `ReprtErr.c` contains the functions `ReportError` (Program 2–2) and `ReportException` (see Program 4–1). Every program executed as a process by other sample programs requires this file, except for the `grep` and `wc` programs and those in Chapter 1.

2. `PrintMsg.c` contains `PrintStrings`, `PrintMsg`, and `ConsolePrompt` (Program 2–1). `ReprtErr.c` calls these functions, so this source file is also required in nearly every project.

3. `Options.c` contains the function that processes command line options and is used frequently starting in Chapter 2. Include this source file in the project for any program that has command line options. The listing is Program A–7.

4. `Wstrings.c` contains the source code for the `wmemchr` function used by `Options.c`. Include this file as necessary. You may find it convenient to add other generic string processing functions.

5. `SkipArg.c` processes a command line by skipping a single argument field with each call. It is listed in Program A–8.

6. `GetArgs.c` converts a character string into the `argc`, `argv [ ]` form. This function is useful when parsing a command line into individual arguments, such as the command line obtained from the `GetCommandLine` function introduced in Chapter 7. The listing is Program A–9.

The functions can be compiled and linked with the calling program. You will find it easiest, however, to build them as a library, either static or dynamic. If they are to be part of a DLL, you will need to define the `_UTILITY_EXPORTS` variable in `support.h` to export their definitions. The `utility` project builds a DLL from these source files, while `utilityStatic` is the project that creates a static library.

The `Include` Directory

The header files defined in the `Include` directory are as follows:

1. `EvryThng.h`, as the name suggests, brings in nearly everything required for normal programs, whether single-threaded or multithreaded. In particular, it includes the files `Envirmnt.h` and `Support.h`. The listing is Program A–1.

2. `Exclude.h` defines a number of preprocessor variables that exclude definitions not required by any of the programs in this book. This arrangement speeds compilation and reduces the size of the precompiled header files.

3. `Envirmnt.h` defines the UNICODE and _UNICODE preprocessor variables consistently as well as the language and sublanguage used by `ReportError`. Program A–2 lists this file.

4. `Support.h` defines many of the common functions, such as `ReportError`, as well as a variety of frequently used symbolic constants. Program A–3 shows this file.

5. `ClntSrvr.h` is used beginning in Chapter 11. It defines the request and response message structures, client and server named pipes and mailslots, time-out values, and so on. See Program A–5.

6. `JobMgt.h` is used in the job management programs at the end of Chapter 7. See Program A–4.

Programs by Chapter

Each chapter directory contains all the programs in that chapter (except for the programs in the `Utility` directory) as well as miscellaneous additional programs. The programs are listed here, with brief descriptions of the additional programs. You will also find a number of programs with an "x" suffix; these programs contain deliberate defects that illustrate common programming errors.

Chapter 1

- `cpC.c` is Program 1–1.

- `cpW.c` is Program 1–2; `cpwFA.c` shows the code modified for better performance. See the results in Appendix C.

- cpCF.c is Program 1–3.

- Other programs include a UNIX version (cpU.c) and one (cpUC.c) built to use the very limited UNIX compatibility library provided with Visual C++.

Chapter 2

- Programs 2–1 and 2–2 are in the Utility directory, which is described later.

- cat.c is Program 2–3.

- atou.c is Program 2–4.

- Asc2Un.c is Program 2–5; Asc2UnFA.c and Asc2UnNB.c are performance-enhanced versions. All three files implement the Asc2Un function called by Program 2–5.

- pwd.c is Program 2–6; pwda.c is modified to allocate the required memory for the pathname.

- cd.c is an implementation of the UNIX directory change command; it is not an example in Chapter 2.

Chapter 3

- tail.c is Program 3–1.

- ls.c is Program 3–2. rm.c is a similar program to remove files.

- touch.c is Program 3–3.

- getn.c is an additional program that reads a specified fixed-size record, illustrating file access and computing file positions.

- lsReg.c is Program 3–4.

- FileSize.c is an exercise solution that determines whether or not file space is allocated sparsely.

- TestLock.c exercises file locking.

Chapter 4

- Program 4–1 is part of ReprtErr.c in the Utility directory.

- toupper.c is Program 4–2.

- Excption.c is Program 4–3 and contains a filter function, Program 4–4.

- `Ctrlc.c` is Program 4–5.

Chapter 5

- `chmod.c` is Program 5–1.

- `lsFP.c` is Program 5–2.

- `InitUnFp.c` is the code for Programs 5–3, 5–4, and 5–5. Programs 5–1 and 5–2 require these functions. The source module also contains code showing how to obtain the name of an owning group, which is Exercise 7–11.

- `TestFp.c` is an additional test program that was useful during testing.

Chapter 6

- `sortBT.c` is Programs 6–1 and 6–2; `sortBTSR.c` omits the no-serialization option on memory management calls to determine whether there is any performance impact in a simple application. The reader can verify that there is very little effect.

- `Asc2UnMM.c` is the function for Program 6–3.

- `sortFL.c` is Program 6–4, and `sortHP.c` is a similar program except that it reads the file into an allocated memory buffer rather than using mapped memory.

- `sortMM.c` is Programs 6–5 and 6–6.

- `atouEL.c` is Program 6–7, and `Asc2UnDll.c` and `Asc2UnmmDLL.c` are the source files for the required DLLs.

- `HeapNoSr.c` is a test program that measures the effect of memory allocation with and without the `HEAP_NO_SERIALIZE` flag. This program can be used with Exercise 6–1.

- `clear.c` is a simple program that allocates and initializes virtual memory in large units, continuing until failure. This program is used between timing tests to ensure that data is not cached into memory, distorting the measurements.

Chapter 7

- `grepMP.c` is Program 7–1. `grep.c` is the source for a C library-based pattern search program to be invoked as a process by `grepMP.c`.

- `timep.c` is Program 7–2.

- `JobShell.c` is Program 7–3, and `JobMgt.c` provides the support functions of Programs 7–4, 7–5, and 7–6.

- `catHA.c` and `grepMPha.c` are modified versions of other programs designed to show how to pass a handle on the command line, solving Exercise 7–2.

Chapter 8

- `grepMT.c` is Program 8–1.

- `sortMT.c` is Program 8–2.

- `wcMT.c` solves Exercise 8–6.

Building the multithreaded applications requires the `LIBCMT.LIB` library when using Visual C++, and it is necessary to suppress the default library. This can be accomplished with the following steps:

1. From the main menu, select `Build...Settings...Link`.

2. Select the `Ignore All Default Libraries` checkbox.

3. Enter `LIBCMT.LIB` in the `Object/Library Modules:` window.

An even better method, used with all the supplied projects, is the following, with Visual C++:

1. From the main menu, select `Build...Settings...C/C++`.

2. Under `Category`, select `CodeGeneration`.

3. Select the appropriate multithreaded library.

This technique will define `_MT` on the command line generated to invoke the compiler.

Chapter 9

- `simplePC.c` is Program 9–1.

- `eventPC.c` is Program 9–2.

- `statsMX.c` is Program 9–3. Variations are `statsNS.c`, `statsCS.c`, and `statsIN.c`.

- `TimeMutualExclusion.c` is used for timing studies suggested in Exercise 9–10.

Chapter 10

- Program 10–1 contains part of `SynchObj.h`; Program 10–3 contains the rest.

- `ThbObject.c` is Program 10–2. `testTHB.c` is the associated test program.

- `QueueObj.c` is Program 10–4, and variations include `QueueObjCS.c` (uses a `CRITICAL_SECTION`), `QueueObjSOAW.c` (uses `SignalObjectAndWait`), and signal model versions.

- `ThreeStage.c` is Program 10–5, and its project requires `Messages.c` and `QueueObj.c`.

- `MultiSem.c`, along with the test program, `TestMultiSem.c`, is the solution to Exercise 10–12.

Chapter 11

- `pipe.c` is Program 11–1. `wc.c` is used as a convenient command to demonstrate its operation.

- `clientNP.c` is Program 11–2.

- `serverNP.c` is Program 11–3.

- `SrvrBcst.c` is Program 11–4.

- `LocSrver.c` is Program 11–5.

Chapter 12

- `clientSK.c` is Program 12–1.

- `serverSK.c` is Program 12–2.

- `command.c` is Program 12–3.

- `SendReceiveSKST.c` is Program 12–4, and `serverSKST.c` and `clientSKST.c` are slight modifications of `serverSK.c` and `clientSK.c` for streaming I/O. `SendReceiveSKST.c` should be built as a DLL, and the DLL should be implicitly linked with the client and server projects.

- `SendReceiveSKHA.c` is Program 12–5, and `serverSKHA.c` is the corresponding server that uses the DLL. `clientSKST` will work with this server.

Chapter 13

- `SimpleService.c` is Program 13–2 and includes all of Program 13–1.

- `ServiceShell.c` is Program 13–3.

- `serviceSK.c` is `serverSK.c` (Program 12–2) converted to a service.

Chapter 14

- `atouOV.c` is Program 14–1.

- `atouEX.c` performs the same task with extended I/O and is Program 14–2.

- `atouMT.c` performs the same task with multiple threads rather than with Win32 asynchronous I/O.

- `atouMTCP.c` uses I/O completion ports.

- `TimeBeep.c` is Program 14–3.

- `serverCP.c`, Program 14–4, is a version of `serverMT` that uses I/O completion ports and overlapped I/O.

Chapter 15

- `SysCommands.IDL` is Program 15–1.

- `SysCommandClient.c` and `SysCommandServer.c` represent Programs 15–2 and 15–3, respectively.

- `SysCommand_c.c` and `Syscommand_s.c` are the MIDL-generated client and server stubs, and `SysCommand.h` is the generated header file.

Include File Listings

EvryThng.h

Program A–1 `EvryThng.h` Include File

```
/* EvryThng.h - All standard and custom include files. */
#include "Exclude.h"
        /* Excludes definitions not required by sample programs. */
#include "envirmnt.h"
#include <windows.h>
#include <tchar.h>
```

```
#include <stdio.h>
#include <io.h>
#include "support.h"
#ifdef _MT
#include <process.h>
```

Envirmnt.h

Program A-2 Envirmnt.h Include File

```
/* Envirmnt.h - define UNICODE and _MT here. */
/* It is best and easiest to define UNICODE within the project. */
/* Use Project...Settings...C/C++. Then, in the "Project Options" */
/* window on the bottom, add /D "UNICODE". */
/* Do the same for _MT, and _STATIC_LIB. */

//#define UNICODE
#undef UNICODE
#ifdef UNICODE
#define _UNICODE
#endif

#ifndef UNICODE
#undef _UNICODE
#endif

//#define _MT
//#define _STATICLIB
        /* Define _STATICLIB if you are either building a */
        /* static library or linking with one. */
//#undef _STATICLIB
```

Support.h

Program A-3 Support.h Include File

```
/* Support.h */
/* Definitions of all symbolic constants and common
   utility functions used throughout the example programs. */

/* IT IS BEST TO DEFINE UTILITY_EXPORTS AND _STATICLIB WITHIN THE
   PROJECT RATHER THAN HERE, BUT THE DESCRIPTIONS ARE INCLUDED. */
/* The name "UTILITY_EXPORTS" is generated by Dev Studio when you
   create a DLL project named "Utility" and it is defined on the
   C command line. */
```

```
//#define UTILITY_EXPORTS Commented out; define within the project.

#ifdef UTILITY_EXPORTS
#define LIBSPEC _declspec (dllexport)
#else
#define LIBSPEC _declspec (dllimport)
#endif

#endif

#define EMPTY _T ("")
#define YES _T ("y")
#define NO _T ("n")
#define CR 0x0D
#define LF 0x0A
#define TSIZE sizeof (TCHAR)

/* Limits and constants. */
#define TYPE_FILE 1    /* Used in ls, rm, and lsFP. */
#define TYPE_DIR 2
#define TYPE_DOT 3

#define MAX_OPTIONS 20 /* Max # of command line options. */
#define MAX_ARG 1000    /* Max # of command line arguments. */
#define MAX_COMMAND_LINE MAX_PATH+50
        /* Max size of a command line. */

/* Commonly used functions. */
LIBSPEC BOOL ConsolePrompt (LPCTSTR, LPTSTR, DWORD, BOOL);
LIBSPEC BOOL PrintStrings (HANDLE, ...);
LIBSPEC BOOL PrintMsg (HANDLE, LPCTSTR);
LIBSPEC VOID ReportError (LPCTSTR, DWORD, BOOL);
LIBSPEC VOID ReportException (LPCTSTR, DWORD);
LIBSPEC DWORD Options (int, LPCTSTR *, LPCTSTR, ...);
LIBSPEC LPTSTR SkipArg (LPCTSTR);
LIBSPEC VOID GetArgs (LPCTSTR, int *, LPTSTR *);

/* Collection of generic string functions modeled after string.h.
   Created as required - there was only one! Implementation is
   derived from Plauger: The Standard C Library. */

LIBSPEC LPCTSTR wmemchr (LPCTSTR, TCHAR, DWORD);

#ifdef _UNICODE /* This declaration had to be added. */
#define _tstrrchr wcsrchr
#else
#define _tstrrchr strrchr
#endif
#ifdef _UNICODE /* This declaration had to be added. */
```

```
#define _tstrstr wcsstr
#else
#define _tstrstr strstr
#endif

#ifdef _UNICODE /* This declaration had to be added. */
#define _memtchr wmemchr
#else
#define _memtchr memchr
#endif

/* Security Functions. */
LPSECURITY_ATTRIBUTES InitializeUnixSA (DWORD, LPCTSTR,
      LPCTSTR, LPDWORD, LPHANDLE);
DWORD ReadFilePermissions (LPCTSTR, LPTSTR, LPTSTR);
BOOL ChangeFilePermissions (DWORD, LPCTSTR, LPDWORD);

/* Constants needed by the security functions. */
#define LUSIZE 1024
#define ACCT_NAME_SIZE LUSIZE
```

JobMgt.h

Program A–4   JobMgt.h Include File

```
/* JobMgt.h - Definitions required for job management.
   Chapter 7. */
/* Job management exit code for killed jobs. */

#define JM_EXIT_CODE 0x1000

typedef struct _JM_JOB
{
   DWORD ProcessId;
   TCHAR CommandLine [MAX_PATH];
} JM_JOB;
#define SJM_JOB sizeof (JM_JOB)

/* Job management functions. */
DWORD GetJobNumber (PROCESS_INFORMATION *, LPCTSTR);
BOOL DisplayJobs (void);
DWORD FindProcessId (DWORD);
BOOL GetJobMgtFileName (LPTSTR);
```

ClntSrvr.h

Program A–5 ClntSrvr.h Include File

```c
/* Definitions for client/server communication. */
/* Request and response messages. Messages are in ASCII as
   the request may be coming from a Windows 95 system. */

#define MAX_RQRS_LEN 0x1000

typedef struct {
   CHAR Command;
   BYTE Record [MAX_RQRS_LEN];
} REQUEST;

typedef struct {
   CHAR Status;
   BYTE Record [MAX_RQRS_LEN];
} RESPONSE;

#define RQ_SIZE sizeof (REQUEST)
#define RS_SIZE sizeof (RESPONSE)

/* Mailslot message structure. */
typedef struct {
   DWORD msStatus;
   DWORD msUtilization;
   TCHAR msName [MAX_PATH];
} MS_MESSAGE;

#define MSM_SIZE sizeof (MS_MESSAGE)

#define CS_TIMEOUT 5000
            /* Time-out period for named pipe
               connections and performance monitoring. */

#define MAX_CLIENTS 20

/* Client and server pipe & mailslot names. */
#define SERVER_PIPE _T ("\\\\.\\PIPE\\SERVER")
#define CLIENT_PIPE _T ("\\\\.\\PIPE\\SERVER")
#define SERVER_BROADCAST _T ("SrvrBcst.exe")
#define MS_SRVNAME _T ("\\\\.\\MAILSLOT\\CLS_MAILSLOT")
#define MS_CLTNAME _T ("\\\\.\\MAILSLOT\\CLS_MAILSLOT")
#define MX_NAME _T ("ClientServerMutex")
#define SM_NAME _T ("ClientServerSemaphore")

/* Commands for the statistics maintenance function. */
#define CS_INIT        1
#define CS_RQSTART     2
```

```
#define CS_RQCOMPLETE   3
#define CS_REPORT       4
#define CS_TERMTHD      5

/* Client/Server support functions. */

BOOL LocateServer (LPTSTR);
```

Exclude.h

Program A–6 defines numerous variables that will exclude definitions not required by the programs in the book. Rector and Newcomer discuss this in detail.

Program A–6 Exclude.h Include File

```
/* Exclude.h - Define variables to exclude selected header files.
   For a complete explanation, see Rector & Newcomer, Win32
   Programming, pp 25ff. */

#define WIN32_LEAN_AND_MEAN
        /* This has the largest impact, halving the precompiled
           header (pch) file size. */

/* These definitions also reduce the pch and improve compiling
   time. All the programs in the book will still compile with
   these definitions. You can also eliminate security with
   #define NOSECURITY. */

#define NOATOM
#define NOCLIPBOARD
#define NOCOMM
#define NOCTLMGR
#define NOCOLOR
#define NODEFERWINDOWPOS
#define NODESKTOP
#define NODRAWTEXT
#define NOEXTAPI
#define NOGDICAPMASKS
#define NOHELP
#define NOICONS
#define NOTIME
#define NOIMM
#define NOKANJI
#define NOKERNEL
#define NOKEYSTATES
#define NOMCX
#define NOMEMMGR
```

```
#define NOMENUS
#define NOMETAFILE
#define NOMSG
#define NONCMESSAGES
#define NOPROFILER
#define NORASTEROPS
#define NORESOURCE
#define NOSCROLL
#define NOSERVICE
#define NOSHOWWINDOW
#define NOSOUND
#define NOSYSCOMMANDS
#define NOSYSMETRICS
#define NOSYSPARAMS
#define NOTEXTMETRIC
#define NOVIRTUALKEYCODES
#define NOWH
#define NOWINDOWSTATION
#define NOWINMESSAGES
#define NOWINOFFSETS
#define NOWINSTYLES
#define OEMRESOURCE
```

Additional Utility Programs

Three additional utility programs—Options, SkipArg, and GetArgs—are sufficiently useful to list here. None, however, is dependent on Win32.

Options.c

This function scans the command line for words with the "–" (hyphen) prefix, examines the individual characters, and sets Boolean parameters. It is similar to the UNIX getopt function.

Program A–7 Options Function

```
/* Utility function to extract option flags from the command line. */

#include "EvryThng.h"
#include <stdarg.h>
DWORD Options (int argc, LPCTSTR argv [], LPCTSTR OptStr, ...)

/* argv is the command line. The options, if any, start
   with a '-' in argv [1], argv [2], ....
```

OptStr is a text string containing all possible
options, in one-to-one correspondence with the addresses of
Boolean variables in the variable argument list (...). These
flags are set if and only if the corresponding option character
occurs in argv [1], argv [2], ... The return value is the argv
index of the first argument beyond the options. */

```
{
    va_list pFlagList;
    LPBOOL pFlag;
    int iFlag = 0, iArg;

    va_start (pFlagList, OptStr);

    while ((pFlag = va_arg (pFlagList, LPBOOL)) != NULL
            && iFlag < (int) _tcslen (OptStr)) {
        *pFlag = FALSE;
        for (iArg = 1;
            !(*pFlag) && iArg < argc && argv [iArg] [0] == '-';
            iArg++)
            *pFlag = _memtchr (argv [iArg], OptStr [iFlag],
                    _tcslen (argv [iArg])) != NULL;
        iFlag++;
    }
    va_end (pFlagList);
    for (iArg = 1; iArg < argc && argv [iArg] [0] == '-'; iArg++);
    return iArg;
}
```

SkipArg.c

This function processes a command line string to skip over a white-space-
delimited field. It is first used in timep, Program 7–2.

Program A–8 SkipArg Function

```
/* SkipArg.c
    Skip one command line argument - skip tabs and spaces. */

#include "EvryThng.h"

LPTSTR SkipArg (LPCTSTR targv)
{
    LPTSTR p;
    p = (LPTSTR) targv;
            /* Skip up to the next tab or space. */
    while (*p != '\0' && *p != TSPACE && *p != TAB) p++;
            /* Skip over tabs and spaces to the next arg. */
```

```
    while (*p != '\0' && (*p == TSPACE || *p == TAB)) p++;
    return p;
}
```

GetArgs.c

This function scans a string for space- and tab-delimited words and puts the results in a string array passed to the function. It is useful for converting a command line string into an argv [ ] array, and it is used initially with JobShell in
Chapter 7. The Win32 function CommandLineToArgvW performs the same function but is limited to Unicode characters.

Program A–9 GetArgs Function

```
/* GetArgs. Process a command line string to put it in
   argc/argv form. */

#include "EvryThng.h"

VOID GetArgs (LPCTSTR Command, int *pArgc, LPTSTR argstr [])
{
    int i, icm = 0;
    DWORD ic = 0;

    for (i = 0; ic < _tcslen (Command); i++) {
        while (ic < _tcslen (Command) &&
                Command [ic] != TSPACE && Command [ic] != TAB) {
            argstr [i] [icm] = Command [ic];
            ic++; icm++;
        }
        argstr [i] [icm] = '\0';
        while (ic < _tcslen (Command) &&
                (Command [ic] == TSPACE || Command [ic] == TAB))
            ic++;
        icm = 0;
    }
    *pArgc = i;
}
```

B | Win32, UNIX, and C Library Comparisons

The tables in this appendix show the Win32 functions described in the main text along with the corresponding UNIX and ANSI Standard C library functions, if any.

The tables are arranged by chapter (some chapters are combined). Within each chapter, they are sorted first by functionality area (file system, directory management, and so on) and then by the Win32 function name.

Each table row gives the following information:

- The functionality area (subject).

- The Win32 function name.

- The corresponding UNIX function name. In some cases, there are more than one.

- The corresponding C library function name, if any.

- Comments as appropriate.

The notation used in the tables requires some explanation.

- The Microsoft Visual C++ library contains some UNIX compatibility functions. For example, _open is the compatibility library function for UNIX open. If the UNIX function is in italics, there is a compatibility function. An asterisk next to the name indicates that there is also a wide character Unicode version. For example, there is a _wopen function.

- A program that uses just the Standard C library, and no Win32 or UNIX system functions, should compile, build, and run on both systems if normal precautions are taken. Such a program will, however, be limited to simple file and I/O operations.

- Commas separating functions indicate alternatives, often with different characteristics or emulating one aspect of the Win32 function.

- Semicolons separating functions indicate that you use the functions in sequence to emulate the Win32 function. Thus, `fork; exec` corresponds to `CreateProcess`.

- An underlined entry indicates a global variable, such as `errno`.

- In a few cases, the UNIX equivalent may be stated imprecisely in terms such as "terminal I/O" for Win32 functions such as `AllocConsole`. Often, "Use the C library" is the appropriate comment, as in the case of `GetTempFileName`. In other cases, the situation is reversed. Thus, under the UNIX signal management functions (`sigaddset` and so on), the Win32 entry is "Use SEH" to indicate that the programmer should set up exception handlers and filter functions to get the desired behavior. Unlike UNIX, Win32 does not support process groups, so the Win32 entries are "N/A," although job management, as done by the programs in Chapter 8, could emulate process relationships.

- There are numerous "N/A" entries, especially for the C library, if there is no comparable function or set of functions. This is the case, for example, with directory management.

- The POSIX threads (Pthreads) functions are the UNIX equivalents shown in the table for Chapters 9 and 10, even though they are not properly a part of UNIX. Furthermore, even though many UNIX implementations have their own synchronization objects similar to events, mutexes, and semaphores, there is no attempt to list them here.

Generally, the correspondence is more precise in the earlier chapters, particularly for file management. The systems tend to diverge with the more advanced functionality and, in many cases, there is no C library equivalent. For example, the UNIX and Win32 security models differ significantly, so the relationships shown are approximations.

These functional correspondences are not exact. There are many differences, small and large, among the three systems. Therefore, these tables are only for guidance. The chapters discuss many of these differences.

The book's disc contains a spreadsheet with all this information. You may find it convenient to sort the spreadsheet in some other way, such as by UNIX function name.

Chapters 2 and 3: File and Directory Management

Subject	Win32	UNIX	C Library	Comments
Console I/O	AllocConsole	terminal I/O	N/A	
Console I/O	FreeConsole	terminal I/O	N/A	
Console I/O	ReadConsole	*read*	getc, scanf, gets	
Console I/O	SetConsoleMode	ioctl	N/A	
Console I/O	WriteConsole	*write*	putc, printf, puts	
Directory Mgt	CreateDirectory	*mkdir*[*]	N/A	Make a new directory
Directory Mgt	FindClose	*closedir*[*]	N/A	Close a directory search handle
Directory Mgt	FindFirstFile	*opendir*[*], *readdir*[*]	N/A	Find first file matching a pattern
Directory Mgt	FindNextFile	*readdir*[*]	N/A	Find subsequent files
Directory Mgt	GetCurrentDirectory	*getcwd*[*]	N/A	
Directory Mgt	GetFullPathName	N/A	N/A	
Directory Mgt	GetSystemDirectory	well-known pathnames	N/A	
Directory Mgt	RemoveDirectory	*rmdir, unlink*[*]	remove	
Directory Mgt	SearchPath	Use opendir, readdir	N/A	Search for a file on a specified path
Directory Mgt	SetCurrentDirectory	*chdir*[*], fchdir	N/A	Change the working directory
Error Handling	FormatMessage	strerror	perror	
Error Handling	GetLastError	<u>errno</u>	<u>errno</u>	Global variable
Error Handling	SetLastError	<u>errno</u>	<u>errno</u>	Global variable
File Locking	LockFile	fcntl (cmd=F_GETLK, ...)	N/A	
File Locking	LockFileEx	fcntl (cmd=F_GETLK, ...)	N/A	
File Locking	UnlockFile	fcntl (cmd=F_GETLK, ...)	N/A	

Chapters 2 and 3: File and Directory Management (cont.)

Subject	Win32	UNIX	C Library	Comments
File Locking	UnlockFileEx	fcntl (cmd=F_GETLK, ...)	N/A	
File System	CloseHandle (file handle)	close*	fclose	CloseHandle is not limited to files
File System	CopyFile	open; read; write; close	fopen; fread; fwrite; fclose	Duplicate a file
File System	CreateFile	open*, creat*	fopen	Open/create a file
File System	DeleteFile	unlink*	remove	Delete a file
File System	FlushFileBuffers	fsynch	fflush	Write file buffers
File System	GetFileAttributes	stat*, fstat*, lstat	N/A	
File System	GetFileInformation-ByHandle	stat*, fstat*, lstat	N/A	Fill structure with file info
File System	GetFileSize	stat*, fstat*, lstat	ftell, fseek	Get length of file in bytes
File System	GetFileTime	stat*, fstat*, lstat	N/A	
File System	GetFileType	stat*, fstat*, lstat	N/A	Check for character stream device or file
File System	GetStdHandle	Use file desc 0, 1, or 2	Use stdin, stdout, stderr	
File System	GetTempFileName	Use C library	tmpnam	Create a unique file name
File System	GetTempFileName, CreateFile	Use C library	tmpfile	Create a temporary file
File System	GetTempPath	/temp path	N/A	Directory for temp files
File System	MoveFile	Use C library	rename	Rename a file
File System	MoveFile	Use C library	rename	Rename a directory
File System	MoveFileEx	Use C library	rename	Rename a file
File System	N/A	link, unlink*	N/A	Win32 does not support links
File System	N/A	link	N/A	Win32 does not support links
File System	N/A	symlink	N/A	Create a symbolic link

Chapters 2 and 3: File and Directory Management (cont.)

Subject	Win32	UNIX	C Library	Comments
File System	N/A	`readlink`	N/A	Read name in a symbolic link
File System	N/A, `ReadFile` returns 0 bytes	N/A, `read` returns 0 bytes	`feof`	Rest for end of file
File System	N/A, use multiple `ReadFiles`	`readv`	N/A, use multiple `freads`	Scatter read
File System	N/A, use multiple `WriteFiles`	`writev`	N/A, use multiple `fwrites`	Gather write
File System	`ReadFile`	`read`	`fread`	Read data from a file
File System	`SetEndOfFile`	`chsize`*	N/A	
File System	`SetFileAttributes`	`fcntl`	N/A	
File System	`SetFilePointer`	`lseek`	`fseek`	Set file pointer
FileSystem	`SetFilePointer` (to 0)	`lseek (0)`	`rewind`	
File System	`SetFileTime`	`utime`*	N/A	
File System	`SetStdHandle`	`close, dup`*, `dup2`*, or `fcntl`	`freopen`	`dup2` or `fcntl`
File System	`WriteFile`	`write`	`fwrite`	Write data to a file
System Info	`GetDiskFreeSpace`	N/A	N/A	
System Info	`GetSystemInfo`	`getrusage`	N/A	
System Info	`GetVersion`	`uname`	N/A	
System Info	`GetVolume-Information`	N/A	N/A	
System Info	`GlobalMemoryStatus`	`getrlimit`	N/A	
System Info	Various defined constants	`sysconf, pathconf, fpathconf`	N/A	
Time	`GetSystemTime`	Use C library	`time, gmtime`	
Time	See `ls` program, Program 3–2	Use C library	`asctime`	

Chapters 2 and 3: File and Directory Management (cont.)

Subject	Win32	UNIX	C Library	Comments
Time	CompareFileTime	Use C library	difftime	Compare "calendar" times
Time	FileTimeToLocal-FileTime, File-TimeToSystemTime	Use C library	localtime	
Time	FileTimeToSystem-Time	Use C library	gmtime	
Time	GetLocalTime	Use C library	time, localtime	
Time	See touch program, Program 3–3	Use C library	strftime	
Time	SetLocalTime	N/A	N/A	
Time	SetSystemTime	N/A	N/A	
Time	Subtract file times	Use C library	difftime	
Time	SystemTimeToFile-Time	Use C library	mktime	

Chapter 4: Structured Exception Handling

Subject	Win32	UNIX	C Library
SEH	`_try — _except`	Use C library signals	Use C library signals
SEH	`_try — _finally`	Use C library signals	Use C library signals
SEH	`AbnormalTermination`	Use C library signals	Use C library signals
SEH	`GetExceptionCode`	Use C library signals	Use C library signals
SEH	`RaiseException`	Use C library signals	`signal, raise`
Signals	Use `_finally` block	Use C library	`atexit`
Signals	Use C library or terminate process	`kill`	`raise`
Signals	Use C library	Use C library	`signal`
Signals	Use SEH	`sigemptyset`	N/A
Signals	Use SEH	`sigfillset`	N/A
Signals	Use SEH	`sigaddset`	N/A
Signals	Use SEH	`sigdelset`	N/A
Signals	Use SEH	`sigismember`	N/A
Signals	Use SEH	`sigprocmask`	N/A
Signals	Use SEH	`sigpending`	N/A
Signals	Use SEH	`sigaction`	N/A
Signals	Use SEH	`sigsetjmp`	N/A
Signals	Use SEH	`siglongjmp`	N/A
Signals	Use SEH	`sigsuspendf`	N/A
Signals	Use SEH	`psignal`	N/A
Signals	Use SEH or C library	Use C library	`abort`

Note: Many UNIX vendors provide proprietary exception handling capabilities.

Chapter 5: Securing Win32 Objects

Subject	Win32	UNIX	Comments
Security	AddAccessAllowedAce	chmod, fchmod	C library does not support security
Security	AddAccessDeniedAce	chmod, fchmod	
Security	AddAuditAce	N/A	
Security	CreatePrivateObjectSecurity	N/A	
Security	DeleteAce	chmod, fchmod	
Security	DestroyPrivateObjectSecurity	N/A	
Security	GetAce	*stat*[*], *fstat*[*], lstat	
Security	GetAclInformation	*stat*[*], *fstat*[*], lstat	
Security	GetFileSecurity	*stat*[*], *fstat*[*], lstat	
Security	GetPrivateObjectSecurity	N/A	
Security	GetSecurityDescriptorDacl	*stat*[*], *fstat*[*], lstat	
Security	GetUserName	getlogin	
Security	InitializeAcl	N/A	
Security	InitializeSecurityDescriptor	*umask*	
Security	LookupAccountName	getpwnam, getgrnam	
Security	LookupAccountSid	getpwuid, getuid, geteuid	
Security	N/A	getpwend, setpwent, endpwent	
Security	N/A	getgrent, setgrent, endgrent	
Security	N/A	setuid, seteuid, setreuid	
Security	N/A	setgid, setegid, setregid	
Security	OpenProcessToken	getgroups, setgroups, initgroups	

Chapter 5: Securing Win32 Objects (cont.)

Subject	Win32	UNIX	Comments
Security	SetFileSecurity	*chmod**, fchmod	C library does not support security
Security	SetPrivateObjectSecurity	N/A	
Security	SetSecurityDescriptorDacl	*umask*	
Security	SetSecurityDescriptorGroup	chown, fchown, lchown	
Security	SetSecurityDescriptorOwner	chown, fchown, lchown	
Security	SetSecurityDescriptorSacl	N/A	

Chapter 6: Memory Management, Memory-Mapped Files, and DLLs

Subject	Win32	UNIX	C Library
Mapped Files	CreateFileMapping	shmget	N/A
Mapped Files	MapViewOfFile	mmap, shmat	N/A
Mapped Files	MapViewOfFileEx	mmap, shmat	N/A
Mapped Files	OpenFileMapping	shmget	N/A
Mapped Files	UnmapViewOfFile	munmap, shmdt, shmctl	N/A
Memory Mgt	GetProcessHeap	N/A	N/A
Memory Mgt	GetSystemInfo	N/A	N/A
Memory Mgt	HeapAlloc	sbrk or C library	malloc, calloc
Memory Mgt	HeapCreate	N/A	N/A
Memory Mgt	HeapDestroy	N/A	N/A
Memory Mgt	HeapFree	Use C library	free
Memory Mgt	HeapReAlloc	Use C library	realloc
Memory Mgt	HeapSize	N/A	N/A
Shared Memory	CloseHandle (map handle)	shmctl	N/A
Shared Memory	CreateFileMapping, OpenFileMapping	shmget	N/A
Shared Memory	MapViewOfFile	shmat	N/A
Shared Memory	UnmapViewOfFile	shmdt	N/A
DLLs	LoadLibrary	dlopen	N/A
DLLs	FreeLibrary	dlclose	N/A
DLLs	GetProcAddress	dlsyn	N/A
DLLs	DllMain	pthread_once	N/A

Chapter 7: Process Management

Subject	Win32	UNIX	C Library	Comments
Process Mgt	CreateProcess	fork (); *execl ()**	N/A	There are 6 execxx functions
Process Mgt	ExitProcess	_exit	exit	
Process Mgt	GetCommandLine	argv []	argv []	
Process Mgt	GetCurrentProcess	*getpid**	N/A	
Process Mgt	GetCurrentProcessId	*getpid**	N/A	
Process Mgt	GetEnvironmentStrings	N/A	getenv	
Process Mgt	GetEnvironmentVariable	N/A	getenv	
Process Mgt	GetExitCodeProcess	wait, waitpid	N/A	
Process Mgt	GetProcessTimes	times, wait3, wait4	N/A	
Process Mgt	GetProcessWorkingSetSize	wait3, wait4	N/A	
Process Mgt	N/A	*execl**, *execv**, *execle**, *execve**, *execlp**, *execvp**	N/A	Win32 does not have a direct equivalent
Process Mgt	N/A	fork, vfork	N/A	Win32 does not have a direct equivalent
Process Mgt	N/A	getppid	N/A	No parent/child relationships in Win32
Process Mgt	N/A	getgid, getegid	N/A	No process groups in Win32
Process Mgt	N/A	getpgrp	N/A	
Process Mgt	N/A	setpgid	N/A	
Process Mgt	N/A	setsid	N/A	
Process Mgt	N/A	tcgetpgrp	N/A	
Process Mgt	N/A	tcsetpgrp	N/A	
Process Mgt	OpenProcess	N/A	N/A	

Chapter 7: Process Management (cont.)

Subject	Win32	UNIX	C Library	Comments
Process Mgt	SetEnvironmentVariable	putenv	N/A	putenv is not part of the Standard C library
Process Mgt	TerminateProcess	kill	N/A	
Synch: Process	WaitForMultipleObjects (process handles)	waitpid	N/A	
Synch: Process	WaitForSingleObject (process handle)	wait, waitpid	N/A	
Timers	KillTimer	alarm (0)	N/A	
Timers	SetTimer	alarm	N/A	
Timers	Sleep	sleep	N/A	
Timers	Sleep	poll or select, no file descriptor	N/A	

Chapter 8: Threads and Scheduling

Subject	Win32	UNIX/Pthreads	Comments
Thread Mgt	`CreateRemoteThread`	N/A	
TLS	`TlsAlloc`	`pthread_key_alloc`	
TLS	`TlsFree`	`pthread_key_delete`	
TLS	`TlsGetValue`	`pthread_getspecific`	
TLS	`TlsSetValue`	`pthread_setspecific`	
Thread Mgt	`CreateThread,` `_beginthreadex`	`pthread_create`	
Thread Mgt	`ExitThread,` `_endthreadex`	`pthread_exit`	
Thread Mgt	`GetCurrentThread`	`pthread_self`	
Thread Mgt	`GetCurrentThreadId`	N/A	
Thread Mgt	`GetExitCodeThread`	`pthread_yield`	
Thread Mgt	`ResumeThread`	N/A	
Thread Mgt	`SuspendThread`	N/A	
Thread Mgt	`TerminateThread`	`pthread_cancel`	`pthread_cancel` is safer
Thread Mgt	`WaitForSingleObject` (thread handle)	`pthread_join`	
Thread Priority	`GetPriorityClass`	`pthread_attr_getschedpolicy`	
Thread Priority	`GetThreadPriority`	`pthread_attr_getschedparam`	
Thread Priority	`SetPriorityClass`	`pthread_attr_setschedpolicy`	
Thread Priority	`SetThreadPriority`	`pthread_attr_setschedparam`	

Note: Pthreads, while a part of most UNIX offerings, are available on non-UNIX systems as well.

Chapters 9 and 10: Thread Synchronization

Subject	Win32	UNIX/Pthreads	Comments
Synch: CritSec	DeleteCriticalSection		C library is not applicable
Synch: CritSec	EnterCriticalSection	Use mutexes to emulate critical sections	
Synch: CritSec	InitializeCriticalSection		
Synch: CritSec	LeaveCriticalSection		
Synch: Event	CloseHandle (event handle)	pthread_cond_destroy	
Synch: Event	CreateEvent	pthread_cond_init	
Synch: Event	PulseEvent	pthread_cond_signal	Manual-reset event
Synch: Event	ResetEvent	N/A	
Synch: Event	SetEvent	pthread_cond_broad-cast	Auto-reset event
Synch: Event	WaitForSingleObject (event handle)	pthread_cond_wait	
Synch: Event	WaitForSingleObject (event handle)	pthread_timed_wait	
Synch: Mutex	CloseHandle (mutex handle)	pthread_mutex_destroy	
Synch: Mutex	CreateMutex	pthread_mutex_init	
Synch: Mutex	ReleaseMutex	pthread_mutex_unlock	
Synch: Mutex	WaitForSingleObject (mutex handle)	pthread_mutex_lock	
Synch: Sem	CreateSemaphore	semget	
Synch: Sem	N/A	semctl	Win32 does not directly support all these options
Synch: Sem	OpenSemaphore	semget	
Synch: Sem	ReleaseSemaphore	semop (+)	
Synch: Sem	WaitForSingleObject (semaphore handle)	semop (-)	Win32 can wait for only one count

Chapter 11: Interprocess Communication

Subject	Win32	UNIX	C Library	Comments
IPC	CallNamedPipe	N/A	N/A	CreateFile, WriteFile, ReadFile, CloseHandle
IPC	CloseHandle (pipe handle)	close, msgctl	pclose	Not part of the Standard C library—see Stevens
IPC	ConnectNamedPipe	N/A	N/A	
IPC	CreateMailslot	N/A	N/A	
IPC	CreateNamedPipe	mkfifo, msgget	N/A	
IPC	CreatePipe	*pipe*	popen	Not part of the Standard C library—see Stevens
IPC	DuplicateHandle	*dup, dup2,* or *fcntl*	N/A	Or use file names CONIN$, CONOUT$
IPC	GetNamedPipeHandleState	*stat, fstat,* lstat64	N/A	
IPC	GetNamedPipeInfo	*stat, fstat,* lstat	N/A	
IPC	ImpersonateNamedPipeClient	N/A	N/A	
IPC	PeekNamedPipe	N/A	N/A	
IPC	ReadFile (named pipe handle)	read (fifo), msgsnd	N/A	
IPC	RevertToSelf	N/A	N/A	
IPC	SetNamedPipeHandleState	N/A	N/A	
IPC	TransactNamedPipe	N/A	N/A	WriteFile; ReadFile
IPC	WriteFile (named pipe handle)	write (fifo), msgrcv	N/A	
Misc.	GetComputerName	uname	N/A	
Misc.	SetComputerName	N/A	N/A	
Security	SetNamedPipeIdentity	Use directory sticky bit	N/A	

Chapter 14: Asynchronous I/O

Subject	Win32	UNIX	C Library	Comments
Asynch I/O	GetOverlappedResult	N/A	N/A	
Asynch I/O	ReadFileEx	N/A	N/A	Extended I/O with completion routine
Asynch I/O	SleepEx	N/A	N/A	Alertable wait
Asynch I/O	WaitForMultipleObjects (file handles)	poll, select	N/A	
Asynch I/O	WaitForMultipleObjectsEx	N/A	N/A	Alertable wait
Asynch I/O	WriteFileEx	N/A	N/A	Extended I/O with completion routine
Asynch I/O	WaitForSingleObjectEx	waitpid	N/A	Alertable wait

C | Performance Results

The example programs have shown a variety of alternative techniques for carrying out the same tasks, such as file copying and ASCII to Unicode file conversion, and it is natural to speculate about the performance advantages of these various techniques. Application design requires knowledge of, rather than speculation about, the performance impacts of alternative implementations and the potential performance advantages of various Win32 features, such as threads and asynchronous I/O. The timep program, Program 7–2, measures the real (elapsed) time, user time, and system (kernel) time required to execute a program and provides a convenient way to measure performance and determine the effects of alternative programming techniques and designs.

Test Configurations

Testing was performed with a representative variety of applications, based on examples in the book and a range of host systems.

Applications

The tables in this appendix show the times measured with timep for the test programs running on several different systems. The five functionality areas are as follows:

1. **File Copying**. Several different techniques, such as using the C library and the Win32 CopyFile function, are measured to determine the performance impact. File copying stresses file I/O without any data processing.

2. **ASCII to Unicode Conversion**. This shows the effect of memory mapping, larger buffers, the Win32 sequential scan flags, and asynchronous I/O. Conversion stresses file I/O with a small amount of data processing as the data is moved, and converted, from one buffer to another.

3. **Pattern Searching**. This uses the grep program in its multiprocess and multithreaded forms. Simple sequential processing is also tested and turns out to be competitive with the two parallel search methods on a single processor. Pattern searching increases the amount of data processing required and minimizes the output.

4. **File Sorting**. This shows the effect of memory mapping, in-memory techniques, and multithreading. Sorting, at least for large files, emphasizes CPU processing speed over file I/O.

5. **Multithreaded Producer/Consumer System**. This shows the effects of different synchronization techniques for implementing a multithreaded queueing system in order to evaluate the trade-offs discussed in Chapters 9 and 10 among CRITICAL_SECTIONs, mutexes, SignalObjectAndWait, and the signal and broadcast condition variable models.

All application programs were built with Microsoft Visual C++ as release versions rather than debug versions. Running in debug mode can add significant performance overhead. Nearly 80 percent overhead was observed in one CPU-intensive test, and the debug executable images can be two or three times larger than the release versions.

Host Systems

Performance was measured on seven systems with a wide variety of CPU, memory, disc, and OS configurations.

1. A 100MHz, 32MB Intel Pentium-based system running Windows 95 to measure the effect of Windows 95 and the FAT file system. These measurements show only the real time, because the GetProcessTimes function works only with NT.

2. A four-processor 400MHz Digital Alpha system using the FAT file system and NT Version 4.0. The processors were 400MHz EV5/400s. The system contained 1GB RAM. This system shows the effects of a high-performance CPU and multiple processors. An additional goal was to verify program portability to a non-Intel architecture. This system was designed for high I/O throughput as well as for fast CPU processing.

3. A 448MHz Pentium III system running NT 4.0.

4. A 450MHz Pentium III system running Windows 98.

5. A 333MHz AMD K6 laptop system running Windows 2000. Note: This system will demonstrate relatively slow file processing but competitive CPU processing. *The slow file processing should not be taken to mean that Windows 2000 file processing is slower than Windows NT or 9x file processing; the disc system used in the laptop is the cause of the slow file processing.* Other experiments on comparable systems yielded comparable file system performance for NT and 2000.

6. A 500MHz Pentium III system running Windows 2000, a FAT file system, and 64MB of RAM.

7. The same 500MHz Pentium III system, but using an NTFS partition.

Systems 6 and 7 allow us to compare the FAT and NTFS. System 2 shows how an SMP system can improve performance under the right conditions. Some of the tests were also run with only one of the four processors enabled, and many were also run on a four-processor 166MHz Intel system and on an NT 4.0/NTFS system, allowing a direct comparison of NT and Windows 9x. These extra results are cited as appropriate.

All file systems were less than 50 percent full and were not significantly fragmented. In addition, the systems were all idle, except for running the test programs. The CPU-intensive applications—the sort programs in particular—gave a good indication of relative processing speeds. The last five systems were newer and faster (with one exception), so they were timed on larger tasks.

Performance Measurements

Each application was run five times on the host system. Physical memory was cleared before each run so that performance figures would not be improved as the files and programs became cached in memory or the swap file. The averages are shown in the tables in the following sections. Times are in seconds. The complete results are in a spreadsheet on the disc.

Comments are listed after the tables. Needless to say, generalizations about performance can be perilous because numerous factors, including test program characteristics, contribute to a program's time performance. These tests do, however, show some of the possibilities and show the potential impacts of various file and operating systems and different programming techniques. Also bear in mind that the tests measure the time from program start to end but do not measure the time that the system might take to flush buffers to the disc. Finally, there was no attempt to exploit specific system features or parameters, such as stripped discs, disc block sizes, multiple disc partitions, and so on.

The Windows 2000/NT performance monitor, available under the Administrative Tools, displays CPU, kernel, user, and other activities graphically. This tool is invaluable in gaining insight into program behavior beyond the measurements given here.

The results show that performance varies widely based on your CPU, file system, disc configuration, program design, and many other factors. The timing programs are all on the disc so that you can perform these tests on your own system.

File Copying

Five file copy implementations were used to copy a 5MB file (first two columns of Table C–1) and a 25.6MB file (last five columns).

1. cpC (Program 1–1) uses the C library. This test measures the effect of an implementation layered on top of Win32, although the library has the opportunity to perform efficient buffering and other techniques.

2. cpW (Program 1–2) is the straightforward Win32 implementation with a small buffer (256 bytes).

3. cpwFA is a "fast" implementation, using a large buffer (8,192 bytes, a multiple of the sector size on all host systems) and the sequential scan flags on both the input and output files.

4. cpCF (Program 1–3) uses the Win32 CopyFile function to determine whether the implementation within a single system call is more efficient than what can be achieved with other techniques.

5. cpUC is a UNIX implementation using a small buffer (similar to cpW). It is modified slightly to use the Visual C++ UNIX compatibility library.

Table C-1 File Copy Performance

		Pentium	4x Alpha	Pentium III	Pentium	AMD K6	Pentium III	Pentium III
	CPU	Pentium	4x Alpha	Pentium III	Pentium	AMD K6	Pentium III	Pentium III
	OS	W95	NT 4.0	NT 4.0	W98	W2000	W2000	W2000
	File System	FAT	FAT	NTFS	FAT	NTFS	FAT	NTFS
cpC	Real	0.74	0.11	11.86	9.49	39.39	8.62	14.69
	User	N/A	0.04	0.27	N/A	0.28	0.12	0.12
	System	N/A	0.08	2.42	N/A	2.37	0.24	0.52
cpW	Real	2.69	0.30	15.50	21.61	48.72	8.49	13.35
	User	N/A	0.04	0.36	N/A	0.47	0.13	0.12
	System	N/A	0.27	11.64	N/A	10.27	0.88	1.37
cpwFA	Real	0.44	0.09	8.67	8.59	37.38	8.35	12.59
	User	N/A	0.01	0.02	N/A	0.03	0.01	0.02
	System	N/A	0.08	2.34	N/A	1.91	0.40	0.50
cpCF	Real	0.35	0.08	12.33	8.08	36.29	8.00	11.69
	User	N/A	0.01	0.01	N/A	0.02	0.02	0.01
	System	N/A	0.08	2.16	N/A	1.44	0.19	0.25
cpUC	Real	1.90	0.53	14.68	12.67	41.12	7.84	13.14
	User	N/A	0.43	0.91	N/A	1.53	0.72	0.66
	System	N/A	0.09	5.13	N/A	4.91	0.40	0.67
		5MB File		*25.6MB File*				

Comments

1. The NTFS does not necessarily give better performance than the FAT file system. On the contrary, the FAT can be faster, as can be seen by comparing columns 6 and 7.

2. The C library gives competitive performance that is superior to the simplest Win32 implementation in many cases.

3. You can gain significant performance advantages by using large buffers, sequential scan flags, or a function such as CopyFile. Notice the very small user times for cpwFA and cpCF.

4. The laptop Windows 2000 file processing performance is much slower than that of other systems. As noted previously, however, W2000 file processing performance is comparable to NT performance on similar systems, as shown in the last two columns.

5. The UNIX compatibility library is usable, giving performance that is comparable to that of the Win32 counterpart in most cases.

ASCII to Unicode Conversion

Eight programs were measured, all converting the same 5MB file to a 10MB file (first two columns of Table C–2) and a 12.8MB file to a 25.6MB file (last five columns).

1. atou is Program 2–4 and is comparable to cpW using a small buffer.

2. atouSS is the first "fast" implementation based on atou. It uses the sequential scan flags but a small buffer.

3. atouLB uses a large buffer (8,192 bytes) but does not use the sequential scan flags.

4. atouLBSS uses both a large buffer and sequential scan flags, making it comparable to cpwFA.

5. atouMM uses memory mapping for file I/O and calls the functions in Program 6–3.

6. atouMT is a multithreaded implementation of Chapter 14's multiple buffer scheme without asynchronous I/O.

7. atouOV, Program 14–1, uses overlapped I/O and does not run on the two Windows 9x systems.

8. atouEX, Program 14–2, uses extended I/O and does not run on the two Windows 9x systems.

Table C-2 ASCII to Unicode Performance

	CPU	Pentium	4x Alpha	Pentium	Pentium	AMD K6	Pentium III	Pentium III
	OS	W95	NT 4.0	NT 4.0	W98	W2000	W2000	W2000
	File System	FAT	FAT	NTFS	FAT	NTFS	FAT	NTFS
atou	Real	5.09	0.49	12.47	14.33	49.92	3.24	7.16
	User	N/A	0.15	0.42	N/A	0.42	0.31	0.33
	System	N/A	0.31	6.82	N/A	8.49	0.46	0.72
atouSS	Real	4.52	0.50	9.73	14.61	41.95	3.77	6.21
	User	N/A	0.14	0.35	N/A	0.46	0.20	0.23
	System	N/A	0.34	6.91	N/A	8.23	0.52	0.81
atouLB	Real	1.19	0.27	10.30	5.71	34.53	4.38	6.41
	User	N/A	0.14	0.11	N/A	0.33	0.10	0.07
	System	N/A	0.13	3.30	N/A	1.40	0.26	0.34
atouLBSS	Real	1.04	0.28	12.94	6.80	31.04	4.63	6.05
	User	N/A	0.12	0.17	N/A	0.23	0.11	0.14
	System	N/A	0.14	3.82	N/A	1.47	0.21	0.27
atouMM	Real	3.16	3.13	2.29	8.02	28.47	4.35	2.75
	User	N/A	0.23	0.32	N/A	0.73	0.27	0.29
	System	N/A	0.09	1.74	N/A	0.83	0.19	0.19
atouMT	Real	9.40	0.62	15.27	12.57	38.95	4.84	6.18
	User	N/A	0.15	0.15	N/A	0.42	0.14	0.15
	System	N/A	0.43	2.61	N/A	1.30	0.45	0.46
atouOV	Real	N/A	0.31	13.32	N/A	39.36	9.54	8.85
	User	N/A	0.15	0.16	N/A	0.37	0.14	0.12
	System	N/A	0.17	1.00	N/A	1.16	0.24	0.23
atouEX	Real	N/A	0.31	12.46	N/A	32.89	5.67	5.92
	User	N/A	0.16	3.90	N/A	3.10	1.10	1.50
	System	N/A	0.16	5.00	N/A	3.51	1.19	1.74

| *5MB File* | | | *25.6MB File* | | | | |

Comments

1. These results reinforce the importance of using large buffers and the sequential scan flags in conjunction. Using large buffers is the more important of the two.

2. Overlapped I/O, in addition to being limited to Windows NT and very difficult to program, gives poor performance. Notice that the time is predominantly real time and not user or system time. It appears that the system has difficulty scheduling the disc access, and experiments with different buffer sizes (larger and smaller) did not help until 65K buffers were used.

3. Extended I/O and multiple threads do not provide any significant benefit.

4. Memory-mapped I/O can give very good performance on the NTFS, but FAT performance with memory mapping can be poor. Tests with Windows 3.51 show that `atouMM` performance on NTFS improved dramatically with Version 4.0. Using an NTFS, the four-processor Alpha system (column 2) gave competitive results (0.32 second). `atouMM` results are not as good, however, when the files are larger than about one-third of the physical memory size; this is discussed in Chapter 6.

Pattern Searching

Three pattern searching methods were tested to compare the efficiencies of multiple threads and processes as well as sequential processing (see Table C–3).

1. `grepMP`, Program 7–1, searches with parallel processes, each processing a separate file. The system and user times are not given, because `timep` measures only the parent process.

2. `grepMT`, Program 8–1, uses parallel threads.

3. `grepSQ` is a DOS batch file that searches each file in sequence. Again, only the real time is available.

The 20 target files used in the test varies in size from a few kilobytes to more than one megabyte. As before, the last five columns show results obtained with larger files.

Table C-3   Pattern Searching Performance

		Pentium	4x Alpha	Pentium	Pentium	AMD K6	Pentium III	Pentium III
	CPU							
	OS	W95	NT 4.0	NT 4.0	W98	W2000	W2000	W2000
	File System	FAT	FAT	NTFS	FAT	NTFS	FAT	NTFS
grepMP	Real	12.79	1.06	1.77	5.32	28.59	5.77	4.04
	User	N/A	N/A	N/A	N/A	N/A	N/A	N/A
	System	N/A	N/A	N/A	N/A	N/A	N/A	N/A
grepMT	Real	10.94	0.43	1.33	3.52	27.48	4.57	1.49
	User	N/A	1.36	0.97	N/A	1.76	0.90	0.90
	System	N/A	0.14	0.35	N/A	0.60	0.10	0.11
grepSQ	Real	6.33	1.94	1.76	6.24	24.67	1.62	1.56
	User	N/A	N/A	N/A	N/A	N/A	N/A	N/A
	System	N/A	N/A	N/A	N/A	N/A	N/A	N/A

Smaller Files   *Larger Files*

Comments

1. In most cases, all three techniques provide similar results on single-processor systems.

2. Multithreading offers a slight advantage over multiple processes, even on single-processor systems. SMP systems show the performance gains that are possible using threads or multiple single-threaded processes. Notice that the total user time exceeds the real time, because the user time represents all four processors. Tests on a four-processor 166MHz Intel system showed similar improvements (1.75, 1.45, and 4.77 seconds real time). When the tests were performed on the same Alpha system with only a single processor enabled, the times were 2.15, 2.10, and 2.04 seconds.

3. There is some indication, particularly from the last two columns, that the NFTS provides superior performance with multiple threads, although there was wide variation within a single test case.

4. The fact that the sequential processing gave such similar results on single-processor systems indicates that the simplest solution is sometimes the best.

File Sorting

A target sort file of about a megabyte (15,949 64-byte records) was used to test four sort implementations from Chapter 8, as shown in the first two columns in Table C–4. The sorted file output was suppressed in all cases so as to emphasize the time required to perform the sorting itself. Then a multithreaded sort, Program 8–2, of an 8MB file with about 128,000 64-byte records was tested with one, two, and four threads. Each individual run used a different file, created by the RandFile program that is in the Chapter 6 directory. There was considerable variation from one run to the next (see Table C–4). CPU performance is more significant than file system performance in these tests, although the FAT times are generally lower than the NTFS times because the files still must be loaded into memory.

The performance data in the last five columns is for a 6.4MB file for the single-threaded sorts and a 25.6MB file for the sortMT test cases.

1. sortBT is Program 6–1, which creates a binary search tree, requiring a memory allocation for each record. This program is CPU-intensive.

2. sortFL is Program 6–4, which maps the file before using qsort. sortFLSR (heap access was serialized) was also tested but showed no measurable difference.

3. sortHP is not listed in the text. It preallocates a buffer for the file and then reads the file into the buffer for sorting rather than mapping the file as sortFL does.

4. sortMM is Program 6–5, which creates a permanent index file.

5. sortMT is Program 8–2, the multithreaded sort-merge. The results are shown as sortMT1, sortMT2, and sortMT4, according to the number of parallel threads.

6. Results can differ significantly depending on the nature of the file to be sorted. This is a characteristic of the underlying quicksort algorithm used to implement the qsort C library function.

Table C-4 File Sorting Performance

	CPU	Pentium	4x Alpha	Pentium	Pentium	AMD K6	Pentium III	Pentium III
	OS	W95	NT 4.0	NT 4.0	W98	W2000	W2000	W2000
	File System	FAT	FAT	NTFS	FAT	NTFS	FAT	NTFS
sortBT	Real	46.83	5.71	154.45	184.72	54.10	17.57	19.52
	User	N/A	0.76	19.52	N/A	13.09	5.33	5.15
	System	N/A	4.96	134.33	N/A	38.27	12.13	14.22
sortFL	Real	0.90	0.30	3.69	3.08	6.84	1.98	2.42
	User	N/A	0.28	1.17	N/A	3.87	1.84	1.84
	System	N/A	0.02	0.25	N/A	0.35	0.08	0.08
sortHP	Real	0.55	0.27	0.98	1.40	1.45	0.89	0.73
	User	N/A	0.26	0.74	N/A	0.98	0.66	0.66
	System	N/A	0.02	0.08	N/A	0.29	0.06	0.07
sortMM	Real	2.16	N/A	10.82	15.64	7.06	1.14	1.41
	User	N/A	N/A	0.80	N/A	1.01	0.60	0.57
	System	N/A	N/A	10.00	N/A	5.67	0.48	0.74
sortMT1	Real	7.37	2.64	0.43	4.45	27.18	2.51	5.03
	User	N/A	2.55	0.01	N/A	0.01	0.01	0.01
	System	N/A	0.10	0.41	N/A	1.23	0.30	0.31
sortMT2	Real	8.11	1.51	1.53	2.93	22.44	2.21	3.92
	User	N/A	2.58	0.01	N/A	0.01	0.01	0.01
	System	N/A	0.11	0.32	N/A	1.14	0.30	0.33
sortMT4	Real	8.12	1.04	0.44	2.88	21.06	2.20	3.96
	User	N/A	2.68	0.02	N/A	0.01	0.01	0.01
	System	N/A	0.15	0.42	N/A	1.31	0.23	0.30

Smaller Files　　　　　　　　*Larger Files*

Comments

1. The binary tree implementation, sortBT, is CPU-intensive; it must allocate storage for each record one at a time. Heap serialization had no significant impact in this example.

2. Memory mapping and reading the file into a preallocated buffer yield similar performance, but the memory mapping was not as good in these tests.

3. sortMT demonstrates the potential of SMP systems, and these results were confirmed on the four-processor Intel SMP system. Additional threads also helped, in general, on single-processor systems.

Multiple Threads Contending for a Single Resource

This test sequence compares different strategies for implementing the queue management functions of Program 10–4, using Program 10–5 (the three-stage pipeline) as a test application. The tests were run using 1, 2, 4, 8, 16, 32, and 64 threads, but in all seven cases each thread was asked to perform 1,000 units of work. The host system was a 500MHz Pentium III running Windows 2000. Ideally, we would then expect real time to increase linearly with the number of threads, but contention for a single mutex (or CS) causes nonlinear degradation as the number of threads increases.

Note that these tests do not exercise the file system.

Six different implementation strategies were used, and the results are shown in separate columns in Table C–5. The comments following Program 10–4 discuss the results and explain the merits of the different implementations, but notice that the signal model is more scalable than the broadcast model.

1. Broadcast model, mutex, event, separate release and wait calls. The tunable time-out was set to 5 ms, which optimized the 16-thread case.

2. Broadcast model, CRITICAL_SECTION, event, separate release and wait calls. The tunable time-out was set to 25 ms, which optimized the 16-thread case.

3. Broadcast model, mutex, event, atomic SignalObjectAndWait call.

4. Signal model, mutex, event, separate release and wait calls.

5. Signal model, CRITICAL_SECTION, event, separate release and wait calls.

6. Signal model, mutex, event, atomic SignalObjectAndWait call.

Table C-5 Multithreaded Pipeline Performance

Number of Threads		Broadcast Model Mtx, Evt 5-ms T/O	Broadcast Model Crit Sec, Evt 25-ms T/O	Broadcast Model Mtx, Evt `SigObjWait`	Signal Model Mtx, Evt Time-out N/A	Signal Model Crit Sec, Evt Time-out N/A	Signal Model Mtx, Evt `SigObjWait`
1	Real	1.02	0.08	0.12	0.10	0.80	0.10
	User	0.01	0.08	0.05	0.09	0.60	0.08
	System	0.01	0.01	0.06	0.01	0.30	0.03
2	Real	0.74	0.16	0.02	0.20	0.16	0.19
	User	0.01	0.12	0.11	0.12	0.15	0.13
	System	0.05	0.05	0.10	0.09	0.20	0.07
4	Real	2.56	0.35	0.43	0.40	0.31	0.39
	User	0.01	0.23	0.30	0.30	0.21	0.29
	System	0.02	0.13	0.14	0.11	0.11	0.11
8	Real	2.98	0.80	1.02	0.80	0.62	0.79
	User	0.14	0.49	0.58	0.49	0.49	0.54
	System	0.10	0.30	0.45	0.31	0.14	0.26
16	Real	5.51	1.88	2.64	1.71	1.37	1.69
	User	0.50	1.10	1.48	1.61	1.09	1.03
	System	0.56	0.79	1.16	0.56	0.29	0.66
32	Real	11.54	5.66	8.43	3.81	3.13	3.73
	User	2.39	2.72	3.23	2.37	2.36	2.51
	System	2.97	2.93	5.18	1.47	0.77	1.22
64	Real	42.76	25.73	33.63	7.96	6.60	7.80
	User	10.68	9.53	11.10	5.34	5.00	5.29
	System	18.22	16.09	22.51	2.62	1.61	2.46

Running the Tests

The `TimeTest` directory includes the following batch files for both Windows 2000/NT and Windows 9x operation:

- `cpTIME.bat`

- `atouTIME.bat`

- `grepTIME.bat`

- `sortTIME.bat`

- `threeST.bat`

To perform each timing sequence, the program `RandFile` creates a large ASCII file that is used for the first two test sequences.

Bibliography

Beveridge, Jim, and Wiener, Robert. *Multithreading Applications in Win32*, Addison-Wesley, Reading, MA, 1997, ISBN: 0-201-44234-5.

Box, Don. *Essential COM*, Addison-Wesley, Reading, MA, 1998, ISBN: 0-201-63446-5.

Box, Don (Editor) et al. *Effective COM: 50 Ways to Improve Your COM and MTS-Based Applications*, Addison-Wesley, Reading, MA, 1999, ISBN: 0-20-1-37968-6.

Brain, Marshall. *Win32 System Services: The Heart of Windows 95 and Windows NT*, Prentice Hall, Englewood Cliffs, NJ, 1996, ISBN: 0-13-324732-5.

Butenhof, David. *Programming with POSIX Threads*, Addison-Wesley, Reading, MA, 1997, ISBN: 0-201-63392-2.

Cohen, Aaron, Woodring, Mike, and Petrusha, Ronald. *Win32 Mutltithreaded Programming*, O'Reilley & Associates, Sebastopol, CA, 1998, ISBN: 1-565-92296-4.

Comer, Douglas E., and Stevens, David L. *Internetworking with TCP/IP, Volume III: Client-Server Programming and Applications, Windows Sockets Version*, Prentice Hall, Upper Saddle River, NJ, 1997, ISBN: 0-13-848714-6.

Custer, Helen. *Inside Windows NT*, Microsoft Press, Redmond, WA, 1993, ISBN: 1-55615-481-X. *Second edition (see below) by David Solomon replaces this book.*

Custer, Helen. *Inside the Windows NT File System*, Microsoft Press, Redmond, WA, 1994, ISBN: 1-55615-660-X.

Davis, Ralph. *Win32 Network Programming: Windows 95 and Windows NT Network Programming Using MFC* (also see the predecessor, *Windows NT Programming: How to Survive in a 32-bit Networking World*), Addison-Wesley, Reading, MA, 1996, ISBN: 0-201-48930-9.

Department of Defense. *DoD Trusted Computer System Evaluation Criteria*, DoD 5200.28-STD, DoD Computer Security Center, 1985. Available via anonymous `ftp` from `ftp.cert.org` as `/pub/info/orange-book.Z`.

Eddon, G., and Eddon, D. *Inside Distributed COM*, Microsoft Press, Redmond, WA, 1998, ISBN: 1-57231-849-X.

Feuer, Alan. *MFC Programming*, Addison-Wesley, Reading, MA, 1997, ISBN: 0-201-63358-2.

Gilly, Daniel, and the staff of O'Reilly & Associates, Inc. *UNIX in a Nutshell*, O'Reilly & Associates, Inc., Sebastopol, CA, 1992, ISBN: 1-56592-001-5.

Hipson, Peter D. *Expert Guide to Windows NT 4 Registry*, Sybex, 1999, ISBN: 0-7821-1983-2.

Kano, Nadine. *Developing International Applications for Windows 95 and Windows NT*, Microsoft Press, Redmond, WA, 1995, ISBN: 1-55615-840-8.

Kernighan, Brian W., and Ritchie, Dennis M. *The C Programming Language (2nd ed.)*, Prentice-Hall, Englewood Cliffs, NJ, 1988, ISBN: 0-13-110370-9.

Miller, Kevin. *Professional NT Services*, WROX, 1998, ISBN: 1-86100-130-4.

Myers, Brian, and Hamer, Eric. *Mastering Windows NT Programming*, Sybex, Alameda, CA, 1993, ISBN: 0-7821-1264-1.

Nottingham, Jason P., Makofsky, Steven, and Tucker, Andrew. *SAMS Teach Yourself Windows CE Programming in 24 hours*, SAMS, 1999, ISBN: 0-6723-1658-7.

O'Donnell, Sandra Martin. *Programming for the World: A Guide to Internationalization*, Prentice-Hall, Englewood Cliffs, NJ, 1994, ISBN: 0-13-722190-8.

Pham, Thuan, and Garg, Pankaj. *Multithreaded Programming with Win32*, Prentice-Hall, Englewood Cliffs, NJ, 1998, ISBN: 0-130-10912-6.

Plauger, P. J. *The Standard C Library*, Prentice-Hall, Englewood Cliffs, NJ, 1992, ISBN: 0-13-131509-9.

Quinn, Bob, and Shute, Dave. *Windows Sockets Network Programming*, Addison-Wesley, Reading, MA, 1996, ISBN: 0-201-63372-8.

Rector, Brent, and Newcomer, Joseph M. *Win32 Programming*, Addison-Wesley, Reading, MA, 1997, ISBN: 0-201-63492-9.

Richter, Jeffrey. *Programming Applications for Microsoft Windows* (formerly *Advanced Windows NT: The Developer's Guide to the Win32 Application Programming Interface* in previous editions), Microsoft Press, Redmond, WA, 1999, ISBN: 1-57-231996-8.

Richter, Jeffrey, and Clark, Jason. *Programming Server-Side Applications for Microsoft Windows 2000*, Microsoft Press, Redmond, WA, 2000, ISBN: 0-73-560753-2.

Robbins, Kay A., and Robbins, Steven. *Practical UNIX Programming: A Guide to Concurrency, Communication, and Multithreading*, Prentice-Hall, Englewood Cliffs, NJ, 1995, ISBN: 0-13-443706-3.

Rosenberry, Ward, Kenney, David, and Fisher, Gerry. *Understanding DCE*, O'Reilly & Associates, Sebastapol, CA, 1992, ISBN: 1-56592-005-8.

Rosenberry, Ward, and Teague, Jim. *Distributing Applications Across DCE and Windows NT*, O'Reilly & Associates, Sebastapol, CA, 1993, ISBN: 1-56592-047-3.

Sedgewick, Robert. *Algorithms in C*, Addison-Wesley, Reading, MA, 1990, ISBN: 0-201-51425-7.

Shirley, John. *Guide to Writing DCE Applications*, O'Reilly & Associates, Sebastapol, CA, 1993, ISBN: 1-56592-004-X.

Silberschatz, Abraham, and Galvin, Peter B. *Operating System Concepts (4th ed.)*, Addison-Wesley, Reading, MA, 1994, ISBN: 0-201-50480-4.

Sinha, Alok K. *Network Programming in Windows NT*, Addison-Wesley, Reading, MA, 1996, ISBN: 0-201-59056-5.

Solomon, David. *Inside Windows NT, Second Edition*, Microsoft Press, Redmond, WA, 1998, ISBN: 1-57-231677-2 .

Standish, Thomas A. *Data Structures, Algorithms and Software Principles in C*, Addison-Wesley, Reading, MA, 1995, ISBN: 0-201-59118-9.

Stevens, W. Richard. *Advanced Programming in the UNIX Environment*, Addison-Wesley, Reading, MA, 1992, ISBN: 0-201-56317-7.

Stevens, W. Richard. *TCP/IP Illustrated, Volume 3: TCP for Transactions, HTTP, NNTP, and the UNIX Domain Protocols*, Addison-Wesley, Reading, MA, 1996, ISBN:0-201-63495-3.

Stevens, W. Richard. *UNIX Network Programming—Networking APIs: Sockets and XTI, Volume I*, Prentice-Hall, Upper Saddle River, NJ, 1998, ISBN: 0-13-490012-X.

Sutton, Stephen A. *Windows NT Security Guide*, Addison-Wesley, Reading, MA, 1997, ISBN: 0-201-41969-6.

Unicode Consortium, The. *The Unicode Standard, Version 2.0*, Addison-Wesley, Reading, MA, 1996, ISBN: 0-201-48345-9.

Weiss, Mark Allen. *Data Structures and Algorithm Analysis in C*, Addison-Wesley, Reading, MA, 1993, ISBN: 0-8053-5440-9.

Index

Essential COM
Don Box

Written by a leading COM authority, this unique book reveals the essence of COM, helping developers truly understand the why, not just the how, of COM. Understanding the motivation for the design of COM and its distributed aspects is critical for developers who wish to go beyond simplistic applications of COM and become truly effective COM programmers. As the COM programming model continues to evolve, such insight also becomes essential to remaining current with extensions, such as Microsoft Transaction Server and COM+. By showing you why Distributed COM works as it does, Don Box enables you to apply the model creatively and effectively to everyday programming problems.

0-201-63446-5 • Paperback • 464 pages • ©1998

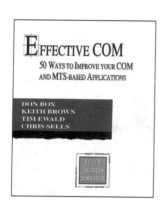

Effective COM
50 Ways to Improve Your COM and MTS-based Applications
Don Box, Keith Brown, Tim Ewald, and Chris Sells

Effective COM offers 50 concrete guidelines for creating COM-based applications that are more efficient, robust, and maintainable. Drawn from the authors' extensive practical experience working with and teaching COM, these rules of thumb, pitfalls to avoid, and experience-based pointers will enable you to become a more productive and successful COM programmer. These guidelines appear under six major headings: the transition from C++ to COM; interfaces, the fundamental element of COM development; implementation issues; the unique concept of apartments; security; and transactions. Throughout this book, the issues unique to the MTS programming model are addressed in detail. Readers will gain a deeper understanding of COM concepts, capabilities, and drawbacks, and the know-how to employ COM effectively for high-quality distributed application development.

0-201-37968-6 • Paperback • 240 pages • ©1999

ATL Internals
Brent Rector and Chris Sells

The Active Template Library (ATL) is a set of small, efficient, and flexible classes that facilitate the creation of interoperable COM components. Written for experienced COM and Visual C++ programmers, this book provides in-depth coverage of ATL's inner workings. It offers insight into the rationale behind ATL design, explains its architectural underpinnings, shows how ATL maps to COM, and describes important implementation details. With coverage current through ATL version 3.0, *ATL Internals* includes an overview of the Wizards but then goes well beyond the basics. The authors provide the detailed information needed to utilize ATL to its greatest advantage and work around its shortcomings.

0-201-69589-8 • Paperback • 656 pages • ©1999

Transactional COM+
Building Scalable Applications
Tim Ewald

Transactional COM+ explains how COM+ works and shows readers how to use the technology to its fullest potential as a framework for developing scalable applications. It examines the theory behind COM+, including the nature of scalability, why traditional object-oriented models are inappropriate for scalable systems, and the importance of transactions. Ewald shows how just-in-time activation and object pooling together change the relationship between a client and an object and he reveals the importance of HTTP and MSMQ as communication protocols that offer significant advantages over DCOM. And most importantly, he explains the influence all these factors have on the design of scalable COM+-based systems. Practical in its approach, *Transactional COM+* goes beyond the rationale behind the technology and the details of its implementation.

0-201-61594-0 • Paperback • 304 pages • ©2001

Programming Windows Security
Keith Brown

Windows security has often been considered a dry and unapproachable topic. For years, the main examples of programming security were simply exercises in ACL manipulation. *Programming Windows Security* is a revelation—providing developers with insight into the way Windows security really works. This book shows developers the essentials of security in Windows 2000, including coverage of Kerberos, SSL, job objects, the new ACL model, COM+, and IIS 5.0. Also included are highlights of the differences between security in Windows 2000 and in Windows NT 4.0.

0-201-60442-6 • Paperback • 608 pages • ©2000

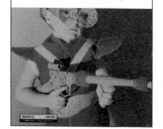

Debugging Windows Programs
Strategies, Tools, and Techniques for Visual C++ Programmers
Everett N. McKay and Mike Woodring

For professional software developers, debugging is a way of life. This book is the definitive guide to Windows debugging, providing developers with the strategies and techniques they need to fulfill one of their most important responsibilities efficiently and effectively. *Debugging Windows Programs* shows readers how to prevent bugs by taking full advantage of the Visual C++ development tools and writing code in a way that makes certain types of bugs impossible. They also will learn how to reveal bugs with debugging statements that force bugs to expose themselves when the program is executed and how to make the most of debugging tools and features available in Windows, Visual C++, MFC, and ATL. The authors provide specific solutions to the most common debugging problems, including memory corruption, resource leaks, stack problems, and release build problems.

0-201-70238-X • Paperback • 592 pages • ©2000

Register
Your Book
at www.aw.com/cseng/register

You may be eligible to receive:

- Advance notice of forthcoming editions of the book
- Related book recommendations
- Chapter excerpts and supplements of forthcoming titles
- Information about special contests and promotions throughout the year
- Notices and reminders about author appearances, tradeshows, and online chats with special guests

Contact us

If you are interested in writing a book or reviewing manuscripts prior to publication, please write to us at:

Editorial Department
Addison-Wesley Professional
75 Arlington Street, Suite 300
Boston, MA 02116 USA
Email: AWPro@aw.com

Addison-Wesley

Visit us on the Web: http://www.aw.com/cseng

CD-ROM Warranty

Addison-Wesley warrants the enclosed disc to be free of defects in materials and faulty workmanship under normal use for a period of ninety days after purchase. If a defect is discovered in the disc during this warranty period, a replacement disc can be obtained at no charge by sending the defective disc, postage prepaid, with proof of purchase to:

Editorial Department
Addison-Wesley Professional
Pearson Technology Group
75 Arlington Street, Suite 300
Boston, MA 02116
e-mail AWPro@awl.com

After the ninety-day period, a replacement disc will be sent upon receipt of the defective disc and a check or money order for $10.00, payable to Addison-Wesley.

Addison-Wesley makes no warranty or representation, either express or implied, with respect to this software, its quality, performance, merchantability, or fitness for a particular purpose. In no event will Addison-Wesley, its distributors, or dealers be liable for direct, indirect, special, incidental, or consequential damages arising out of the use or inability to use the software. The exclusion of implied warranties is not permitted in some states. Therefore, the above exclusion may not apply to you. This warranty provides you with specific legal rights. There may be other rights that you may have that vary from state to state. The contents of this CD-ROM are intended for personal use only.

More information and updates are available at:

http://www.awl.com/cseng/titles/0-201-70310-6